"Anyone who has wandered the ruins of a biblical site like Ephesus has probably noticed graffiti that looked like a pie cut into eight slices. On my first visit, I asked my professional guide about it and was told (incorrectly) the graffito was a board game, commonly played by Roman soldiers. Open this book and learn like I did how this symbol initially was a subversive sign of persecuted Christianity and later became a public sign similar to the cross. Christian symbols (including this one) played a visual role in Christian victory over paganism, protection from the spirits, and the cleansing of spaces. There are 'Aha!' moments throughout this wonderfully readable book. I highly commend it to all curious Christians looking for a view into our past."
—E. Randolph Richards,
Research Professor of New Testament,
Palm Beach Atlantic University

"Not just a book about pictures and symbols, this beautifully engrossing study uses the Ichthus Christogram to induct readers into the lived reality of early Christians over the first several centuries. As Hays narrates the Christian focus on Jesus, he provides engaging historical vignettes that help one get a sense of the local flavor of the places where Christianity grew and flourished. This book achieves the rare feat of being a true advance in scholarship that will also captivate those considering these topics for the first time."
—Ben C. Blackwell,
Professor of Early Christianity,
Westminster Theological Centre

"J. Daniel Hays thoroughly surveys the eight-spoked wheel symbol carved into marble floors and walls in many Greco-Roman sites such as Ephesus and Rome. Although tour guides sometimes identify these as game boards, Hays argues these ubiquitous carvings are Christian symbols. He provides extensive evidence that the eight-spoke wheel was formed by stacking the Greek word ΙΧΘΥC, 'fish.' The letters of this word are the first letters of Jesus Christ, Son of God, Savior. Just as the symbol of the cross was used to ward off demons in the early century of the church, the eight-spoked wheel symbol may have been carved by Christians to cleanse pagan temples or other places where idols were placed. He demonstrates the transition of this eight-spoked wheel from Christian graffiti in a pagan world to a common Christian symbol in churches by the sixth century. The book is richly illustrated with recent photographs from Hays's exploration of ancient sites."
—Phillip J. Long,
Professor of Biblical Studies,
Grace Christian University

T0370031

"The author's extensive research traces the development of early Christian symbols and abbreviations for Jesus Christ. He documents numerous sites where clearly Christian symbols (including crosses) occur near eight-spoked wheels. He also shows that these symbols occur in strategic locations in ancient pagan temples, reflecting Christians' desire to cleanse these places from demonic forces and to declare Christ's victory over them following the Great Persecution of AD 303–313 and the subsequent spread of Christianity following Constantine's victory in AD 313. This book is extensively researched and accessibly written. The numerous photos illustrate examples of Christian symbols and abbreviations. Hays makes a compelling, cumulative, and perhaps definitive case for understanding the eight-spoked 'wheel' as a pervasive early Christian symbol—not a gameboard—that came to be used throughout the Roman Empire. This book makes an important contribution to the material culture of the earliest Christians and offers new insights into their faith and courage."

—Dana M. Harris,
Professor and Department Chair, New Testament,
Trinity Evangelical Divinity School

"The artifacts of material culture sometimes exist without any literary records of the beliefs and daily lives of those who created various objects as symbols of their religious and social convictions. Yet both ancient writings and material remains inform and enrich our understanding of the faith and practice of early Christians. In this book, Daniel Hays offers the reader an opportunity to appreciate the devotional lives of early Christians through the visual world of some of their symbols. Beautifully illustrated by a scholar with the heart of a teacher and pastor, by his words and pictures, Hays takes us on a journey back in time to many cities of antiquity where we can almost touch the artifacts that stirred and inspired others in Christian fidelity."

—D. Jeffrey Bingham,
Research Professor of Historical Theology,
Jesse Hendley Professor of Biblical Theology,
Southwestern Baptist Theological Seminary

THE ICHTHUS CHRISTOGRAM AND OTHER EARLY CHRISTIAN SYMBOLS

J. DANIEL HAYS

KREGEL
ACADEMIC

Published by Kregel Academic, an imprint of Kregel Publications, 2450 Oak Industrial Dr. NE, Grand Rapids, MI 49505-6020.

Cataloging-in-Publication Data is available from the Library of Congress

ISBN 978-0-8254-4821-8

Printed in the United States of America

25 26 27 28 29 / 5 4 3 2 1

To my wife Donna, my colleagues Scott and Judy Duvall,
and all of the Ouachita Baptist University students who
have walked the streets of these ancient cities with me.

CONTENTS

FIGURES

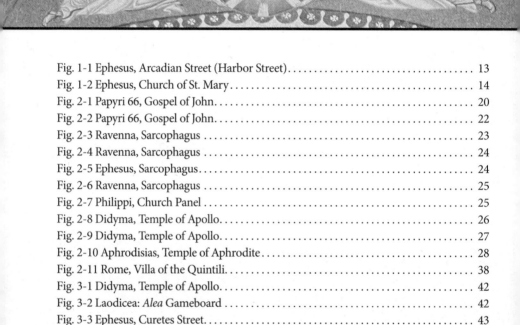

ACKNOWLEDGMENTS

I would like to acknowledge and thank a few of the many people who helped me along the way with this project. First and foremost is my colleague, Scott Duvall, who co-led with me several student biblical studies trips to the eastern Mediterranean world and who has scoured the ruins of Greco-Roman cities with me looking for ancient graffiti. Several of my former Ouachita Baptist University (OBU) students were particularly helpful—Levi Dade for help with the ICHTHUS wheel graphics; and Sara Patterson and Jael Shumaker for help with pictures from Beth Shean, Jerusalem, and Philippi. A number of my colleagues at OBU have been encouraging and insightfully helpful, especially Doug Nykolaishen, Marvin Pate, and Jeremy Greer. I am thankful to the Pruet School of Christian Studies at OBU for funding the trips and travel required to gather the firsthand information needed for this study. Also, I am particularly grateful to the invaluable OBU librarians Janice Ford and Rachel Martinez, who graciously acquired the many international and multilingual interlibrary loan sources that I needed.

In 2023, I attended a very helpful conference near Izmir, Turkey, entitled "The Second Global Smyrna Meeting on the Seven Cities of Revelation," sponsored by Tutku Educational Travel. A number of people at that conference, especially Ryan Black and Phillip J. Long, joined me in searching for and locating eight-spoked-wheel graffiti at the sites we visited. Also helpful to me at that conference were Mark Wilson and Tutku VP Cenk Eronat.

I also want to express my appreciation to my niece Kim Cragin-Padilla and my great-niece Alethea Cragin-Padilla for acquiring and providing important pictures from Delphi. Finally, I would be remiss if I did not thank my good friend and scholar Randy Richards, who has encouraged me along the way and also invited me to write a short article on this topic ("The Eight-Spoked Wheel Graffito") for the volume *Inscriptions, Papyri, and Other Artifacts*, edited by James R. Harrison and E. Randolph Richards, vol. 10 in *Ancient Literature for New Testament Studies* (Zondervan, 2024).

INSCRIPTION DATABASES

Most of the ancient inscriptions that are cited by database number in this book are accessible online through the Europeana Eagle Project (EAGLE: Electronic Archive of Greek and Latin Epigraphy) or through Packard Humanities Institute (PHI) Greek inscriptions. These two large accessible databases are, in turn, collections of and connections to earlier inscription corpora and databases. Often the identifying number for the inscription refers to one of these specific inscription collections. The abbreviations for the main collections, containing most of the cited inscription database numbers, are below.

CIL	*Corpus Inscriptionum Latinarum*
IAph	*Inscriptions of Aphrodisias*
ICG	*Inscriptiones Christianae Graecae*
ICUR/ICVR	*Inscriptiones Christianae Urbis Romae*
IEph	*Die Inschriften von Ephesos*
IG	*Inscriptiones Graecae*
MAMA	*Monumenta Asiae Minoris Antiqua*
SB	*Sammelbuch Griechischer Urkunden aus Ägypten*
SEG	*Supplementum Epigraphicum Graecum*

CHAPTER 1

INTRODUCTION

Years ago, on a student biblical studies trip to Turkey that Dr. Scott Duvall and I were leading, we came upon an eight-spoked wheel, about thirty inches in diameter, etched into one of the paving stones on the Harbor Road in Ephesus. It was a stone's throw from the famous theater and right next to the agora, or market, where the riot that threatened Paul and his companions took place (Acts 19:23–41).

"What do you think this is?" I asked Scott, completely unaware of its significance.

"It's probably a Christian symbol," Scott replied, "formed by overlaying the Greek letters from the Greek word for fish (*ichthus*). The five letters in the Greek word for fish are also an acrostic, developed by taking the first letters of 'Jesus Christ God's Son Savior.'"

Using his toe as a pointer, Scott proceeded to draw the Greek capital letters for me on the circle—I (*iota*, the first letter from Ἰησοῦς, Jesus), X (*chi*, the first letter of *Christus*, Christ), and so forth (as shown later in the chapter), spelling out ICHTHUS, the Greek word for fish.

"On the other hand," Scott continued to explain, "some top scholars think it is a game board for gambling."

Fig. 1-1 Ephesus, Arcadian Street (Harbor Street): Eight-Spoked Wheel (ICHTHUS Christogram)

As we continued our tour, we walked a hundred yards or so past the theater and the Harbor Road and came to the Church of St. Mary, built in the mid-fifth century. There, on one of the stone wall panels from the front of the church, was a professionally engraved eight-spoked wheel. Next to the wall panel with the eight-spoked wheel was a panel engraved with a traditional cross. So, in the front interior of this church, on the side wall panels, there were two symbols—a cross and an eight-spoked wheel.

After a moment of contemplating the images, Scott said, "This eight-spoked wheel is certainly not a game board. It seems to be used interchangeably with the Christian cross. It probably carries a similar significance as the cross does. This seems to support the ICHTHUS (fish) explanation of the eight-spoked wheel."

Since that trip years ago with Dr. Duvall, I have come across the eight-spoked wheel, or ICHTHUS, in dozens of places across the Mediterranean world of late antiquity (AD 200–600) in a wide range of contexts. In many cases, as on the Harbor Road of Ephesus, it is etched into stone paving blocks on main streets. Yet it also frequently appears on the floors and steps of pagan temples, as well as at bathhouses and public fountains. Because of the informality of the etchings, it is often referred to as graffiti. Yet keep in mind that the graffiti of the early-church era (i.e., late antiquity) was quite different

Fig. 1-2 Ephesus, Church of St. Mary: Eight-Spoked Wheel (ICHTHUS Christogram)

than graffiti today. In today's world, graffiti can be produced easily with cans of spray paint purchased from any number of stores, then quickly sprayed on surfaces. In addition, today's graffiti falls into the category of vandalism, is assumed to be done mostly by youth, and is typically unsanctioned by authorities.

The ICHTHUS graffiti of late antiquity that we are analyzing in this book, however, was typically etched into hard stone, often marble. This not only took quite a bit of time, but it required a chisel and hammer—expensive specialty tools that were not owned by many people. There were not giant hardware stores in every town where these tools could be purchased. Even in a sizable urban center like Ephesus, there were probably only a small group of people (most likely professional stone masons or professional stone inscription artists) who owned the tools necessary for etching graffiti onto hard stone surfaces. It is highly unlikely that this ancient graffiti was produced as an act of vandalism without the consent and against the wishes of some ruling or controlling entity. The eight-spoked-wheel graffiti that we are studying took time to inscribe, and many of them were in public areas, such as on main streets or in major monumental buildings.

Nonetheless, this wheel graffito was etched on stone surfaces in cities all across the Greco-Roman and early Christian world. A list of sites containing known inscribed wheel graffiti—a list, no doubt, far from being complete—includes Turkey (Ephesus, Aphrodisias, Didyma, Laodicea, Priene, Sardis, and Sagalassos); Greece (Philippi and Delphi); Italy (Ostia and Rome); and Israel (Jerusalem). At several of these sites the wheels are found in many-places.[1]

This is the case even though most of the ancient graffiti inscribed in the late antiquity era did not survive. In many of the large, monumental buildings, like the famous temples of Apollo in Didyma and the Temple of Athena in Pirene, the walls were often plastered with a stucco-like material and then painted. Over time, this plastered wall covering has not survived, so almost everything written or inscribed on the walls has been lost. Significant exceptions are the extensive underground catacombs on the outskirts of Rome and the cities of Pompeii and Herculaneum, which were buried quickly by the ash and lava of the eruption of nearby Mount Vesuvius in 79. Another significant exception is from a wealthy home just outside Rome, called the Villa of the Quintili. Here a section of wall plaster (with the word ICHTHUS in Greek along with an eight-spoked wheel) fell off the wall to the floor, where it was buried by rubble and debris, and preserved. At Scythopolis (Beth Shean) in Israel, there is a small room (niche) on the side of the Western Bathhouse that still retains some of its original wall plaster. Painted on this plaster in red is a Latin cross.

Throughout the years, most of these ancient cities and their buildings have been ravaged by earthquakes, invading armies, and the effects of time. Throughout this period, it was common practice for people involved in later construction projects to take the cut paving stones, blocks, columns, and other architectural elements of existing buildings (especially if they had been abandoned or destroyed) and reuse them in constructing new buildings.

---

1. There are at least twenty-two instances of eight-spoked-wheel graffiti at Ephesus and two each in Philippi and in Sagalassos. I've located twenty-eight at the Temple of Apollo in Didyma. Glenn Maffia, however, a newspaper reporter and amateur archaeologist, lives nearby in Didim, Turkey. One of his interests is the study of the Temple of Apollo at Didyma, where he has spent hours exploring and documenting. He states that he has located thirty-two eight-spoked wheels there. See Glenn Maffia, *Faint Whispers from the Oracle: Archaeological environment surrounding the Temple of Apollo at Didyma* (n.p.: Aslan Publishing House, 2019), 15–16.

Even in cities where archaeological excavations and study have been extensive, due to limited resources and time, only a small fraction of each ancient city has actually been excavated and studied. Archaeologists tend to focus on the areas of the city where the impressive monumental buildings and streets were located and not on the residential areas, especially the residences of the average person. Also, in some cases (Rome, Jerusalem, Izmir/Smyrna, etc.), a modern city sits on the ancient site, restricting the areas where archaeologists can excavate.

Within the limited, surviving archaeological ruins that have been discovered and excavated, the fact that quite a number of these wheels appear implies that there must have been many, many more occurrences of the eight-spoked-wheel graffito in the cities of late antiquity.

Throughout the early Christian era, the eight-spoked wheel shows up as an important and significant Christian symbol in numerous contexts other than graffiti. As noted above, in one instance where the plaster of the Villa of the Quintili did survive, an eight-spoked wheel was discovered on the walls. Another one appears on a Christian gravestone in Pannonia (modern-day Croatia) and on a gold pendant discovered inside the sarcophagus of the Empress Maria (d. AD 407) in Rome. The eight-spoked wheel appears professionally inscribed on the capitals of columns and on interior stone wall panels from the front of churches in Ephesus (the Church of St. Mary and the Church of St. John), Labraunda, Samos, and Stobi (North Macedonia). In the city of Laodicea, the eight-spoked wheel appears in the paved brick floor of a house church alongside the depiction of a fish. In Israel, it appears in the mosaics of the main street (*Cardo*) at Sepphoris, in the floor mosaics of a church at Hippos, and in the mosaics of the converted Western Bathhouse at Scythopolis (Beth Shean). In Istanbul, an eight-spoked wheel is used interchangeably with traditional crosses in the mosaics on the ceiling at the famous church Hagia Sophia. It is featured prominently, and in a similar parallel usage with the cross, in the beautiful wall mosaics at the front of the Church of San Vitale in Ravenna, Italy. Finally, the eight-spoked wheel appears repeatedly alongside several traditional crosses and Chi-Rho Christograms on the spectacular Kurşunlugerme Bridge—part of the impressive aqueduct system in Thrace that transported water to ancient Constantinople (modern-day Istanbul).

To see the significance for Christians within the eight-spoked wheel, we must go back to the Greek. The Greek word IXΘΥC (*ichthus*)[2] is the regu-

---

2. Throughout this book, for the Greek letter *sigma* the lunate *sigma* C will typically be used instead of the more familiar Σ, in keeping with the practice reflected in most inscriptions of this era (second to sixth centuries). In cases where Σ is used in an ancient text, this book will also use Σ. The font shape of Greek letters was evolving throughout the early Christian and late antiquity period, and a number of variations occur for several letters, especially in informal writing. Thus, in addition to variations for the letter *sigma*, occasionally the Greek letter Θ (*theta*) will appear in a rectangular shape rather than a rounded shape. See the discussion in B. H. McLean, *An Introduction to Greek Epigraphy of the Hellenistic and Roman Periods from Alexander the Great*

lar word for "fish." Yet early on, Christians recognized that these letters also formed an acrostic by putting together the first letters of the phrase "Jesus Christ God's Son Savior": Ἰησοῦς Χριστός θεοῦ Υἱός Cωτήρ (*Iēsous Christos Theou Huios Sōtēr*).[3] If those same five Greek letters are stacked on top of each other, they produce an eight-spoked wheel. This stacking of the letters is illustrated below:[4]

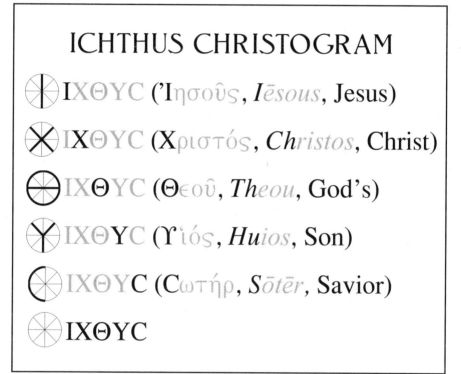

ICHTHUS CHRISTOGRAM

IXΘYC (Ἰησοῦς, *Iēsous*, Jesus)

IXΘYC (Χριστός, *Christos*, Christ)

IXΘYC (Θεοῦ, *Theou*, God's)

IXΘYC (Υἱός, *Huios*, Son)

IXΘYC (Cωτήρ, *Sōtēr*, Savior)

IXΘYC

Since this Christogram occurs with high frequency in many ancient Greco-Roman cities, this book attempts to notate as many occurrences of this symbol as possible and place them into their historical context by asking several questions. Where do these symbols occur? Do we know when they

down to the Reign of Constantine (323 B.C.–A.D. 337) (Ann Arbor: The University of Michigan Press, 2002), 40–42.

3. For extensive discussions on how the early Christians connected the fish symbol and the IXΘYC (ICHTHUS) acrostic with Jesus Christ, see Franz Joseph Dölger, *ICHTHYS*, 5 vols., 2nd ed. (Münster: Aschendorf, 1928–1943); and Josef Engermann, "Fisch, Fischer, Fischfang," in *Reallexikon für Antike und Christentum: Sachworterbuch zur Auseinandersetzung des Christentums mit der antiken Welt*, ed. Theodor Klauser, Ernst Dassmann, and Georg Schöllgen (Stuttgart: Anton Hiersemann, 1969), 959–1094.

4. This particular graphic presentation of the ICHTHUS wheel was developed by my former student Levi Dade.

were made? What was happening at the time in each city that suggests a context for these Christian symbols? Why were they placed at the location in which we find them? What was their purpose? How does that purpose relate to the ICHTHUS meaning?

This discussion about historical contexts includes stories about real people, especially those early Christians who were committed to the Lord Jesus and who took a stand publicly for their faith. It reveals the incredible spread of Christianity throughout the Roman Empire (and beyond) for the next several hundred years—right after the book of Acts ends. It shows how early Christians, born into a world dominated by interconnected yet hostile pagan and Roman imperial powers, overcame that opposition and proclaimed publicly and loudly all across the cities of the Roman world that Jesus Christ is the Son of God, the Savior, and the victor over all forces of evil.

With some confidence, we can place the production of most of the ICHTHUS Christograms we will study in the period of early Christianity that runs from AD 100 to 600. Therefore, we will provide a historical, social, and religious context for this time period, especially as it pertains to the various cities in which we find the ICHTHUS wheel. As we study the generalities and the specifics of the social background and religious settings, we can correlate them into the momentus historical events, and then identify as many examples of the Christogram as possible, we will then be able to develop the most plausible and probable explanation for the meaning behind each appearance of this symbol.

CHAPTER 2

THE VISUAL SYMBOLIC WORLD
OF EARLY CHRISTIANITY

SYMBOLS AND ABBREVIATIONS FOR JESUS CHRIST

There is extensive evidence supporting the identification of the eight-spoked wheel as a Christian symbol representing the acrostic ICHTHUS/ΙΧΘΥC (fish). This evidence is comprised of both literary and archaeological sources. The first line of evidence we will explore is to show that this kind of complex combination of abbreviation, acrostic, and letter symbolism was quite common in early Christianity.

In fact, the practice of using abbreviations, as well as various, creative, and complex combinations of letters and symbols was widespread across the Greco-Roman world,[1] especially from the second century on. Typically, the abbreviations only contained the first letter or the first few letters of the word. The word Καισαρ (Caesar), for example, was often abbreviated as K or ΚΑΙΣ.[2]

The early Christians picked this up and developed a system of abbreviating words. The earliest Christian writings were written on papyri and are often referred to as papyri manuscripts. These manuscripts, some of which date as early as AD 200, extensively employed a special abbreviation system called *nomina sacra* ("sacred names"). This developed fairly quickly into a

---

1. For example, see the extremely complex overlapping and interconnected series of letters in a small square monogram at Aphrodisias that, when deciphered, translates to "The fortune of the Greens triumphs" (the "Greens" refers to one of the major Roman chariot teams and their extensive, fanatical fanbase). This and other complex monograms, including Christian monograms incorporating crosses, are presented and discussed in Charlotte Roueché, *Aphrodisias in Late Antiquity*, Journal of Roman Studies Monographs 5 (London: The Society for the Promotion of Roman Studies, 1989), 161–63; 226–28.

2. McLean, *An Introduction to Greek Epigraphy*, 53. McLean provides a substantial list of the most commonly occurring abbreviated Greek words (52–54).

standardized system of abbreviations for special, divine-related words, such as "Lord," "God," "Jesus," "Christ," "Father," "Son," "Spirit," "cross," and "savior," among others. The *nomina sacra* abbreviation was typically formed by taking the first and last letters of the word and then adding a horizontal stroke directly above the letters (see fig. 2-1). Occasionally, three letters from the word were used.

This practice became quite common among early Christian writers.[3] In fact, Larry Hurtado writes, "The *nomina sacra* are so familiar a feature of Christian manuscripts that papyrologists often take the presence of these forms as sufficient to identify even a fragment of a manuscript as indicating its probable Christian provenance."[4]

The *nomina sacra* abbreviation system was used not only in manuscripts but in Christian inscriptions. For example, in Israel, near Megiddo, a third-century Christian prayerhouse was discovered with distinctively Christian floor mosaics. Included in the mosaics is an inscription honoring the donor who paid for the floor. The terms "God," "Jesus," and "Christ" are all abbreviated in *nomina sacra* style, including the horizontal line drawn over each of the two-letter abbreviations.[5] Also in Israel, the mosaic floors of a church discovered at Horbat Hadat, dating to the late fifth century, contain the *nomina sacra* abbreviation for "God" alongside a Tau-Rho Staurogram, which we will discuss more later in this chapter.[6]

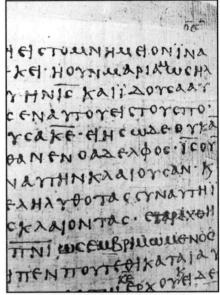

Fig. 2-1 Papyri 66, Gospel of John: Counting Down from the Top, Clear *Nomina Sacra*. Abbreviations Are on Lines 3, 5, 6, and 10.

---

3. For examples of *nomina sacra* in early Christian papyri, see P. Chester Beatty II, P46 (1 Cor. 7:37–8:7) and P. Chester Beatty I, P45 (Luke 12:18–37).

4. Larry Hurtado, *The Earliest Christian Artifacts: Manuscripts and Christian Origins* (Grand Rapids: Eerdmans, 2006), 96. See his extensive discussion of *nomina sacra* in Christian writings on pages 95–134. See also Anton Herman Reinier Everhard Paap, *Nomina Sacra in the Greek Papyri of the First Five Centuries AD: The Sources and Some Deductions* (Leiden: Brill, 1959), 76–99, who lists out hundreds of examples.

5. Yotam Tepper, Leah Di Segni, and Guy Stiebel, *A Christian Prayer Hall of the Third Century CE at Kefar 'Othnay (Legio): Excavations at the Megiddo Prison 2005* (Jerusalem: Israel Antiquities Authority, 2006), 36 (with a picture of the mosaic).

6. Lehi Habas, "Mosaic Floors of the Church at Horbat Hadat, Israel," *Journal of Mosaic Research* 15 (2022): 167–84. See the picture of this mosaic on page 171 (fig. 3).

Nomina sacra abbreviations also show up in graffiti (see fig. 5–8). Although the preservation of original plaster walls is quite rare, several sections have survived from the House Church of St. Peter in Capernaum. Written on these plaster walls are a number of Christian abbreviations and phrases dating from the third to fifth centuries, likely placed there by pilgrim travelers. One text translates as, "Lord Jesus Christ, help!" All three divine words are in *nomina sacra* abbreviation form.[7] The verb βοήθι (*boēthi*, "help!") is common in early Christian graffiti and inscriptions, especially throughout Anatolia/Asia Minor (see chapter 5 for more). It is normally used next to the word "Lord" (*kyrios*), as it is here, written out in full, unabbreviated form. Yet it also appears numerous times elsewhere in abbreviated form and in combination with a variety of cross-related symbols.[8] Also of interest, one of the other abbreviated words used on the plaster of this early house church in Capernaum, but not one that regularly occurs in abbreviated form, is the word ΙΧΘΥC (ICHTHUS), abbreviated only by dropping the first letter (I).[9]

In addition to using abbreviations, non-Christian Greek inscriptions across the Greco-Roman world after the first century would frequently combine two or more letters into a single shape, creating a kind of new letter and thus saving space. These are often called "ligatures." Similarly, sometimes new letters (called "compendia") were formed by putting one adjacent letter within or on top of the other letter.[10]

Christians also followed this practice both in their scribal literary writings and in their inscriptions, especially for words relating to Jesus. Thomas Kraus writes,

According to archaeological evidence, Christians rather early used several symbols and/or signs for self-identification for a variety of reasons and for diverse purposes. Among these, the fish symbol (ΙΧΘΥC) from the late second century onwards and the pleomorphic representations of the name of Jesus Christ, collectively referred to as "Christograms," were the most popular and widespread ones.[11]

7. James R. Wicker, "Pre-Constantinian *Nomina Sacra* in a Mosaic and Church Graffiti," *SWJT* 52.1 (2009): 59–63.
8. Emmanuele Testa, *Il Simbolismo Dei Giudeo-Cristiani*, Publicazioni Dello Studium Franciscanum 14 (Gerusalemme: Tipografia Dei PP. Francescani, 1962), 399, along with Wicker, "Pre-Constantinian *Nomina Sacra*," 60, suggest that βοήθι (*boēthi*) is probably not abbreviated here because the word carries numerical significance. That is, if the number values of each letter are added up (β = 2, etc.) the total is 99—the number of sheep Jesus had after one was lost. Testa, 396–400, cites some examples, along with drawings, that illustrate the wide range of usage involving βοήθι (*boēthi*). It is used with regular crosses, Tau-Rho Staurograms, Chi-Rho Christograms, *alpha* and *omega* letters, and various abbreviations for Jesus Christ. In numerous instances, it is abbreviated simply with the Greek letter *beta* (B).
9. Paap, *Nomina Sacra in the Greek Papyri*, 63, 66; Wicker, "Pre-Constantinian *Nomina Sacra*," 62.
10. McLean, *An Introduction to Greek Epigraphy*, 55.
11. Thomas J. Kraus, "Christograms," in *The Reception of Jesus in the First Three Centuries*, ed. Chris Keith, Helen K. Bond, Christine Jacobi, and Jens Schröter, vol. 3, *From Celsus to the Catacombs:*

It is important to underscore two aspects of Kraus's summarizing state-ment. First, there were a number of symbols used by the early Christians. Second, the acrostic ΙΧΘΥC (ICHTHUS), along with several other combina-tions using the letters of the name of Jesus Christ, were very common.

One of these "pleomorphic representations" or compendia shapes was the Tau-Rho Staurogram, a symbol formed by superimposing the Greek letters *tau* (T) and *rho* (P). This symbol was used in Christian writings, both biblical and nonbiblical, in place of the Greek words for "cross" (*stauros*) and "crucify" (*stauraō*) appearing as early as 175 to 225 (see fig. 2-2).[12] The staurogram also appears frequently in Christian inscriptions across the Roman Empire in late antiquity (200–600), espe-cially in funerary-related contexts. In inscriptions on stone surfaces, it does not normally serve as a substi-tute in a text for the words *stauros* ("cross") or *stauraō* ("crucify"), as in the papyri literature, but it stands apart from the text, in similar usage as crosses or the Chi-Rho Christo-gram (see below). This Tau-Rho symbol also appears in church floor mosaics, sometimes with the *alpha* and *omega* letters below the arms of the cross, such as on the floor mosa-ics of a church at Zahrani, Lebanon (ca. AD 389–390).[13] In early Christi-anity the Tau-Rho Staurogram was a popular symbol, and it occurs in Christian inscriptions frequently, often with the letters *alpha* and *omega* (see fig. 2–4).[14]

Fig. 2-2 Papyri 66, Gospel of John: Tau-Rho Staurogram in Third Line from the Top

Visual, Liturgical, and Non-Christian Reception of Jesus in the Second and Third Centuries CE, ed. Chris Keith (London: T&T Clark, 2020), 221.

12. For examples of the Tau-Rho Staurogram in early Christian manuscripts, see P. Bodmer XIV, P75 (Luke 14:26b–15:3) and P. Bodmer XV, P75 (John 1–15). For a discussion on the staurogram, see Hurtado, *Earliest Christian Artifacts*, 135–54; Bruce W. Longenecker, *The Cross before Constantine: The Early Life of a Christian Symbol* (Minneapolis: Fortress, 2015), 106–110; and Dieter T. Roth, "Staurogram," in Keith, *From Celsus to the Catacombs*, 349–58.

13. Hugo Brandenburg, "Christussymbole in frühchristlichen Bodenmosaiken," *Römische Quartalschrift für christliche Altertumskunde und Kirchengeschichte* 64 (1969): 105.

14. From the *ICG* database, some examples include *ICG* 2248 (Athens, 300–450); *ICG* 188, 274, 374, 436, 503 (Laodicea Combusta, 200–600); *ICG* 304 (Iconium, 300–450); *ICG* 316 and 437, both containing the staurogram plus *alpha* and *omega* (Iconium, 400–700); *ICG* 740, containing the staurogram plus *alpha* and *omega* (Lystra, 200–350); *ICG* 61 (Ekdaumaua, 200–700); and *ICG* 72 and 81, both containing the staurogram plus the *alpha* and *omega* (Ekdaumaua, 400–500). Dates

Fig. 2-3 Ravenna, Sarcophagus:
Tau-Rho Staurograms with Alpha-Omega

Early Christians also combined various Greek letters taken from the name Jesus Christ to form symbols representing Christ. The Greek letters *chi* (X) and *rho* (P), for example—the first two letters of Χριστός (*Christos*, "Christ")— were combined and superimposed to form the Chi-Rho Christogram (see figs. 2-5, 8-3, and 8-13). As will be discussed in chapter 4, church historians Eusebius and Lactantius popularized the story of the Emperor Constantine associating the Chi-Rho Christogram with a critical military victory in 312. After Constantine legalized and supported Christianity, the Chi-Rho Christogram became popular as a Christian symbol. Frequently the Christogram was encircled by a victory wreath or placed inside of a circle.[15] Like the Tau-Rho Staurogram, the Chi-Rho Christogram often appears with *alpha* and *omega* (taken from Rev. 1:8; 21:6; 22:13), which are typically placed inside the arms of the *chi* and on each side of the *rho*. Throughout the years 300 to 600, the Chi-Rho symbol appeared hundreds of times in different contexts—in church architecture, on coins, bowls, plates and cups, on signet rings, necklaces, and other jewelry, on amulets, in funerary contexts (sarcophagi and monuments, the walls of tombs), on public-works projects like city walls and aqueducts, in inscriptions, and in literature (see figs. 2-4, 2-5, and 8-13).[16]

Another popular letter combination used by early Christians was the Iota-Chi. This involved superimposing the letters I (*iota*) and X (*chi*), taken from the first letters of the name Jesus Christ ᾿Ιησοῦς Χριστός; *Iēsous Christos*).

are taken from the database page. There is also a Tau-Rho graffito inscribed on the paving of Curetes Street in Ephesus.

15. See the sarcophagus of Domitilla and the sarcophagus of Catervius and Severina, both from the fourth century in Felicity Harley-McGowan, "Picturing the Passion," in *The Routledge Handbook of Early Christian Art*, ed. Robin M. Jensen and Mark D. Ellison (New York: Routledge, 2018), 297; and Mark D. Ellison, "'Secular' Portraits, Identity, and the Christianization of the Roman Household," in Jensen and Ellison, *The Routledge Handbook*, 331. Other fourth-century examples of the Chi-Rho placed within a wheel or round wreath can be seen in Jeffrey Spier, ed., *Picturing the Bible: The Earliest Christian Art* (New Haven, CT and London: Yale University Press, 2007), 20, 95, 105, and 247–48.

16. See the discussion and dozens of examples in Ildar Garipzanov, *Graphic Signs of Authority in Late Antiquity and the Early Middle Ages, 300–900* (Oxford: Oxford University Press, 2018), 50–80.

This symbol occurs frequently in graffiti,[17] on funerary monuments, and in formal church architecture. This Iota-Chi, when placed inside of a wreath or circle rim, produces a six-spoked wheel, similar in appearance to the eight-spoked ICHTHUS Christogram (see figs. 2-6, 2-7, and 5-30). Another symbol came from the Greek word for Jesus in all caps (IHCOYC) with the first two letters I (*iota*) and H (*eta*) combined to produce the symbol,[18] similar in appearance to the modern logo for the farm equipment company International Harvester.

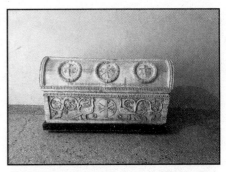

Fig. 2-4 Ravenna, Sarcophagus: Top Level, Wreathed Chi-Rho Christogram with Alpha-Omega, Flanked by Wreathed Tau-Rho Staurograms with Alpha-Omega; Lower Level, Chi-Rho Christogram with Alpha-Omega

In this era, the simple cross symbol was not yet standardized as we commonly have today in the West, typically called the Latin cross (where the vertical bottom leg is much longer than the other arms of the cross). Among the early Christians, sometimes the cross was rotated to look more like an X. Also appearing early is the T-shaped cross.[19] Particularly in early inscriptions, and especially at the beginning and the end of a written inscription, a cross with equal-sized arms that looks like a plus sign (+) can be found. This is sometimes called the "equilateral cross" or the Maltese cross (usually with flared ends) or, using the Latin term, *crux quadrata*. These equilateral crosses were common in early Christianity, perhaps rivaling the traditional Latin cross in popularity.[20]

Fig. 2-5 Ephesus, Sarcophagus: Chi-Rho Christogram with Alpha-Omega

---

17. One of these Iota-Chi symbols occurs inscribed on a stone fragment in the Basilica at Aphrodisias. See the picture in P. T. Stinson, "New Incised Architectural Drawings from the Basilica," in *Aphrodisias Papers 5: Excavations and Research at Aphrodisias, 2006–2012*, ed. R. R. R. Smith, Julia Lenaghan, Alexander Sokolicek, and Katherine Welch, *Journal of Roman Archaeology Supplement* 103 (Portsmouth, RI: Journal of Roman Archaeology, 2016), 233.

18. Hurtado, *Earliest Christian Artifacts*, 154. For dozens of examples of these and numerous other similar symbols from the third to sixth centuries, see Margherita Guarducci, *Epigrafia Greca IV: Epigraphi Sacre Pagane E Cristiane* (Rome: Instituto Poligrafico Dello Stato, 1978), 317–556.

19. Longenecker, *The Cross before Constantine*, 12–13.

20. From the *ICG* database, see, for example: *ICG* 119, 145, 381, 744, 1298. There are dozens and dozens of these in this database. See the discussion on the various shapes of crosses occurring in

Fig. 2-6 Ravenna, Sarcophagus: Iota-Chi Christogram   Fig. 2-7 Philippi, Church Panel: Iota-Chi Christogram

In Revelation 1:8, 21:6, and 22:13 the Lord declares, "I am the Alpha and Omega" (i.e., the beginning and the end). These two letters, *alpha* (A)— and the actual shape of the letter *alpha* appears in a variety of forms—along with the letter *omega* (Ω, often appearing as the lower case ω), are frequently added to each side of the various cross symbols. Although the letters *alpha* and *omega* appear most frequently with the Chi-Rho Christogram, they also appear with a wide range of other crosses and symbols for Christ as well, especially the Tau-Rho Staurogram (see fig. 2–3).[21] The letters *alpha* and *omega* also can stand alone as symbols of Christ.[22] Serving as bookends around the book of Revelation (1:8; 21:6 and 22:13), these two letters not only reflect theological realities about Christ (e.g., his eternality), but they also carry strong connotations of the victory that Christ has won.[23]

early Christianity in Bruce W. Longenecker, *The Crosses of Pompeii: Jesus-Devotion in a Vesuvian Town* (Minneapolis: Fortress, 2016), 30–33; and Longenecker, *The Cross before Constantine*, 73–119.

21. From epitaphs in Iconium, Laodicea Combusta, and Lystra, for example, *alpha* and *omega* appear on each side of a Tau-Rho Staurogram (*ICG* 316, 437, 740).

22. Margherita Guarducci, *The Tomb of St. Peter: The New Discoveries in the Sacred Grottoes of the Vatican*, trans. Joseph McLellan (New York: Hawthorn Books, 1960), 100–109.

23. Mark Wilson, *The Victor Sayings in the Book of Revelation* (Eugene, OR: Wipf & Stock, 2007); Mark Wilson, *Victory through the Lamb: A Guide to Revelation in Plain Language* (Bellingham, WA: Lexham Press, 2019).

Throughout early Christianity and late antiquity, symbols and abbreviations for the name of Jesus Christ and the cross symbol itself appear frequently in a wide range of forms,[24] and for each of these symbols or abbreviations there were half a dozen or so creative variations.[25]

Almost all of these cross symbols and abbreviated names for Jesus also appear inside circles or within circular wreaths (see the discussion on victory wreaths in chapter 4). This is especially true of the Chi-Rho Christogram[26] and the equilateral cross.[27] Likewise, the Tau-Rho Staurogram[28] and the Iota-Chi Christogram[29] occur frequently within a circle or circular wreath.

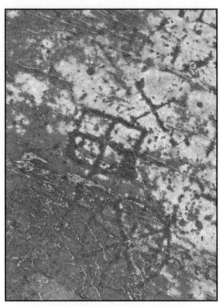

Fig. 2-8 Didyma, Temple of Apollo: ICHTHUS Christogram, Crosses, and Crosses Inside Squares (Four-Square Boxes)

Crosses can appear inscribed within square boxes and grids too. Testa, for example, presents a chart with twenty-four different drawings of creative combinations of crosses and squares from Christian contexts across the Roman world. Although it would be hard to verify conclusively, Testa includes the simple four-square box as a variation of a Christian cross (i.e., a simple equilateral cross inscribed within a square).[30] Yet there is substantial evidence that this identification is correct. At Aphrodisias, Didyma, and Laodicea (see chapter 5), for example, four-square boxes occur in the inscribed graffiti right beside regular crosses, crosses within circles, and ICHTHUS Christograms (see figs. 2–8 and 2-9).

Ine Jacobs summarizes the overall situation by declaring, "Cross graffiti are omnipresent in the cities of the eastern Mediterranean. They appear on

24. See also the discussion of these various forms and the many examples provided in Longenecker, *The Cross before Constantine*, 82–92; and Bruce W. Longenecker with Chris Keith, "Cross Symbol," in Keith, *From Celsus to the Catacombs*, 235–49.
25. Testa, *Il Simbolismo Dei Guideo-Cristiani*, 25–40, 153–96, 261–67, 400–425.
26. *ICG* 259.
27. *ICG* 10 (Anzulada, Lycaonia), *ICG* 14 (Tyraion, Lycaonia), *ICG* 82 and 83 (Gdanmaa, Lycaonia), *ICG* 392 and 441 (Laodicea Combusta), *ICG* 630 (Lycaonia), *ICG* 666 (Barata, Lycaonia), *ICG* 1298 (Amorion, Phrygia).
28. *ICG* 61 and 728.
29. *ICG* 89.
30. Testa, *Il Simbolismo Dei Guideo-Cristiani*, 304–9.

Fig. 2-9 Didyma, Temple of Apollo:
Cross and Cross Inside a Square (Four-Square Box)

city gates, on the walls and doors of houses and monumental buildings, on the benches of theaters, on columns of agorae and streets, on statues and statuary bases, on church walls and furniture, and so on."[31] We can expand on Jacobs's statement by noting that not only crosses but a wide range of cross-related and Jesus-name symbols appear as well, often appearing side by side with the regular crosses. These symbols, however, are not limited to graffiti, nor are they limited to the eastern Mediterranean. These crosses and Jesus-name symbols appear both in graffiti informally inscribed on stone pavement as well as in professionally inscribed church architecture and on Christian funerary stones throughout the entire Mediterranean world.

MONOGRAMS AND "CRYPTIC" LETTER COMBINATIONS

A number of complex, artistically crafted letter combinations, or monograms, also appear in graffiti and in professionally crafted church architectural elements, both in Christian and non-Christian contexts. There are a number of these in the city of Aphrodisias (western Turkey) that also have crosses adjacent to them or within them. They were discovered in churches, thus identifying them as Christian monograms. Some of these are even more complicated than the ICHTHUS wheel.[32]

---

31. Ine Jacobs, "Cross Graffiti as Physical Means to Christianize the Classical City: An Exploration of Their Function, Meaning, Typographical, and Socio-Historical Contexts," in *Graphic Signs of Identity, Faith, and Power in Late Antiquity and the Early Middle Ages* (Cursor Mundi, 27), ed. Ildar Garipzanov, Caroline Goodson, and Henry Maguire (Turnhout: Brepols, 2017), 175.

32. See Ildar Garipzanov "Monograms, Early Christians, and Late Antique Culture," in Garipzanov, Goodson, and Maguire, *Graphic Signs of Identity*, 109–30; and Roueché, *Aphrodisias in Late Antiquity*, 161–77, figs. 101–121. See also the discussion by Hurtado, *Earliest Christian Artifacts*, 136–39. He writes (137–38), "Technically, a 'monogram' is an interweaving or combination of two (or sometimes more) alphabetic characters, the component letters of the resultant device typically referring to a person's name or title. But such 'compendia' (also called 'ligatures') can also serve other purposes. . . . In any case, the basic technique of joining various letters to form a ligature was familiar to readers of the time, especially in documentary texts and inscriptions." These continue to be used frequently throughout the Byzantine era.

For example, in figure 2–10 is a collection of Christian graffiti carved on the west doorjamb of the Temple of Aphrodite in Aphrodisias, which was later converted to a church. There are three panels with similar informal inscriptions,[33] which Roueché interprets as Christian prayers (see also fig. 5–8). She suggests translating the combined symbols as follows, moving from top to bottom, noting the frequent use of abbreviations:

Fig. 2-10 Aphrodisias, Temple of Aphrodite: Doorjamb with Christian Graffiti, Including a Peter Monogram (top center)

1. The top symbol, shaped like a cross with letters attached on the end of each arm is a monogram reading Πέτρο(ς) (Peter)
2. Reading the Greek script above the cross on the left and continuing into the cross-like symbol in the middle yields Ἀνάληψης τ(ου) Κ(υρίο)υ (Ascension of the Lord)
3. Reading the third line, starting with the cross on the left and moving into the figure in the middle reads *cross* Κ(ύρι)ε Βοίθι το σο δ(οὐ)λο PO ("Lord help your servant Ro[…]" followed by a string of unidentified abbreviated single letters).[34]

In the Baths of Neptune in Ostia (near Rome), a number of complicated symbols were discovered on the mosaic floors. Several scholars have argued that these are Christian symbols, some of them derived from the name of Jesus in quite a complex manner. For example, Longenecker demonstrates that one symbol uses a combination of vertical strokes (representing the letters *iota* and *eta*), along with *sigma* and *upsilon*, to make a creative symbol that says, in Latin, *IESUS* (Jesus).[35]

In the grotto in Rome that is probably the burial site of St. Peter, there are dozens and dozens of complicated graffiti. Guarducci explains that these early Christians were using a kind of cryptographic language not to hide their iden-

33. See Roueché, *Aphrodisias in Late Antiquity*, plate XXXI, figs. 117, 118, and 121.
34. Roueché, *Aphrodisias in Late Antiquity*, 176–77.
35. Longenecker, *The Cross before Constantine*, 78–81.

tity, but to add a level of mystery to their adoration.[36] Thus, there are many letters that are combined with each other and with Christian symbols (like crosses) in creative ways. For example, the Latin P, which was used to abbreviate Peter, often had the three lines of an E (the second letter in Peter) added to the lower vertical line below the loop of the P. This contraction stood for PE, abbreviating Peter, but the shape also looked like a key, recalling Matthew 16:19 where Christ tells Peter he is giving him the keys of heaven.[37] These complicated Christian monograms also show up in the Roman catacombs, many of them dating to the third and fourth centuries.[38]

Another related phenomenon are several instances of early Christians interpreting numbers in written text as references to Jesus Christ when the Greek letters used as numbers align with the letters used for the name Jesus Christ. For example, in the Epistle of Barnabas 9 (AD 135) attention is drawn to Genesis 14:14, where the number of men in Abraham's household is 318. In Greek, the number 318 is represented by the letters TIH (*tau, iota, eta*). Barnabus concludes that the letter T (*tau*) represents the cross and the letters IH (*iota, eta*) are from the first two letters of Jesus ('Ιησοῦς; *Iēsous*).[39] Later in history (mid-fourth century), Athanasius, bishop of Alexandria, claimed that the number of bishops who attended the Council of Nicaea (AD 325) was 318 (*tau, iota, eta*), a reference to Genesis 14:14 and to the cross (*tau*) and Jesus (*iota-eta*). This identification of the number of bishops with the number 318 was widely viewed as highly and divinely significant and was cited to add validity and authority to the results of the Council of Nicaea during the fourth century.[40]

A reference back to these 318 bishops at Nicaea, "anathema from the 318 fathers," appears in a graffiti inscription along with three crosses at Aphrodisias. Roueché observes that this formula ("anathema from the 318 fathers") is widely attested in inscriptions. This particular one at Aphrodisias appears to have a horizontal line above the 318 (TIH), similar to the line normally designating the *nomina sacra* abbreviations.[41]

THE ICHTHUS (FISH) ACROSTIC

In light of the evidence presented above, it would not have been unusual at all for the early Christians to note the connection between the Greek word for

---

36. Guarducci, *The Tomb of St. Peter*, 100–109.
37. Guarducci, *The Tomb of St. Peter*, 100–109. For pictures of the "key-shaped" PE representation for Peter, see pages 108–9.
38. Rachael Helen Banes, "Scratch That: A Comparative Approach to Graffiti in the Late Antique Eastern Mediterranean C. 300–700 CE" (PhD diss., University of Birmingham, 2022), 302. Banes presents drawings of nine different monograms from the catacombs.
39. This point is also made by Clement of Alexandria, *Stromateis* 6.11.
40. See the discussion by Everett Ferguson, *Church History*, vol. 1, *From Christ to Pre-Reformation* (Grand Rapids: Zondervan, 2005), 52, 204.
41. See the inscription text, translation, and discussion in Roueché, *Aphrodisias in Late Antiquity*, 170–71.

"fish" (ICHTHUS, ΙΧΘΥC) and the acrostic taken from the first letters of the phrase "Jesus Christ God's Son Savior" and to combine them into a graphic symbol—the eight-spoked wheel. In fact, the depiction of fish and the use of the word ΙΧΘΥC itself as a symbol of Jesus Christ is widely attested, appearing as early as the end of the second century or early third century. Since church buildings were often prohibited prior to the early fourth century, much of the earliest Christian art and inscriptions available from that period are found in funerary settings. Indeed, the depiction of fish, as well as the acrostic ΙΧΘΥC, appear numerous times in the Christian catacombs and on gravestones of Christians from the third (perhaps even late second) to the sixth centuries.[42]

These ΙΧΘΥC (ICHTHUS) inscriptions occur throughout the Mediterranean world of the Roman Empire, and often there are other Christian symbols or texts in the same inscription. ΙΧΘΥC especially appears in the following contexts: 1) with regular equilateral crosses; 2) with crosses and the letters *alpha* and *omega*; 3) with the Tau-Rho Staurogram and the letters *alpha* and *omega*; 4) with the Greek word βοηθέω (*boētheō*, "help")—this word appears frequently in early Christian inscriptions, usually in the imperative, "Lord, help so-and-so"; and 5) with the Greek words (or abbreviations of) Φωϛ (*phōs*, "light") and Ζωή (*zōē*, "life").[43]

One of the earliest known examples to date of ΙΧΘΥC occurring in an inscription is in the epitaph on the tombstone of Aberkios, bishop of Hierapolis in Phrygia, who died around 200. Part of the epitaph translates as, "Having Paul in the carriage, Faith led the way everywhere and set before me as nourishment everywhere a fish from a spring, immense, spotless, which a holy virgin caught." Most scholars concur that the "fish" refers to Jesus Christ. The rest of the epitaph contains other Christian references as well. Hurtado concludes that this particular use of ΙΧΘΥC is a "graphic sign" for Jesus and an expression of Christian faith referring to the acronym "Jesus Christ God's Son Savior."[44]

---

42. The Epigraphic Database (Europeana Eagle Project) lists twenty-six examples of the inscribed word ΙΧΘΥC from Rome alone, mostly from the catacombs and other funerary settings. From other locations across the Roman Empire, there are fifty-nine different texts that have been documented. See also the dozens and dozens of examples in Franz Joseph Dölger, *ICHTHYS*, vol. 1, *Das Fisch-Symbol in frühchristlicher Zeit: ΙΧΘΥC als Kürzung der Namen Jesu IHCOYC XPICTOC ΘEOY YIOC CΩTHP*, 2nd ed. (Münster: Aschendorf, 1928), 192–231. For a more recent discussion, along with numerous examples, see Robin M. Jensen, "Fish Symbol," in *From Celsus to the Catacombs: Visual, Liturgical, and Non-Christian Reception of Jesus in the First Three Centuries CE*, ed. Chris Keith, vol. 3, *The Reception of Jesus in the First Three Centuries*, ed. Chris Keith, Helen Bond, Christine Jacobi, and Jens Schröter (London: T&T Clark, 2020), 275–80.

43. From the Epigraphic Database (European Eagle Project), see the following inscriptions: *RIChrM* 25, *RIChrM* 80, *IG* X.2 1 1017, *IGLSyr* 2 425, *IGLSyr* 2 428, *IGLSyr* 2 458, *IGLSyr* 2 659, *IGLSyr* 2 662, *IGLSyr* 4 1249, *IGLSyr* 4 1422, *IGLSyr* 4 1635, *IGLSyr* 4 1648, *IGLSyr* 5 2457, *IGLSyr* 5 2415, *SEG* 29:1611, *SEG* 31:1418, *AGLSyr* 21.2.60, *ICKarth* 3.271, *IG* XIV 238, *I.Akrai* 44, and *I.Ravenna* 21.

44. Larry W. Hurtado, "Earliest Christian Graphic Symbols: Examples and References from the Second/ Third Centuries," in Garipzanov, Goodson, and Maguire, *Graphic Signs of Identity, Faith, and Power*, 37–38. Coming to this same conclusion, see also William Tabbernee, "Epigraphy," in *The Oxford Handbook*

Also dating to fairly early in the Christian movement, not far away in the city of Apamea in Phrygia, a gravestone epitaph has six lines of Greek text describing the couple buried in the grave. At the bottom of the inscription, standing alone in the center below the last line, is the Greek word IXΘΥΣ (ICHTHUS).[45]

Another example can be seen in the Mausoleum of the *Innocentiores*, part of the catacombs underneath the Basilica of San Sebastiano along the Via Appia just south of Rome. In the mausoleum, the word IXΘΥC is informally scratched on the wall. In between the first two letters (I and X, the letters standing for Jesus Christ), a large *tau* is inscribed, probably representing the cross. This graffito dates to the late second to early third century.[46]

Additional evidence of the widespread familiarity of Christians with the IXΘΥC acrostic comes from the Pectorius inscription (*IG* XIV–2525; *SEG* 29, 825), a funerary monument discovered in France, probably dating to the fourth century (earlier scholars placed it in the third century). Written in Greek, this epitaph mentions IXΘΥC four times. Furthermore, reading vertically down the left-hand column, the first letters of the first word in the first five lines also form the acrostic IXΘΥC.[47]

In Rome, an early Christian tombstone dating to the late second century was discovered on Vatican Hill. It depicts two fish and an anchor with the inscribed words IXΘΥC ZWNTWN[48] (*ichthys zōntōn*, "fish of the living").[49] An important observation is that, although IXΘΥC (fish) is a Greek word and the

---

of Early Christian Studies, ed. Susan Ashbrook Harvey and David G. Hunter (Oxford: Oxford University Press, 2008), 127–28; Everett Ferguson, "Aberkios," in *The Eerdmans Encyclopedia of Early Christian Art and Archaeology*, ed. Paul Corby Finney (Grand Rapids: Eerdmans, 2017), 1:2–3; R. A. Kearsley, "The Epitaph of Aberkios: The Earliest Christian Inscription?", in *New Documents Illustrating Early Christianity*, ed. S. R. Llewlyn and R. A. Kearsley (Marrickville, NSW, Australia: Macquarie University Press, 1992), 177–81; C. R. Morey, "The Origin of the Fish-Symbol: The Inscriptions of Abercius and Pectorius," *Princeton Theological Review* (1910): 282–89; and Dölger, *ICHTHYS*, 1:87–112.

45. *ICG* 962. The old *ICG* database dates this to 212–300.
46. *ICVR* v 12899. Antonio E. Felle, "Late Antique Christian Graffiti: The Case of Rome (Third to Fifth Centuries CE)," in *Cultic Graffiti in the Late Antique Mediterranean and Beyond*, ed. Antonio E. Felle and Bryan Ward-Perkins (Turnhout: Bepols, 2021), 60; Longenecker, *The Cross before Constantine*, 84–85; Robin M. Jensen, Peter Lampe, William Tabbernee, and D. H. Williams, "Italy and Environs," in *Early Christianity in Contexts: An Exploration across Cultures and Continents*, ed. William Tabbernee (Grand Rapids: Baker, 2014), 401.
47. See Henry Preston Vaughan Nunn, *Christian Inscriptions* (New York: Macmillan, 1920), 21–22; Morey, "The Origin of the Fish-Symbol," 282–89; and Dölger, *ICHTHYS*, 1:177–83.
48. The text is in all capitals but uses the small form of the *omega* as a capital.
49. Jutta Dresken-Weiland, "Response to Peter Lampe's *Paul to Valentinus: Christians at Rome in the First Two Centuries*: The Archaeology of *Die stadtrömischen Christen* in 2016," in *The First Urban Churches 6: Rome and Ostia*, ed. James R. Harrison and L. L. Welborn, Writings from the Greco-Roman World Supplement Series 18 (Atlanta: SBL Press, 2021), 452–54; Dölger, *ICHTHYS*, 1:159–77; Spier, *Picturing the Bible*, 197. Dresken-Weiland, 454, and Dölger, 161, date this inscription to the late second century (around 200), while Spier, 197, dates it to the late third century. Each of these sources also presents a good picture of this Christian gravestone.

IXΘΥC acrostic is based on the Greek phrase "Jesus Christ God's Son Savior," this acrostic frequently appears in contexts where the primary language is Latin (e.g., Italy, especially Rome), as in the example above. There are numerous other inscriptions that contain both the Greek word IXΘΥC along with Latin text.[50] For example, Dölger presents a gravestone containing numerous lines of inscribed Latin, including quite a few abbreviated words. Written above the inscription is IXΘΥC (in Greek), and then, written vertically down the left-hand margin, just prior to the Latin lines of text, is the word IXΘΥC. That is, the Greek I (*iota*) is written right before the first line of Latin text, and the Greek X (*chi*) is written right before the second line of Latin text, and so forth. Interestingly, added to the end of the IXΘΥC is the Greek letter N, so the acrostic actually reads IXΘΥCN. In all likelihood, the N is an abbreviation for the Greek word for victory (Νίκη, *Nikē*), a word that is often associated with the cross (especially the Chi-Rho Christogram) and other symbols used in early Christianity for Jesus Christ (see the discussion on "victory" below).[51]

Another place that combines the Greek word IXΘΥC with Latin words and in a Latin context is in Classe, near Ravenna, Italy at the spectacular cross mosaic located in the apse (at the very front and in the most prominent location) of the Basilica of Sant'Apollinare. Below the cross is the Latin phrase SALVSMVNDI ("salvation of the world"), while right above the cross is IXΘΥC in Greek (see fig. 8-5).[52]

Literarily, early in the Christian movement, writers also refer to Jesus Christ as the IXΘΥC. For example, around 198–203, the Christian writer and apologist Tertullian refers to Jesus Christ as "our IXΘΥC" (*Baptism* 1.10). Adding to the probability that Tertullian is referring to the acrostic (Jesus Christ God's Son Savior) and not just to "fish" in general is that Tertullian writes in Latin. In this quote, however, in referring to Jesus Christ, he does not use the Latin word for "fish" (*piscis*) but switches to Greek for this one word. The most logical explanation for this language shift is that he is aware of the acrostic that is associated with the Greek word fish (which doesn't work in Latin) and wants to allude to it.[53]

Writing in Greek, Clement of Alexandria (AD 150–215) tells his people to inscribe Christian symbols on their signet rings, such as a dove, a fish, or a ship's anchor (*Christ the Educator* 3.59.2).[54] Indeed, the word IXΘΥC, with and without a visual depiction of a fish, appears on numerous Christian signet

50. See Dölger, *ICHTHYS*, 1:192–94, 204–6, 214–18.
51. Dölger, *ICHTHYS*, 1:184–87. Dölger notes the possibility that the N is an abbreviation of νικᾷ ("victory"), but he alternately proposes that the N is an abbreviation for Νηπίων ("child"), indicating the early age of the one buried.
52. Herbert L. Kessler, "Bright Gardens of Paradise," in Spier, *Picturing the Bible*, 128–29.
53. Graydon F. Snyder, *Ante Pacem: Archaeological Evidence of Church Life before Constantine* (Macon, GA: Mercer University Press, 2003), 32.
54. For an extensive list and discussion of the symbolic use of the Greek word for fish in the literature of the church fathers, see Liselotte Wehrhahn-Stauch, "Christliche Fischsymbol von den Anfänger bis zum hohen Mittelalter," *Zeitschrift für Kunstgeschichte* 35 (1972): 54–68.

rings from the third and fourth centuries.[55] One of these rings, dating to the third century, has the letters from IXΘΥC in the shape of a cross (with the letter *theta* [Θ] in the center).[56]

Christian writers in the fourth and fifth centuries likewise mention the IXΘΥC acrostic frequently, including Eusebius (*Oration of Constantine to the Assembly of the Saints* 18–19; 260–339), Jerome (*Epistles* 7.3; 342–420), Zeno of Verona (*Tractate on Baptism* 2.13.2; 300–380), Optatus of Milevis (*Against Parmenian* 3.2.1–8), and Quodvultdeus of Carthage (*The Book of Promises and Prophecies of God* 2.39).[57]

Beginning early in the Christian movement, Christians also began to combine their various signs and symbols or to use them in parallel, closely associated situations. The term IXΘΥC, for example, appears numerous times alongside or within the Chi-Rho Christogram and the Tau-Rho Staurogram. Dölger documents pictures and discussions of a large number of inscriptions that contain both the word IXΘΥC and either a Chi-Rho Christogram or the Tau-Rho Staurogram.[58] From the fourth century, for example, there is a red jasper gem containing the Greek word IXΘΥC, but on top of the second letter, *chi* (X), is a *rho* (P), forming a Chi-Rho Christogram within the acrostic.[59] Testa presents two examples in which *rho* (P) has been added to the letter *chi* (X) in IXΘΥC, thus adding a Chi-Rho Christogram on top of, or in addition to, IXΘΥC.[60] This is strong evidence that, beginning early in the Christian movement, the IXΘΥC acrostic was closely associated with other popular and widely used Christian symbols.

Discovered in the ancient city of Sidon (in modern Lebanon), on the four sides of a fourth-century lead sarcophagus, are ten Chi-Rho Christogram symbols. Interestingly, each one of the symbols has the Greek letters forming the word IXΘΥC written clockwise in a circle with each letter appearing in the space created by the intersecting lines of the Chi-Rho Christogram.[61]

In the ancient city of Cibalae in the Roman province of Pannonia Secunda (now modern-day Croatia), a gravestone was discovered with an eight-spoked wheel. The inscribed Latin text above the wheel suggests that the two people buried here were martyred. On the top of the vertical line of the wheel (i.e.,

55. Dölger presents pictures of dozens of examples. Franz Joseph Dölger, *ICHTHYS*, vol. 4, *Die Fischdenkmäler in der frühchristlichen Plastik Malerei und Kleinkunst* (Münster: Aschendorf, 1928), tables 208–209. Spier shows photos of two late third–early fourth century rings that have the word IXΘΥC along with an inscribed fish in Spier, *Picturing the Bible*, 5, 196.

56. Longenecker, *The Cross before Constantine*, 87.

57. Jensen, "Fish Symbol," 279.

58. Dölger, *ICHTHYS*, 1:192, 220 (with four Tau-Rho Staurograms, two of which also have *alpha* and *omega*), 228, 235–39, 251, 254–57, 262–63.

59. Michael Squire and Christopher Whitton, "*Machina Sacra*: Optatian and the Lettered Art of the Christogram," in Garipzanov, Goodson, and Maguire, *Graphic Signs of Identity, Faith, and Power*, 72.

60. Testa, *Il Simbolismo Dei Giudeo-Cristiani*, 38.

61. Dölger, *ICHTHYS*, 1:235–39.

the capital letter *iota*, I) a loop has been added, changing this letter to a *rho* as in the Chi-Rho symbol.[62] Or perhaps one could view this as a Chi-Rho Christogram to which a horizontal line was added and around which a circle was inscribed (i.e., the *theta*, Θ). Some have suggested that perhaps this is a combination of the Chi-Rho Christogram and the Tau-Rho Staurogram. Yet putting the symbols in a circle (creating the Θ, *theta*) argues that this is more likely a combination of the Chi-Rho Christogram and the ICHTHUS Christogram. As discussed above, variations of cross symbols were frequent.[63] That the wheel occurs with some creative variation is in keeping with the variety of ways the other Christian symbols are used. In addition to the Chi-Rho incorporated into the ICHTHUS Christogram through the simple addition of the loop from the letter *rho*, the eight-spoked wheel also occurs with the top horizontal line of the *tau* (T) added to the central vertical line (the *iota*).[64]

This combination of the ICHTHUS with a Chi-Rho Christogram was found on a pendant of the Roman Empress Maria (AD 384–407). Maria was the daughter of Stilicho, a famous general of the western Roman Empire. Married to the Emperor Honorius at an early age, Maria died in 407 at a fairly young age (perhaps twenty-three to twenty-four years old). Her sarcophagus was discovered in the Mausoleum of Honorius near Old St. Peter's Basilica in Rome. A number of jewelry items were found inside her sarcophagus, including a beautiful gold pendant, which was perhaps a bridal gift (now in the Louvre, no. OA9523). On both sides of the pendant is an eight-spoked wheel, with the loop from the *rho* added to the *iota* in the middle, as in a Chi-Rho symbol. Thus, as in the gravestone at Pannonia above, it appears to be a combination of the ICHTHUS and the Chi-Rho Christogram. Forming the IΧΘΥC and Chi-Rho letters on both sides of the pendant are the names of Maria's family—husband, parents, and other close relatives—in Latin.[65]

Starting in the fourth century and continuing into the fifth century, after Constantine ended the Great Persecution and gave imperial support to Christianity, churches were built by the hundreds all across the Roman Empire. The ruins of many of these churches have survived, and the mosaic floor of the church (or monastery) is one of the features that is most likely to have survived. On three church floors, one in Stobi, North Macedonia, and two

---

62. This tombstone is in the City Museum of Vinkovci (GMVi inv. A–736). See Branka Migotti, "The Archaeological Material of the Early Christian Period in Continental Croatia," in *From the Invincible Sun to the Sun of Justice: Early Christianity in Continental Croatia*, ed. Zeljko Demo (Zagreb, Croatia: The Archaeological Museum in Zagreb, 1994); and Gaetano S. Bevelacqua, "Observations on Christian Epigraphy in Pannonia," *Studia Patristica* 73 (Leuven: Peeters, 2014), 109.

63. Guarducci, *The Tomb of St. Peter*, 114, presents a seal in which the letter P is used as a Greek letter P (*rho*) in a Chi-Rho Christogram as well as a Latin letter P as part of the phrase *Spes Dei* ("the hope of God").

64. Testa, *Il Simbolismo Dei Giudeo-Cristiani*, 373. See the photo on Plate 40, photo 1.

65. See the discussion in Garipzanov, *Graphic Signs of Authority in Late Antiquity*, 78–79. Garipzanov suggests that the "graphic composition . . . is neither text nor image. It belongs to the realm of early Christian graphicacy." He also implies that the combination is of the Chi-Rho and the Tau-Rho.

in modern Israel (in the Church of the Nativity at Bethlehem and in the monastery at Beth-Hashitta), the IXΘΥC acrostic appears (see the discussion on each below). In addition, at the city of Cyrene in North Africa, IXΘΥC appears in an inscription probably dating to the fourth century, suggesting that the teacher and the students referred to in the inscription are Christians.[66]

From these examples, it can be seen that the acrostic IXΘΥC was in fairly wide usage as a reference to Jesus Christ throughout the third to sixth centuries (AD 200–600). The popular notion, however, that the fish was somehow a secret sign that the early Christians used to make discreet contact is highly unlikely, and there is no historical evidence for that use.[67]

THE ICHTHUS ACROSTIC IN THE SIBYLLINE ORACLES

One of the most fascinating and strongest pieces of evidence demonstrating the popularity of the IXΘΥC acrostic comes from the Sibylline Oracles. The Sibyl in Greek legend, tradition, and literature was a female oracle or prophet. According to this widely accepted ancient legend, she was not consulted for specific advice like the Pythia at Delphi but spoke on her own accord as moved by the gods. The earliest reference in Greek literature to the Sibyl and her prophecies dates to 500 BC (Heraclitus). From ancient times, her oracles were written down in Greek hexameter poetry, and the frequent use of acrostics was deemed a mark of authenticity. According to legend, the official collection of Sibylline Oracles was kept in Rome in the temple of Jupiter. When the temple was destroyed in a fire in 83 BC, this original collection of Sibylline Oracles perished. From the third century BC on, Greek-language Jewish Sibylline literature began to appear. Later on in the Christian era, Christian material was apparently added as well. The current collection referred to as the Sibylline Oracles (some suggest that "pseudo-Sibylline" might be more appropriate) dates from around 180 BC to the third century AD (and includes both Jewish and Christian material). Numerous early Christian writers, however, referred to the Sibylline Oracles as authentic ancient prophecies.

One of the texts in the Sibylline Oracles that was frequently cited by early Christian writers as evidence of prophecy pointing to Jesus Christ occurs in Book 8, lines 217 to 250.[68] This text contains a clear example of the IXΘΥC

66. Richard George Goodchild, *Kyrene und Apollinia* (Zurich: Raggi, 1971), 141–42; Joyce Reynolds, "The Christian Inscriptions of Cyrenaica," *The Journal of Theological Studies* 11.2 (1960): 287–88; Edwin M. Yamauchi, *Africa and the Bible* (Grand Rapids: Baker, 2004), 201.
67. Tabbernee concludes, "There is no evidence to support the view that the fish acrostic or fish iconography accompanying inscriptions ever functioned as clandestine signs, meant to suppress or disguise rather than reveal associated meanings and identities." Tabbernee, "Epigraphy," 1:476–81.
68. See John J. Collins, "Sibylline Oracles," *ABD* 6:2–6; Ursula Treu, "Christian Sibyllines," in *New Testament Apocrypha*, ed. Wilhelm Schneemelcher, rev. ed. (Louisville: Westminster John Knox, 1992), 2:652–56, 673–74; Thomas J. Kraus, "Christianized Texts," in *From Thomas to Tertullian: Christian Literary Receptions of Jesus in the Second and Third Centuries CE*, ed. Chris Keith, Helen K.

acrostic. The first letter of each line combines to form the phrase "Jesus Christ God's Son Savior" (Ἰησοῦς Χριστός θεοῦ Ὑιός Σωτήρ). In capitals, as presented below, it is ΙΗΣΟΥΣ ΧΡΕΙΣΤΟΣ ΘΕΟΥ ΥΙΟΣ ΣΩΤΗΡ, plus an additional word at the end: ΣΤΑΥΡΟΣ ("cross"). The Greek text is presented below to illustrate this acrostic clearly. Even if you are not able to read Greek, you should be able to spot the Greek letters ΙΗΣΟΥΣ (Jesus) ΧΡΕΙΣΤΟΣ (Christ) ΘΕΟΥ (God's) ΥΙΟΣ (Son) ΣΩΤΗΡ (Savior) ΣΤΑΥΡΟΣ (cross) running down the left-hand margin in the text of the Sibylline Oracles presented below:

[217] Ἰδρώσει δὲ χθών, κρίσεως σημεῖον ὅτ᾽ ἔσται.
[218] Ἥξει δ᾽ οὐρανόθεν βασιλεὺς αἰῶσιν ὁ μέλλων,
[219] Σάρκα παρὼν πᾶσαν κρῖναι καὶ κόσμον ἅπαντα.
[220] Ὄψονται δὲ θεὸν μέροπες πιστοὶ καὶ ἄπιστοι
[221] Ὕψιστον μετὰ τῶν ἁγίων ἐπὶ τέρμα χρόνοιο.
[222] Σαρκοφόρων δ᾽ ἀνδρῶν ψυχὰς ἐπὶ βήματι κρίνει,
[223] Χέρσος ὅταν ποτὲ κόσμος ὅλος καὶ ἄκανθα γένηται.
[224] Ῥίψουσιν δ᾽ εἴδωλα βροτοὶ καὶ πλοῦτον ἅπαντα.
[225] Ἐκκαύσει δὲ τὸ πῦρ γῆν οὐρανὸν ἠδὲ θάλασσαν
[226] Ἰχνεῦον, ῥήξει τε πύλας εἱρκτῆς Ἀίδαο.
[227] Σὰρξ τότε πᾶσα νεκρῶν ἐς ἐλευθέριον φάος ἥξει
[228] Τῶν ἁγίων· ἀνόμους δὲ τὸ πῦρ αἰῶσιν ἐλέγξει.
[229] Ὁππόσα τις πράξας ἔλαθεν, τότε πάντα λαλήσει·
[230] Στήθεα γὰρ ζοφόεντα θεὸς φωστῆρσιν ἀνοίξει.
[231] Θρῆνος δ᾽ ἐκ πάντων ἔσται καὶ βρυγμὸς ὀδόντων.
[232] Ἐκλείψει σέλας ἠελίου ἄστρων τε χορεῖαι.
[233] Οὐρανὸν εἱλίξει· μήνης δέ τε φέγγος ὀλεῖται.
[234] Ὑψώσει δὲ φάραγγας, ὀλεῖ δ᾽ ὑψώματα βουνῶν,
[235] Ὕψος δ᾽ οὐκέτι λυγρὸν ἐν ἀνθρώποισι φανεῖται.
[236] Ἴσα δ᾽ ὄρη πεδίοις ἔσται καὶ πᾶσα θάλασσα
[237] Οὐκέτι πλοῦν ἕξει. γῆ γὰρ φρυχθεῖσα τότ᾽ ἔσται
[238] Σὺν πηγαῖς, ποταμοί τε καχλάζοντες λείψουσιν.
[239] Σάλπιγξ δ᾽ οὐρανόθεν φωνὴν πολύθρηνον ἀφήσει
[240] Ὠρύουσα μύσος μελέων καὶ πήματα κόσμου.
[241] Ταρτάρεον δὲ χάος δείξει τότε γαῖα χανοῦσα.
[242] Ἥξουσιν δ᾽ ἐπὶ βῆμα θεοῦ βασιλῆος ἅπαντες.
[243] Ῥεύσει δ᾽ οὐρανόθεν ποταμὸς πυρὸς ἠδὲ θεείου.
[244] Σῆμα δέ τοι τότε πᾶσι βροτοῖς, σφρηγὶς ἐπίσημος
[245] Τὸ ξύλον ἐν πιστοῖς, τὸ κέρας τὸ ποθούμενον ἔσται,
[246] Ἀνδρῶν εὐσεβέων ζωή, πρόσκομμα δὲ κόσμου,
[247] Ὕδασι φωτίζον κλητοὺς ἐν δώδεκα πηγαῖς·

Bond, Christine Jacobi, and Jens Schröter, vol. 2, *The Reception of Jesus in the First Three Centuries*, ed. Jens Schröter and Christine Jacobi (London: T&T Clark, 2020), 394–96; and Daniel M. Gurtner, *Introducing the Pseudepigrapha of Second Temple Judaism* (Grand Rapids: Baker, 2020), 124–41.

²⁴⁸ Ῥάβδος ποιμαίνουσα σιδηρείη γε κρατήσει.
²⁴⁹ Οὗτος ὁ νῦν προγραφεὶς ἐν ἀκροστιχίοις θεὸς ἡμῶν
²⁵⁰ Σωτὴρ ἀθάνατος βασιλεύς, ὁ παθὼν ἕνεχ' ἡμῶν.⁶⁹

Each line in this section of the Sibylline Oracles emphasizes theological and eschatological themes relating to Jesus Christ (his sovereignty and authority, death and resurrection, etc.). Note especially the translation of the last two lines, which conclude, "This is our God, now proclaimed in acrostics/ the king, the immortal savior, who suffered for us."[70]

Note also that the word for "cross" was added to the end of the ΙΧΘΥC acrostic. That is, the word "Savior" ends at line 243, and lines 244–250 start with the letters ΣΤΑΥΡΟΣ (STAUROS, "cross"). This is an interesting, but not surprising, phenomenon in light of the frequent way that the ΙΧΘΥC acrostic and the eight-spoked wheel are so often used in close conjunction with traditional crosses. Longenecker writes, "It does illustrate . . . that the artisan who crafted this third-century poem thought that the cross was inseparable from reflection on the identity of 'Jesus Christ, Son of God, Savior.' "[71]

It is not known when this Christianized portion of the Sibylline Oracles was produced, but it has to be before the early fourth century, for, according to the church historian Eusebius (writing around AD 330–339), the Emperor Constantine gave a speech in which he cited this entire portion of the Sibylline Oracles as a prophecy foretelling Jesus Christ.[72] Writing later in 426, the early church theologian Augustine cites this entire acrostic passage from the Sibylline Oracles (*Civ.* 18:23). Also, Maximus of Turin (AD 380–465) references this part of the Sibylline Oracles and specifically points out the ΙΧΘΥC acrostic and its meaning (*Against the Pagans*, 4).[73] These three examples from well-known and widely read churchmen provide strong evidence that this acrostic was considered quite significant and was well-known.[74]

THE EIGHT-SPOKED WHEEL AND THE ICHTHUS ACROSTIC

While the evidence for ΙΧΘΥC as a frequently used acrostic for Jesus Christ in the early church is extremely strong, what case can be made to connect it

---

69. Sibylline Oracles 8:217–250. Ken Penner and Michael S. Heiser, "Old Testament Greek Pseudepigrapha with Morphology" (Bellingham, WA: Lexham Press, 2008), exported from Logos Bible Software.

70. Kraus, "Christianized Texts," 396.

71. Longenecker, *The Cross before Constantine*, 149–51.

72. Eusebius, *Oration of Constantine to the Assembly of the Saints*, chapter 18.

73. For the actual text, see A. Spagnolo and C. H. Turner, "Maximus of Turin: Against the Pagans/Contra Paganos," *The Journal of Theological Studies* 17.7 (1916): 332. Some scholars have questioned whether Maximus actually wrote *Against the Pagans*. Even if it is a forgery, this document still demonstrates the widespread acceptance and belief that the Sibylline Oracles prophesied Jesus Christ with the ΙΧΘΥC acrostic.

74. Jensen, "Fish Symbol," 278–79; Dölger, *ICHTHYS*, 1:52–68.

to the eight-spoked wheel graffito or to the eight-spoked wheel in church architecture? The evidence for the connection between the ΙΧΘΥC acrostic and the eight-spoked wheel is strong and derives from a number of different sources. Many of these will be discussed in more detail in chapters 5–8, but it will be helpful to include a few short summaries here.

Just south of Rome, along the ancient road referred to as Via Appia, was an impressive, lavish residence called the Villa of the Quintili (see more in chapter 8). Discovered in the excavations of this villa was a section of alabaster wall plaster that has an eight-spoked wheel painted on it. Underneath the wheel is a title box,[75] and written in the title box is the word ΙΧΘΥC (see fig. 2–11).[76] Dating to the fourth century, this combination of the word ICHTHUS

Fig. 2-11 Rome, Villa of the Quintili: Wall Plaster with Eight-Spoked Wheel Fragment and the Greek Word ΙΧΘΥC (ICHTHUS)

with the eight-spoked wheel is powerful evidence for connecting the two and concluding that the wheel is a Christogram developed from the letters in the word ΙΧΘΥC.[77]

Another strong piece of evidence comes from the recently discovered Peristyle House Church at Laodicea (in modern Turkey). In one of the central rooms, the floor paving consists of a terra-cotta-style brick arranged in panels

75. This was initially discovered in the latter half of the eighteenth century. An initial drawing of this alabaster wall painting was made by the archaeologist before the panel was further damaged. This drawing reveals the rest of the circle, clearly identifying it as an eight-spoked wheel. For a discussion and a replication of this drawing, see Dölger, *ICHTHYS*, 1:231–35. This alabaster painting does seem to combine the ΙΧΘΥC Christogram with the Chi-Rho Christogram, for to the vertical line (capital *iota*) a small loop has been added, making it serve also as a *rho*. As discussed below, a very similar eight-spoked wheel with a *rho* was discovered in Pannonia on a tombstone (funerary block) also dating to the second half of the fourth century (Inscription of Venatorinus and Martoria, ILJ 283).

76. Rita Paris, ed., *Via Appia: The Villa of the Quintili* (Milan: Electa, 2000), 15, 70.

77. *ICUR* 5.15413; Paris, *The Villa of the Quintili*, 15, 70–71; Lucrezia Spera, "The Christianization of Space along the Via Appia: Changing Landscape in the Suburbs of Rome," *American Journal of Archaeology* 107.1 (2003): 35–37; Tuomas Rasimus, "Revisiting the *ICHTHYS*: A Suggestion Concerning the Origins of Christological Fish Symbolism," in *Mystery and Secrecy in the Nag Hammadi Collection and Other Ancient Literature: Ideas and Practices: Studies for Einar Thomassen at Sixty*, ed. Christian H. Bull, Liv Ingeborg Lied, and John D. Turner (Leiden and Boston: Brill, 2012), 337–44; and Dölger, *ICHTHYS*, 1:231–35.

to create images or designs. There are two panels next to each other—the design for one panel is the eight-spoked wheel; the design for the other panel is a fish. Near these two panels, on the street paving adjacent to the house church, inscribed on stone and centered in the middle of the main entrance to the house church, is an eight-spoked-wheel graffito. While the house itself dates to the first century, the conversion to a house church (or perhaps the house of a wealthy Christian, a bishop, or other leader) probably took place in the early fourth century (see chapter 5). The side-by-side layout of the eight-spoked wheel and the fish present strong evidence that the wheel stood for ICHTHUS.

The archaeological remains at Ephesus also contain an eight-spoked wheel intricately and professionally carved into a stone wall panel from the interior/front side in the Church of St. Mary (early fifth century) (see fig. 1-2 and chapter 6). There are only two symbols on this wall—a cross and an eight-spoked wheel. This phenomenon, a cross and an eight-spoked wheel used in parallel, occurs quite frequently, especially, but not exclusively, in church architecture. This implies that the eight-spoked wheel carried a strong theological significance, a symbolic meaning similar in importance to the cross. The IXΘΥC acrostic explanation is, by far, the most plausible understanding for the significance of the eight-spoked wheel when it is used in parallel with the cross.

Discovered on the lintel of a house door in the village of Bābiskā (Syria) were a number of Christian symbols, including various crosses, perhaps serving an apotropaic function to protect and keep demons away. One of the symbols is an eight-spoked wheel inscribed inside of a box. The presence of this symbol among other Christian symbols strongly suggests that it is also Christian. The Greek inscription beside the wheel translates as "One God and Christ, be (the) helper of Flavius Eusebios." The inscription is clearly dated as well, placing this inscription at 350.[78]

Across the Roman/Byzantine Empire, especially during the fourth to sixth centuries, ICHTHUS Christograms proliferated alongside traditional crosses and Chi-Rho Christograms as graffiti on streets and in the remains or reuse of once-powerful pagan temples; as architectural features in churches, such as mosaics and stone wall panels; and in professionally inscribed stonework, as well as in floor and wall mosaics of public spaces, such as colonnaded walkways, converted bathhouses, and aqueducts.

---

78. William Kelly Prentice, *Greek and Latin Inscriptions*, The Publications of the American Archaeological Expedition to Syria in 1899–1900, Part III (New York: Century, 1908), 84–85 (no. 66); Testa, *Il Simbolismo Dei Guideo-Cristiani*, 305–6.

CHAPTER 3

GRAFFITI GAME BOARDS
IN GRECO-ROMAN CITIES

INTRODUCTION

A mong the informally inscribed graffiti that appears in the paving stones and on other stone surfaces throughout the archaeological remains of Greco-Roman cities are a number of rectangular shapes and patterns that appear to be the playing boards for various games. Occasionally, these playing boards are inscribed more professionally as well. Because the eight-spoked ICHTHUS Christogram sometimes appears near these game boards (see fig. 3–1), a number of scholars and other writers have concluded that both the circles and the rectangular shapes are *all* game boards. For our study, it will be helpful to explore the occurrences of stone-inscribed graffiti game boards in Greco-Roman cities.

THE POPULARITY OF RECTANGULAR GAME BOARDS

Board games are widely attested in the Greco-Roman world throughout late antiquity, both in literature and in archaeology. Ovid (43–17 BC), for example, in his work of poetry entitled *The Art of Love*, writes that in courtship it is helpful, even for the woman, to know how to compete in games. Ovid specifically mentions "dice" and "the battle of the brigands." He also describes one of the games, writing, "There is a sort of game confined by subtle method into as many lines as the slippery year has months [i.e., twelve]: a small board has three counters on either side, whereon to join your pieces together is to conquer."[1]

---

1. Ovid, *The Art of Love* 3.355–380 (Mozley, LCL).

Ovid is describing the game known as *Ludus Duodecim Scriptorum* (the Game of Twelve Lines), sometimes generically referred to as *alea*. While the majority of the game boards used to play this game were probably made of wood and have not survived, many of them were etched into stone, both professionally and informally, and a number of these have survived. They are easily recognizable, for they typically have two columns of small squares or circles divided by a series of three small geometric shapes. In each column are three rows with six small squares or circles. Reading across the columns, the rows have two groups of six, for a total of twelve squares or circles. With three rows of twelve, the board has a total of thirty-six small squares or circles. Several examples of this game board can be seen at Aphrodisias, Didyma, Laodicea, and Ephesus (see figs. 3–2 and 3–3).

There is a popular variant of this game in which letters are used instead of the small squares or circles (often the letters are inside of the small squares). These letters are also arranged in two columns that each have three groups of six letters, for a total of thirty-six letters (see fig. 3–4). This particular game board appears with some frequency in Greco-Roman cities (with differing letter combinations), particularly in Italy and North Africa, and especially in Rome (where they are usually written in Latin).[2] While the

Fig. 3-1 Didyma, Temple of Apollo: *Alea* Gameboard next to ICHTHUS Christograms

Fig. 3-2 Laodicea: *Alea* Gameboard

2.   Nicholas Purcell, "Literate Games: Roman Urban Society and the Game of Alea," *Past and Present* 147 (1995): 18–19.

Fig. 3-3 Ephesus, Curetes Street:
Fragment of an *Alea* Gameboard

Fig. 3-4 Ephesus, Museum:
Alea Gameboard with Letters

specific letters played a role in this complex literary game, the letters also often spelled out something clever (e.g., "no one can play with lucky right hand on all occasions"; "hunting, bathing, playing, laughing: this is living"), while frequently abbreviating some of the longer words to stay within the six-letter-per-unit requirement.[3] These short, pithy sayings typically fell into one of three categories: 1) luck; 2) circus factions (the Blues and Greens chariot teams); and 3) military victories.[4]

One very unusual game board of this type was discovered near Rome and is now in the Capitoline Museums (Museo della Civilta Romana, MCR 3574). Following the typical pattern of six words—with six letters arranged in two columns of three rows—this board reads, in Latin: *ABEMUS* (abbreviated from Habemus to stay with six letters) *INCENA PULLUM PISCEM PERNAM PAONEM*. This can translate as a tavern menu: "we have, for dinner, chicken, fish, ham, peacock."[5]

Then written underneath the "menu" are two more words (*BENA TORES*), probably not part of the game but a reference to the venatores,[6] the trained armed warriors who specifically fought and killed wild animals—lions, bears, elephants, and so forth—in the stadiums and theaters of the

3. Purcell, "Roman Urban Society and the Game of Alea," 23.
4. Anita Rieche, "Board Games and Their Symbols from Roman Times to Early Christianity," in Finkel, *Ancient Board Games in Perspective*, 88.
5. Purcell, "Roman Urban Society and the Game of Alea," 24.
6. In Latin inscriptions, B and V are often used interchangeably.

Roman Empire. However, they most certainly did not fight chickens, fish, pigs, or peacocks. There is some humor involved here, as is typical for these type of game boards.

Most of these *alea*-style game boards, both the ones with letters and the ones with just two columns of squares or holes, have three symbols or geometric designs in the center between the two groups of six letters.[7] On this "tavern menu" game board from Rome, the symbols dividing the two columns, with one placed on each of the three rows, are a leaf, an eight-spoked wheel, and a branch (or peacock feather?). In this case, the eight-spoked wheel could, at first glance, be dismissed as merely a geometric design. But that is unlikely. First of all, the other two (especially the stylized leaf) are common symbols (used particularly with inscriptions and funerary epitaphs, both Christian and non-Christian);[8] they are probably not just random geometric designs. In addition, these three identical symbols (except there is an encircled Chi-Rho Christogram instead of the eight-spoked wheel in the middle) appear on a funerary inscription from Pannonia. The Chi-Rho Christogram establishes this inscription as a Christian inscription.[9]

Second, on the "tavern menu" game board, the eight-spoked wheel sits right next to the word *PISCEM*, Latin for "fish." This could, of course, just be coincidence. Yet keep in mind that this "tavern menu" game board was found in Rome, only a few miles away from the Villa of the Quintili where the word IXΘΥC was written right below an eight-spoked wheel.

A number of questions emerge. Does the function of this game board have anything to do with being a real menu for a tavern? That is, is it a real menu in the form of a game board (unlikely) or a game board that is using a menu as the words needed for the game (more likely)? Why are the venators mentioned, and how are they connected? Is the fact that the eight-spoked wheel, so often associated with the Greek word for fish, is placed adjacent to the Latin word for fish purely coincidental? Is this a "Christian" game board? Or is it a hostile parody of the Christians?[10]

This is complicated by the fact that the popularity of *alea* game boards continued into the post-Constantine era after the cities became predominately Christian. In general, bishops and other influential Christian theologians opposed the practice of public gambling. Probably related to this opposition was the practice among Christians, especially in Rome, to reuse these stone

---

7.   Purcell, "Roman Urban Society and the Game of Alea," 20. See the pictures in Peter Talloen, "Rolling the Dice: Public Game Boards from Sagalassos," *Journal on Hellenistic and Roman Material Culture* 7.1–2 (2018): 103, 106, 111, 113–14, 117–18. Talloen, 118, also presents a picture of a stone *alea* game board with two columns of blank squares instead of letters but with three Maltese crosses inscribed in circles dividing the columns. This game board is from the State Agora at Ephesus.

8.   See, for example, Roueché, *Aphrodisias in Late Antiquity*, PL IX, 31; PL XVI, 62, 64, 65.

9.   Bevelacqua, "Observations on Christian Epigraphy in Pannonia," 107 (plate V, fig. 14).

10. During the Great Persecution, a number of Christians had been executed in the stadiums and theaters by facing (unarmed) the same wild animals that the venatores normally fought.

Fig. 3-5 Ephesus, Street: 2 x 6 Grid Gameboard

alea game boards as the covers for tombs.[11] This may have been for economic or convenience reasons (these large stone game boards had been abandoned and were inexpensive) or perhaps an indication that the deceased had once been a gambler (perhaps prior to conversion).[12]

Not surprisingly, in spite of official church opposition to public gambling, the practice continued even after Christians gained political control of the empire. There even seems to have been an attempt by some of these gamblers to bring their Christian "belief" into the gambling process or to "sanctify" the game. A modern comparison would be the prayers offered up in Las Vegas while gamblers desperately seek to win. Some clutch small crucifixes, angels, or saints in their hands, and it is not unusual to see someone make the sign of the cross right before they pull the lever on the slot machine. Likewise, in the letters of one ancient *alea* game board is an invocation (in Greek) for Jesus to help the gambler to win. In addition, there are a few *alea* game boards with crosses on them (one at Ephesus and one at Sagalassos).[13]

There are other shapes that have been discovered in archaeology that are probably game boards as well. In the ruins of many Greco-Roman cities there are a number of grid-type graffiti, both square and rectangular. These are subdivided into smaller squares (like a chessboard), and they come in a wide variety of combinations in regard to the number and the layout of the smaller squares in the grid. The number of squares in the square-style grid can be 4 (2 x 2), 64 (8 x 8), 100 (10 x 10), or 225 (15 x 15), and in the rectangular-style grid there can be 10 (2 x 5), 12 (2 x 6), 16 (2 x 8), or 20 (2 x 10) (see figs. 3–5 and 3–6). Sometimes there are small, cup-sized holes in the stone instead of squares. These game boards with holes are also usually in grids with a wide variety of combinations (2 x 3, 2 x 4, 3 x 6, 7 x 7, etc.).[14]

11. Rieche, "Board Games and Their Symbols," 88; Purcell, "Roman Urban Society and the Game of Alea," 18–19.
12. Purcell, "Roman Urban Society and the Game of Alea," 19.
13. CIG 8083; see Purcell, "Roman Urban Society and the Game of Alea," 19; and Talleon, "Public Game Boards from Sagalassos," 120.
14. For a discussion on these shapes and locations for them, see R. C. Bell, "Notes on Pavement Games of Greece and Rome," in Finkel, *Ancient Board Games in Perspective*, 98–99; Bell and Roueché, "Graeco-Roman Pavement Signs and Game Board," 106–9.

Many of these squares, rectangles, and grids are undoubtedly game boards. As noted above, scholars have even been able to name some of the games played on these various types of game boards.[15] A bit more speculative are those writers who have presented the rules for these games, for this involves quite a bit of conjecture.[16] One scholar summarizes the challenge in determining the rules for these ancient games: "While literary sources have been extensively used for the interpretation of better known games such as the *ludus latrunculorum* . . . the interpretation of most Roman games relies entirely on the physical evidence. As a result, some games are satisfactorily understood, while our understanding of others is limited."[17]

Fig. 3-6 Aphrodisias, Theater Seat: 2 x 5 Grid Gameboard

ARE THERE CIRCULAR GRAFFITI GAME BOARDS?

Circular-shaped graffiti, especially four-spoked wheels and eight-spoked wheels, occur in Greco-Roman cities even more frequently than the rectangular and square shapes. Another huge conjecture, without any corroborating literary evidence, is the assumption made by a number of writers that, simply because *some* of the graffiti shapes (the rectangles and squares) are game boards, then *all* inscribed graffiti shapes (including circles) are game boards.[18] Indeed, again without any ancient literary evidence, some go so far as to declare names for the games played on these circular shapes, such as "three men's morris," "circular merel," "wheel-type mill," "round mill" (*Rundmühle*), or simply "mill games."[19] Often the rules for these "circle games" are

---

15. For a good discussion of the literary sources that assist in providing these names for Roman games, see Ulrich Schädler, "Scripta, Alea, Tabula: New Evidence for the Roman History of 'Backgammon,' " *New Approaches to Board Games Research: Asian Origins and Future Perspective*, Working Papers Series 3 (Leiden: International Institute for Asian Studies, 1995), 73–98.

16. Purcell, "Roman Urban Society and the Game of Alea," 3–37; H. J. R. Murray, *A History of Board-Games Other Than Chess* (Oxford: Clarendon, 1952), 30–34; David Parlett, *Parlett's History of Board Games* (Brattleboro, VT: Echo, 2018), 70–72.

17. Francesco Trifilò, "Movement, Gaming, and the Use of Space in the Forum," in *Rome, Ostia, Pompeii: Movement and Space*, ed. Ray Laurence and David J. Newsome (Oxford: Oxford University Press, 2011), 320.

18. Murray, for example, in discussing an eight-spoked wheel graffito, states, "It is difficult to see any reason for the cutting of these diagrams other than for use in playing board-games" (*A History of Board Games*, 18–19).

19. Carl Blümlein, *Bilder aus dem römisch-germanischen Kulturleben* (München and Berlin: R. Oldenbourg, 1918), 101–2; Parlett, *Parlett's History of Game Boards*, 116–18. For a discussion of

not addressed at all, but when they are addressed, the suggested rules of the game are frequently similar to the modern, simplistic game of tic-tac-toe.

The source of this speculative interpretation for the circle-type graffiti, especially for the eight-spoked wheel (but also the four-spoked wheel), can be traced back to writers in the early twentieth century. For example, Carl Blümlein (1918) assumed that the eight-spoked wheel was a game board and then, without any outside evidence, speculated on the rules of the game, proposing rules similar to the modern tic-tac-toe.[20] Thédenat (1904), assuming that the eight-spoked wheels were game boards, suggested a cultural setting for making the game boards and playing them—that of idle people just killing time.[21] These two speculations were uncritically accepted and disseminated widely throughout the twentieth century.[22] Even today, a popular view among authors of guidebooks, scholars of game-board history, and other scholars and writers engaging with ancient Greco-Roman culture and archaeology is that the eight-spoked wheel graffito is a game board, one of many different types of game boards used for public gambling.[23]

In recent years, however, this view has been seriously challenged from several different fields. From the field of game board studies, Schädler points out the lack of *any* evidence connecting graffiti circles or "wheels" to the "merel" or "mill" type game, calling the identification "mere conjecture."[24] Roueché, one of the primary archaeologists and inscription scholars of Aphrodisias, cautions against simply identifying *all* shapes of graffiti as game boards. She points out that at Aphrodisias, some of the graffiti are probably "*topos* inscriptions—that is, names, monograms, or other phrases, apparently reserving spaces—whether for peddlers or for spectators or participants at public gatherings . . . a 'place' indication to show where people should stand on particular occasions."[25]

A number of scholars have pointed out that the suggested tic-tac-toe-style rules of the game for these circles are too simplistic and noncompetitive for a

this development, see Florian Ulrich Maximilian Heimann and Ulrich Schädler, "The Loop within Circular Three Men's Morris," *Board Games Studies Journal Online* 8 (2014): 51–53.

20. Blümlein, *Bilder aus dem römisch-germanischen Kulturleben*, 101–2.

21. Thédenat, *Le Forum Romain*, 218.

22. For a brief discussion of this history, see Heimann and Schädler, "The Loop within Circular Three Men's Morris," 51–61.

23. Jerome Murphy-O'Connor, *The Holy Land: An Oxford Archaeological Guide*, 5th ed. (Oxford: Oxford University Press, 2008), 36; Parlett, *Parlett's History of Board Games*, 116–17; Maffia, *Temple of Apollo at Didyma*, 16–17; Bell, "Notes on Pavement Games of Greece and Rome," 98–99; and Murray, *A History of Board-Games*, 18–34.

24. Ulrich Schädler, "Games, Greek and Roman," in *The Encyclopedia of Ancient History*, ed. R. S. Bagnall, K. Broderson, A. Erskine, and S. Huebner (London: Blackwell, 2013), 2841–44. See also Heimann and Schräder, "The Loop within Circular Three Men's Morris," 51–61.

25. Charlotte Roueché, "Late Roman and Byzantine Game Boards at Aphrodisias," in *Ancient Board Games in Perspective: Papers from the 1990 British Museum Colloquium, with Additional Contributions*, ed. I. L. Finkel (London: The British Museum, 2007), 100.

public gambling game. While perhaps games played in private homes may have *sometimes* been casual, the public gambling games were intense and serious, as considerable sums of money were often involved and tempers frequently flared. Purcell writes, "The game was about money, and the point of playing was profit. . . . Gambling made *alea* both deceptive and violent."[26] Tic-tac-toe-style rules are just too simplistic. With only a low level of skill, as in tic-tac-toe, the game would always result in a stalemate, challenging perhaps for small children but highly unlikely to be played by serious, competitive, gambling-addicted adults. Schädler also underscores that this circular tic-tac-toe-style game is not attested anywhere else in the world.[27] This makes it improbable that these rules could be used for a serious gambling game played upon an eight-spoked wheel. This is even less likely in the case of a four-spoked wheel, where no rules at all have been proposed, just the assumption that it must be a game board.

The assumption that if some graffiti shapes are game boards, then all graffiti shapes are game boards is just that—an assumption, one contradictory to much of the evidence. As we have noted throughout this book, there are quite a few clear Christian symbols that show up as graffiti—Latin crosses, equilateral crosses, Tau-Rho Staurograms, and Chi-Rho Christograms. Furthermore, Jewish menorahs appear in graffiti at Ephesus and Laodicea. Clearly the crosses and the menorahs are not game boards but religious symbols, so one cannot just assume that all of the graffiti shapes that appear in Greco-Roman cities are game boards.

In some cases, the location of the eight-spoked wheel graffiti argues strongly, even *conclusively*, against viewing them as game boards. For example, as discussed in chapter 6, inscribed on top of the altar at the famous Temple of Apollo at Delphi are five eight-spoked wheels along with over one hundred crosses. These are clearly not game boards but Christian symbols.

Finally, the frequent appearance of the eight-spoked-wheel symbol along with the four-spoked-wheel symbol in Christian church architecture, often used in parallel with the cross, clearly establishes these two shapes as prominent and important Christian symbols. This forms a very strong argument that, when appearing in graffiti, especially alongside crosses, the eight-spoked wheel and the four-spoked wheel are Christian symbols. Other than occasional proximity to game boards, there is no evidence at all that the eight-spoked wheel (or the four-spoked wheel) is a game board.

---

26. Purcell, "Roman Urban Society and the Game of Alea," 9–10. Lanciani provides a substantial list of Roman literary sources in which sizable sums of money changing hands because of gambling wins and losses are cited. Likewise he cites several sources that refer to altercations and hard feelings deriving from these gambling games. See Rodolfo Lanciani, "Gambling and Cheating in Ancient Rome," *The North American Review* 155.428 (1892): 97–105. See also Schädler, "Games, Greek and Roman," 1.

27. Schädler, "Games, Greek and Roman," 1–2; Heimann and Schädler, "The Loop within Circular Three Men's Morris," 51–53; Claudia-Maria Behling, "Der sog. Rundmühle auf der Spur—Zug um Zug zur Neudeutung römischer Radmuster," in *Akten des 14. Österreichischen Archäologentages am Institut für Archäologie der Universität Graz*, ed. Elisabeth Trinkl (Wien: Phoibos70, 2014), 63–70.

CHAPTER 4

THE CHRISTIANIZATION OF THE PAGAN ROMAN WORLD

INTRODUCTION

By the end of the first century (AD 100) the New Testament canon was complete, and the church had been planted in cities (and in the countryside) all across Asia Minor (modern-day Turkey), Greece, Italy, North Africa, and Syria/Judea/Palestine. During the second and third centuries (AD 100–300) Christianity continued to spread, both to the west and to the east, even though there were a number of sporadic and sometimes regionally severe persecutions against the church. In general, while the Christians grew in numbers and continued to become more and more organized, with bishops appointed over regional groups of churches, these Christians were largely marginalized from mainstream political power and civic life, which was centered on pagan temple worship, including the veneration of the Roman imperial cult. Most churches at this time met in houses, and there were few church buildings constructed.

At the center of the complex socio-religious-economic life, being, and civic identity of Greco-Roman cities at the beginning of the fourth century (ca. AD 300) were the pagan temples. These included temples dedicated to pagan gods such as Artemis, Athena, Apollo, and Zeus (among many others), as well as those temples dedicated to the Roman imperial cult, with deified emperors such as Augustus, Domitian, and Trajan. Socioeconomically and politically, these temples were some of the most powerful entities in the Roman world.

Operation and maintenance of these temples and the payroll for their extensive personnel came primarily from wealthy people in the city who, as benefactors of the temple, received civic prestige. In exchange, they expected to be able to place their relatives in key positions at the temple. Occasionally, especially for major repairs like those needed after an earthquake, funding was provided by the Roman emperor, who also played the role of supreme benefactor. Some of the temples owned land and estates from which they received income as well.

The temples in the Roman world also served as banks. They held and guarded deposits, made loans and investments, and collected loan payments. Not only did the temples have their own guards to protect the money, but there was a general belief that the god of the temple also guarded the deposited money. The Temple of Artemis (Latin: Diana) in Ephesus, for example, was particularly famous for its significant deposits of money. Julius Caesar writes that twice the bank in this temple was threatened and twice he sent legions to Ephesus to protect it (*Civil Wars* 3.33; 3.105; on the large sum of money deposited there from all across the world, see Dio Chrysostom, *To the People of Rhodes* 54–55 [*Orations* 31.54–55]).[1]

The entire Roman Empire, however, underwent a dramatic change during the fourth century (the 300s) and into the early fifth century (the 400s). The thoroughly paganized and pagan-worship-centric cities of the Roman Empire went through a "Christianization" process. Visible pagan elements, especially idol statues that were prominent throughout the cities, were destroyed or defaced. Temples were closed. As discussed later in this chapter, a common belief in early Christianity was that the pagan gods were demons. This meant not only did the idol statues need to be destroyed or removed but the presence of the demons needed to be driven away and kept away. While hammers, chisels, and ropes were effective in removing the idols, to drive the demons away and to keep them away, the sign of the cross along with other Christian symbols like the ICHTHUS Christogram were etched into the pavement and painted on walls. As the pagan idols and their demonic influence were removed from the city, hundreds of churches were built—dramatically changing the look and the very fabric of life in the urban centers across the Roman Empire.

In the year 300, these pagan temples, most of them spectacular architectural structures and the pride of the cities, exerted tremendous power and influence in all aspects of civic life across the Roman Empire. Within a hundred years, however, everything had changed. By the year 400, practically all public pagan religious ceremonies, especially the sacrifices, had ceased, and most of the temples had been abandoned or destroyed. Any remaining persistent and defiant pagan practices were systematically and totally eliminated by a series of additional laws issued during the reign of Theodosius II (AD 408–450).[2] By the end of the reign of Theodosius II, almost every single

---

1.   See the discussion by Jerome Murphy-O'Connor, *St. Paul's Ephesus: Texts and Archaeology* (Collegeville, MN: Liturgical Press, 2008), 52–53, 64–66.

2.   See the discussion in Frank R. Trombley, *Hellenic Religion and Christianization c. 370–529*, vol. 1, 2nd ed., Religions in the Graeco-Roman World 115 (Leiden: Brill, 1995), 1–35; and Peter Talloen

pagan temple in the Roman world (hundreds of them) had been either abandoned, destroyed, or converted into a Christian church.

THE GREAT PERSECUTION

The primary precursor event that shaped the historical, cultural, and theological background for the Christianization of the pagan Greco-Roman world was the Great Persecution. From 50 to 300, persecution against the early Christians, either with the tacit approval of the Roman emperors or instigated specifically by them, was sporadic and inconsistently applied—that is, it was severe in some areas and mild in others and generally short in duration. The major persecutions in literary records (and evidenced by Christian funerary monuments) were that of Nero (ca. AD 64–66) and Decius (AD 250). There is also some evidence of persecution during the reigns of Domitian (AD 81–96), Marcus Aurelius (AD 161–180), and Severus (AD 193–211), but these are disputed with no consensus among scholars. While some of these persecutions were intense, even deadly, for some Christians in particular areas (North Africa seemed to be hit especially hard), they were in general short in duration and not applied widely across the empire.

The Great Persecution of 303–313, however, was quite different, both in its duration and in its widespread application. It was the deadliest and most devastating for the Christians. It lasted ten years, and the terror and horror that the Christians endured during this time were unimaginable for most of us modern readers. A brief history and a look at the accounts of some of the contemporary sources will help us to have a clearer understanding of this terrible time and a better understanding of the Christians' response (and retaliation) to it throughout the decades that followed.

Overwhelmed with trying to control the entire Roman Empire, in 285 to 286 the Emperor Diocletian (ruled AD 284–305) appointed a co-ruler to provide direct military leadership to the western part of the empire due to encroaching invaders. In 293, Diocletian expanded this to four rulers, further dividing up the empire (Constantine's father, Constantius, was the ruler in the west—Gaul and Britain). Diocletian himself ruled in the east, with his capital in the city of Nicomedia in Anatolia (now northwest Turkey).

As is the case in many major events in history, there were a number of interrelated causes leading up to the Great Persecution. One was simply the rapid expansion of Christianity in the second half of the third century. While in general building activity in the empire was being curtailed, the Christians were building substantial-sized churches in visible areas (which were later

---

and Lies Vercauteren, "The Fate of Temples in Late Antique Anatolia," in *The Archaeology of Late Antique "Paganism,"* ed. Luke Lavan and Michael Mulryan, Late Antique Archaeology 7 (Leiden: Brill, 2011), 347–58.

destroyed in the Great Persecution), probably to the growing annoyance of those committed to the old ways and the old gods.[3]

Another cause was the attack from within the Greco-Roman intellectual world. Led by a philosopher and teacher named Porphyry, an ever-increasing volume of vitriolic anti-Christian literature was produced throughout the second half of the third century, to which the Christian writers tried to respond, often with equally scathing criticism. These writers accused Christians of being a threat to the well-being—even the survival—of the Roman Empire. Temple priests and oracles joined in this criticism, complaining that when Christians were present, the gods did not honor sacrifices. The belief was circulated that because of the Christians' presence, the pagan gods that traditionally protected the cities had fled to be replaced with evil demons. Throughout the latter years of the third century, a number of oracles of Apollo gave negative and hostile messages against the Christians.[4]

The Emperor Diocletian believed strongly in these oracles, and he was frequently involved in seeking to receive "divine" predictions of the future from the gods. Along with others in his court, he became convinced that the presence of Christians was sabotaging his ability to receive this guidance (and good favor) from the gods. In response to this, he imposed restrictions on the Christians. In 299, he purged the army of Christians. At first, Diocletian was a bit reluctant to impose a severe empire-wide persecution. Galerius, however, one of the four co-rulers and the adopted son of Diocletian, vehemently opposed the Christians, and in 303, he strongly urged Diocletian to institute a serious, empire-wide persecution of the Christians—one that included executions.

To get divine guidance on whether to embrace Galerius's proposed persecution, Diocletian sent one of his court soothsayers south from the palace at Nicomedia to the Temple of Apollo at Didyma to inquire of the oracle Pythia there, who told him to persecute the Christians. Diocletian then issued an edict in February 303 that decreed that churches were to be demolished, Christian Scriptures confiscated and destroyed, Christians of rank stripped of their status, and Christian imperial freedmen to be re-enslaved. Galerius pushed for even harsher punishments. Later in 303, church clergy were arrested and often executed if they did not apostatize by sacrificing to the gods. A further stipulation requiring universal sacrifice was added in 304. These edicts were enforced quickly throughout the Roman Empire, except in the west (Gaul and Britain), where Constantius complied only minimally.[5]

---

3.   Min Seok Shin, *The Great Persecution: A Historical Re-Examination*, Studia Antiqua Australiensia 8 (Turnhout: Brepols, 2018), 26–59.

4.   See the discussion of these events leading up to the Great Persecution in Elizabeth DePalma Digeser, *A Threat to Public Piety: Christians, Platonists, and the Great Persecution* (Ithaca, NY and London: Cornell University Press, 2012), 164–91; and Shin, *The Great Persecution*, 17–103.

5.   Simon Corcoran, "Before Constantine," in *The Cambridge Companion to the Age of Constantine*, ed. Noel Lenski, rev. ed. (Cambridge: Cambridge University Press, 2012), 40–52; Elizabeth DePalma

Lactantius (AD 250–325), who lived through the Great Persecution and who wrote his account (*The Death of the Persecutors*) shortly afterward, provides a chilling description of what happened. First, he witnessed the burning of the Scriptures and the destruction of the church at Nicomedia, the capital city. But soon the persecution became even more deadly. Lactantius writes:

> Presbyters and other officers of the Church were seized, without evidence by witnesses or confession, condemned, and together with their families led to execution. In burning alive, no distinction of sex or age was regarded; and because of their great multitude, they were not burnt one after another, but a herd of them were encircled with the same fire; and servants, having millstones tied about their necks, were cast into the sea. Nor was the persecution less grievous on the rest of the people of God; for the judges, dispersed through all the temples, sought to compel everyone to sacrifice. The prisons were crowded; tortures, hitherto unheard of, were invented. (*The Death of the Persecutors* 15)

Eusebius (AD 265–339), also a firsthand witness to the Great Persecution, gives an equally horrific account in book 8 of his *Ecclesiastical History*. He recounts quite graphically and in great detail the number of martyrs (men, women, and children) beheaded, burned alive (some quickly and some slowly), ripped in two, tortured, crucified, fed to the wild beasts in the stadiums, sold into brothels not only in Nicomedia (the capital) but all across the empire (except in Gaul and Britain). Others committed suicide rather than face the terrible tortures. In one account, in the city of Antioch, a wealthy Christian woman and her two daughters threw themselves into the river to avoid being raped by the Roman soldiers. Like a modern investigator gathering evidence against a mass murder by some evil ruling faction, toward the end of book 8 Eusebius provides a long list of the specific names of bishops—along with other men and women—who were killed and the cities in which they were executed. This persecution continued for ten years.

Corroborating the testimony of Lactantius and Eusebius, at least regarding the scale of the persecution, are a number of funerary inscriptions, along with other literary records explicitly recounting the martyrdom of Christians during this time. This evidence from funerary inscriptions only reveals a small percentage of the Christians who actually died because inscriptions on stone were quite expensive and only the wealthier Christians (or the bishops) could afford them. In this regard, the contributors of Tabbernee's edited volume, *Early Christianity in Contexts*, seek to identify early Christian martyrs in various areas of the Roman Empire. Working primarily with funerary inscriptions

---

Digeser, "An Oracle of Apollo at Daphne and the Great Persecution," *Classical Philology* 99.1 (2004): 57–77. For this information they are primarily relying on Eusebius (*Ecclesiastical History* 8.1–17; *Life of Constantine* 2.48–60) and on Lactantius (*The Death of the Persecutors* 1–24).

and literary sources (other than Lactantius and Eusebius), they identify 112 Christian martyrs from all across the empire (except Gaul and Britain) whose deaths can be attributed to the Great Persecution.[6]

In comparison, Min Seok Shin, in the appendix to *The Great Persecution*, pulls from a wider range of inscriptions and literary records and provides a larger compilation of those killed. He lists out by name, occupation, and region 850 identified martyrs who died in the Great Persecution. In addition, he estimates that there were more than 20,000 other unidentified, unnamed martyrs who were killed at this time.[7]

These ten horrifying years were not quickly forgotten, and the memory of this horror no doubt remained with those who lived through it and was passed on to the next generation. In the years following the Great Persecution, as surviving bishops and other preachers returned to their churches and new bishops were appointed to fill the vacancies of those executed, the memory of these martyrs was kept vividly alive. The stories of the martyrs—now in the hero category—were recounted over and over from church pulpits, and the bravery, faith, and sacrifice of the martyrs was extolled as exemplary for the growing Christian congregations.[8] Both Eusebius and Lactantius published their accounts within ten to fifteen years after the persecution ended. As discussed in more detail in the next section, in 325 the emperor Constantine called together the bishops from all over the empire for a church council at Nicaea. Around three hundred bishops came to the conference. Of these three hundred, most of them had either been tortured and imprisoned, or else they had replaced the prior bishop who had been brutally martyred. No doubt, as they interacted at this conference, they shared stories of what had happened at each of their localities. In all probability, this continual reminder of the terrible Great Persecution, which was still fresh in the experience of all Christians across the empire, fanned the flames of resentment, perhaps even anger, at those people and institutions who had carried out the atrocities.

CONSTANTINE AND THE CHRISTIAN EMPERORS

Several years into the Great Persecution, in the west, Constantine, who had replaced his father as the ruling augustus (a title similar but secondary to that of emperor), marched against Rome and its currently ruling augustus, Maxentius. The church historians Lactantius and Eusebius record that, just prior to Constantine's decisive victory outside Rome (at the Milvian Bridge), Constantine saw a dramatic, life-impacting vision. Lactantius writes,

---

6.   Tabbernee, *Early Christianity in Contexts*, 39–40, 250, 276, 287–88, 291, 306–8, 314, 348, 360–61, 429–31, 443.

7.   Shin, *The Great Persecution*, 227–53.

8.   See Lucy Grig, *Making Martyrs in Late Antiquity* (London: Duckworth, 2004).

Constantine was directed in a dream to cause the heavenly sign to be delineated on the shields of his soldiers, and so to proceed to battle. He did as he had been commanded, and he marked on their shields the letter X, with a perpendicular line drawn through it and turned round thus at the top [i.e., the Chi-Rho symbol], being the cipher of Christ. (*The Death of the Persecutors* 44)

Soon after Constantine's victory, he and his main ally, an augustus named Licinius, produced the edict of Milan (AD 313), which reversed the edicts of the Great Persecution and granted Christians freedom of worship.[9] It also stated that all confiscated Christian property be returned. By 326, Constantine had defeated Licinius too and became the sole ruler of the Roman Empire. In 330, he renamed the city of Byzantium to Constantinople and moved the capital of the Roman Empire there. During this time, the Roman Empire was undergoing drastic changes, and the reemerging Christian church, which had suffered so badly during the Great Persecution, now had imperial support and backing. Numerous new churches were built throughout the empire.

Except for the brief reign of Julian the Apostate (AD 361–363), who tried unsuccessfully to take the empire back to paganism, every Roman/Byzantine emperor after Constantine professed and supported Christianity. This was in sync with the religious changes already taking place across the empire, for Christianity was spreading rapidly at all levels of society. While exact demographic statistics from the ancient world are difficult to determine, some scholars estimate that by the time Julian the Apostate died (AD 363), the population in most of the cities of the eastern Mediterranean was split about fifty-fifty between Christians and "traditional pagans."[10] While Constantine himself seemed to embrace a pragmatic policy of tolerance for paganism while advocating and supporting Christianity (paganism was still quite strong and very much entrenched in many city power structures when Constantine came to power), the emperors who followed him became more and more aggressive in seeking to eliminate pagan worship in the empire altogether. Throughout the fourth and fifth centuries, they enacted several edicts and laws that sought to restrict and eventually eliminate functioning temples and pagan worship, particularly in the cities.[11] As early as 346, the pagan temples were ordered

---

9. H. A. Drake, "The Impact of Constantine on Christianity," in Lenski, *The Cambridge Companion to the Age of Constantine*, 121–22.

10. Trombley, *Hellenic Religion and Christianization*, 110. Trombley, 110–111, notes that in 370, based on a homily by John Chrysostom, the largest church in Antioch by itself had a congregation numbering 100,000.

11. For discussions and explanations of these various decrees and edicts, see Trombley, *Hellenic Religion and Christianization*, 1–97; Richard Bayliss, *Provincial Cilicia and the Archaeology of Temple Conversion*, BAR International Series 1281 (Oxford: BAR, 2016), 8–11, 116–20; and Luke Lavan, "The End of the Temples: Towards a New Narrative," in Lavan and Mulryan, *The Archaeology of Late Antique "Paganism,"* xxii–xxiii.

to be closed. The implementation of this decree was carried out with various levels of zeal and success, depending on the power structures of each area. The transition from pagan-worship control of the city to Christian control of the city was underway all across the empire at this time, even if it was far from complete or universal.[12] Decades later, in 435, Theodosius II issued a stronger and more definitive edict (along with publishing a list of earlier anti-temple edicts) prohibiting all pagan worship and encouraging the destruction of temples or their transformation into churches, with their walls to be purified by the sign of the cross.[13]

DEMONS AND THE FORCES OF EVIL

Related to the Christianization of the empire and the destruction of the pagan temples was the understanding of most Christians that demons were closely associated with the pagan gods and their temples. Indeed, the informal inscription of ICHTHUS Christograms in pagan temples was probably part of the attempt by Christians to drive out the demons who lived there with the name of Jesus and by the power of the cross. To fully appreciate this, we need to explore and explain the belief in demons during this time (AD 200–600).

In the pre-Christian pagan world, the term "demons" was used of a wide range of nonmaterial beings that were between the gods and people (although sometimes overlapping somewhat with the gods). Demons were believed to inhabit the "in-between" spaces and were neither—just by the term "demon"— wholly good or wholly bad.[14] Many of them, however, were very bad, and they were frequently viewed as responsible for tragic, harmful events such as sickness, death, famine, plague, warfare, stillborn children, and so on. Although there was considerable variation across the Roman Empire regarding specific beliefs about demons and how to protect oneself and one's family from them, one commonality is that, for the average person, the demons and all that went with them (curses, evil eyes, etc.) were an integral aspect of everyday life. Moyer Hubbard writes, "Far more important for daily life than the Olympian deities or the major imports from the east like Isis and Cybele were the innumerable demons and malevolent spirits that had to be kept at bay or placated as best one could."[15] For the modern Western reader, it is difficult to grasp the extent to which fear of demons permeated so many aspects of life for the people in the ancient world.

As inhabitants of the in-between spaces, demons were thought to be especially present at entrances, doorways, thresholds, and street intersections.

---

12. Bayliss, *Archaeology of Temple Conversion*, 9–10.
13. Codex Theodosianus 16.10.25. See the discussion by Talloen and Vercauteren, "The Fate of the Temples," 373–74; and especially Trombley, *Hellenic Religion and Christianization*, 1–97.
14. Eva Elm, "Introduction," in *Demons in Late Antiquity*, ed. Eva Elm and Nicole Hartmann, Transformationen der Antike 54 (Berlin: De Gruyter, 2019), 2–3.
15. Moyer V. Hubbard, *Christianity in the Greco-Roman World* (Grand Rapids: Baker Academic, 2010), 24.

Hubbard says, "All throughout the Roman world the intersection of two roads was believed to be the gathering place of spirits (*daemones*) of the underworld, 'the most harmful beings in the universe,' according to Plutarch."[16] John Clarke writes:

> If we were to ask an ancient Roman, "Who protects you from misfortune and evil spirits within the city?" he or she would probably first name the city's titular deity, then—in the context of moving from place to place within the city—the various temples and shrines that defined specific neighborhoods. He would then name the guardian spirits, worshipped at certain crossroads—liminal places *par excellence*. Numerous altars to the protector-deities of the crossroads . . . attest to the common belief that individuals needed protection from evil forces lurking out in the open.[17]

Many of those living in Greece or in Anatolia (Asia Minor) turned, somewhat fearfully, to a dangerous goddess name Hecate (or Hekate) for protection from the demons. While there was one large temple dedicated to Hecate at Lagina, near the city of Stratonikeia (southwest Turkey, not far from Ephesus), in general she was more of a personal, household type of deity with hundreds of small shines dedicated to her all across Asia Minor and Greece.[18] Hecate was venerated as the goddess with power over the transitional, liminal places, and thus she was associated with demons, ghosts, magic, witchcraft, the moon, and the underworld. Shrines to Hecate were placed at intersections or crossroads and at entrances, sometimes even entrances into major pagan temples. There is evidence that a statue of Hecate stood near or in the Temple of Artemis in Ephesus (see chapter 5). Plutarch (AD 46–119) seems to imply that placing evening meals in these shrines each night for Hecate and "the hostile spirits" (ἀποτροπαίοις, *apotropaiois*) was a normal and common activity.[19] Images of Hecate depict her in triplet form—that is, there are usually three statues of her back to back, facing in three different directions, probably connecting to her relationship with street intersections. Likewise, inscriptions to her containing curses and spells are found on doorways.[20]

---

16. Hubbard, *Christianity in the Greco-Roman World*, 25, citing Plutarch, *Moralia* 153A. See also Sarah Iles Johnston, "Crossroads," *Zeitschrift für Papyrologie und Epigraphik* 88 (1991): 217–24; and Longenecker, *The Crosses of Pompeii*, 233–34.

17. John R. Clarke, *Looking at Laughter: Humor, Power, and Transgression in Roman Visual Culture, 100 BC–AD 250* (Berkeley: University of California Press, 2007), 64.

18. In *The Life of Porphyry* (64), the text states that the bishop Porphyry, along with the governor of Gaza and his troops, overturned the places of the idols of Gaza, including eight public temples, one of which was dedicated to Hecate. Mark the Deacon, *The Life of Porphyry, Bishop of Gaza*, trans. G. F. Hill (Oxford: Oxford University Press, 1913).

19. Plutarch, *Moralia* 9.7.708–9.

20. Amanda Herring, "Hekate of Lagina: A Goddess Performing Her Civic Duty," *Anatolian Studies* 72 (2022): 141–65; Hubbard, *Christianity in the Greco-Roman World*, 25.

The popularity of Hecate and the numerous references to demons through-out early Greco-Roman literature underscore how widespread and entrenched belief in demons, especially bad ones, was throughout the cultures of the Greco-Roman world. As the Christians encountered this pagan world and then worked to convert it and transform it into a Christian world, they discounted the reality and power of the pagan pantheon of gods, but to a large extent, they incorporated the common belief in demons into Christian doctrine.

Christians recognized that, both in the Gospels and in the book of Acts and reinforced throughout the rest of the New Testament, demons were part of Satan's hostile spiritual forces that Christ and his followers battled against. It was natural to place the common, culturally inherited belief in demons into this context. Christianity clarified that good spiritual beings are known as angels, while the bad ones would keep the name demons.

Early Christian writers discussed demons quite extensively.[21] They connected the pagan gods with demons, although there was no clear consensus on the exact relationship between the pagan gods and the demons. Tertullian (AD 155–220) equated the gods themselves with demons (*The Apology* 22–23; *The Shows* 13; *The Chaplet* 7). Origen (AD 185–253) equates the pagan gods with demons too (*Against Celsus* 7.62–67), underscoring that the temples are the dwelling places of demons (*Against Celsus* 7.35). He also points out that the good demons are angels (*Against Celsus* 4.24). Others argued that the pagan gods themselves were nothing but that demons were everywhere entrenched throughout the pagan system of idols, temples, sacrifices, and sacred processions.

The early Christians believed that demons were especially active and present in the temples, but they were also everywhere that the pagan system, with its numerous statues, had a presence throughout the city. That is to say, there was no real neutral public space; every public road, building, fountain, plaza, or gate was interconnected to pagan belief, tied in especially with the proliferation of idol statues in those areas. One scholar writes, "Indeed, early Christians felt constantly surrounded by demons; they sensed them lurking under the statues and images, and behind pagan oracles and divinations."[22] Likewise, the belief that the demons haunted intersections and entrances continued to be held popularly even into the Christian era. Demons were associated with witchcraft, sorcery, divination, the "evil eye," and occult activities.

The Christian understanding of demons in the early fourth century can be seen in the writings of Lactantius (AD 250–325), a Christian scholar who was part of the imperial court of Diocletian in Nicomedia and who converted to Christianity and became a prolific writer and apologist for the faith. He became an advisor for Constantine and a tutor for his son. In a chapter entitled, "Of the Demons, and their Evil Practices," he states:

---

21. Stephen Benko, *Pagan Rome and the Early Christians* (Bloomington: Indiana University Press, 1986), 115–32.
22. Benko, *Pagan Rome and the Early Christians*, 120.

These are the demons. . . . For they so persuaded men by their entice-
ments and deceits, that they believed that the same were gods. . . . They
also brought to light astrology, and augury, and divination. . . . They also
invented the tricks of the magic art, to deceive the eyes. . . . They themselves
invented necromancies, responses, and oracles, to delude the minds of men
with lying divination. . . . They are present in the temples and at all sacrifices; and by the exhibition of some deceitful prodigies . . . they so deceive
men that they believe that a divine power is present in images and statues.
(*The Epitome of the Divine Institutes* 28)[23]

The reality and danger of demons and their role as evil servants of Satan,
in parallel to the good angels of God, is widely expressed by Christian writers throughout the latter part of the fourth and into the fifth centuries. John
Chrysostom (AD 347–407) addresses the demons repeatedly not only in his
two homilies, *Concerning the Power of Demons* and *Concerning the Statues*,
but in several other homilies.[24] Augustine (AD 354–430) addresses demons
repeatedly and extensively in his work *City of God* (see especially 8.14–27 and
9.1–19).

Furthermore, there was a strong, oft-repeated belief among Christians
during the third to fifth centuries that the sign of the cross, along with the
name of Jesus Christ, had power to drive away the demons associated with
the pagan gods. For example, summarizing the situation in Ephesus during
the fourth century, Foss writes, "Belief that they [pagan temples] were
haunted by demons was common and usually caused crosses or inscriptions
to be carved on them."[25] As noted above, it was not just the temples that
were associated with demons but other areas in the city, especially those
associated with idols, like public fountains and bathhouses. One scholar
remarks, "The widespread Christian belief that the baths of the pagan world
were linked with the devil could be conveniently reversed by formally purifying them."[26]

This understanding is repeated frequently by Christian writers, especially
throughout the fourth century. Lactantius refers to this phenomenon several
times. In the chapter of *The Divine Institutes* entitled "Of the Wonders Effected
by the Power of the Cross, and of Demons," Lactantius declares:

---

23. Translations of Lactantius are from *Ante-Nicene Fathers: the Writings of the Fathers Down to A.D. 325*,
    ed. Alexander Roberts and James Donaldson (1886; repr., Peabody, MA: Hendrickson, 1994).
24. Dayna S. Kalleres, in *City of Demons: Violence, Ritual, and Christian Power in Late Antiquity*
    (Oakland: University of California Press, 2015), spends half of her book exploring John Chrysostom's
    understanding of demonology and his homiletical efforts to help his congregation in Antioch purge
    the city of demons, *City of God.* Her title, *City of Demons*, perhaps plays off Augustine's classic work addressing
    demons, *City of God.*
25. Clive Foss, *Ephesus after Antiquity: A Late Antique, Byzantine and Turkish City* (Cambridge:
    Cambridge University Press, 1979), 35.
26. Fikret Yegül, *Bathing in the Roman World* (Cambridge: Cambridge University Press, 2010), 202.

At present it is sufficient to show what great efficacy the power of this sign has. How great a terror this sign [i.e., the cross] is to the demons . . . when adjured by Christ, they flee from the bodies which they have besieged. . . . So now his followers, in the name of their Master, and by the sign of His passion, banish the same polluted spirits from men. (*Inst.* 27)

In *The Epitome of the Divine Institutes*, in a chapter entitled "Of the Death of Christ on the Cross," Lactantius writes:

All the host of demons is expelled and put to flight by this sign. . . . And as He Himself before His passion put to confusion demons by His word and command, so now, by the name and sign of the same passion, unclean spirits . . . are driven out. . . . What therefore can the Greeks expect from their superstitions and with their wisdom, when they see that their gods, whom they do not deny to be demons also, are subdued by men through the cross? (*Epit.* 51)

Athanasius (AD 296–373), bishop of Alexandria during the fourth century, writes:

By the sign of the Cross the demons fly, oracles cease, magic and witch-craft brought to naught. . . . By his Name being named, all madness of the demons is uprooted and chased away. (*On the Incarnation* 48.3–8)

In several written hagiographic accounts (stories about early monastic, holy people), the heroes often encountered demons as they moved into aban-doned temples. Frequently, they overcame the demons with crosses, driving them out of the temples. Helen Saradi, who presents quite a number of these encounters, concludes that these demons "could be defeated by the faith of the holy men and the sign of the cross."[27]

Demons were encountered and driven away from places other than the temples as well. In one account, Porphyry (bishop of Gaza AD 395–420) entered the city of Gaza while carrying a cross, with a procession of Christians following him. At a street intersection, they came upon a statue of the goddess Aphrodite, in which a demon was thought to dwell. The demon could not tolerate the sight of the cross and came out of the statue, breaking it to piec-es.[28] This story illustrates an aspect that we will encounter throughout our study—the need to drive away the demons not only in the temples but in statues outside of the temples, especially at intersections.

---

27. Helen Saradi, "The Christianization of Pagan Temples in the Greek Hagiographical Texts," in *From Temple to Church: Destruction and Renewal of Local Cultic Topography in Late Antiquity*, ed. Johannes Hahn, Stephen Emmel, and Ulrich Gotter (Leiden: Brill, 2008), 115–33.
28. Saradi, "The Christianization of Pagan Temples," 118.

There was a widespread understanding in the fourth century that the combination of the cross and the name of Jesus was effective in driving away the demons and keeping them away. Both the cross and the name of Jesus were associated with the ICHTHUS Christogram. It was regularly used in parallel with various types of crosses—that is, it was used as a symbol of Christ in a similar manner to crosses. Thus, in the realm of using the cross to drive out the demons, the wheel was likely viewed as one of the symbols that could be used quite effectively. In addition, the ICHTHUS Christogram represented an extended and powerful form of the name of Jesus, specifically "Jesus Christ God's Son Savior."

It is interesting to note that alongside the various forms and features of the cross, the acrostic word IXΘΥC was also often used for individual protection. It was written on amulets or on doorways (entrances have special religious significance), where it appears to serve a similar function—to keep demonic forces away (prophylactic) or to drive them away (apotropaic) from someone's residence or business. Different types of crosses and related symbols were used in these "magic formula" apotropaic purposes on doorframes and on amulets that people wore. This included equilateral crosses as well as Tau-Rho Staurograms and Chi-Rho Christograms and the word IXΘΥC.[29]

For example, a papyrus textual amulet from Egypt (dating to the fourth to fifth centuries) contains a spell seeking to protect the owner's house from all sorcery and evil spirits. It invokes the names of several divinities in addition to Jesus Christ. At the end of the incantation, adding power to the spell, are several Christian symbols—a cross with the letters *alpha* and *omega*; a Tau-Rho Staurogram; and the word IXΘΥC.[30]

In summarizing the data, one scholar writes that the early Christians in the post-Constantine era, "in their attempt to avert the demons, used apotropaic amulets or the sign of the cross marked on the doors, accompanied with a written invocation of Christ's name or the acrostic IXΘΥC."[31] Since we also find ICHTHUS wheels in such places and contexts, the implication is that the ICHTHUS Christogram was used similarly for the purpose of cleansing or de-demonizing areas where the demons had been dwelling (especially pagan temples, but at street intersections and other places, like public fountains, where pagan idols abounded).

---

29. William K. Prentice, "Magical Formulae on Lintels of the Christian Period in Syria," *American Journal of Archaeology* 10.2 (1906): 138, 141, 145–48. One text (141), which has a cross right before the words, he translates as "Of this house (the) Lord shall guard the entrance and the exit: for the cross being set before, no malignant eye shall prevail (against it)." He also cites several instances (143–44) where the cross occurs with the Greek word *nika* ("to conquer," "be victorious"), meaning "this sign conquers."

30. Garipzanov, *Graphic Signs of Authority in Late Antiquity*, 103–4.

31. Anastasia D. Vakaloudi, "ΔΕΙΣΙΔΑΙΜΟΝΙΑ and the Role of the Apotropaic Magic Amulets in the Early Byzantine Empire," *Byzantion* 70.1 (2000): 188. See also Henry Maguire, "Magic and Geometry in Early Christian Floor Mosaics and Textiles," in *Rhetoric, Nature and Magic in Byzantine Art*, ed. Henry Maguire (Aldershot, UK and Brookfield, VT: Ashgate, 1998), 265–88.

Based on the teachings of the New Testament, most Christians today acknowledge the reality of demons, but the extent and the degree to which the early Christians believed that demons inhabited their cities is rather foreign to us, and the actions of these early Christians in regard to the demons seems rather extreme. A modern parallel, however, might be helpful. Suppose that you (or your son or your daughter) are moving into a new apartment. As you are moving in, the people across the hall tell you that the previous occupants were Satan worshipers and that very strange things had occurred in that apartment. Upon hearing this, you might view the apartment quite differently. If you decided to continue moving in, perhaps you would have a special prayer or Scripture reading in the apartment, just to be sure that all evil influence was totally removed. You might even put a cross on the wall or on a desktop. Then before you went to sleep there for the first night, you might offer up another special prayer asking the Lord for protection. It is this same fear and concern that the early Christians felt all across their cities due to their belief that evil demons had occupied those spaces and still posed a real threat.

THE END OF THE PAGAN TEMPLES

Both literary and archaeological evidence from the fourth and fifth centuries indicate that the manner and speed in which the pagan temples in the Roman Empire came to an end—institutions that had dominated civic life for nearly a millennium—varied to some degree throughout the empire. In some cities, wealthy benefactors of the temples converted to Christianity and therefore shifted their resources away from the temples to pay for the construction of the hundreds of new Christian churches that were being built. Or, due to the rising unpopularity of the temples, especially in the eyes of the Christian emperors, these wealthy benefactors decided to spend their money in other areas (many shifted to building up their private villas).[32] In some locations, the temples had traditionally been able to collect their own taxes to cover operations, especially for the huge city-wide annual festivals. This power was stripped by imperial edicts against the temples.[33] Likewise, temple estates, which often had been extensive and were able to generate substantial sums of money,[34] were sometimes confiscated. Worried about the future legal status of the temples, many of the banking depositors who had kept their money in the temple banks withdrew their money and invested it elsewhere.

---

32. Talloen and Vercauteren, "The Fate of the Temples," 350.
33. Bayliss, *Archaeology of Temple Conversion*, 11.
34. A fascinating inscription (*IEph.* Ia.17, 18, 19a, 19b) related to temple finances (the Temple of Artemis at Ephesus) is a proconsular edict from 44 in which the proconsul notes that the temple's abundant revenues had been restored by Emperor Augustus but that the temple personnel were misusing these funds. He also reprimands the existing priests for selling the office of priesthood and yet keeping the proceeds for themselves. See the text and discussion in G. H. R. Horsley, "The Inscriptions of Ephesos and the New Testament," *Novum Testamentum* 34.2 (1992): 147–48.

Monetary support from the emperor, which in the past had been available for major repairs to temples, especially after earthquakes, completely disappeared. Temples that were damaged or destroyed by earthquakes during the fourth and fifth centuries did not have the resources to rebuild, and many of them never were restored.[35] For example, a devastating earthquake hit Ephesus at the end of the fourth century. Unlike earlier years, there were no imperial funds available this time to repair the many damaged temples. Several of these temples simply became inexpensive quarries, providing already-cut stone blocks and columns to be used in the reconstruction of other buildings in the city, including new churches.[36]

Outside of the rise of Christianity, two additional phenomena brought serious damage to the pagan temples of many cities in the Roman Empire. One cause was natural events, especially the frequently occurring earthquakes, and, as was the case for the huge Temple of Artemis at Sardis, flooding and sedimentation from a nearby stream. The other phenomenon was invading armies. For much of the Imperial Period of Rome (50 BC to AD 200), the Pax Romana was in effect. This meant that the Roman army worked to keep foreign invaders out of the empire. During the third century AD, however, there was a breakdown in Roman power, and foreign armies (especially the Goths) invaded various parts of the empire several times. For instance, in the 260s, the Goths intruded far enough into the empire to capture Ephesus and Didyma, plundering the famous pagan temples there.

There were also incursions from the east by the powerful Sasanian Empire (from Persia, modern-day Iran).[37] There was a short period of relative peace from foreign invaders in much of the eastern empire during the fourth century (after AD 330) and throughout much of the fifth century. But in the first half of the sixth century, the emperor Justinian was constantly fighting off invaders and striving to reconquer areas that had been lost to the Ostrogoths or the Lombards.[38]

Throughout the second and into the third century (AD 100–300), serious financial aid from the emperors was often available to fund the reconstruction of prominent pagan temples of the Roman Empire that were damaged by earthquakes or by invading foreign armies. Yet the instability caused by the rule of several inept emperors in the third century, coupled with these consequential invasions, was already starting to restrict funding for reconstruction, and in general, the construction of new public monuments or the renovation of older facilities was already waning by the second half of the

---

35. Bayliss, *Archaeology of Temple Conversion*, 25.
36. Talloen and Vercauteren, "The Fate of the Temples," 356; note that at Ephesus this was the fate of the Temple of the Sebastoi and of the huge Olympieion.
37. Ine Jacobs, "The Creation of the Late Antique City: Constantinople and Asia Minor During the Theodosian Renaissance," *Byzantion* 82 (2012): 117. (See bib. on pp. 113–164.)
38. A. D. Lee, "The Empire at War," in *The Cambridge Companion to the Age of Justinian*, ed. Michael Maas (Cambridge: Cambridge University Press, 2005), 113–33.

third century, especially when compared to the heyday of construction in the second century. Although Constantine (ruled AD 324–337) brought a certain amount of stability to the empire after he came to power, the rise and spread of Christianity became a driving theological and political force, and throughout the rule of the following Christian emperors, imperial funding for temple repair vanished almost completely.

Politically, after Constantine became the sole emperor, the influence and power of the temples and their associated priestly personnel diminished quickly in most cities but not everywhere. Christian bishops were appointed in almost all major cities to serve the rapidly growing churches throughout the Roman Empire, and many of these bishops became quite powerful in civic politics. Soon governors and other imperially appointed leaders were also required to be Christians. Although the situation and speed of development varied from city to city, as the fourth century progressed, pagan temples and their priests all across the Roman Empire eventually found themselves short on cash, making them unable to sustain a guard or police force to protect them from the hostility of the Christians who were ever-growing in numbers and in power. Most of the Christian bishops and other early church leaders, often supported by the local governor and the emperor, viewed the complete removal of pagan worship as one of their primary goals in leading the spread of Christianity.[39] They particularly targeted the temples. This was true not only of the traditional pagan temples but those of the imperial cult. The new Christian emperors after Constantine, while still striving to maintain the idea of divine favor and appointment, nonetheless abandoned the imperial-cult emphasis of earlier imperial Roman emperors and cut off all support.

Despite these changes, the effects and consequences of the earlier pagan-driven Great Persecution (AD 303–313) continued into the rest of the fourth century, even after it had ended. To personalize this, imagine your family had been prominent in one of the cities of the Roman Empire but you had become Christians and perhaps were even using your home as a house church. Then your family experienced terrible things during the Great Persecution. These horrific events had often been initiated and carried out in conjunction with the local temples. Consequently, if you knew that certain temple priests had been the ones to push for the execution (or torture) of your father and mother, as well as the destruction of your home and the confiscation of all your family property, your hostility toward the temples and priests no doubt stayed with you throughout your life. You could be easily motivated by your local Christian bishop to destroy or deface the gods in the temple and to drive out the associated demons with crosses and other Christian symbols, proclaiming victory over the forces that had persecuted you and your family.

At some point, probably starting early in the fourth century in some areas but certainly well underway by the mid-fourth century, many of the money-

---

39. Bayliss, *Archaeology of Temple Conversion*, 19–22.

strapped pagan institutions could no longer maintain any way to guard or defend the temple. The prominent theology being advocated by the numerous newly appointed Christian bishops and other influential Christian leaders regarding the temples and pagan gods was not merely that these gods were false myths representing nothing but that they were demons (or that demons were closely associated with them and the temple areas)—evil forces that needed to be dealt with. So even if the temple personnel had withdrawn and the temple had lain vacant, to the Christians these temples had become the haunts of demons, often right in the central areas of their cities. Organized and led by the local bishops and other church leaders (and occasionally with soldiers involved) with either the support or blind-eye indifference of the local governors, Christians marched into the pagan temples all across the empire to cleanse them from demons and to declare victory over the pagan world that had caused so much suffering for them during the Great Persecution.

After analyzing a number of written reports describing this era, Trombley proposes that a fairly common pattern of action occurred across the empire. He writes:

> By taking different elements from variously reported incidents, one can almost reconstruct a composite liturgy that included, "One God" acclamations, the recitation of the psalms, the erasure of the gods' names, the smashing of their faces, the incision of crosses, Christograms, and the Alpha-Omega on temple walls and spolia, the degrading treatment of temple spolia.[40]

Commentating on this same literary collection of temple-cleansing actions, Bayliss summarizes:

> The bishop might let forth a series of "One God" acclamations, whilst warding off evil spirits by brandishing a cross at the pagan statues, which were then smashed or at least mutilated. The stones of the temple then might have been incised with a variety of Christian symbols, and some temples might have been ruined with fire.[41]

This is the most likely historical context in which many of the eight-spoked ICHTHUS Christogram graffiti, along with crosses and other Christian symbols, were etched into the stones at pagan temple sites all across the Roman Empire.

Based on extensive archaeological and literary evidence, it is clear that one of the first things that the Christians did—and this was widespread—was destroy or deface the many pagan idols not only in the temples but throughout

---

40. Trombley, *Hellenic Religion and Christianization*, 245.
41. Bayliss, *Archaeology of Temple Conversion*, 12.

the city. The most common action was to lop off the head of the statue. This could be accomplished with a wooden mallet or even with a large piece of wood (used like a modern baseball bat). Often the body of the statue itself was knocked over and broken. Indeed, in the many Greco-Roman exhibits in museums all across the world there are rooms full of headless statues, testifying to this action (see fig. 5-22). In the excavation process in many of the ancient Greco-Roman cities, the archaeologists were able to recover the body of the idol (or emperor or other famous person) and put it back together if it was broken, but often they were unable to even locate the head. So, either the Christians had smashed the heads into small pieces or buried them somewhere else. Interestingly, in Laodicea, the head of the Emperor Augustus, from a statue in an imperial cult temple, was discovered in a public latrine across town.[42] In some locations, the defaced heads were placed in wells or cisterns, while the bodies were used either as building material (rubble used in constructing new walls, a feature common in the fourth century) or burned in kilns to produce lime, which was used in making cement.[43]

Sometimes rather than removing the heads, the Christians defaced the idol's face by whacking off the nose or etching away as much of the face as possible, as can be also seen in the Greco-Roman exhibits in modern museums. This is true especially in situations where the pagan god was not a stand-alone statue but rather incorporated into a wall-panel scene.

In discussing the destruction of the Temple of Serapis in Alexandria in 391, details of which were recorded by the Christian historian Rufinus, Johannes Hahn notes that pagan idol statues were not removed or destroyed in silence or in private, but they were profaned in public as trophies of victory. Fragments from the huge statue of Serapis, for example, were taken from the temple by the Christians, dragged through the streets, and then set on fire. The main torso was burned before a huge crowd in the theater. Hahn writes:

> This burning was celebrated as a religious statement; it is probable that the event was orchestrated centrally and quite consciously to symbolize the ritual cleansing of the city from the pagans' erroneous beliefs. The same conclusion can be drawn from the systematic destruction of the countless small Serapis busts that could be found on pedestals on the streets and crossings of Alexandria. They were demolished and replaced by signs of the cross, all apparently within a few hours or days. Thus the city now belonged to Christ and the God of the Christians, no longer to Serapis.[44]

---

42. Celal Şimşek, "Laodikeia Yontuculuğu" [Eng. Laodicea Sculpting], in *Laodikeia (Laodicea ad Lycum)*, *Laodikeia Çalişmalari* 2 (Istanbul: Ege Yayinlari, 2013), 461.

43. Amelia R. Brown, "Crosses, Noses, Walls, and Wells: Christianity and the Fate of Sculpture in Late Antique Corinth," in *The Afterlife of Greek and Roman Sculpture: Late Antique Responses and Practices*, ed. Troels Myrup Kristensen and Lea Stirling (Ann Arbor: University of Michigan Press, 2016), 167.

44. Johannes Hahn, "The Conversion of the Cult Statues," in Hahn, Emmel, and Gotter, *From Temple to Church*, 356–57.

There is considerable evidence that the standard Christian understanding of the day was that these idols represented demons and that this demonic presence could only be driven away by the name of Jesus Christ and the sign of the cross. Thus, sometimes crosses were etched on the faces, legs, or backs of idols, as seen on statues at Corinth,[45] as well as at Ephesus and Laodicea (see chapter 5).[46]

As the Christians sought to cleanse the entire temple of demonic presence, they etched crosses and Christograms into various parts of the temple.[47] For example, at the Temple of Apollo at Delphi (in Greece), there are more than one hundred small crosses etched into the top surface of the huge stone altar. This altar also has a number of ICHTHUS Christograms etched into it along with the crosses,[48] indicating that this symbol was used in a similar fashion to the cross, probably representing both the cross and the name of Jesus (Jesus Christ God's Son Savior).[49] The Temple of Apollo at Didyma has numerous crosses as well as a multitude of ICHTHUS Christograms etched into the floor of the temple itself, most of them near the front entrance of the church.

Some of these temples had an elaborate entryway structure called the propylon. Often the cross and other Christian graffiti were etched in these formal entryways. At the Temple of Aphrodite at Aphrodisias, for example, just inside the monumental entrance (referred to as the Tetrapylon instead of the propylon because of its shape and size) are numerous ICHTHUS Christograms along with other Christian symbols (see chapter 5). The etching of the crosses and wheels served to not only drive away the demons but to keep them away. These Christian symbols often were placed at the entrances or near the entrances of the temples because it was believed that the demons had a special presence and power in entrances and over thresholds.[50]

45. Brown, "Crosses, Noses, Walls, and Wells," 150–76.

46. Troels Myrup Kristensen, "Miraculous Bodies; Christian Viewers and the Transformation of 'Pagan' Sculpture in Late Antiquity," in *Patrons and Viewers in Late Antiquity*, ed. Stine Birk and Birte Poulsen (Aarhus, Denmark: Aarhus University Press, 2012), 31–66; Jacobs, "Cross Graffiti," 209.

47. Talloen and Vercauteren, "The Fate of the Temples," 355.

48. Pierre Amandry, "Chronique delphique," *Bulletin de correspondance hellénique* 105.2 (1981): 739–40.

49. Trombley, *Hellenic Religion and Christianization*, 55, cites a magic papyrus from Egypt (fourth or fifth century) that was used to protect a household from evil things by the repetition of magic words and the extensive use of names for God and Jesus. It reads: "Protect this house with those living in it from every evil influence or the spirits of the air, and of the human [evil] eye, and of dangerous illness, and of the bite of the scorpion and snake through the power of the name of the God most high. . . . Protect me, Lord, son of David according to the flesh, who are begotten holy highest God of the holy virgin Maria of the Holy Spirit. Glory to you, celestial king! Amen." Next in this text is an *alpha* and *omega*, then a Tau-Rho Staurogram, then another *alpha* and *omega*, and then the word ΙΧΘΥΣ. This indicates that the symbols of *alpha* and *omega*, as well as the Tau-Rho Staurogram and the ICHTHUS acrostic, were seen as effective as signs of the cross and names of Jesus Christ in keeping evil away.

50. Bayliss, *Archaeology of Temple Conversion*, 13. Sitz observes this phenomenon at the Temple of Hecate (goddess of boundaries and crossroads) in the city of Lagina, where crosses and other Christian graffiti are inscribed on the front of the temple and especially at the propylon but absent in the stoa of the temple. Anna M. Sitz, "Inscribing Caria: The Perseverance of Epigraphic Traditions in Late

The purpose of etching these crosses and ICHTHUS Christograms, however, was not just related to driving away demons or cleansing the temples. There was an element of a victory proclamation being declared—the victory of the cross of Jesus Christ over the demons and all the forces of darkness.[51] This emphasis on victory can be seen in a literary account about how a bishop named Porphyry destroyed a temple and then built a new church right in the religious center (the temenos, where the main idol had stood) of what had been the temple. Organized and led by the bishop, a large group of Christians with shovels and other tools paraded into the temple in a religious procession. As they began digging the foundation of the new church, the congregation sang "Christ has conquered" (ὁ Χριστός ἐνίκησεν).[52]

In the archaeological inscription evidence there are several examples where the cross is associated with the Greek word νίκη (nikē, "victory, triumph").[53] For example, at the temple to Isis in Philae, Egypt, there is a cross and then the Greek words declaring, "The cross has triumphed; it will always triumph."[54] This exact same phrase occurs on one of the huge arch spans of the Kurşunlugerme Bridge—part of the aqueduct system that served Constantinople. In this case, professionally engraved on the stone facing of the bridge is not only a cross and the Greek statement about the victory of the cross but an eight-spoked wheel.[55]

The ICHTHUS proclamation is that Jesus Christ is God's Son, the Savior. This may have carried a particular irony in light of the similar terminology used in the imperial cult, which was especially popular and widely venerated in the many cities of Anatolia. The Roman emperor Augustus—the one most responsible for launching the imperial cult as an institution and extension of imperial power—often referred to himself in Latin as *divi filius* ("son of divinity") similar to "son of God." Augustus had proclaimed his adoptive father, Julius Caesar, as *divi Julius*, thus giving him divine status as his adopted son.

Antiquity," in *Early Christianity in Asia Minor and Cyprus: From the Margins to the Mainstream*, ed. Cilliers Breytenbach, Martin Goodman, Christoph Markschies, and Stephen Mitchell, Ancient Judaism and Early Christianity 109 (Leiden: Brill, 2019), 216–17.

51. Talloen and Vercauteren, "The Fate of the Temples," 378.

52. Talloen and Vercauteren, "The Fate of the Temples," 378; Trombley, *Hellenic Religion and Christianization*, 107–8. See the extensive discussion of this event in Saradi, "The Christianization of Pagan Temples," 117–121.

53. Christopher Walter, "IC XC NI KA: The Apotropaic Function of the Victorious Cross," *Revue des études byzantines* 55 (1997): 195.

54. Johannes Hahn, "Die Zerstörung der Kulte von Philae: Geschichte und Legende am Ersten Nilkatarakt," in Hahn, Emmel, and Gotter, *From Temple to Church*, 203.

55. For discussion, along with numerous pictures, see James Crow, "Blessing or Security? Understanding the Christian Symbols of a Monumental Aqueduct Bridge in the Hinterland of Late Antique Constantinople," in Garipzanov, Goodson, and Maguire, *Graphic Signs of Identity, Faith, and Power*, 147–74; and James Crow, "The Christian Symbols and Iconography of the Aqueducts of Thrace," in *The Water Supply of Byzantine Constantinople*, ed. James Crow, Jonathan Bardill, and Richard Bayliss, Journal of Roman Studies Monograph 11 (London: The Society for the Promotion of Roman Studies, 2008), 157–80.

Even more significant is the fact that the word σωτήρ (*sōtēr*; "savior") was used frequently as part of the title honoring those deified Roman emperors within the imperial cult during the entire Roman imperial era (50 BC–AD 300).[56] It was used in the sense of the savior being the one who brings in the golden age of peace and prosperity.[57] This was particularly true in Asia Minor (western Anatolia), where the imperial cult was so popular and powerful.[58] Indeed, Fredrick Long writes, "In Ephesus and Asia Minor, Caesar was 'Savior.' "[59] The Greek term σωτήρ (*sōtēr*; "savior") was used especially in acclamations and inscriptions regarding the Emperor Hadrian (AD 117–138). Sometimes the acclamations called him "savior of the world" or savior of a certain city.[60] The terminology and concepts relating to "son of God" and "savior" were closely associated with the imperial cult, and the Christian usage of these same terms and concepts, starting in the New Testament writings and continuing into the early Christian era, represented a strong theological and sociological counterclaim—even perhaps an ironic polemic.[61]

For most cities across Asia Minor, these imperial cult inscriptions and the statues that often accompanied them stood in public view at the most prominent places in the city. There was an imperial cult temple dedicated to Hadrian in Ephesus as well as in Sagalassos. There was a bathhouse dedicated to (and funded by) Hadrian in Aphrodisias. Ephesus in particular was heavily committed to venerating the imperial cult in addition to their traditional god, Artemis. As in the New Testament, the public acclamation of Jesus Christ as God's Son, and especially as Savior, was both an acclamation of victory and a rejection of and counterclaim to the entire Roman imperial cult system. This was probably another reason why the Christians etched these ICHTHUS wheels all across the cities of Asia Minor and beyond.

CLEANSING THE REST OF THE CITY

Although the pagan temples were the power center and the focus of the pagan world, pagan idols were not limited to the temples. Most public

---

56. Craig Koester, "'The Savior of the World' (John 4:42)," *JBL* 109 (1990): 665–68; Walter Otto, "Augustus Soter," *Hermes* 45.3 (1910): 448–60.
57. Werner Foerster, "σωτήρ," *TDNT* 7:1010–12.
58. S. R. F. Price, *Rituals and Power: The Roman Imperial Cult in Asia Minor* (Cambridge: Cambridge University Press, 1984).
59. Fredrick Long, "'Εκκλησία in Ephesians as Godlike in the Heavens, in Temple, in γάμος, and in Armor: Ideology and Iconography in Ephesus and Its Environs," in *The First Urban Churches 3: Ephesus*, ed. James R. Harrison and L. L. Welborn, Writings from the Greco-Roman World Supplement Series 9 (Atlanta: SBL Press, 2018), 223.
60. Foerster, "σωτήρ," 7:1011.
61. Allen Brent, *The Imperial Cult and the Development of Church Order: Concepts and Images of Authority in Paganism and Early Christianity before the Age of Cyprian*, Supplements to Vigiliae Christianae: Texts and Studies of Early Christian Life and Language XLV (Leiden: Brill, 1999), 71–72, 91–93, 180–81, 194.

areas—monumental buildings, bathhouses, theaters, city gates, streets and street intersections, as well as other facilities, especially in the centers of the cities—had numerous pagan idols. While these pagan god statues could be found throughout the city centers, they were heavily concentrated at the public fountains. These impressive water fountains were called "nymphaeum" because they were originally dedicated to the nymphs—the gods of mountain water springs. But by the Roman era, these extravagant public fountains were dedicated to, and contained numerous statues of, a wide range of gods, as well as deified emperors. Regarding these public fountains, Jacobs writes, "They were the most prominent show facades of their community, located in highly conspicuous locations on nodal points in the traffic network or on civic agora."[62]

Many of the headless statues in the museums all across the world today are from these public fountains. The Christians destroyed or defaced these idol statues, probably at the same time the idols in the temples were being destroyed and the temples cleansed. In some cases, we also find graffiti crosses and ICHTHUS Christograms at these public fountains (e.g., Ephesus and Laodicea), and sometimes the Christians replaced the front stone panels of the fountain pools with panels formally inscribed with crosses (Ephesus). Keep in mind that, while the temples could be destroyed and completely abandoned, the huge public water fountains needed to be kept running, as they provided a significant part of the city population with water. Thus, the Christians removed the pagan idols or renamed them (at Laodicea the statue of the deified Trajan was renamed Constantine and then kept at the fountain) and then cleansed or consecrated the fountain with crosses or ICHTHUS wheels so that the fountain could continue to be used. Jacobs notes that there were probably many painted and chalked crosses added as well, but few of these have survived.[63]

It is highly likely that at the same time the Christians sought to destroy or cleanse the temples, perhaps even before, they also destroyed or defaced all the pagan idols that lined the streets or that stood in other facilities such as bathhouses and theaters. The many crosses, ICHTHUS Christograms, and other Christian symbols that we find in the ancient streets (e.g., Philippi, Ephesus, Laodicea) in front of where these idols once stood or inscribed on the doorways and walls were probably made at the same time—during the fourth century as the Christians sought to cleanse and Christianize the city and, particularly, to drive the demons away and keep them away.

The reason that most of these eight-spoked wheels and other cross-related graffiti usually appear on the floor and not on the walls, particularly in temples such as the Temple of Apollo at Didyma and the Temple of Athena at Priene, is that the walls of temples (as well as many other monumental

---

62. Jacobs, "Cross Graffiti," 199–200.
63. Jacobs, "Cross Graffiti," 200.

buildings at that time) were covered with plaster stucco and then painted. While the stone floor often survived, as well as the basic stone walls, little of the wall plaster and paint that originally covered the walls in ancient cities has survived.[64] In a few cases where the original plaster and paint have survived, we do find crosses and eight-spoked wheels painted on the walls, such as at the Villa of the Quintili in Rome and the niche at the Western Bathhouse at Scythopolis (see chapter 7).

In a number of instances, such as at the Temple of Artemis at Sardis and the Temple of Aphrodite in Aphrodisias (see chapter 5), cross-related graffiti and other Christian inscriptions are etched directly on the vertical faces of stone doorjambs and walls, suggesting that either this portion of the temple was not plastered and painted or, more likely, that the plaster and paint for this section was removed prior to the Christian inscription activity. Perhaps there were pagan symbols and inscriptions painted on this part of the wall and the Christians scraped it off, or perhaps the temple had been abandoned for a time and regular weathering removed the plaster.

THE THREE PHASES OF CHRISTIANIZING THE ROMAN CITY

At the risk of oversimplifying, we might refer to the defacing and removal of idols, along with the etching of graffiti-type crosses and ICHTHUS Christograms on temples and streets, as Phase I in the Christianization of the Roman pagan cities. This took place primarily in the fourth century, from about 325 to 400. In Phase II, the Christians pushed things a step further. This includes the actual destruction of the temples, as well as the construction of churches using material from the destroyed or abandoned temples (or other abandoned or destroyed facilities). Phase II overlapped some with Phase I, depending on the speed of change taking place in each city. We can roughly estimate Phase II to run from 350 to 450. Hundreds of churches were built during this time, many of them in prominent and visible areas, sometimes replacing earlier facilities (temples, gymnasiums, bathhouses, etc.). This was the primary urban construction done during this time, and it drastically changed the landscape of the ancient cities. Numerous churches, of course, would continue to be built after 450 (into Phase III, 450–565), but 450 is a good ballpark date for the end of the pagan temples and their complete replacement on the city landscape by the Christian churches.

---

64. John W. Stamper, "Urban Sanctuaries: The Early Republic to Augustus," in *A Companion to Roman Architecture*, ed. Roger B. Ulrich and Caroline K. Quenemoen (West Sussex, UK: Wiley and Sons, 2014), 216, writes, "The entire structure was covered with a thin coat of stucco at the time of its initial construction. Somewhat later, elements of decoration were added to the walls . . . but now disappeared." See also Nancy L. Klein, "How Buildings Were Constructed," in *A Companion Guide to Greek Architecture*, ed. Margaret M. Miles (West Sussex, UK: Wiley and Sons, 2016), 215.

The actions in Phase I could be carried out with a minimal amount of organization, special equipment (only clubs, hammers, and chisels were needed), or funding. In some recorded cases, when the Christians first tried to destroy the temples, they discovered that dismantling the huge stone blocks and massive stone columns required the same construction skill and special equipment that it took to build the temples.[65] The wooden doors and roofs to the temples could be burned, but the structures themselves were difficult to destroy without specialized construction workers. Furthermore, the attempt to destroy these massive structures could be dangerous. One literary account of a temple destruction notes that one of the soldiers was killed by a falling burning beam.[66]

It is highly improbable that game boards (see chapter 3) were in use while the temples were operating. With the exception of a few temples that allowed people inside in order to try to be healed (for example, temples associated with Asclepius), most functioning pagan temples (especially in the eastern part of the empire, like Anatolia) did not allow regular people inside of the temple proper. Therefore, the picture some writers describe of people lounging around a functioning pagan temple and casually playing games on game boards to kill the time is extremely improbable.[67] Sometime during Phase II the temples sat vacant for many years. This is probably the context for when the occasional rectangular game board graffito was etched into some of the temple floors. A vacated temple that was centrally located in the city and still provided a certain amount of shade does seem to be a plausible location for public game board gambling (see chapter 3).

In some locations, the Christians converted the temple area itself into a church (for example, at Aphrodisias), using many of the same columns and walls but with some reconfiguration. At other locations, the Christians built churches nearby the temple, freely taking blocks and columns from the temple to use in the church, especially if the project had proper funding and trained construction crews. To reuse blocks and columns that were available nearby instead of purchasing new ones was cost-effective, and this happened frequently.[68] For example, many of the blocks and columns of the Temple of Artemis at Ephesus were reused to construct the nearby Church of St. John.

---

65. Marcellus, bishop of Apamea in the province of Syria Secunda, aggressively tried to destroy pagan temples. In one of his early attempts (AD 391), even though he had two units of soldiers with him, he found the massive stones and manner in which they were attached to be daunting, until an individual in his group, skilled in how to dismantle such stones, demonstrated the method to him (using fire). Eventually, however, a group of enraged pagans captured Marcellus and burned him alive, indicating that in some regions, even as late as the end of the fourth century, pagan resistance was still strong. See Saradi, "The Christianization of Pagan Temples," 116–17; and especially Trombley, *Hellenic Religion and Christianization*, 123–29.

66. Trombley, *Hellenic Religion and Christianization*, 217.

67. See, for example, Maffia, *Temple of Apollo at Didyma*, 16–17, who probably picked up this image from earlier writers such as Henry Thédenat, *Le Forum Romain et les Forums Impériaux* (Paris: Librairie Hachette, 1904), 218.

68. Talloen and Vercauteren, "The Fate of the Temples," 358–68.

It was not only local Christian church construction projects (which comprised a significant portion of new construction at this time) but other construction projects, both local and distant, that frequently took the stone blocks and columns from the abandoned pagan temples for reuse. These projects included new government buildings, public fountains and other public facilities, and palaces, especially in newly developing capital cities like Constantinople. These factors, along with the frequent earthquakes in the region, led to the constant, continuing deterioration of the ancient pagan temples down to the condition in which we find them today.

During Phase II (AD 350–450), as hundreds of churches were being constructed, the architects and builders for these churches incorporated existing elements of Roman architecture (e.g., the basilica, the arch, etc.). For theological statement and identity, these early Christians largely used the same symbols that were already well established within the Christian tradition—the Latin cross, the equilateral cross, the Chi-Rho Christogram with *alpha* and *omega*, the Tau-Rho Staurogram with the *alpha* and *omega*, and the ICHTHUS Christogram. The ICHTHUS wheel was used in these churches interchangeably with traditional crosses and sometimes even with emphasis (i.e., placed centrally with the cross on the side). The ICHTHUS Christogram shows up at the front of churches on chancel screens, on the ceiling of churches in mosaics, and in the floor mosaics. In several locations (e.g., Stobi and Bethlehem), the actual acrostic IXΘΥC was used in the floor mosaics.

At this point, and certainly continuing into Phase III (AD 450–565), as the cities became dominated by churches and crosses rather than pagan temples, the primary meaning and purpose of the ICHTHUS Christogram probably transitioned away from being the means to drive out demons or keep out demons, as it had been used earlier in graffiti etched on pagan temples and on the streets of the cities.[69] It then began to function more like the cross, serving as a well-known symbol of Jesus Christ and emphasizing the orthodox Christology of "Jesus Christ God's Son Savior." Brandenburg, however, in his discussion on the use of Christian symbols (primarily crosses) in the floor mosaics of early Christianity, notes that the function of crosses (and other Christian symbols), especially when they were near or centrally located at entrances probably still carried some apotropaic connotations. He notes that the use of these crosses (and other symbols) also carried other significant meanings—they underscored the sanctity of the building and pointed to Christ, the one who was being honored there and from whom all salvation emanates.[70]

---

69. Some scholars disagree with this and contend that the use of crosses and other Christian symbols, especially on the floors and near entrances, continued to be apotropaic in nature, even when used in sacred areas, such as churches. See, for example, Hans Buchwald and Anne McClanan, *Churches EA and E at Sardis* (Cambridge, MA: Harvard University Press, 2015), 44.

70. Brandenburg, "Christussymbole," 98–99.

There are several instances in large churches where crosses were placed at critical structural locations (e.g., the center top of arches) and sometimes in locations that would rarely have been seen (e.g., in upper windows, sills, and niches that were often over one hundred feet from the ground). An example of this can be seen at the monastery of St. John of Stoudios in Constantinople (AD 450s) and Agios Titos at Gortyna (Crete, end of sixth century).[71] These examples suggest an attempt to protect the structure rather than proclaiming meaning to the viewers.

During Phase III (AD 450–565), church construction moved to a higher level and spectacular churches were constructed (e.g., Basilica of St. John in Ephesus, Hagia Sophia in Constantinople, and Basilica of San Vitale in Ravenna). These churches were lavish enough to rival even the most grandiose of the ancient pagan temples. When Justinian I (AD 527–565) completed the Hagia Sophia Church in 537, it was the largest cathedral in the world and remained so for nearly one thousand years. These impressive churches continued to employ the use of crosses and ICHTHUS Christograms. At this point, especially during the reign of Justinian I, the battle against paganism was practically over, especially in the cities, and the power of the pagan temples was but a faint memory. Yet the battle over orthodox Christology still raged. In this context, the theological meaning of the ICHTHUS Christogram, as well as with the cross itself, was still valid. The powerful proclamation of "Jesus Christ God's Son Savior" through the acrostic symbolism of the eight-spoked wheel was still exceedingly meaningful.

VICTORY (*NIKĒ*) OVER PAGANISM AND PERSECUTION

A number of concepts related to the Greek verb νικάω (*nikaō*) and the noun νίκη (*nikē*) interconnect in early church history and relate to our study. Throughout Greek literature (as well as in the New Testament) the word νικάω (*nikaō*) and its associated word group had a basic meaning of "victory" (with connotations sometimes of "superiority"). Greek literature outside the New Testament often presents the understanding that "victory cannot be an achievement of mortals; only divine power can bring it about. A god alone conquers, is unconquered and unconquerable."[72]

Not surprisingly, the New Testament uses this word group over thirty times, and our English Bibles typically translate the word as "victory," "triumph," or "overcomes." For example, Jesus declares, "In this world you will have trouble. But take heart! I have *overcome* the world" (John 16:33, emphasis added). This word is especially prominent in the book of Revelation, used

---

71. Slobodan Ćurčić, "Design and Structural Innovation in Byzantine Architecture Before Hagia Sophia," in *Hagia Sophia from the Age of Justinian to the Present*, ed. Robert Mark and Ahmet Ş. Çakmak (Cambridge: Cambridge University Press, 1992), 17.

72. O. Bauernfeind, "νικάω," TDNT 4:942.

Fig. 4-1 Ephesus, Near the Temple of Domitian: Nike, Greek Goddess of Victory

with regard to the victory of Jesus Christ and his saints.[73] Revelation 17:14 reads: "They will wage war against the Lamb, but the Lamb will *triumph* over them because he is Lord of lords and King of Kings" (emphasis added).[74] John exhorts the church in Laodicea: "To the one who is *victorious*, I will give the right to sit with me on my throne, just as I was *victorious* and sat down with my Father on his throne" (Rev. 3:21, emphasis added).

A related word is στέφανος (*stephanos*), often translated as "crown." The English word "crown," however, is a little misleading, for in most instances the Greek word στέφανος refers to a laurel wreath. In the Greco-Roman world the laurel wreath was a sign of victory—for the Greeks it was in athletics (see 1 Cor. 9:25), but for the Romans, this victory was primarily triumph in war.[75]

Nike was the winged Greek goddess of victory. She is often depicted with the victory wreath in her hand as she awards it to an athletic champion (see fig. 4-1). For the Romans, however, Nike became Victoria, and rather than being associated only with athletic competition, she became the goddess of victory in war and conquest. The wreaths she awarded were often to returning generals and caesars after a great military victory. Because of her role in Roman military conquest, Victoria played a wider, more central and embedded role in Roman government and society than Nike did in Greek government and society. Entire temples were built and dedicated to Victoria.

Indeed, one of the most famous statues of Victoria (which was originally created as a statue of Nike but taken over by the Romans) was the one inside the Roman senate building Curia Julia. Placed here by Augustus, this "statue

---

73. Wilson, *The Victor Sayings*, and Wilson, *Victory through the Lamb*.

74. Frequently in Revelation this term is translated as "the one who overcomes," or something similar (2:7, 11, 17, 26; 3:5, 12, 21; 21:7). As in Revelation, this term occurs elsewhere in clusters. For example, 1 John 5:4–5 (emphasis added): "For everyone born of God *overcomes* the world. This is the *victory* that has *overcome* the world, even our faith. Who is it that *overcomes* the world? Only the one who believes that Jesus is the Son of God." Consider also 1 Corinthians 15:54–57 (emphasis added): "'Death has been swallowed up in *victory*.' 'Where, O death, is your *victory*? Where, O death, is your sting?' The sting of death is sin, and the power of sin is the law. But thanks be to God! He gives us the *victory* through our Lord Jesus Christ."

75. Grundmann notes, "The simplest form of the crown is a bent twig or two twigs tied together. . . . The Roman victor's crown was originally a simple wreath of grass." He points out that although the crowns in athletics and in war were two of the most popular usages, crowns were awarded and worn in a wide range of social situations. Walter Grundmann, "στέφανος," *TDNT* 7:615–36.

became one of the most vital links between the Roman state and Roman religion and also a tangible reminder of Rome's great past and her hopes for the future."[76] Prudentius, a Roman Christian poet, later provides a detailed description of this statue: "golden, that is, made of gilded bronze, winged, barefooted, and dressed in a flowing robe; she was poised on a globe and held a laurel wreath in the right hand."[77] This image matches the depictions of Victoria on Roman coins from the Augustan era down through late antiquity into the Byzantine era (when the Victoria image apparently evolved into an angel).[78] See the discussion in chapter 8 about the struggle in the late fourth century led by Bishop Ambrose to remove this statue and the associated altar from the Senate building, Curia Julia, in the Forum in Rome.

As discussed earlier in this chapter, the Great Persecution raged from 303–313. This horrific and devastating time for Christians was enforced by the current powers in their cities—the intertwined civic powers of pagan Roman government, imperial cult, and pagan temples—and it affected every Christian in the empire (except perhaps in the west where it was not enforced with such severity). As we discuss the actions and attitudes of Christians in the years that followed, as the power structures in the cities became reversed, it is important to remember that the memories and scars of the Great Persecution were still fresh.

Thus, during the years that followed Constantine's rise to power, several things happened that show up in the archaeological and literary records. The Chi-Rho Christogram, often accompanied by *alpha* and *omega* (usually the *omega* is shown as ω but in capital size), not only became popular, occurring throughout the Roman Empire, but it also started to appear circumscribed within victory wreaths (very similar to the wreaths used by Nike and Victoria).[79]

The cross symbol in general became associated with victory over the pagan powers and pagan world.[80] Thus, regular crosses of all types were frequently depicted inside these victory wreaths, as were the eight-spoked ICHTHUS

76.   James J. Sheridan, "The Altar of Victory: Paganism's Last Battle," *L'Antiquité Classique* 35 (1966): 187.

77.   H. A. Pohlsander, "Victory: The Story of a Statue," *Historia: Zeitschrift für Alte Geschichte* 18.5 (1969): 590.

78.   Pohlsander, 590–91, notes that there is a statue of Nike in the Museo Nazionale in Naples that may be modeled after the statue of Victoria in the Roman senate.

79.   The cross as a symbol of victory has continued to be an important theological component in the Eastern Orthodox tradition, even today. Payton, for example, writes, "St. John of Damascus gave voice to the way the Greek church fathers and, in their train, Orthodoxy, approach the cross: 'We venerate the Cross of Christ, by which the power of the demons and the deceit of the devil were destroyed.' This betokens a different emphasis than prevails in Western Christianity, which sees the crucified Christ as a suffering victim, enduring the divine judgment and paying the legal penalty for our sins. By contrast, Orthodoxy sees the cross as an emblem of victory. This approach has deep roots, both in Scripture and in the writings of the early church fathers, and it is celebrated in the rich liturgical traditions of Orthodoxy." James R. Payton Jr., *The Victory of the Cross: Salvation in Eastern Orthodoxy* (Downers Grove, IL: IVP, 2019), 8–9.

80.   Walter, "IC XC NI KA," 214.

Christograms, where the victory wreath forms the outer circle.[81] The words στέφανος (*stephanos*, "wreath") and σταυρός (*stauros*, "cross") are used together in inscriptions to mean "the wreathed [i.e., victorious] cross."[82] In an inscription in Scythopolis, a new word was apparently formed when the two words were combined to form a new verb: στεφανοσταυρίον (*stephanostaurion*), perhaps meaning "to make a wreathed cross."[83]

Under the Christian emperors following Constantine, the images used earlier of the goddesses Nike and Victoria were now used to portray angels, and these angels were the ones depicted as crowning the Christian Byzantine emperors. This appears regularly on coins from this era, although the coins sometimes, especially in the earlier years, still designate the winged female as Victoria, leaving the chronology of this conversion to an angelic being somewhat murky but a transition that, nonetheless, definitely took place.[84]

This image of angels (like Nike and Victoria, but now usually in pairs) then starts to appear in Christian art but with crosses or Christograms prominently displayed inside their victory wreaths (see fig. 4-2). For example, a fourth-century sarcophagus shows two angels holding a wreathed Iota-Chi symbol.[85] Similarly, a mid-sixth century ivory book cover shows two scenes of two winged angels holding a wreathed cross (over the apostles and over the Virgin Mary).[86] As discussed in more detail in chapter 8, the Basilica of San Vitale at Ravenna (mid-sixth century) contains three sets of angels—two pairs holding wreathed crosses (on the left and right sides as one walks through

---

81. From Spier, *The Earliest Christian Art*, see the following pictures: sarcophagus with wreathed Chi-Rho (c. 350), 105, 220; gold glass medallion with Peter, Paul, and wreathed Chi-Rho (late fourth century), 247–48; ivory book cover with a doubly-wreathed lamb in the center (fifth century), 256–57. From Jensen and Ellison, *Routledge Handbook of Early Christian Art*, see: sarcophagus with wreathed Chi-Rho (perhaps fifth to sixth centuries), 65; sarcophagus with wreathed Chi-Rho (late fourth century), 329–31. From Crow, Bardill, and Bayliss, eds., *The Water Supply of Byzantine Constantinople*, see pictures of the following, all inside wreaths from the fifth century: cross with *alpha* and *omega*, 169, 178; eight-spoked Christograms, 172–73, 175.

82. See the examples in Adam C. Chambers, "Re-Centering the Temple: The Origin and Expansion of the Decapolis Churches, 4th to 7th c. CE" (PhD diss., Miami University, 2009), 184–85.

83. G. M. Fitzgerald, *A Sixth Century Monastery at Beth-Shan (Scythopolis)* (Philadelphia: University of Pennsylvania Press, 1939), 3, 15.

84. During the pre-Christian Roman era, the goddess Victoria was often also associated with the trophy-post (*tropaeum*). Sometimes, rather than holding a wreath, she is depicted as holding this trophy-post. This was a tall post, usually set up in Rome after a victorious battle, that held the armor of the vanquished enemy ruler. Roman coins from this time period often had the emperor on one side and Victoria, holding the *tropaeum*, on the other side. As early as the second century, however, Christian writers such as Justin Martyr (AD 100–165) identified the cross as the Christian *tropaeum*, an imagery that caught on quickly, especially after Constantine. By the time of Theodosius II, the winged woman (probably now an angel and not Victoria, but the imagery is the same) on the back of the emperor's coins held a tall Christian cross as the *tropaeum*. See R. H. Storch, "The Trophy and the Cross: Pagan and Christian Symbolism in the Fourth and Fifth Centuries," *Byzantion* 40.1 (1970): 105–18.

85. Guntram Koch, "Early Christian Sarcophagi Outside of Rome," in Jensen and Ellison, *The Routledge Handbook of Early Christian Art*, 58.

86. Herbert L. Kessler, "The Word Made Flesh in Early Decorated Bibles," in Spier, *Picturing the Bible*, 143.

the presbytery toward the front) and one climactic pair of angels holding a wreathed ICHTHUS Christogram above the exalted Christ seated on the globe in the center of the apse (see figs. 7–5 and 7–6).[87] This underscores the ultimate victory of Christ and the cross.

Relatedly, from an early date, Christians were using abbreviations of the word *nikē* (and the related form *nika*) in creative ways. Usually in inscriptions, this word appears as NIKA (grammatically this can be either the imperative or the third-person present indicative form). For example, at Aphrodisias NIKA appears several times (see chapter 5). In one case the inscription has a cross, and in the four quadrants formed by the arms of the cross are Greek letters that, when put together,

Fig. 4-2 Ravenna, Engraved Ivory Book Cover: Top Panel Depicts Winged Angels Holding a Wreathed Cross

spell out Χριστε νικα ("Christ, be victorious" or "Christ is victorious").[88] Guarducci argues that even in Latin inscriptions, the letter N was often used as an abbreviation of the Greek work *nika*, such as in complex monograms. In several cases the Latin inscriptions use the Latin letters NICA to spell out the Greek *nika*.[89] In one inscription, the acrostic IXΘΥC is followed by the letter N, probably abbreviating *nika*.[90]

Also, recall the cross and eight-spoked Christogram carved into the Kurşunlugerme Bridge in the aqueduct serving Constantinople discussed earlier in the chapter. The inscription (using abbreviations as is typical) is spread across the four quadrants formed by the arms of the cross and reads as follows (the missing, abbreviated letters are in brackets): O CTA[ΥP]OC EN[I]KHCE[N] AEI NIKA (see fig. 5-13). Crow translates this as "the Victorious Cross will always be triumphant."[91] This could also be translated as, "The cross has been victorious; it will always be victorious," or perhaps "The cross has been victorious; be ever victorious!"

---

87. See the beautiful pictures in Gianfranco Malafarina, ed., *The Basilica of San Vitale and the Mausoleum of Galla Placidia in Ravenna*, 2nd ed. (Modena, Italy: Franco Cosimo Panini, 2017), 48–79.

88. Roueché, *Aphrodisias in Late Antiquity*, 185. For other examples of NIKA in the inscriptions of Aphrodisias, often with crosses and/or references to Christ, see pp. 180–88.

89. Guarducci, *The Tomb of St. Peter*, 101, 115, 122.

90. Testa, *Il Simbolismo Dei Giudeo-Cristiani*, 417–18.

91. Crow, "A Monumental Aqueduct Bridge," 164.

Interestingly, this exact text shows up at the other end of the empire, at the temple to Isis in Philae in southern Egypt. It was converted to a church during the reign of Justinian (AD 527–565), one of the last pagan temples in the Byzantine Empire to be converted and a conversion that required military force.[92] On an interior temple wall, right on the doorway to the inner holy place where the goddess Isis once stood, a cross has been professionally inscribed into the wall.[93] Written below the cross is Greek text identical to the inscription on the Kurşunlugerme Bridge, but without any abbreviations, proclaiming the victory of the cross.[94]

CHURCH COUNCILS AND CHRISTOLOGY CONTROVERSIES

Theological disputes and heretical false teaching surfaced quickly in the early church. Almost as soon as Paul and the other early evangelists planted a church, aberrations and syncretizations of the gospel emerged. Much of the New Testament was written in this context with the dual, but interrelated, purposes of teaching correct Christian theology while countering false doctrine. Warnings about false teaching and exhortations to stand firm in the received apostolic teaching occur all across the New Testament epistles as well as in Revelation. Not surprisingly, doctrinal disputes and attempts to counter and correct theological heresies continued through the second and third centuries, even though the church was hampered by the sporadic persecutions imposed by the governing authorities and by Christianity's unofficial and unrecognized status in the Roman Empire. Church leaders (largely bishops) could gather locally to deal with regional doctrinal issues, but dealing with empire-wide doctrinal problems was challenging. Nonetheless, the church kept spreading.

The situation changed drastically in the fourth century after Constantine came to power. Not only did Constantine legalize Christianity, but he and his successors provided imperial support for Christianity. Soon after Christianity was legalized in 313 (ending the Great Persecution), a divisive (and explosive) theological dispute arose over the teachings of a man in Alexandria named Arius about the nature of Jesus Christ. Meanwhile, Constantine consolidated power and control of the eastern portion of the empire by defeating Licinius in 324. Shortly afterward, hoping to establish unity among the churches, he provided imperial transportation assistance, allowing bishops to come from across the empire to gather at the city of Nicaea (in what is now western Turkey) to deal with this issue. More than three hundred bishops attended (although reports of the actual number of bishops varies) along with their associates. The ecumenical council of Nicaea met in 325 and hammered out the Nicene Creed,

---

92. Hahn, "Die Zerstörung der Kulte von Philae," 203.
93. Walter, "IC XC NI KA," 195.
94. Hahn, "Die Zerstörung der Kulte von Philae," 214.

a positive statement of Christian orthodoxy that also condemned Arius's teaching of Christology ("there was a time when Christ was not").[95]

Most of the bishops and associate church leaders who came to Nicaea had suffered terribly in the Great Persecution, which had ended only twelve years earlier. Most had suffered personally, and, in many cases, they had stepped into the office of bishop after the prior bishop had been martyred. Now they gathered together openly and freely, with the emperor paying for the conference. The drastic change in fortunes was astounding, and the bishops, of course, attributed this to the Lord. These bishops and their associates, along with the next generation, would play a major role in spreading Christianity throughout the Roman Empire (and beyond) and in transforming their cities from pagan-temple dominated to Christian-church dominated.

Nicaea set a precedent for how to deal with major empire-wide doctrinal disputes and heretical teachings. Although regional church councils continued to be held (e.g., the Council of Laodicea in 363–364, attended by thirty bishops from the province of Asia), four critically important, ecumenical church councils were held during the fourth and fifth centuries to deal with major doctrinal issues in the church: Nicaea I (AD 325); Constantinople I (AD 381); Ephesus (AD 431); and Chalcedon (AD 451).

For our study, it should be noted that these church councils and the disputes on which they sought to rule occurred concurrently with the Christianization process of the pagan Greco-Roman cities of the empire (Phases I and II, which ran from AD 320 to 450).[96] As background for our study of the ICHTHUS Christogram, it is significant to realize that the largest and most divisive controversies dealt with by these councils, especially Nicaea and Chalcedon, were in regard to christological and Trinitarian theology. They dealt with issues concerning the relationship of Jesus Christ to the Father, especially regarding substance (was Christ of the same substance as the Father?); time, creation, and divinity (was there a time when Christ was not?); and nature (does Christ have two natures—fully God and fully human—or just one nature?).

While we cannot draw any firm conclusions, it is still interesting to note some parallels between the creeds of the councils and the theology conveyed by the ICHTHUS Christogram (Jesus Christ God's Son Savior). The creed adopted at Nicaea, which was to become the basic theological statement for what orthodox Christianity affirmed, stressed critical doctrinal beliefs: "We believe in one God the Father All-sovereign . . . and in one Lord Jesus Christ,

---

95. For a discussion of the events that led to the Council of Nicaea, see Ferguson, *Church History*, 191–93.

96. Another interesting observation is that during this general era (especially AD 370–430), quite a number of influential and prolific Christian theologians were writing and addressing these (and other) issues. This included Ambrose, Jerome, Augustine, and Cassian (in Latin), as well as Basil, Gregory of Nyssa, Gregory of Nazianzus, John Chrysostom, Cyril of Jerusalem, and Cyril of Alexander (in Greek). See the discussion in Adrian Hastings, "150–550," in *A World History of Christianity*, ed. Adrian Hastings (Grand Rapids: Eerdmans, 1999), 57.

the Son of God . . . Light of Light . . . who . . . for our salvation came down and was made flesh . . . and rose on the third day, ascended into the heavens, is coming to judge the living and the dead."[97] At the same time, as often-heated and sometimes violent christological battles were being waged by bishops and theologians within the church all across the empire, Christians were inscribing ICHTHUS Christograms in the pagan temples and in the streets, proclaiming "Jesus Christ God's Son Savior." As the number of new Christian churches being built multiplied, the eight-spoked wheel was regularly incorporated into the symbolic architecture alongside the other Christian symbols of Jesus Christ (the cross, the Tau-Rho Staurogram, the Chi-Rho Christogram, *alpha* and *omega*, etc.). And not surprisingly, similar or identical terms from the Nicene Creed (e.g., "all-sovereign," παντοκράτορος, *pantokratoros*; "light," Φως, *phōs*) appear in inscriptions and graffiti that occur across the cities of the Roman Empire during the fourth to sixth centuries, several of which we will discuss in the next chapter.

---

97. Taken from Ferguson, *Church History*, 195.

CHAPTER 5

THE EIGHT-SPOKED ICHTHUS CHRISTOGRAM IN ANATOLIA AND THRACE (WESTERN TURKEY)

INTRODUCTION

Many of the ancient cities discussed in this section—Aphrodisias, Didyma, Ephesus, Labraunda, Laodicea, Priene, Sagalassos, Samos (Pythagoria), and Sardis—are all located in southwestern Turkey. Up until around 200 this entire area was included in the Roman provinces of either Asia or Lycia and Pamphylia. If one marked a center at Aphrodisias or nearby Laodicea and then drew a circle with a 150-mile radius around that center, all of these cities would fall into that circle. These cities were close enough together that we should not be surprised to find some common cultural affinities between them, especially during the early Christian era (AD 200–600).

In Acts 13–14, Paul and Barnabas first bring the gospel into Anatolia, planting churches in Galatia and Phrygia—the region that is now central Turkey. Paul revisits this area on his second journey (Acts 16–18:22), also briefly visiting the western region of Anatolia (e.g., Ephesus) as he returns back to Antioch. On his third journey (Acts 18:23–21:16), Paul revisits Galatia and Phrygia but then travels to Ephesus in the Roman province of Asia (western Turkey), where he stays for two years and three months (Acts 19:8–10). During this time, the gospel spreads throughout the province of Asia (Acts 19:10), no doubt carried into many cities in this region by the coworkers of Paul. We can assume with some assurance that it is at this time that churches are planted in most of the cities that are discussed in this section. Revelation 2–3 addresses Ephesus, Laodicea, and five other cities in this region, indicating both the presence of a significant church in each city and the problems these churches were already facing as the first century draws to a close.

Christianity continued to spread throughout this region during the second and third centuries. This can be seen from literary evidence in the writings produced by (or about) significant Christian leaders from this time and region (Polycarp, Melito, Polycrates, etc.), as well as from Christian funerary inscriptions. As in other regions, the grim records of the Great Persecution list many Christian martyrs from this area.[1]

By 300 there were many strong churches in this area. After Constantine came to power and the Great Persecution ended, Christianity exploded throughout this region. Strong evidence for the rapid and widespread Christianization of Asia Minor in the fourth century comes from funerary inscriptions, which transition from being almost completely non-Christian at the beginning of the fourth century to being almost totally Christian by the end of the century. Stephen Mitchell writes:

> With very rare exceptions, the inscribed texts of the period AD 350 and 600 displayed the hall-marks of Christianity and thus through their very presence helped to create the Christian environment in a material and monumentalized format. Purely secular inscriptions are almost unknown after the mid-4th century. . . . Crosses were also routinely displayed on other monuments, especially building inscriptions.[2]

APHRODISIAS (STAUROPOLIS)

The City of Aphrodisias

The city of Aphrodisias was located in southwestern Turkey (the ancient Roman province of Asia), about 100 miles (160 km) inland from Ephesus and the western coast of Turkey. Its origins date back several millennia before the arrival of Christianity. The name Aphrodisias comes from the cult of Aphrodite (goddess of love); the Temple of Aphrodite (which probably developed from the worship of the Mesopotamian goddess Ishtar) and the veneration and worship of Aphrodite were at the heart of the life and reputation of the city.

Brought into the Roman Empire in the first century BC, Aphrodisias acquired the status and rights of a free city. During the first two centuries AD, the city experienced a time of prosperity and rising importance. A number

---

1. William Tabbernee, "Asia Minor and Cyprus," in *Early Christianity in Contexts*, 261–88, 315–19; Shin, *The Great Persecution*, 229–30, 252–53.
2. Stephen Mitchell, "The Christian Epigraphy of Asia Minor in Late Antiquity," in *The Epigraphic Cultures of Late Antiquity*, ed. Katharina Bolle, Carlos Machado, and Christian Witschel (Stuttgart: Franz Steiner Verlag, 2017), 279.

of impressive and lavish structures were constructed during this time, and the remains of many of these can still be seen at the site today. This included the huge Temple of Aphrodite, with a grandiose gateway called the Tetrapylon. There was also a temple-like structure called the Sebasteion, dedicated to the imperial cult and built to honor both Aphrodite and the Roman emperors. Another impressive structure was the eight-thousand-seat theater, which included a bust of Aphrodite and statues of Nike (the goddess of victory).

Modifications to the theater in the mid-second century included lowering the orchestra area (the central ground area between the seats and the stage) and installing a net in front of the bottom rows. This conversion was to accommodate gladiatorial combat and fights with wild beasts (those who fought the wild beasts were called *venatores*). Public executions were also held here. Close to the theater were the Theater Baths, but the more impressive bathing facility was the Hadrianic Bathhouse. There were also two agoras, although some have suggested that the South Agora is misnamed; it was comprised primarily of a huge oval-shaped fountain-fed pool, 556 feet long (168 m) and 62 feet wide (19 m).[3] There was also a small government building shaped into an amphitheater for official meetings (called the Odeon or the Bouleuterion).

Aphrodisias also had an oval-shaped stadium with thirty rows of seats and a seating capacity of thirty thousand. In addition, there was an impressive palace or lavish private residence, often called the Bishop's Palace. This was originally the home of a wealthy aristocrat or perhaps the governor, but later it became the residence and office of the Christian bishop. The city was enclosed with a system of walls and gates. Many of these structures are well preserved and can be seen on a site visit.[4] Around 250, the Roman rulers broke up the province of Asia into smaller units, and Aphrodisias became the capital of the new province of Caria-Phrygia.

Throughout the second and third centuries, Christianity was spreading and growing throughout the area. In 325, soon after Constantine legalized and provided imperial support of Christianity, Aphrodisias became an episcopal see—the headquarters and residence of a regional bishop.[5] As was typical for cities all across the Roman Empire, Aphrodisias went through several phases in the Christianization process. Probably at some point soon after the arrival of the first bishop, depending on the events relating to the power structures in the city and the power of the pagan temples, Christians sought to

---

3.   Andrew Wilson, "Water, Nymphs, and a Palm Grove: Monumental Water Display at Aphrodisias," in *Aphrodisias Papers 5: Excavations and Research at Aphrodisias, 2006–2012*, ed. R. R. R. Smith, J. Lenaghan, A. Sokolicek, and K. Welch, Journal of Roman Archaeology Supplement Series 103 (Portsmouth, RI: 2016), 109.

4.   Henry Matthews, *Greco-Roman Cities of Aegean Turkey: History, Archaeology, Architecture* (Istanbul: Ege Yayinlari, 2014), 177–202. On the stadium and theater see Katherine Welch, "The Stadium at Aphrodisias," *American Journal of Archaeology* 102.3 (1998): 547–69.

5.   Rou<eché>, *Aphrodisias in Late Antiquity*, 154. Rouché, 322, notes that Bishop Ammonius of Aphrodisias attended the Council of Nicaea.

destroy the pagan idols throughout the city and to cleanse and drive out demons throughout the city, especially at the pagan temples, the fountains, and perhaps the bathhouses. Probably by the mid-fourth century, the famous statue of Aphrodite had been defaced and buried (to be uncovered later by archaeologists).[6] By the mid-fifth century, the Temple of Aphrodite had been converted into a church. Eventually, the Christian government of the city changed the pagan-associated name of the city (Aphrodisias) to the Christianized name Stauropolis (city of the cross).[7]

Christian Graffiti at Aphrodisias: Crosses, Eight-Spoked Wheels, and Four-Spoked Wheels

Aphrodisias is helpful for our study because it is filled with graffiti, perhaps more so than any other ancient Greco-Roman city. Indeed, we might call Aphrodisias the "graffiti capital of the Greco-Roman world." More than 630 graffiti inscriptions, including texts, drawings, and symbols, have been documented and published.[8] This published list includes five eight-spoked wheels, forty-three simple crosses, two Chi-Rho Christograms (with *alpha* and *omega*), one Tau-Rho Staurogram inscribed in a circle, and three Jewish menorahs. There are also more than fifty recognizable rectangular and square game boards along with a variety of circles.[9] Among the circle shapes, there are at least twenty circles that have a simple cross inscribed within them (like a four-spoked wheel).[10] If these circles with crosses are viewed as Christian crosses,[11] as noted above and argued below, then there are sixty-three known (published) Christian crosses etched in stone as graffiti in Aphrodisias.

---

6.   Matthews, *Greco-Roman Cities*, 175–78; Roueché, *Aphrodisias in Late Antiquity*, 1–2.
7.   Roueché, *Aphrodisias in Late Antiquity*, 149.
8.   Most of these are included in the online database *Inscriptions of Aphrodisias*, edited by J. Reynolds, C. Roueché, and G. Bodard (2007). See https://insaph.kcl.ac.uk/insaph/iaph2007/inscriptions/index.html. They are nicely compiled into a chart by Banes, "A Comparative Approach to Graffiti," 368–430.
9.   After cautioning that not all of these shapes, especially the simpler circles, are game boards, Roueché describes the locations for most of the square, rectangular, and circular shapes that are inscribed on the pavement or stadium seats at Aphrodisias. See Roueché, "Game Boards at Aphrodisias," 100–105.
10. Bell and Roueché have attempted to collect as many different variations of circles, squares, and rectangular shapes appearing in graffiti as they could find (including a number of these from Aphrodisias) and to organize them by shape. Then they assigned a letter and number designation for each of these so that scholars could use this typology to identify these shapes in their excavations and writings. To the eight-spoked wheel they assign the designation of C4. The circle with a simple equilateral cross within they designate as C2. This typology is helpful in that it allows scholars to discuss these shapes using a common typology to differentiate between them. See R. C. Bell and C. M. Roueché, "Graeco-Roman Pavement Signs and Game Boards: A British Museum Working Typology," in Finkel, *Ancient Board Games in Perspective,* 106–9.
11. The same symbol appears frequently in the city of Sagalassos, east of Aphrodisias (see the discussion below). Lavan refers to this shape as "a simple cross in a circle." See Luke Lavan, "The Agorai of Sagalassos in Late Antiquity: An Interpretive Study," in *Field Methods and Post-Excavation Techniques in Late Antique Archaeology*, ed. Luke Lavan and Michael Mulryan (Leiden: Brill, 2013), 334, 336.

Fig. 5-1 Aphrodisias, Theater Seats: Equilateral Cross Inside Circle

What interests us the most in this study are the eight-spoked ICHTHUS Christograms that appear in Aphrodisias. The five eight-spoked wheels cited in the publication above are identified at the following locations: one at the bishop's palace, three in the stadium, and one in the theater baths. These published lists are not complete, however, for during my visit to Aphrodisias in June 2023, I found an additional eight-spoked wheel within the Temple of Aphrodite and eight more eight-spoked wheels on the paving just inside the Tetrapylon, or the elaborate entryway to the Temple of Aphrodite, yielding a total of *fourteen* ICHTHUS Christograms at Aphrodisias (see figs. 5–4 and 5–5).

Roueché notes that the circle with a simple equilateral cross inscribed inside (resembling a bull's-eye target, which she designates as style C2) is one of the most common shapes occurring at Aphrodisias. I was able to locate seventeen of these just in the theater on the seats (see fig. 5–1). Although a number of writers assume these four-spoked wheels are game boards, it is hard to imagine what kind of game could be played on this four-quadrant circle. Indeed, Roueché doubts that these are game boards and suggests instead that they served as a kind of place marker for people to stand or sit.[12] Others writing about this symbol at Aphrodisias likewise question its use as a game board. In regard to the presence of several of these circles on the seats around the pool in the South Agora, Wilson, Russell, and Ward write: "The circle in cross motifs cannot be gameboards of the same kind [i.e., like tic-tac-toe]. . . . The cross in circle motif would either have to be a game of a different type whose rules are currently unknown, or not a game at all, but a symbol, perhaps a Christian one."[13] It is highly likely that this symbol is Christian—a simple equilateral cross inscribed inside of a circle (which doesn't rule out the "place marker" possibility as it could identify the group sitting there or gathering there as a Christian group).

Testa points out that early Christianity used a wide variety of symbols that involved crosses and circles together. He presents a chart with drawings of over forty examples of how crosses and circles are combined, several of which are the equilateral cross inscribed in the circle—the type that appears so frequently at Aphrodisias.[14]

12. Roueché, "Game Boards at Aphrodisias," 100.
13. Andrew Wilson, Ben Russell, and Andrew Ward, "Excavations in an urban park ("South Agora"), 2012," in Smith, Lenaghan, Sokolicek, and Welch, *Aphrodisias Papers 5*: 84.
14. Testa, *Il Simbolismo Dei Giudeo-Cristiani*, 297, with discussion on pp. 297–304.

As we noted in chapter 2, in early Christianity the shape of the cross had not yet standardized into the one with a long vertical leg and shorter arms (i.e., the Latin cross), as we normally depict it today. In fact, a quick survey through the hundreds of crosses appearing in the database *Inscriptiones Christianae Graecae* (AD 200 to 700) shows the majority are equilateral crosses, where each arm is equal in length. Not surprisingly, these equilateral crosses appear frequently in the inscriptions at Aphrodisias.[15] A variation of this is the Maltese Cross, a thick equilateral cross with flared ends. Maltese-type crosses also appear frequently in the early Christian inscriptions recorded in the database mentioned above.

Throughout the Mediterranean world during the early Christian era, Christians inscribed the equilateral cross inside of a circle, which is identical to the C2 style (the four-spoked circle) that is ubiquitous at Aphrodisias. There are dozens and dozens of examples of these C2-style circles that are clearly used in Christian contexts within funerary epitaphs and other inscriptions from sites across the early Christian world, especially throughout Asia Minor.[16]

The evidence is strong that the four-spoked circles that occur in Aphrodisias are actually equilateral crosses inscribed within a circle. Two of these published equilateral-cross circles are in the Hadrianic Baths, seven are on stadium seats, and eleven are on theater seats,[17] and as mentioned above, in my last visit, I located seventeen equilateral-cross circles etched on the theater seats.

Another interesting group of inscriptions at Aphrodisias include the Greek word τόπος (*topos*), which means "place." There are fifty-one graffiti inscriptions that contain *topos* in full or in abbreviated form. Twenty-one of these are personal names (e.g., "place of Theodosius"). Ten of them are blank regarding whose place it was ("place of . . ."). Five of the place inscriptions seem to refer to associations or guilds (e.g., "the gold-workers"; the "gardeners"). Three refer to the Blues, one of the Circus Factions (a chariot team fan club and political group). Both the Jews and the Christians made use of this practice. Two place inscriptions refer to the "place of the Jews." Six of the inscriptions have crosses as part of the inscription, strongly implying that these are Christian inscriptions. For example, in the theater baths one inscription reads "place of Alexandros, barber," with a cross before and after the inscription. One inscription reads ΤΟΠ (abbreviation for *topos*) followed by a cross ("place of the cross" perhaps).

15. For pictures of several examples, see Roueché, *Aphrodisias in Late Antiquity*, figs. 153, 155, 156, and 158.

16. For example, see *ICG* 1, 10, 14, 82, 83, 85, 392, 441, 630, 666, 1411, 1434, 1561, 1582, 1659, and 2388. There is another group that has the Maltese-style cross inscribed within the circle, or the regular equilateral-style cross with slightly flared ends. These include *ICG* 1298, 1887, 2284, 2285, 2293, 2308, 2370, 2465, 2511, and 3637.

17. J. Reynolds, C. Roueché, and G. Bodard, eds., *Inscriptions of Aphrodisias*, (2007) IAph dataset, https://kclpure.kcl.ac.uk/portal/en/publications/inscriptions-of-aphrodisias-iaph2007; Banes, "A Comparative Approach to Graffiti," 368–430.

A number of graffiti inscriptions are illegible, and many of them consist of only a few letters. Most of the time these letters do not form recognizable words; they are probably abbreviations for people's names.

The Theater Graffiti

There are hundreds of inscriptions and graffiti on the stone seats of the theater at Aphrodisias. A few of these are rough drawings of people. One of these drawings (*IAph*2007 8.60.9i) depicts a man's torso and head (without arms). Over the center of his torso is an eight-spoked wheel (see fig. 5-2). Above the wheel are four Greek letters, ΘΡΑξ (THRAX), which means "Thracian," or someone from Thrace. Often this man is assumed to be a Thracian gladiator. In the early years of the Roman Empire, this special type of gladiator fought with a small, curved sword and a round or rectangular shield. It seemed reasonable to assume that the eight-spoked circle covering this man was a shield and that the letters ΘΡΑξ (THRAX) indicate that this was a Thracian gladiator. Since this graffito was on a theater seat, and since the theater was often the venue for gladiator fights (until around AD 300–350), this identification seemed to fit well, even if the actual purpose for the drawing remained obscure.

Fig. 5-2 Aphrodisias, Theater Seats: The Thracian

In her dissertation, "Seating and Spectacle in the Graeco-Roman World," Tamara Jones analyzes hundreds and hundreds of seating inscriptions from eighty-one Greco-Roman seating venues (theaters, stadiums, amphitheaters, and Odeons), both in the western and eastern Roman Empire. She cites several examples where a gladiator, actor, or venator (the animal-fighter) won a victory of some sort and was awarded a section of seating reservations, assumedly for family, friends, and influencers.[18] Perhaps this sketch of a man was honoring a Thracian gladiator and indicated the reserved area for his family and friends.

Yet the details of this etched graffito and the overall context may be a little more complicated than it appears at first glance, and the quick

18. Tamara Jones, "Seating and Spectacle in the Graeco-Roman World" (PhD diss., McMaster University, 1988), 114, 139.

conclusion that this represents a gladiator may be premature or at least questionable. Gladiator contests (where trained warriors fought each other as entertainment for large audiences) were popular across the Roman Empire until the middle of the fourth century when the expense of the fights, along with the aversion and strong opposition from the newly empowered Christians, brought them to an end. By the mid-fourth century (AD 350), gladiator fights in the eastern part of the Roman Empire (especially Asia Minor) were rare, and by the year 400, gladiator fights had ended all across the empire.[19] No doubt this was also the case in Aphrodisias. There were still fights between the venatores and wild animals, but these fighters were not called gladiators and were not associated with Thrace, as some gladiators were.

Furthermore, it is curious that this man etched on the theater seat in Aphrodisias does not wear a helmet, for the Thracian gladiators were famous for their unique, colorful helmets.[20] Gladiators in general are typically portrayed with their helmets on, even in graffiti. There are nearly a dozen graffiti depictions of gladiators scrawled on the basilica at nearby Smyrna, and they all are wearing helmets.[21] Another peculiarity is the absence of any kind of sword (or even arms or hands, for that matter) on this so-called gladiator. The circle is assumed to be a shield, but nowhere in any of the many visual depictions of gladiators extant today do round shields with eight spokes appear.[22]

Yet if the word ΘΡΑΞ, "Thracian," does not refer to gladiators, to what or to whom might it refer, and why would it be used? Although not conclusive, several interesting observations may bear on this question. First of all, starting with Marcian, the emperor of the eastern Roman Empire from 450 to 457, a number of emperors (and their generals) of the eastern empire were Thracian, or at least were rumored to be from Thrace. Leo I, for example, who followed Marcian, ruling 457–474, was often called "The Thracian" ὁ Θραξ). If this

---

19. Alan Cameron, *Circus Factions: Blues and Greens at Rome and Byzantium* (Oxford: Clarendon, 1976), 214–17; and Welch, "The Stadium at Aphrodisias," 568. Both Wiedemann and Meijer provide an overview of the decline and then disappearance of gladiatorial fights in the face of the growing Christian opposition from 200–400, starting with the opposition by Tertullian and Clement of Alexandria and climaxing with Augustine. See Thomas Wiedemann, *Emperors and Gladiators* (London and New York: Routledge, 1992), 147–60; and Fik Meijer, *The Gladiators: History's Most Deadly Sport* (New York: St. Martin's, 2003), 200–205.

20. See Anne Hrychuk Kontokosta, "Gladiatorial Reliefs and Elite Funerary Monuments at Aphrodisias," in *Aphrodisias Papers 4: New Research on the City and Its Monuments*, ed. C. Ratté and R. R. R. Smith, Journal of Roman Archaeology Supplement Series 70 (Portsmouth, RI: 2008), 193. See the elaborate helmets (with characteristic feathers on top) of the Thracian gladiators depicted in Meijer, *The Gladiators*, 41, 83, and 92.

21. Roger S. Bagnall et al., *Graffiti from the Basilica in the Agora of Smyrna* (New York: Institute for the Study of the Ancient World and New York University Press, 2016), 78–79, 164, 196, 230, 258, 278, 282, 285, 287, 301.

22. See the many depictions from ancient mosaics and stone reliefs shown in Wiedemann, *Emperors and Gladiators*, figs. 3–17; Meijer, *The Gladiators*, 27, 41, 62, 64–65, 67, 69, 72, 78, 83, 92, 94, 138, 143, 160–61, 169, and 172–74.

inscription (ΘΡΑξ) was made, say, in 470, during Leo's reign, then gladiatorial fights and Thracian gladiators would be a distant memory. It would have been several generations since the last gladiatorial fight occurred in Aphrodisias. Leo I (The Thracian), however, had his face on most of the coinage being used and was perhaps the most well-known name in the empire at that time. Coins bearing Leo's image were discovered in the excavations of the Church at Aphrodisias that had been converted from the Temple of Aphrodite.[23] The inscription ΘΡΑξ in this context would have been understood to have reference to this emperor.

The Council of Chalcedon, a gathering of bishops and other church leaders from across the Byzantine Empire, was held in 451 during the reign of the Emperor Marcian. The resulting decree from Chalcedon led to a split of Christianity in the east over the nature of Christ. The church in the east (where Aphrodisias was), as well as the emperors in Constantinople, struggled with this split throughout the next two centuries. The opponents to the Council of Chalcedon, called non-Chalcedonians (or sometimes called Monophysites) were strong in Egypt and in parts of Palestine, as well as in Aphrodisias.[24] As discussed below, it is possible, although not at all conclusive, that the ICHTHUS Christogram, referring to Jesus Christ God's Son Savior, became a visible statement in support of Chalcedonian orthodoxy. Thus, the figure inscribed on this theater seat in Aphrodisias with an ICHTHUS Christogram and the title ΘΡΑξ, "Thracian," could be referencing Marcian, Leo I, or one of the other Thracian, Chalcedonian-affirming emperors. While this is far from certain, it has about as much support as the gladiator option does.

If this figure of a man with the word ΘΡΑξ, "Thracian," does *not* refer to a gladiator, then the eight-spoked wheel that dominates the drawing is not a shield. It may not even be connected to the drawing of the man. It could have been added later.

Another interesting group of graffiti are the eighteen that refer to the "Greens" or the "Blues," mostly on theater seats. These are the well-documented Circus Factions, and they show up all over the eastern part of the Greco-Roman world. The "Greens" and "Blues" supported chariot-racing teams, and the prominent associations based on these names functioned as a combination of fanatic sports fan club and political party. The reference to the Blues or Greens on the theater seats probably indicated the area of the theater in which they sat. They probably sat in groups, dressed in their blue or green shirts. They are well known in late antiquity for being loud and rowdy.[25]

---

23. Anna M. Sitz, "Hiding in Plain Sight: Ephigraphic Reuse in the Temple-Church at Aphrodisias," *Journal of Late Antiquity* 12.1 (2019): 143.

24. Roueché, *Aphrodisias in Late Antiquity*, 144–46, who notes that the conflict between the Chalcedonians and the non-Chalcedonians would have been intense and quite damaging in Aphrodisias.

25. Cameron, *Circus Factions*, 214–15, 244–245, points out that in the fifth century the Blues and Greens became quite popular and powerful throughout the eastern part of the Byzantine Empire, and they appear frequently in theaters and amphitheaters, both in literature and in archaeology. They are

In these inscriptions, the Blues and the Greens frequently are associated with the Greek word Νικα (*nika*, meaning "victory" or "triumph").[26] A common inscription is the phrase Νικα ἡ τύχη τῶν Βενέτων ("Victory is the fortune of the Blues"), a phrase used also by the Greens. In the theater and stadium of Aphrodisias, this formula, "Victory is the fortune of so-and-so" or closely related slogans using Νικα, appears in the graffiti twenty-four times. Twelve times it is referring to the Blues or the Greens, and five times the referent is blank ("Victory is the fortune of ____"). Seven times the referent is related to something Christian, usually the cross (see chapter 4 regarding the role of the word NIKA or NIKE in early Christian history). One inscription reads ΤΟΥΤΟ ΝΙ(cross)ΚΑ ("This is victory," with a cross inserted in between NI and KA, "victory"). This inscription would be saying that the cross is victorious (and probably implying that it is not the Blues or the Greens that are really victorious). Another inscription (see the discussion below) includes abbreviations of the words "Jesus," "Christ," and "victory," interspersed with crosses, meaning "Jesus Christ is victorious."

There are also a number of crosses inscribed on the seats of the theater (nine are listed in the databases).[27] This includes both Latin-type crosses (longer vertical member) (see fig. 5-3) and equilateral-type crosses. As mentioned above, there are also at least seventeen equilateral crosses inside circles, and there are small squares divided into four quadrants, perhaps a box with a cross in the middle. As noted in chapter 2, Testa suggests that these are crosses inscribed within a square, and he presents a number of other square-and-cross-related symbols. These small, four-square boxes are frequently found at other sites often among regular crosses and crosses inscribed within circles.

One interesting seat has a fascinating collection of symbols and texts, although not all of it is

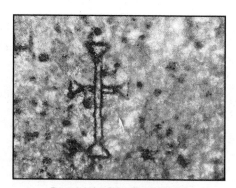

Fig. 5-3 Aphrodisias, Theater Seats: Cross with Flared Ends

also closely associated with public disturbances. They are known for rowdy cheering and chanting, especially to honor (or dishonor) civic leaders.

26. The Circus Factions are infamously connected to the terrible Nika revolt in Constantinople. Starting in the Hippodrome, they started a week-long riot, which threw the city into chaos and included igniting the nearby church, Hagia Sophia. The emperor Justinian finally responded by sending in the imperial troops, who trapped many of them in the Hippodrome and killed thirty thousand of them. See Cameron, *Circus Factions*, 278–79.

27. Reynolds, Roueché, and Bodard, eds., *Inscriptions of Aphrodisias*; and Banes, "A Comparative Approach to Graffiti," 368–430; Roueché, *Aphrodisias in Late Antiquity*, 172.

completely legible. The first line reads, "Lord, help." The second line is a Chi-Rho Christogram with the letters *alpha* and *omega*. The third line has "prayer [or vow, dedication, Gr. εὐχή, *euchē*] of Stephanas." The fourth line reads, "Help your servant Geo(rge?)" (part of this line is unfinished). The fifth line reads, "The fortune of [a cross symbol is inscribed here] is victory (Νικα)."[28]

The Bishop's Palace
One of the eight-spoked Christograms, embellished with vines and leaves, was discovered in the courtyard of the bishop's palace, a governmental palace that was converted into a bishop's house. This is the most decorative of the ICHTHUS Christograms at Aphrodisias, which is fitting for the splendor of the building. Also in the bishop's palace is a blue marble column with a half dozen crosses, cross monograms, and several graffiti inscriptions, mostly fragmentary, along with numerous illegible letters informally inscribed on it (*IAph*2007 2.402). Included is an inscription that reads ΙΣ (abbreviation for "Jesus"), then a cross, and then ΧΣ (abbreviation for "Christ"). Below it is ΝΙ, then a cross, and then ΚΑ, forming ΝΙΚΑ. All together the inscription is proclaiming "Jesus Christ is victorious." The informal nature of the inscription and the unplanned-looking appearance of this graffito on this column convey a certain spontaneity. It could be that it was inscribed during the (perhaps chaotic) transformation from the pre-Christian government ruler's house to the residence of the newly appointed Christian bishop. The proclamation of "victory" seems to imply a strong statement of conquering or overcoming not only of victory over the earlier era of Christian persecution but of overcoming the integrated powers of imperial rule and pagan worship along with the many demons associated with the pagan rulers. The ΙΧΘΥΣ inscription in the courtyard may be saying the same thing as it proclaims "Jesus Christ God's Son Savior."

The Temple of Aphrodite and the Tetrapylon
The spectacular temple dedicated to the goddess Aphrodite was constructed in the first century BC. With huge columns numbering eight across and thirteen deep, it was almost as big as the famous temple to Artemis in Ephesus. The importance of this temple to the city is underscored by the fact that the city Aphrodisias is named after the goddess Aphrodite. In the early second century AD, during the reign of Emperor Hadrian, this temple was modified by the addition of surrounding colonnades. Then in about 200, an impressive and intricate entranceway was added, located over one hundred yards away and connected to the temple with a paved road and walls. This impressive structure, known as the Tetrapylon, is still standing, although most of the

---

28. Roueché, *Aphrodisias in Late Antiquity,* 184 (inscription 137).

connecting roadway and walls are gone.[29]

At some point in Aphrodisias, perhaps as early as the mid-fourth century or perhaps the early fifth century, Christians invaded this temple and removed the idols. The central idol of Aphrodite in the temple was defaced and buried nearby (to be discovered later by archaeologists; the idol is in the museum at Aphrodisias). Similarly, at the Tetrapylon, the bust of Aphrodite, located centrally at the top, was removed and a cross inscribed instead.[30] As throughout the empire, in addition to proclaiming victory over the pagan power structures in the city, these Christians probably were intent on "de-demonizing" this pagan sacred space, especially the entrances. It is probably at this time that they inscribed the extensive Christian graffiti that we see there today.

In our discussion in chapter 4, we observed that in the ancient world thresholds and entryways played important religious and theological roles, as did the paving area just before and after the doorway.[31] As the Christians cleansed the pagan temples and other pagan areas of the demons and sought to keep them away, they often placed crosses and Christograms at the entrances.[32] To enter the Temple of Aphrodite you had to first came through the Tetra-

Fig. 5-4 Aphrodisias, The *Tetrapylon*, Monumental Entrance to the Temple of Aphrodite: Several Eight-Spoked Wheel ICHTHUS Christograms Along with Other Christian Graffiti Are Etched in the Stone Pavement in Front

Fig. 5-5 Aphrodisias, The *Tetrapylon*, Monumental Entrance to the Temple of Aphrodite: ICHTHUS Christogram on the Stone Pavement

---

29.   Matthews, *Greco-Roman Cities*, 198–201.
30.   Jacobs, "Cross Graffiti," 192–93.
31.   Emilie M. Opstall, *Sacred Thresholds: The Door to the Sanctuary in Late Antiquity*, Religions in the Graeco-Roman World 185 (Leiden: Brill, 2018).
32.   Bayliss, *Archaeology of Temple Conversion*, 13.

Fig. 5-6 Aphrodisias, The *Tetrapylon*,
Monumental Entrance to the Temple of Aphrodite:
ICHTHUS Christogram, Crosses, Crosses Inside
Squares (Four-Square Boxes) and Circles

Fig. 5-7 Aphrodisias, West Doorway
to the Temple of Aphrodite

Fig. 5-8 Aphrodisias, West Doorway to the Temple of
Aphrodite: Christian Inscriptions

pylon (see fig. 5–4). Inscribed on the stone threshold of this gateway and on the stone paving immediately after entering the temple complex through this gate are eight ICHTHUS wheels along with several equilateral crosses inside of circles and several four-square boxes (a cross inside of a box, perhaps) (see figs. 5–5 and 5–6).[33]

After walking the one hundred yards or so along the paved roadway (which is mostly grass now), you can then enter the temple proper through the main doorway (the west door) (see fig. 5–7). Inscribed on both stone side panels (doorjambs) of this doorway into the temple are Christian graffiti consisting of prayers, monograms of names, and crosses (one or two of the crosses may have been professionally inscribed after the graffiti). The graffiti inscriptions on one of these doorway side panels are discussed in chapter 2 (see fig. 2–10). The inscription on the other doorway side panel (see fig. 5–8) has a monogram at

---

33. There are other puzzling, non-identifiable graffiti in this area as well.

the top that perhaps is the name Theophilus. Below the monogram is the text (using abbreviations) that translates as "Lord, help your servant, the butcher." The word for "Lord" (*kurie*) is abbreviated as κε, but there is a horizontal line above these two letters, indicating it is a *nomina sacra* abbreviation. The term "butcher" likely refers to the occupation of Theophilus, who probably inscribed this prayer on this doorjamb just as the Christians were destroying idols and bringing the operation of this temple to an end.

Fig. 5-9 Aphrodisias, Pavement Inside of the Temple of Aphrodite: ICHTHUS Christogram

Right past this doorway, as one steps into the main temple area itself, there is another ICHTHUS Christogram etched into the paving stones. This one was placed in the center of the paving of the temple's atrium (see fig. 5–9).

On a broken block, perhaps part of a doorway, another interesting series of graffiti texts was discovered. There are three groups of texts. Translated from the Greek, the first one says, "In fear approach the gate of the judgment seat [Gr. *bema*, βεμα]," followed by a cross. Traces of red paint were found in this inscription. The next text has the Greek letters I (for "Jesus," *Iēsous*, Ἰησοῦς) and X (for "Christ," *Christos*, Χριστος), along with NI and KA, which form the Greek word for "victorious." Each of these four are placed in one of the four quadrants formed by the cross. An additional, similar cross with letters in the four quadrants then follows, but this text translates as "Lord, help your servant, Philip, a sinner. Amen." Several other crosses are inscribed next to these texts.[34]

Later, perhaps in the mid-fifth century[35] or late fifth century,[36] this temple complex was structurally reconfigured and converted into a Christian church in a major, expensive, multiyear reconstruction. The archaeological remains from this conversion include stone wall panels and chancel screens with professionally inscribed equilateral crosses in circles (see fig. 5–10), similar to those seen in other churches across the Byzantine Empire at

---

34. See Roueché, *Aphrodisias in Late Antiquity*, 179–80, fig. 129 on plate XXXII. In the database, this is *IAph*2007 1.193i, ii, iii.

35. Matthews, *Greco-Roman Cities*, 199.

36. Sitz, "Epigraphic Reuse in the Temple-Church," 143–44. Some have suggested that the dedication of this church could perhaps be associated with the visit of Emperor Theodosius II in 443. See Matthews, *Greco-Roman Cities*, 199, and Roueché, *Aphrodisias in Late Antiquity*, 153.

this time. The informality of the etched graffiti on the entryway doorjambs, as well as that seen in the nine ICHTHUS Christograms on the pavement, are in stark contrast to the professionally cut and inscribed wall panels and other architectural features of the church. While we cannot be certain, this strongly implies that the informal Christian graffiti and ICHTHUS Christograms were etched prior to the formal church construction and were not part of it.

The City Walls

At the southeast corner of the city walls, inscribed facing each other on either side of a vaulted passageway near the east gate, are two parallel and fascinating inscriptions. Similar to the examples cited above, each one includes a Latin cross and an inscribed text. Each text, however, is split up into four parts with each part in one of the quadrants created by the cross. On one side, split up into the four quadrants, are the two Greek words Χριστὲ ("Christ") and νίκα ("victory," "be victorious"). On the other side are the two words Φῶς (*phōs*, "light") and Ζωή (*zōē*, "life").[37] These two words Φῶς ("light") and Ζωή ("life") also appear with crosses inscribed on the walls of the Temple of Artemis at Sardis (see section on Sardis below).

Fig. 5-10 Aphrodisias, Temple of Aphrodite, after Conversion to Christian Church: Stone Panel with Equilateral Cross Inside Circle

Two other interesting inscriptions on the city walls are on the northeast gate of the city. These two formally inscribed inscriptions are together—one above the other. The top one, dating to the mid-fourth century, honors the one who built the gate. The bottom one, dating to the mid-fifth century, honors the one who rebuilt the gate. The bottom inscription includes crosses at the beginning and at the end of the inscription. Yet both inscriptions have been modified. Inscribed on top of the upper inscription is a Latin cross inside of a circle along with the letters *alpha* and *omega*. On the bottom inscription, the name of the city (Aphrodisias) has been removed

37. Roueché, *Aphrodisias in Late Antiquity*, 185.

and replaced with the new name, Stauropolis ("city of the cross"),[38] another visible indication of the Christianizing process that took place in this city.

The Bathhouses and the South Agora Pool

There are two bathhouses at Aphrodisias: the Theater Bathhouse and the Hadrianic Bathhouse. There are several Christian inscriptions in these bathhouses. Inside the Hadrianic Bathhouse, for example, are six inscriptions that contain crosses.[39] Likewise, the Theater Bathhouse contains four graffiti inscriptions that contain crosses,[40] as well as one ICHTHUS wheel.[41]

Built in the second century, the Hadrianic Bathhouse continued to operate as a bathhouse throughout the fourth to sixth centuries, even after the Christians de-paganized the city. Several major renovations were apparently done to make the facility more economical to operate and to transition it from a public to a private bathhouse. Whether this was driven by Christian attitudes to public bathing or by pragmatics and economics is debated.[42] As part of the recent archaeological restoration of this bathhouse, one headless statue has been recovered and restored, a reminder that these bathhouses probably had numerous pagan statues at the beginning of the fourth century, most of which were removed, destroyed, defaced, or beheaded at some point later in the fourth century.

Aphrodisias had several public fountains, but the most visible one was the fountain-fed pool of the South Agora, which has been recently excavated and restored. The perimeter of the pool comprises seats, and on several of these are four-spoked wheels (i.e., crosses inside a circle).[43] This huge monumental fountain likely contained dozens of pagan god statues, but very few were discovered during excavations. As noted in chapter 4, as Christians de-paganized the city, they probably removed the pagan statues from this pool and buried them somewhere (as yet unexcavated), smashed them into small pieces to use as rubble or fill in foundations or walls, or burned them in kilns to produce lime. One statuette of a naked boy riding a dolphin was found in the eastern end of the pool. Although the bottom portion of the dolphin is missing, it is likely that the dolphin's mouth was a spout for water flowing into the pool. As with so many other pagan statues, this one is missing his head.

---

38. *IAph*2007 12.101i and 12.101ii; Roueché, *Aphrodisias in Late Antiquity*, 75; Sitz, "Epigraphic Reuse in the Temple-Church," 142–43.

39. *IAph*2007 5.12i, 5.13, 5.14, 5.15, 5.17, and 5.24.

40. *IAph*2007 8.601iii, 8.603, 8.605, and 8.607.

41. *IAph*2007 8.601v.

42. Allyson McDavid, "Renovation of the Hadrianic Baths in Late Antiquity," in Smith, Lenaghan, Sokolicek, and Welch, *Aphrodisias Papers 5*, 207–24.

43. Two of these circle-inscribed crosses can be seen in an archaeologist's sketch of one small portion of the pool perimeter. See Wilson, "Monumental Water Display at Aphrodisias," 112.

As at other cities, in the bathhouses and at one of the largest pools in the city, there is evidence of Christians removing, destroying, and defacing pagan statues as well as inscribing crosses and other Christian symbols.

CONSTANTINOPLE

The City of Constantinople/Byzantium (Istanbul)

The origins of the ancient city of Byzantium are obscure, clouded by various mythological accounts. It was probably founded as a Greek colony as early as the seventh century BC. Located at a key point—guarding the sole entrance to the Black Sea and one of the major east-west land routes—the city quickly became strategically and economically important. Another key feature was its specific geographical location—on a peninsula, naturally protected by water on three sides, making it easily defensible.[44]

Although Byzantium is not mentioned in the New Testament, Christianity likely arrived there in the mid-first century. The major Roman highway leading west from Byzantium, the Via Egnatia (in Latin, *via* means "road"), led to Philippi and then Thessalonica, where early Christian communities sprang up. To the southeast was Asia Minor, where Paul and his coworkers had planted churches in cities across the region (Ephesus, Laodicea, etc.). Due east was Bithynia and then Pontus. Peter addresses his first epistle to the Christians in Pontus, Galatia, Cappadocia, Asia, and Bithynia (1 Peter 1:1), implying that the churches planted in Bithynia and Pontus were also in the first century. Indeed, in 112, Pliny the Younger, the Roman governor of Bithynia-Pontus, asked the emperor Trajan how to deal with the troublesome Christians in his province.[45] Thus, Christianity appears to have been fairly widespread in the regions surrounding and connecting to Byzantium by the early second century. A later legend, probably inaccurate, attributed the planting of the church in Byzantium to the apostle Andrew.

In 196, as Septimius Severus was battling rival claimants to become sole emperor of the Roman Empire, he besieged and then destroyed most of the city of Byzantium. Later in his reign, however, Severus sponsored much of the rebuilding of the city, and afterward, during the third century, the city flourished and grew. Although when the Roman Empire was split into four administrative sections (the Tetrarchy), Nicomedia—not Byzantium—was selected as the capital of the east.

By the time of the Great Persecution, Christianity had spread throughout the provinces near Byzantium—Thrace, Bithynia, Pontus, Asia. Many

---

44. Noel Lenski, "The Reign of Constantine," in Lenski, *The Cambridge Companion to the Age of Constantine*, 77; Guntram Koch, "Constantinople," in Finney, *The Eerdmans Encyclopedia of Early Christian Art and Archaeology*, 1:358.

45. Pliny, *Epistulae* 10.96–97. For a discussion on Pliny's letter and the expansion of Christianity into Bithynia-Pontus, see Tabbernee, "Asia Minor and Cyprus," 302–8.

Christians were martyred in these provinces during the Great Persecution, which was especially severe in Nicomedia.[46]

After defeating Maxentius in 312 and then Licinius in 324 (who had used Byzantium as one of his last defensive positions), Constantine became the sole ruler of the Roman Empire. His reign ushered in a new era that dramatically changed the history of the Roman Empire. Among the many changes he instituted, one of the more significant ones was shifting the capital of the empire from Rome to Byzantium (bypassing Nicomedia), which he renamed during its dedication in 330 as "Nea Roma" (New Rome). Yet the city quickly became known as Constantinople, after the emperor himself. Striving to make this city worthy of the imperial capital of the Roman Empire, Constantine began building up the city soon after he gained control. This included a fortification wall on the western side, a rationalized street grid (typical of Roman cities), a palace, bathhouse complexes, a capitolium, a circular forum, a senate house, two martyria, and three additional churches. In 330, Constantine dedicated his new capital and moved in.[47]

During the reign of Theodosius II (AD 408–450), an extensive system of city walls and gates was constructed, enlarging the city that had been enclosed in Constantine's smaller wall-and-gate system. Many of Theodosius's walls and gates still stand and dominate the landscape of the old city in modern Istanbul. Throughout the fifth and sixth centuries, Constantinople continued to grow and become more powerful and influential as a city and as the center of Christianity. Churches, residences, public monuments, and government buildings were built. At the time of Justinian (ruled AD 527–565), Constantinople's population topped 500,000 people.[48] Due to the new construction associated with this rapid population growth and the big projects carried out by the emperors across the city during the fifth and sixth centuries, the archaeological remains from the second to the fourth century are meager. Almost nothing remains from the city's pagan past (pre-Constantine). Even most of what Constantine built was replaced or seriously renovated and expanded over the next two centuries, and we know of his building projects largely through literary sources.[49]

Constantinople continued to serve as the imperial capital—first of the Roman Empire and then of the Byzantine Empire—until the fifteenth century. The ecclesiastical influence and power of Constantinople continued to grow. Constantine appointed a bishop over Constantinople. In 381, a church council held at Constantinople elevated the authority and jurisdiction

---

46. Shin, *The Great Persecution*, 160–69, 247–53.
47. Linski, "The Reign of Constantine," 77; Koch, "Constantinople," 1:358.
48. Brian Croke, "Justinian's Constantinople," in Maas, *The Cambridge Companion to the Age of Justinian*, 67.
49. Mark J. Johnson, "Architecture of Empire," in Lenski, *The Cambridge Companion to the Age of Constantine*, 291–92.

of the bishop of Constantinople to number two in the empire, just below the bishop of Rome. In 451, the bishop of Constantinople (now referred to as the patriarch of Constantinople) was given ecclesiastical authority over the entire eastern part of the empire. This formalized a rift that was already taking place, as the western church (to become the Roman Catholic Church, with its capital at Rome, led by the pope) was distancing itself from the eastern church (to become the Eastern Orthodox Church, with its capital at Constantinople, led by the patriarch of Constantinople).

In 1453, Constantinople was captured by the Ottoman Turks and renamed Istanbul. The city served as the imperial capital for the Muslim Ottomans until 1923, when the new Republic of Turkey moved the political capital to Ankara. Today, with more than fifteen million residents, Istanbul is the largest city in Turkey and the largest city in Europe.

The Hagia Sophia

Built by Emperor Justinian in just five years (AD 532–537), the Hagia Sophia ("Church of the Holy Wisdom") is arguably the greatest architectural achievement of the entire Byzantine era (AD 330–1453). This magnificent basilica, also known as "The Great Church," was the largest church structure in Christendom for hundreds of years.[50]

Similar to the architectural style of other churches built during this time (such as the Basilica of San Vitale), the exterior of Hagia Sophia was not elaborate or lavish (although impressive in size) in contrast to the interior of the church, which was beautifully decorated. The high ceilings are covered with colorful mosaics in a multitude of patterns. One of the central themes in these patterns is the Christian cross. Incorporated into this cross theme are a number of eight-spoked ICHTHUS Christograms.[51] Located in multiple bays throughout the narthex, in addition to appearing in the structurally critical location of window arches, are dozens of ICHTHUS wheel mosaics, as well as Latin crosses. Both the ICHTHUS Christograms and the Latin crosses "were positioned for maximum visibility by worshippers."[52] The eight-spoked wheel

---

50. Natalia B. Teteriatnikov, *Justinianic Mosaics of Hagia Sophia and Their Aftermath*, Dumbarton Oaks Studies XLVII (Washington, DC: Dumbarton Oaks Research Library, 2017), 1–7. For a history of the earlier two churches that had been built on this same site, see İlhan Akşit, *The History and Architecture of the Hagia Sophia* (Istanbul: Akşit Kültür Turizm Sanat Ajans Ltd. Şti., 2019), 29–38.

51. For beautiful color pictures of this, see Lord Kinross (John Patrick Balfour), *Hagia Sophia* (New York: Newsweek, 1972), especially the front and back inside cover pages. See also Akşit, *The History and Architecture of the Hagia Sophia*, 76–77, 164–67, who shows several eight-spoked wheels and then observes that "the church was decorated with cross motifs." Another Justinian-era church with a shape similar to the eight-spoked wheel displayed prominently like a cross is the Church of St. Nicholas in Lycia (Demre) on the southern coast of Turkey.

52. Teteriatnikov, *Justinianic Mosaics of Hagia Sophia*, 15, 17, 54–55, 67, 133, 204–7, 274–77. In addition, there are a number of eight-spoked wheels in which the spokes taper down toward the perimeter, creating a star look. Teteriatnikov, 63–65 refers to these as a "star in a medallion." Yet they are used in close association with Latin crosses in the same manner as the regular eight-spoked wheels.

is closely associated with the cross, appearing alongside and often in parallel to this important Christian symbol. This strongly implies that the eight-spoked wheel was not used merely as a geometric or decorative shape, but that it carried symbolic theological meaning.[53] The most plausible explanation for why this eight-spoked wheel was used in such prominent locations and in parallel with standard crosses is that it represented the acrostic ICHTHUS, declaring "Jesus Christ God's Son Savior."[54]

The Constantinople Aqueduct (the Kurşunlugerme Bridge)

Cities of the Roman Empire, including those of the Roman East (e.g., modern Turkey, Syria, Lebanon, Jordan, and Israel), consumed a tremendous amount of water. Besides the demand for drinking water for the residents (often provided through fountains) and a significant demand from urban workshop activity (food production, pottery manufacture, textiles, metal instrument manufacture), a typical Roman city of significant status would have public ornamental fountains (often called nymphaeum), as well as bathhouses with large pools, public latrines with running water, extensive gardens to be watered, and running water in the houses of the elites. Delivering the huge quantities of water to the facilities that required it and at high enough elevations that allowed for it to flow by gravity was a monumental engineering feat at which the Romans excelled.[55] The ability to provide an extravagant amount of water, especially in visible public spaces such as at fountains, was a status symbol and a matter of civic pride. This meant the water systems were both utilitarian as well as decorative. Ann Koloski-Ostrow writes:

---

53. The association between the eight-spoked wheel and the cross are so close that Teteriatnikov, in *Justinianic Mosaics of Hagia Sophia* (without recognizing the ΙΧΘΥϹ connection), calls the wheel a Christogram and views it as a type of cross. After repeatedly labeling pictures and drawings of the eight-spoked wheel as Christograms (54–55), she writes, "Two types of crosses were used in the decoration: the Latin cross and the Christogram" (67).

54. Ćurčić has observed that not only are numerous crosses used in the building, but that they appear in critical structural locations (at the top of arches or domes). He cites a similar phenomenon in other churches built during this era, noting that the crosses, while certainly meaningful signs of Christian identity, also often appear in places that would not be seen by anybody. In those locations, he concludes, while the cross may not lose its theological meaning, its primary meaning may be more apotropaic (spiritual protection to give structural help). See Ćurčić, "Design and Structural Innovation in Byzantine Architecture," 17–18.

55. See Julian Richard, *Water for the City, Fountains from the People: Monumental Fountains in the Roman East*, Studies in Eastern Mediterranean Archaeology IX (Turnhout: Brepols, 2012); James Crow, Jonathan Bardill, and Richard Bayliss, eds., *The Water Supply of Byzantine Constantinople*, Journal of Roman Studies Monograph 11 (London: The Society for the Promotion of Roman Studies, 2008); Elena H. Sánchez López, "Water and Production: Reflections on the Water Supply to Urban Workshops in Roman Times," *Water History* 15 (2023); Andrew Wilson, "Water, Power, and Culture in the Roman and Byzantine Worlds: An Introduction," *Water History* 4 (2012): 1–9; and Fikret Yegül, *Bathing in the Roman World* (Cambridge: Cambridge University Press, 2010). Vitruvius, a Roman engineer and architect (80–15 BC), includes a section of guidelines in his book *De Architectura* for constructing water systems (*Arch* 8.6).

When water was celebrated in lavish public displays in the Roman city, bubbling openly in *nymphaea* (large, architectural water displays), fountains, and luxurious pools in public parks and abundantly available in enormous bath complexes in which latrines often functioned with continuous flush into the sewers, then it took care of utilitarian needs, but it also symbolized the largesse of the empire, and the political power, status, and wealth wished for by many and possessed by few.[56]

Unlike Rome, which had a good water supply, Constantinople's defensible location—on a peninsula surrounded by seawater—made the acquisition of fresh water difficult. For any serious expansion of the city—especially the addition of huge, spectacular fountains, which were expected features in an imperial capital—a massive upgrade was required for the water delivery facilities. A small aqueduct system had been constructed during Hadrian's reign (AD 117–138), but this system only served the lower elevation areas of the city and delivered a limited quantity of water. The higher half of the city was forced to rely on wells and rainfall stored in cisterns, along with the water from a few small springs, which were unable to deliver the huge quantities of running water required for impressive fountains and for lavish bathhouse pools.[57]

Studies on how to bring more water into the city, especially from the water-rich mountains of nearby Thrace, along with the early stages of construction, probably started during the reign of Constantine (or shortly thereafter). Yet it wasn't until 373, during the reign of Valens (reigned AD 364–378), that the first phase of this famous water system was completed and water was delivered into the city, feeding the new public fountain built by Valens. Typically this system is called the Aqueduct of Valens, even though it was expanded and renovated several times by other emperors over the next century.

By the mid-fifth century (AD 450), this aqueduct system was one of the longest and most impressive in the entire Byzantine Empire. It stretched over 200 miles (322 km) to the west, bringing a large quantity of water to Constantinople from the mountains of Thrace. In some parts, during the fifth-century expansion, a parallel channel was added. Other aspects of the expansion included connecting with additional springs in the mountains and then transporting the water from these springs through the mountains via three secondary aqueducts to the main line. Adding these branches to the main aqueduct yielded a total distance of 382 miles (611 km), making this the largest aqueduct system in the empire.[58] It also included an estimated sixty massive bridges that crossed over creeks and valleys, of which nineteen are still standing (in some form) today.

---

56. Ann Olga Koloski-Ostrow, *The Archaeology of Sanitation in Roman Italy: Toilets, Sewers, and Water Systems* (Chapel Hill: University of North Carolina Press, 2015), 73.
57. Crow, Bardill, and Bayliss, eds., *The Water Supply of Byzantine Constantinople*, 10–14.
58. Crow, "Monumental Aqueduct Bridge," 148; Crow, Bardill, and Bayliss, eds., *The Water Supply of Byzantine Constantinople*, 1.

This water transportation system also included several tunnels cut through the mountains. The maximum flow rate, occurring during the rainy season in the mountains, is estimated to be 1.73 cubic meters per second, or 3,950,000 gallons per day.

Although some of the aqueduct has been damaged or destroyed over time, a significant portion remains. The forested mountainous area of Thrace where much of the aqueduct was built has been fairly isolated for

Fig. 5-11 The Constantinople Aqueduct, the Kurşunlugerme Bridge

much of the aqueduct's history, as it is still today, and this has helped preserve much of it.

In the middle section of the aqueduct are spectacular bridges.[59] Carved into the stonework of five of these bridges are Christian symbols, such as crosses and Chi-Rho Christograms.[60] One of the symbols on the Büyükgerme Bridge is an eight-spoked wheel.[61]

Of the five bridges with Christian symbols, the awe-inspiring

Fig. 5-12a The Kurşunlugerme Bridge: ICHTHUS Christogram (damaged), Flanked by Crosses on Either Side

Kurşunlugerme Bridge stands out in its number and range of symbols. This is the largest still-standing bridge in this huge aqueduct system, spanning a steep valley and encompassing three levels of arches. The highest point in the center of the bridge is 115 feet (35 m) above the ground, and at the top, from bank to bank, the bridge is 489 feet (149 m) in length (see fig. 5-11). This bridge is located in an isolated area in Thrace. It is about 50 miles (80 km) west of the modern-day Istanbul International Airport that is just outside the main city of Istanbul.

Carved professionally into the stonework of the Kurşunlugerme Bridge are thirty-one Latin crosses, three Tau-Rho Staurograms, one Chi-Rho Christogram, several textual Christian inscriptions, and four ICHTHUS Christograms (see fig. 5-12a and 5-12b). The christological letters *alpha* and *omega* also appear several times: next to a cross, a Tau-Rho Staurogram, and a Chi-Rho Christogram. Most of these Christian symbols are placed in the most

---

59. One of the largest of these bridges, the Balligerme Bridge, was destroyed with dynamite in 2020 by treasure hunters who apparently thought there might be gold inside.
60. Crow, "Aqueducts of Thrace," 157.
61. Crow, "Monumental Aqueduct Bridge," 156; Crow, "Aqueducts of Thrace," 177.

Fig. 5-12b The Kurşunlugerme Bridge: Equilateral Cross Inside Circle, with Alpha-Omega

Fig. 5-13 The Kurşunlugerme Bridge: ICHTHUS Christogram and Cross

visible areas of the bridge and the most critical structural areas, such as the keystone (the top of the arch).

One of the ICHTHUS Christograms is inscribed inside of a victory wreath and just above a Latin cross (see fig. 5-13). Written across the four panels formed by the cross is an inscription that translates, "The victorious cross will always be triumphant."[62]

There is another example of the wreathed ICHTHUS Christogram in one of the arches. Flanking this Christogram are two Latin crosses with inscriptions in Greek. One says, "Emmanuel" (a Greek transliteration from the Hebrew word), and one says, "God with us," which is the meaning of the word "Emmanuel" in Hebrew.[63]

Another inscription on the bridge states, in Greek, KYPIE BOHΘEI ("Lord, help"). As noted in chapter 2, this is a common Christian inscription, appearing at sites both in graffiti and in professionally inscribed texts.[64]

---

62. For discussion, along with numerous pictures, see Crow, "Monumental Aqueduct Bridge," 147–74; and Crow, "Aqueducts of Thrace," esp. 157–80.

63. See the pictures of these inscriptions in Crow, "Monumental Aqueduct Bridge," 162–63; and in Crow, "Aqueducts of Thrace," 174.

64. Regarding similar inscriptions at Aphrodisias, Roueché writes, "The formulae recognizable in these fragments are largely those standard in Christian inscriptions. The prayer for help (βοήθει, βοήθησον) . . . is one of the most widespread of such formulae; it is common at Aphrodisias . . . and throughout the Byzantine world." Roueché, *Aphrodisias in Late Antiquity*, 97.

The ICHTHUS wheels on the bridges of this aqueduct are used in parallel, or similar to, the other Christian symbols (the cross, the Tau-Rho Staurogram, and the Chi-Rho Christogram). This is strong evidence that the ICHTHUS Christogram was an important Christian symbol.

The arrangement of the symbols on the Kurşunlugerme Bridge points to an emphasis on the ICHTHUS Christogram, in that these Christograms are often depicted as central. For example, one of the Christograms discussed above is located at the center and top of the arch, flanked by Latin crosses and inscriptions. Likewise, in the example containing the inscription "The victorious cross will always triumph," the Christogram is placed above the Latin cross.[65]

What was the purpose of these crosses and Christograms? It could be related to the water-carrying function of the aqueduct. Stephen Humphreys, for example, studies the occurrences of crosses in underground cisterns and proposes that the crosses located in these water facilities are related to the concept of water "purity."[66] As noted in several places in this study, crosses and ICHTHUS wheels show up with some regularity in water-related systems (fountains, bathhouses, etc.).

Crow points out that, while these huge aqueduct bridges were in an isolated area, most of the crosses and Christograms were placed in areas that were quite visible, implying that they were intended to be seen. Some of them were placed in the most critical structural areas of the arches in the bridges, maybe hoping to add some spiritual protection for the bridge, whether from earthquakes (which were quite common in this area) or from demons.[67]

The texts that were placed alongside the symbols (e.g., "the victorious cross") also add a theological component. The meaning of these combined symbols and texts, Crow observes, could be quite complex and involve a number of factors. He concludes, "These were symbols capable of expressing not just the apotropaic power of the cross but also more complex iconographic and doctrinal concepts of faith concerning victory, salvation, and the very nature of Christ."[68]

DIDYMA

The Temple of Apollo

On the southwestern coast of Anatolia (now modern Turkey), going south from Ephesus, it was about thirty-three miles (fifty-four km) to the city of Priene (see section on Priene below). From Priene, it was sixteen miles (twenty-five km) to Miletus. About ten miles (sixteen km) further south of Miletus, connected

---

65. See the pictures in Crow, "Aqueducts of Thrace," 173, 175.
66. Stephen Humphreys, "Crosses as Water Purification Devices in Byzantine Palestine," in *Trends and Turning Points: Constructing the Late Antique and Byzantine World*, The Medieval Mediterranean: Peoples, Economies and Cultures, 400–1500, vol. 117, ed. Matthew Kinloch and Alex MacFarlane (Leiden: Brill, 2019), 229–46.
67. Crow, "Monumental Aqueduct Bridge," 170–71.
68. Crow, "Monumental Aqueduct Bridge," 170–71.

with a paved road called the Sacred Way, was the site of Didyma. The name "Didyma" does not refer to a city but to a sacred worship site where a famous Temple of Apollo was built (there were, no doubt, ancillary facilities as well—a small residential village, a few small temples to other gods, a sacred grove of trees, shops, baths, porticos, and stone benches).[69] Prior to the arrival of Greek colonists in the second millennium BC, this had been a worship site for a local Anatolian god. After the Greeks arrived, they built an open-air altar there, along with a small temple, and dedicated it to their god Apollo. Soon it became known as a place where oracles (predictions of the future or advice for future actions, especially for the royal court) could be obtained. The oracle at Didyma rivaled the famous Pythia oracle of Delphi, located in Greece.[70]

In 560 BC, King Croesus of Lydia financed the construction of a spectacular temple on this site, featuring 120 columns 60 feet high with a diameter of 6 feet. This temple was destroyed by the Persian king Xerxes in 479 BC. Alexander the Great initiated reconstruction of this temple, and his successors established the site as the home of one of the most important oracles in the Greco-Roman world. It was also one of the three largest temples in the Greco-Roman world. Construction on the temple continued into the Roman era.[71] Even though construction was never quite finished, the structure remains awe-inspiring. The oracle at this temple was active during the imperial Roman era and into the third and early fourth centuries AD, even as Christianity began to spread throughout the region.

The Oracle, the Great Persecution, and the Triumph of Christianity

In general, the future-telling oracles at the temples of Apollo (especially at Delphi, Didyma, and Claros) in the Greco-Roman world "played an important role in the pagan attack on Christianity."[72] The oracle in the Temple of Apollo at Didyma, in particular, played a critical role in instigating the Great Persecution.

At the end of the third century AD, the Roman Empire was split up into four parts, each ruled by different emperors. Galerius, one of these rulers, advocated for an empire-wide effort to diminish the rising power and influence of the Christians. Galerius urged his fellow emperor in Asia Minor (the most powerful of the four), Diocletian, to join him in an empire-wide persecution. Diocletian was unsure, and he consulted with the oracle at the Temple of Apollo in Didyma. The oracle gave him a positive response,[73] encouraging

69. Joseph Fontenrose, *Didyma: Apollo's Oracle, Cult, and Companions* (Berkeley: University of California Press, 1988), 30–31.

70. Matthews, *Greco-Roman Cities*, 319–21; Fontenrose, *Didyma*, 1–23.

71. Matthews, *Greco-Roman Cities*, 320–21; Fontenrose, *Didyma*, 15–22.

72. Pier Franco Beatrice, "Monophysite Christology in an Oracle of Apollo," *International Journal of the Classical Tradition* 4.1 (1997): 4.

73. For the text of the response, a list of sources which cite it, and a discussion of the response, see Fontenrose, *Didyma*, 206–8.

him to join Galerius in persecuting Christians. In 303, Diocletian began to issue edicts under which churches were destroyed, Scriptures burned, and Christians forced to sacrifice to the gods or face execution.[74]

Much of the Temple of Apollo at Didyma still remains and can be easily seen if you visit (see fig. 5-14). After bypassing the front courtyard where the huge altar would have been, you encounter a stone staircase across the front of the temple. Ascending the staircase, you enter the pronaos, or front part of the temple proper, consisting of a stone paved floor and rows of gigantic columns, ten across. Many of the columns have been removed and reused elsewhere, but enough of the bases remain to give a feel for the temple's size. Etched on the stone floor in between the columns all across the entire pronaos area are no less than twenty-eight ICHTHUS Christograms of various sizes and degrees of precision (perfect circles or lopsided circles) (see figs. 5-15 and 5-16).[75] There are also a number

Fig. 5-14 Didyma, The Temple of Apollo

Fig. 5-15 Didyma, The Temple of Apollo:
ICHTHUS Christogram

of regular crosses inscribed in the pavement, along with several equilateral crosses inscribed inside circles. The placement of crosses next to some of

---

74. Lactantius, *The Death of the Persecutors*, 1–33; Mark Wilson, *Biblical Turkey: A Guide to the Jewish and Christian Sites of Asia Minor* (Istanbul: Ege Yayinlari, 2010), 274; Digeser, "An Oracle of Apollo at Daphne," 61, 76.

75. Glenn Maffia, a reporter who lives in Turkey nearby and studies this temple as a hobby, writes that he has identified thirty-two eight-spoked wheels and that he suspects there are probably even more. He questions the identification of these circles as Christian symbols, arguing that if they were Christian symbols, they would have been placed on the walls where people could more clearly see them and not on the floor. This argumentation, however, is questionable. These early Christians are probably placing these ICHTHUS wheels and crosses on the floor to drive out the demons by the power of the cross and the name of Jesus Christ. They would not have been concerned with whether the wheels were visible at eye level. More importantly, as discussed in chapter 2, the walls of Greco-Roman temples like this one would have been plastered with stucco and then painted. Very little if any of this stucco or paint remains today; it has all weathered away over the centuries. So we do not know if these Christians painted or inscribed anything on the walls. Maffia, *Temple of Apollo at Didyma*, 15–16.

Fig. 5-16 Didyma, The Temple of Apollo:
ICHTHUS Christogram and Cross

Fig. 5-17 Didyma, The Temple of Apollo:
ICHTHUS Christogram and Cross

these ICHTHUS wheels (see fig. 5-17), as well as the placement of crosses right in the pie-shaped areas in one of the wheels (see fig. 5-18), argue rather convincingly that these are Christian symbols. The wheel with the crosses in each segment is the most prominently placed Christogram, located in the center of the temple pronaos area.[76]

In all likelihood, at some point after Constantine came to power, probably in the mid-fourth century, the Temple of Apollo at Didyma lost its privileged status and its protection. Perhaps this happened as late as 385, after Emperor Theodosius officially shut down this temple. [77] Christians then probably came into this temple—especially because the oracle here told Diocletian to persecute the Christians—after it had been abandoned or after the guards had been dismissed, and they etched these ICHTHUS proclamations of "Jesus Christ God's Son Savior" all across the front of the temple, both proclaiming victory over this famous pagan site and seeking to cleanse it from the demons associated with it. The Great Persecution had a far-reaching and terrible impact on the Christians. The memory of that persecution would have lived on in the Christian culture for several generations, so while we don't know exactly when the Christians claimed this temple and covered it with crosses and ICHTHUS wheels, there were a number of likely opportunities throughout the fourth century to do this as they continued to rectify their suffering.

---

76. Also appearing among the crosses and ICHTHUS Christograms are a number of small four-box squares, possibly reflecting a cross inside of a square. There are also several rectangular game boards.
77. Matthews, *Greco-Roman Cities*, 321.

There is quite a bit of variety in these ICHTHUS wheels, as well as in the other Christian symbols. That is, there is size variation as well as a contrast in precision. Some of the circles have been drawn and etched as perfect circles and with perfectly straight lines, while some of the circles and lines seem to have been drawn and etched freely or spontaneously without patterns or guidelines to follow. This implies that they were inscribed by different people. The Christians didn't hire one stone inscriber to make all twenty-eight ICHTHUS wheels, but different Christians were probably involved in the inscribing process. Some of these Christians took their time, likely using chalk patterns, and they etched precise eight-spoked wheels (and other Christian symbols). Others just started chiseling and shaped as they went, without a well-drawn chalk pattern. These wheels are lopsided, and the lines are often crooked.

Fig. 5-18 Didyma, The Temple of Apollo: ICHTHUS Christogram, with Cross in Each of Eight Segments

It is possible that these Christograms and other Christian symbols were made by a crowd, as described in some literary accounts of temple cleansing from other cities, such as Gaza and Alexandria. Perhaps the etching of these Christian symbols in this temple by individuals (or small groups of people working together on one wheel) was a form of public testimony, a proclamation of Jesus Christ as the Son of God and the Savior—made by new believers or by older believers who had suffered in the Great Persecution.

The Sacred Way, connecting Didyma to Miletus and the route that the prestigious annual religious festival parade followed, displayed statues of former priests and priestesses along it. Many of the earliest statues were from a priestly family known as the Branchidae. When excavating the Sacred Way, archaeologists discovered two statues of Branchidae priests with crosses etched on them. Perhaps this action of etching crosses on the statues of priests associated with the Temple of Apollo occurred at the same time or under the same circumstances as the etching of the ICHTHUS Christograms and crosses in the temple.[78]

---

78. Kristensen, "Miraculous Bodies"; cited by Jacobs, "Cross Graffiti," 209.

Later, toward the end of the fourth century, a church was built within the temple. As at other sites, this church had professionally crafted architectural elements, including crosses.

A comparison can be made with what happened at the other famous Temple of Apollo, the one with the Pythia oracle at Delphi (see chapter 6). The altar of that temple was covered with crosses and eight-spoked Christograms. Christians etched crosses and ICHTHUS wheels on both of the famous temples of Apollo that housed the oracles of the pagan world—probably sometime in the fourth century.

EPHESUS

The City of Ephesus

The ancient city of Ephesus is one of the most developed archaeological sites in Turkey and draws over 3.5 million visitors per year. The city was located in southwest Anatolia on a harbor for the Aegean Sea formed by the Cayster River. Over the years, both the harbor and much of the river valley has silted up, so the ancient port city of Ephesus is now three miles (five km) inland.[79]

The origins of the city, while wrapped in mythology, are quite ancient, going back perhaps as far as 1000 BC. Hills and valleys make up the general area, and the city proper moved to locations in and around these hills several times, attempting to navigate silting and flooding problems. Alexander the Great overran this area in 334 BC. His successor in Asia Minor, Lysimachus, moved the city of Ephesus to the location of the archaeological site we see today. As the terminus of the major east-west road across Anatolia (connecting the Aegean Sea to Syria and Persia), and as a major port on the Aegean Sea, the city of Ephesus grew and prospered in this location throughout the Hellenistic, Roman, and early Byzantine (late antiquity) periods (294 BC–AD 650), after which the population moved a few miles away.[80]

In the New Testament era and throughout the Roman imperial period for the next two hundred years, Ephesus was the leading commercial and financial center for Asia Minor. It was probably the fourth largest urban area in the Roman Empire (after Rome, Alexandria, and Antioch on the Orontes), with a population estimated as high as 250,000 (some estimate as high as 300,000–400,000). Already an impressive city when Paul arrived around AD 52, significant monumental construction and expansion continued throughout the second and third centuries (AD 100–300), although, as all across the empire, building activity slowed down toward the end of the third century.[81]

---

79.   Wilson, *Biblical Turkey*, 199, 203.
80.   Wilson, *Biblical Turkey*, 199–200.
81.   Mark R. Fairchild, *Christian Origins in Ephesus and Asia Minor*, 2nd ed. (Peabody, MA: Hendrickson, 2017), 7–9; Wilson, *Biblical Turkey*, 200–201.

Ephesus was famous throughout the ancient world for the spectacular temple of the goddess Artemis. Thousands of people came to Ephesus each year to attend the annual festival of Artemis. Yet the Ephesians venerated many other gods as well, and there is evidence of that as early as the first century. Ephesus had temples dedicated to at least fourteen other pagan gods.[82] In addition, statues of pagan gods stood throughout Ephesus, particularly in niches at gates, on pedestals along streets (especially intersections), and at monumental public fountains. Based on the extensive inscription evidence from Ephesus, James Harrison concludes, "In sum, the world of the Ephesian elite was full of gods, both in the heavens and on the earth . . . and the Ephesians were scrupulous in showing their allegiance to them."[83]

As one of the major cities in the Roman Empire, Ephesus was committed to the imperial cult—the worship and veneration of deified Roman emperors.[84] There were at least two visible and prominent imperial cult temples in Ephesus. The Temple of Domitian (also called the Temple of the Sebastoi, "the revered ones"), built in 89–90, dominated the upper southeast portion (the State Agora area) of the city. The other imperial cult temple was dedicated to Hadrian, who renamed himself as Hadrian Zeus Olympios. This gigantic temple, second in size only to the temple of Artemis, was completed around 130 and dominated the other side of the city (the lower, northwest portion). In addition, there might have been a temple dedicated to Divine Caesar and Dea Roma (the goddess Rome) on the eastern end of the State Agora, dating back to the time of Augustus (27 BC–AD 14). Nothing remains of it today except several statues that were perhaps originally placed there (see the section on Augustus and his wife, Livia, below). There was also another, smaller temple of Hadrian located on Curetes Street and dedicated to Hadrian, Artemis, and the people of Ephesus. There are gates and fountains likewise dedicated to the Roman emperors.[85]

There is substantial inscription evidence that as early as 40 BC there may have been a Sebasteion (imperial-cult-worship location) in the innermost portion (the temenos) of the Temple of Artemis, where the goddess Roma and Divus Julius (the divine Julius Caesar) were worshiped, at least until the end of the second century AD.[86]

---

82. Wilson, *Biblical Turkey*, 201.

83. James R. Harrison, "An Epigraphic Portrait of Ephesus and Its Villages," in *The First Urban Churches 3: Ephesus*, ed. James R. Harrison and L. L. Welborn, Writings from the Greco-Roman World Supplement Series 9 (Atlanta: SBL Press, 2018), 1.

84. François Kirbihler, "Ruler Cults and Imperial Cults at Ephesos: First Century BCE to Third Century CE," in *Religion in Ephesos Reconsidered: Archaeology of Spaces, Structures, and Objects*, ed. Daniel Schowalter, Sabine Ladstätter, Steven J. Friesen, and Christine Thomas, NovTSup 177 (Leiden: Brill, 2020), 195–210.

85. Wilson, *Biblical Turkey*, 221–48; Dies van der Linde, "Artemis Ephesia, the Emperor and the City: Impact of the Imperial Cult and the Civic Identity on Roman Ephesos," *Ancient Society* 46 (2016): 165–201.

86. Van der Linde, "Artemis Ephesia," 174–75.

Acquiring the rights from the Roman emperor to build an imperial cult temple was highly coveted, and the cities of Asia Minor competed vigorously to win the right to build one (like cities today competing for the right to host the Olympics). Ephesus apparently won this competition twice (and maybe three times). As the second century progressed (AD 100–200), Ephesian civic identity and pride, once reserved for Artemis primarily, now became intertwined with the deified emperors of the imperial cult. Van der Linde writes, "The communal identity of Ephesos was redefined: it was no longer simply the city of Artemis Ephesia, but had gradually turned into the city of *both* Artemis Ephesia *and* the Emperor."[87] Harrison, in studying the inscriptions of Ephesus, comes to the same conclusion.[88]

Ephesus was also famous throughout the world for magical practices, which were most often connected to dealing with demons and how to protect oneself from them.[89] A reference to a magical incantation called "the Ephesian letters" (*ephesia grammata*) appears several times in ancient literature. For example, using this rite as an analogy, the pagan writer Plutarch (AD 46–119) writes, "For just as sorcerers advise those possessed by demons to recite and name over to themselves the Ephesian letters, so we . . ." (*Moralia* 706E). The Christian writer Clement of Alexandria (AD 150–211) actually gives the six-word content of the *ephesia grammata* (*Stromateis* 5.242). These letters (probably divine names) were apparently used in warding off harmful demons.[90]

Although Artemis was not viewed primarily as a goddess of magic, she was closely associated with demons and the underworld. She was believed to possess authority and control over the demons, similar to the goddess Hecate. In magical papyri texts, she is "virtually identified with Hecate, Selene, and the Babylonian goddess Ereschigal, who are even more widely renowned as goddesses of the underworld."[91] According to Pliny (AD 24–79), there was even an image of Hecate in the temple grounds of Artemis (*Natural History* 36.4.32). Indeed, in the magical papyri, Artemis and Hecate are connected as well as with the *ephesia grammata* (Ephesian letters).[92]

The cultural-religious context of Ephesus regarding demons was probably similar in the first century to what it was later in the fourth century and is reflected in the New Testament. In Acts 19:13–19, a group of Jewish exorcists

---

87. Van der Linde, "Artemis Ephesia," 195.
88. Harrison, "An Epigraphic Portrait of Ephesus," 3–7, 12–17.
89. Wilson, *Biblical Turkey*, 202. See also Craig S. Keener, *Acts: An Exegetical Commentary, 15:1–23:35*, vol. 3 (Grand Rapids: Baker, 2014), 2856–57.
90. Murphy-O'Connor, *St. Paul's Ephesus*, 51; Clinton E. Arnold, *Ephesians: Power and Magic: The Concept of Power in Ephesians in Light of Its Historical Setting*, SNTSMS 63 (Cambridge: Cambridge University Press, 1989), 14–16.
91. Arnold, *Ephesians: Power and Magic*, 23.
92. Arnold, *Ephesians: Power and Magic*, 22–243. Underscoring the close association of the goddess Artemis with magic and evil demons is Sandra L. Glahn, *Nobody's Mother: Artemis of the Ephesians in Antiquity and the New Testament* (Downers Grove, IL: IVP Academic, 2023), 88–89, 124–26.

in Ephesus try to use the name of "the Jesus whom Paul preaches" to drive out a demon. The demon answers, "Jesus I know, and Paul I know about, but who are you?" The man with the demon then jumped on these exorcists and gave them a beating. The people in Ephesus were all "seized with fear" and "the name of the Lord Jesus was held in high honor." Afterward, "a number who had practiced sorcery [i.e., dealt with demons] brought their scrolls together and burned them publicly. When they calculated the value of the scrolls, the total came to fifty thousand drachmas." A drachma (silver coin) was worth approximately one day's wages; thus, the value of these books and the monetary sacrifice of these new believers was immense. The encounter with a demon and exorcists, combined with the account of people turning from their magic practices and burning such a huge collection of magic books, all underscore how entrenched in magic and demonology the city of Ephesus was in the mid-first century.

Clinton Arnold argues that the repeated references to "power" and "powers" throughout the book of Ephesians is best understood against this backdrop. While clearly also a problem at Rome and at Corinth, no other Pauline epistle contains as much direct admonition in the area of Christ's power over the demons' powers as does Ephesians. The new Christians in Ephesus were still living in a world where dangerous demons were everywhere. Paul acknowledges this clearly in 6:12: "For our struggle is not against flesh and blood, but against the rulers, against the authorities, against the powers of this dark world and against the spiritual forces of evil in the heavenly realms." Paul then instructs them to take up the armor of God and engage in spiritual warfare (6:13–17). Back in Ephesians 1, Paul pointed out that the power of Christ is "far above all rule and authority, power and dominion, and every name that is invoked, not only in the present age but also in the one to come" (1:21).[93] Similarly, the warnings from Paul to Timothy—who was ministering in Ephesus at the time— against deceiving spirits and demonic teaching (1 Tim. 4:1) are probably polemical references to the cult of Artemis in Ephesus.[94]

As one of the largest and most prosperous cities of the Greco-Roman world, by the year 200, Ephesus boasted many impressive architectural structures, and the remains of these can be seen at the site today (see fig. 5-19). The huge theater, seating 21,500 people, still dominates the lower part of the city. As noted above, not only did Ephesus have the world-famous Temple to Artemis but also two imposing and awe-inspiring imperial cult temples. Squeezed along the valley between two hills and along the harbor coast, Ephesus had city walls and several monumental gates, pagan temples, monumental fountains, gymnasiums and bathhouses, public latrines, a stadium, paved colonnaded streets, two agora areas, commercial shops, an Odeon, and rows of wealthy homes.

---

93. Arnold, *Ephesians: Power and Magic*, see esp. 51–69, 103–29, 165–72.
94. Glahn, *Nobody's Mother*, 126.

Fig. 5-19 Ephesus, The Façade of the Library of Celsus

Acts 18–19 describes the dramatic arrival of Christianity in Ephesus. In Acts 18:19–21, Paul stopped briefly in Ephesus on his way back to Antioch at the end of his second journey. His colleagues, Priscilla and Aquila, remained in Ephesus to continue the work there while Paul returned to Antioch. During this time, Apollos also briefly ministered in Ephesus, where he was corrected doctrinally by Priscilla and Aquila before he moved on to proclaim Christ in Corinth (Acts 18:24–26). In Acts 19:1, Paul returned to Ephesus, where he stayed for two years (AD 53–55), during which time he and his colleagues effectively planted churches throughout this region. Luke summarizes, "All the Jews and Greeks who lived in the province of Asia heard the word of the Lord" (Acts 19:10). The hostile opponents of Paul, in their complaints, verify the effectiveness of Paul's ministry, declaring, "Paul has convinced and led astray large numbers of people here in Ephesus and in practically the whole province of Asia" (Acts 19:26).

There is every indication that Ephesus quickly became a center of the rapidly expanding Christian faith. Paul writes his famous letter to the Ephesians from his Roman jail around 60–62. A few years later (AD 64) he writes to his protégé, Timothy, who was leading the church in Ephesus (1–2 Timothy). There is strong evidence that the apostle John served the church in Ephesus around 85–90, and Ephesus is one of the seven churches of Asia that John writes to in Revelation (AD 90–95).[95] Ignatius, a prominent church leader in Antioch, also writes a letter to the Ephesians, probably sometime in the early second century.[96]

There are a number of later church traditions ("legends") that describe the early second century in Ephesus as a time of hostile confrontation between the Christians and the pagans, especially those associated with the Temple of Artemis. In the apocryphal Acts of Timothy, Paul's companion Timothy,

---

95. For a good discussion on the arrival of Christianity and Paul's ministry in Ephesus, see Fairchild, *Christian Origins in Ephesus*, 27–116. For John's ministry in Ephesus and the surrounding region, see pp. 121–33.

96. For a translation of the letter and discussion of its contents, see Murphy-O'Connor, *St. Paul's Ephesus*, 74–77.

now quite elderly and serving as the bishop of Ephesus, tried to stop the huge annual festival procession of Artemis and was killed.

In the Acts of John, the apostle John fared much better. At the height of the festival of Artemis, probably after the procession with the carried idols had returned to the Temple of Artemis, John went to the temple (wearing black instead of white like everyone else). Those in the temple seized him and attempted to kill him but were unable to. He climbed up on a high platform and prayed, "O God, who art God above all that are called gods . . . at whose name every idol takes flight, and every demon, power and every unclean nature; now let the demon that is here take flight at the name, the deceiver of this great multitude; and show thy mercy in this place, for they have been led astray." Then the huge altar split, and half of the temple fell down. As the people of Ephesus turned to the God of John as a result, he continued, "Where is the power of the demon? Where are her sacrifices? . . . Where is all that sorcery and the witchcraft that is sister to it?" (Acts of John 37–43).[97]

These legends date to a later period (the Acts of John dates to the third or fourth century perhaps),[98] and while their historical accuracy is questioned (scholars are fairly certain the Temple of Artemis was destroyed by the Goths in 262 and not by John), they are, nonetheless, reflective of the attitudes and beliefs of the time period in which they were written. That is, in the fourth century—critical to our study—this confrontation between John and the demons in the Temple of Artemis may well reflect how the Christians imagined things.

Firmly established in the latter half of the first century, the church at Ephesus continued to be active and visible throughout the second and third centuries, even if the emperors at the time occasionally imposed regional persecutions. A letter from Polycrates, the bishop of Ephesus at the end of the second century, addressed to the bishop at Rome, argued for a certain way to determine when Easter should be celebrated. This implies that there was a strong, influential church at Ephesus. By the early fourth century, a number of martyrs in Ephesus are known, especially from the Great Persecution.[99]

In the fourth century, after Constantine and his Christian successors came to power, huge changes took place throughout the urban centers of the Roman Empire as Christians began to Christianize the pagan cities. Ephesus, one of the stronger Christian communities and one of the most populous cities, no doubt was at the forefront of this transition. Foss writes, "During the period, crosses were carved on the city gates, and crosses and pious inscriptions were set up, as pagan monuments were defaced or destroyed."[100]

97. Knut Schäferdiek, "The Acts of John," in *New Testament Apocrypha*, ed. Wilhelm Schneemelcher, 2 vols. (Louisville: Westminster John Knox, 1992), 2:187–88.
98. Schäferdiek, "The Acts of John," 152–54. Murphy-O'Connor, *St. Paul's Ephesus*, 154, states that it was probably written in Egypt not long after the middle of the second century.
99. Izabela Miszczak, *The Secrets of Ephesus*, Tan Travel Guide (Fairfield, CT: Aslan, 2020), 45–47.
100. Foss, *Ephesus after Antiquity*, 37.

During the second half of the fourth century (AD 350–399) and the first half of the fifth century (AD 400–450), most of the impressive pagan temples in Ephesus were not only abandoned but dismantled, and their stone blocks and columns were reused in other projects. Jacobs writes:

> Building elements from the famous Artemision were recycled for the renovation of the Harbour Baths in the second quarter of the 4th century, and blocks of its *temenos* wall were abundantly used in the construction of the Church of St. Mary and its associated 'bishop's palace' in the later 420's or early 430's [*sic*, as noted below, these dates are probably too early]. The altar of the Artemision and the surrounding temenos colonnade, together with its pediment, were further reused in the area of the Basilica of St. John. Likewise, the dismantling of the large Temple of the Sebastoi [the Temple of Domitian] began before the end of the 4th century at the latest, as did that of the Olympieion.[101]

Throughout the fourth and fifth centuries, as Christianity grew in visibility, popularity, and power, it is no surprise that Ephesus stepped into a role as one of the leading Christian cities with one of the more powerful resident bishops. In 431, the third ecumenical council was held in Ephesus, attended by more than 250 delegates from across the empire. During the reign of Emperor Justinian (AD 527–565), a spectacular church (the Church of St. John) was built on Ayasuluk Hill above the tomb of St. John, overlooking the dilapidated remains of the once-glorious Temple of Artemis below.

As noted in chapter 4, the term σωτήρ (*sōtēr*, "savior") was closely associated with the imperial cult, and the deified emperors were referred to frequently as "savior of the world" or "savior of the city." Long notes that "in Ephesus and Asia Minor, Caesar was 'Savior.'"[102] Glahn points out that the goddess Artemis of Ephesus was also regularly called "savior," as evidenced by a great deal of inscriptions in the city.[103] With the heavy involvement and commitment to the veneration of both Artemis and the imperial cult in Ephesus, the statement of the ICHTHUS Christogram that Jesus Christ was God's Son, the Savior, was a loud, public counterstatement against the two central religious cults in which the pagan population of Ephesus trusted.

The Graffiti of Ephesus

From the ancient city of Ephesus, archaeologists and Greek inscription scholars have discovered and published around 3,750 Greek inscriptions (mostly literary texts, but a few have sketches and symbols—the published collection of sketches and symbols reflects only a small portion of what is readily visible

---

101. Jacobs, "Creation of the Late Antique City," 126.
102. Long, "Ἐκκλησία in Ephesians," 223.
103. Glahn, *Nobody's Mother*, 86, 118–22.

on the streets and buildings of Ephesus today). This is more than any other city except Rome and Athens.[104] Most of these are formal, and professionally made inscriptions—edicts, honorific texts for famous individuals as well as for gods, building dedications, donor lists, and such.

There are also informal (non-professional) graffiti texts scattered throughout the city. These texts have not been collected, organized, and studied as thoroughly as the professional inscriptions, and these graffiti texts have just recently started to draw attention from scholars.[105] Similarly, Christian graffiti in Ephesus remains understudied. Banes, in an attempt to catalog all of the graffiti in the eastern Mediterranean during late antiquity, has identified 148 of these published texts and sketches as graffiti (still inscribed in stone but non-professionally and more informally).[106] Yet the vast majority of the graffiti cataloged by Banes are literary texts, and literary texts are only a small part of the graffiti record. She does note twelve rectangular or square game boards, but only a few circles of any type, and none of the many crosses that occur throughout Ephesus.

In contrast, during my brief visit to Ephesus in 2023, I located or identified a total of *twenty-four* eight-spoked wheels—many of them quite visible at eighteen to twenty inches in diameter—in addition to scores of crosses and other Christian symbols, and my search was far from thorough because significant tracts of the ancient city are inaccessible to the public. This is a reminder that much of the Christian graffiti at these ancient cities has not yet been thoroughly documented and published. While Ephesus does not have the same quantity of graffiti as Aphrodisias has, it does have a significant number of texts and symbols.

In addition to the ICHTHUS Christograms and crosses that are discussed below, Ephesus has fifty-one informally inscribed "Lord, help" texts.[107] This category of Christian graffiti texts (also common in Aphrodisias[108] and elsewhere)[109] usually includes invoking the Lord (κύριος, *kyrios*), followed by the imperative of the verb "to help" (βοηθέω, *boētheō*), followed by the name of the person seeking the help. Interestingly, although this phrase "Lord, help so-and-so" appears frequently in the Christian graffiti of Greco-Roman cities

---

104. Harrison, "An Epigraphic Portrait of Ephesus," 1; Horsley, "The Inscriptions of Ephesos," 121. Glahn, *Nobody's Mother*, 81, notes that the figure of 3,750 for the number of inscriptions in Ephesus is outdated and that the current count (as of 2023) is closer to 6,000.

105. See the discussion of graffiti in Ephesus by Harrison, "An Epigraphic Portrait of Ephesus," 49–56.

106. Banes, "A Comparative Approach to Graffiti," 430–55.

107. Banes, "A Comparative Approach to Graffiti," 432–44.

108. For numerous examples from Aphrodisias, see Roueché, *Aphrodisias in Late Antiquity*, 172, 176–77, 179–84, 186–87, 189.

109. Sitz, "Inscribing Caria," 215, notes that these "Lord, help" inscriptions, along with crosses, appear at the temple of Hecate (the goddess of magic, sorcery, and demons) at Lagina (near the city of Stratonikeia), located in southwest Anatolia (modern Turkey).

in late antiquity, there is also one (in Syria) which reads: IXΘΥC ὁ βοηθ(ῶν) ("ICHTHUS is the one who helps").[110]

The ICHTHUS Christogram at Ephesus

In the city proper of ancient Ephesus, I have been able to locate eighteen eight-spoked ICHTHUS Christograms etched informally as graffiti into the pavement of the streets and courtyards. Another ICHTHUS wheel has been identified (and pictured) in a book by Mehlika Seval. This Christogram has a fish inscribed right next to it, but I have not personally been able to verify this Christogram.[111] I did, however, locate another inscribed ICHTHUS Christogram on a wall at the nearby Church of St. John. Counting all of these yields twenty ICHTHUS Christograms in graffiti. I also found four more eight-spoked wheels with variations (i.e., arcs added on the inside perimeter, see fig. 5-20), resulting in a total of twenty-four ICHTHUS Christograms in the graffiti at ancient Ephesus and in the vicinity. Additionally, I found six equilateral crosses inside circles, two Tau-Rho Staurograms, and a number of crosses. There are also ICHTHUS wheels professionally engraved into wall panels and column capitals at the two main early churches—St. Mary and St. John.

For our discussion of the location and significance of the many eight-spoked Christograms at Ephesus, we will start at the upper (southeastern) part of the city where the State Agora and Temple of Domitian are located. Then we will move in a northwesterly direction down Curetes Street, past the terrace houses on the left and the Scholastica Baths on the right. We'll take a slight right turn at the Library of Celsus onto Marble Street. We will pass the Commercial Agora on the left. As we approach the theater (on the right), we will take a left turn onto Arcadian Street (sometimes called Harbor Street). We will pass by the theater gymnasium area and then turn right. We will head north until we come to the Church of St. Mary. This is the route that most tourist groups and study groups follow. Then we leave the central ancient city ruins of Ephesus and drive the short distance into the adjacent city of Selçuk to the Church

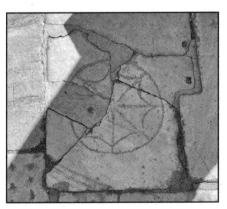

Fig. 5-20 Ephesus, Street Paving: A Variation of the Eight-Spoked ICHTHUS Christogram

---

110. *IGLSyr* 4 1422 (see the PHI Greek Inscriptions database).

111. A picture of this ICHTHUS wheel with a fish, and an equilateral cross inside of a circle inscribed right next to it, is presented by Mehlika Seval, *Ephesus: Step by Step* (Istanbul: Minyatür, 1988), 51. She locates it on the Narrow Street, apparently near the Alytarch's Stoa.

of St. John. We will briefly discuss the Temple of Artemis (located close by in Selçuk and not in the ancient city proper), but there is almost nothing left at the actual temple site to see.

The State Agora/Temple of Domitian

Those who traveled to Ephesus by land from the southeast would have entered through the monumental Magnesian Gate. In general, gates in the ancient world carried religious connotations as a liminal space, or threshold, between two areas (what is in the city and what is outside of the city). In this case, it was "a transient zone between the influential area of the Artemision and the city of Ephesos."[112] This particular gate also played a specific role in the religious procession of Artemis, for here a ritual took place in which the priests who carried idol statues transferred them to the "young men of the city" to carry down to the theater.[113] Etched informally into the major doorjamb of this gate are three crosses.[114]

Heading due west from this gate leads you to the upper part of the city of Ephesus. This is the area you first encounter today when arriving through the north entrance, and our tour begins here. It is dominated by the State Agora, which functioned as the city's administrative center. This agora measured 525 feet (160 m) by 190 feet (58 m) and consisted of a huge open area with impressive colonnaded stoas (roofed walkways, lined on both sides with columns) on three sides. Included in this area were several pagan temples, fountains, an Odeon (often called a bouleuterion, a small theater-like seating facility for city council meetings), and a bathhouse. Adjacent to the west side of the State Agora was the important Temple of Domitian and its associated fountains. Domitian was a Roman emperor who reigned 81–96 and who perhaps instigated an early Christian persecution that might have formed the historical context for the book of Revelation. Sometimes this temple is referred to as the Temple of the Sebastoi ("the revered ones"). It was an integral part of the imperial cult worship in Ephesus.[115] At the eastern entrance to the State Agora stood statues of the Roman emperor Augustus and his wife Livia.

On display at the eastern end of the State Agora a stone block has been discovered in that area that has an ICHTHUS Christogram graffito inscribed on it (see fig. 5-21). Often added in chalk (done recently by the Ephesus Park curators?) as an explanation of the meaning of this graffito is the Greek word ΙΧΘΥΣ and a simple two-stroke fish drawing (as is popular in modern Christian culture). While the inscribed ICHTHUS wheel itself is authentic,

112. Alexander Sokolicek, "The Magnesian Gate of Ephesos," in Schowalter et al., *Religion in Ephesos Reconsidered*, 113–17.

113. Sokolicek, "The Magnesian Gate of Ephesos," 113–17.

114. For a picture, see Andreas Pülz, "Selected Evidence of Christian Residents in Late Antique Ephesos," in Schowalter et al., *Religion in Ephesos Reconsidered*, 74.

115. Steven J. Friesen, *Twice Neokoros: Ephesus, Asia and the Cult of the Flavian Imperial Family*, Religions in the Graeco-Roman World 116 (Leiden: Brill, 1993), 56–75.

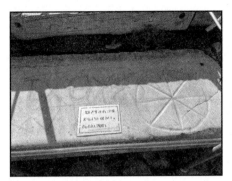

Fig. 5-21 Ephesus, State Agora: ICHTHUS Christogram

dating back to the early Christian era, the explanatory word ΙΧΘΥΣ and the fish drawing are not. Also, sometimes the eight-spoked wheel is enhanced with chalk coloring, which is also not original. Only the eight-spoked wheel dates back to the early Christian era.[116]

Passing by this stone, you turn left at the Odeon, and you enter the area that once was the Basilica Stoa, or the colonnaded porch that ran the length of the north side of the State Agora. In the Greco-Roman world, the term "basilica" originally referred to a large, impressive public building (often used for administrative functions), with a high vaulted ceiling. Later in history, when the Christians started building large, impressive churches, they would use the term "basilica" to refer to the church structure, and thus, in Christian history, "basilica" became synonymous with "church." "Stoa" typically denotes that the building has long colonnaded open sides or walkways.

As noted above, the huge statues of Augustus and his wife Livia stood here at the eastern end, not far from where the ICHTHUS wheel is displayed. At some point the Christians in Ephesus removed these statues, knocking off their noses and inscribing crosses on their foreheads. They are both on display at the Ephesus Museum.[117]

The Odeon, where the city councils met, resembles a small theater. Only the bottom few rows of seats remain from the original. Inscribed on one of the remaining seats is a simple cross. This cross could have been inscribed as a place marker, noting the identity of the one for whom the seat was reserved. On the other hand, this could have been part of the Christianizing or cleansing phase of early Christianity in the fourth century. Since most of the original seats did not survive, we can only guess at what was inscribed on them.

The "street" you walk on as you pass the Odeon (on the right) is really the floor paving of the Basilica Stoa of the State Agora. At the west end of the Agora lies an intersection called Domitian Square. Straight ahead and angling to the right is Curetes Street. To the left is a paved street (often called the Domitian Road) leading to the Temple of Domitian. At the center of this temple stood a sixteen-foot-high (five m) statue of the emperor Domitian (or perhaps his brother Titus, originally). Christians destroyed this pagan statue

---

116. I visited this site in 2021 and then again in 2023, and each time, while the eight-spoked wheel had not changed, the explanatory ΙΧΘΥΣ words in chalk were different, as was the fish drawing. Perhaps the explanatory words get washed off with the rain and then are replaced.
117. Jacobs, "Cross Graffiti," 195–96; Kristensen, "Miraculous Bodies," 44–50.

most likely in the mid-fourth century. Archaeologists recovered only the huge head and part of the right arm of this gigantic statue, which are on display in the Ephesus Museum. There may have been statues (smaller, no doubt) of other emperors in this temple as well. Either in the mid- to late fourth century or early fifth century, this temple was dismantled down to its foundations. Few architectural pieces of the original temple were uncovered during excavations, and two columns from the front facade have been patched and set up in the reconstruction effort.[118]

Back at the street intersection, on the right is the Fountain of Memmius (often called the Memmius Monument). As with most other public monumental fountains, this one contained a number of idol statues, especially of nymphs and satyrs. Several of these were recovered by archaeologists and are on display in the Ephesus Museum. Like most statues discovered from this era, these are all headless (see fig. 5-22).[119] As in other places, the Christians beheaded these statues and then either smashed the heads into unrecoverable pieces or buried them.

On the immediate left, across the street from the Fountain of Memmius, is a lower entrance structure for the Agora Stoa (called the chalcidicum; some suggest that it was associated with the Temple of Domitian, others that it served as an entrance to the Agora) and a fountain of Domitian.[120] There are several headless statues from this fountain on display in the Ephesus Museum. On the paving directly in front of the doorway to the chalcidicum is an ICHTHUS Christogram. It is difficult to determine whether the Christogram is located here in association with the street intersection, the adjacent fountain, or the entrance to the entire Domitian temple. Some of the archaeologists who excavated this area suggested that the two statues of Augustus and Livia with crosses on their foreheads originally stood here,[121] which puts the ICHTHUS wheel inscribed on the pavement right in front of these two statues. Remember that as the Christians sought to cleanse or de-paganize the city by driving out and keeping out the demons associated with the pagan gods, they placed crosses and ICHTHUS Christo-

Fig. 5-22 Ephesus Museum: Headless Statues

---

118. Sabine Ladstätter, "The So-Called Imperial Cult Temple for Domitian in Ephesos," in Schowalter et al., *Religion in Ephesos Reconsidered*, 11–40; Mathews, *Greco-Roman Cities*, 225–26.

119. See the discussion and picture in Seval, *Ephesus: Step by Step*, 40–41.

120. Miszczak, *The Secrets of Ephesus*, 162–70.

121. Kristensen, "Miraculous Bodies," 45.

Fig. 5-23a Ephesus, Curetes Street, Near Fountain of Trajan: ICHTHUS Christogram

Fig. 5-23b Ephesus, Curetes Street, Near Fountain of Trajan: Tau-Rho Staurogram

grams particularly in the entrance areas of temples, in front of fountains and the idols associated with them, and in intersections. The location for this particular ICHTHUS Christogram fits all these criteria.

Curetes Street (Embolos Street)

From the top of Curetes Street[122] at Domitian Square to the bottom of Curetes Street (near the terrace houses) are five regular ICHTHUS wheels inscribed on the pavement of the street. There is also a modified eight-spoked wheel with arcs at its perimeter.[123] There are also two circles with simple equilateral crosses and a Tau-Rho Staurogram. Several of these are clustered in front of the Fountain of Trajan (see figs. 5-23a and 5-23b). This fountain was one of the most lavish and impressive monuments in Ephesus, and it served as the central terminus for a twenty-five-mile-long (forty km) aqueduct that fed the city (one of four water conveyance systems). The water cascaded down from the two-story structure (about thirty-one feet high) into a huge pool adjacent to the street, a pool measuring sixty-six feet (twenty m) wide (parallel to the street) and thirty-three feet (ten m) deep (perpendicular to the street). A two-story facade wrapped around three sides of the pool (with the street on the fourth side). On the second floor were ten niches

---

122. See Andreas Pülz, "Von der Göttin zur Gottesmutter? Artemis und Maria," in *Die Archäologie der ephesischen Artemis: Gestalt und Ritual eines Heiligtums*, ed. Ulrike Muss (Vienna: Phoibos Verlag, 2008), 67.

123. In their typology, Bell and Roueché label this type of circle as C6 ("Graeco-Roman Pavement Signs and Game Boards," 107).

containing life-sized statues of gods. Several of these idols (e.g., Aphrodite, two of Dionysus) were uncovered and placed in the Ephesus Museum. They are all missing their heads and other body parts (of the two statues of Dionysus, one is only missing half of its head and some of its nose). On the bottom floor stood a towering statue of Trajan, twice life size. He stood at the center of the building in a heroic pose with a globe under his feet. The only part of this statue recovered by archaeologists was the globe and his feet.[124] As in other locations, the Christians here kept the fountain operational, but they beheaded, smashed, and removed the idols. To complete the cleansing operation and the removal of the associated demons, the Christians etched eight-spoked ICHTHUS Christograms and other Christian symbols on the pavement in front.

Slightly farther down Curetes Street on the right, across from the terrace houses, is a bathhouse complex. Originally constructed in the early second century by Quintilius Valens Varius (often called the Varius Bathhouse), after being damaged by a severe earthquake in 359, it was renovated at the end of the fourth century by a Christian woman named Scholastica.[125] There is a large (approx. thirty-six in. diameter) ICHTHUS Christogram on the pavement of the main entryway into this bathhouse. While we do not know for sure when this Christogram was etched, it was probably done at the same time that the idol statues of Ephesus were destroyed, prior to the earthquake of 359, and probably not associated with the later renovations and dedication of the bathhouse by Scholastica.

According to the book *Ephesus: Step by Step*, there is another eight-spoked Christogram in this area, just to the left of Curetes Street. Near the Alytarchs' Stoa and before the terrace houses, there is Narrow Street, which climbs the same hill on which the terrace houses are constructed. Up several steps on this Narrow Street, at an intersection, is an ICHTHUS wheel alongside an inscribed fish and an equilateral cross within a circle.[126] The inscribed fish next to this Christogram is not the simple two-stroke, cross-loop fish popular today but rather a sketch attempting a depiction of a real fish (with eyes and fins, etc.).

At the bottom of Curetes Street, after passing the terrace houses on the left and the Baths of Scholastica along with the public latrines on the right, you come to a public fountain known as the Heroon of Androclos. This heroon, or honorific monument, honored Androclos, the legendary founder of Ephesus. Directly in front of this fountain, inscribed in the street pavement, is an eight-spoked Christogram (see fig. 5-24). This Christogram was probably

124. See Miszczak, *The Secrets of Ephesus*, 154–56; Wilson, *Biblical Turkey*, 213; Clyde E. Fant and Mitchell G. Reddish, *A Guide to Biblical Sites in Greece and Turkey* (Oxford: Oxford University Press, 2003), 190–91; and Selahattin Erdemgil, *Ephesus Museum* (Istanbul: Do-Gü, n.d.), see the discussion and pictures of the idol statues in the museum on pp. 35–45.
125. Matthews, *Greco-Roman Cities*, 232; and Miszczak, *The Secrets of Ephesus*, 139–40.
126. Seval, *Ephesus: Step by Step*, 51–52. See the picture of the wheel with the fish and cross on p. 51.

Fig. 5-24 Ephesus, in Front of the Heroon of Androclos (fountain): ICHTHUS Christogram

Fig. 5-25 Ephesus, the Heroon of Androclos (fountain): Stone Panels with Crosses

inscribed in the early to mid-fourth century as the Christians attempted to rid the city of pagan gods and other pagan influences, especially demons. In addition to the statue honoring Androclos, this fountain likely displayed many pagan gods, as was typical for public monumental fountains. It is highly likely that the Christians removed, destroyed, or defaced the pagan statues at this fountain, and then they etched the ICHTHUS Christogram into the pavement in front, incorporating both the name of Jesus and the sign of the cross as a powerful sign to drive away and keep away the demons.

At some point during the early Christian era, this fountain's basin at street level was modified by the addition of several Latin crosses on the front of the stone panels adjacent to the street (see fig. 5-25). These panels can be seen today, and because of these crosses, this fountain is sometimes referred to as the Byzantine Fountains.[127] The addition of crosses and ICHTHUS wheels to public fountains and other water distribution facilities was a common phenomenon across the Greco-Roman world.

Just beyond the Heroon of Androclos (Byzantine Fountains) stood Hadrian's Gate and a three-way intersection called Triodos ("Three Roads"—Curetes Street, Marble Street to the right, and Ortygia Way to the left, going up above the Library of Celsus). The Heroon of Androclos stands on the edge of the plaza for this intersection. The eight-spoked Christogram placed in front of the Heroon of Androclos may be cleansing or counteracting evil forces associated with both the fountain and the intersection.

---

127. Miszczak, *The Secrets of Ephesus*, 143.

Until Christians came into power, a statue of Artemis stood in this Triodos intersection. An inscription on the marble base on which the statue likely stood reads, "Having destroyed a deceitful image of the demonic Artemis, Demeas set up this sign of truth, honouring both God the driver-away of idols, and the cross, that victorious, immortal symbol of Christ."[128] Apparently, a Christian named Demeas not only removed the statue of Artemis but wrote this inscription and set up a cross at the intersection.[129]

Another ongoing public event in Ephesus that probably contributed to the need for the Christians to de-demonize these particular portions of the streets can be seen in the inscription of C. Vibius Salutaris, dated to 104. This long inscription (568 lines have survived), which had been prominently displayed in the theater, spelled out that Salutaris had paid a considerable sum to finance the famous annual procession of Artemis statues through Ephesus. The inscription notes that the procession carried thirty-one statues, nine of which were statues of Artemis, while the rest were of notable people and other gods. While the huge procession, part of the famous festival, took place annually, this inscription states that there should also be a procession of these statues through the streets every two weeks. The route of these statues is specified. The statues were to reside at the Temple of Artemis. They would be lifted from their bases and carried along the Sacred Way from the temple to the Magnesian Gate (this is to the east of the upper State Agora, near the modern-day upper main entrance to the park where we started our discussion). At the Magnesian Gate, the priests carrying the statues would pass them to the young men of the city to carry them in. From there, the procession would go across the State Agora and then down Curetes Street to the theater. At the theater, the statues would be placed on bases for the festivities there. Afterward, they would be picked up again, and the procession would take Theater Street, past the stadium, out through the Coressian Gate, and back to the Temple of Artemis.[130] Therefore, in addition to the regular presence of pagan gods (and the demons behind them) throughout the city and especially at fountains and intersections, if this procession of pagan gods did occur every two weeks, one can imagine the concern of the Christians to cleanse this route.

This famous procession passed by several sites associated with Androclos, along with imperial cult locations like the Fountain of Trajan. The growing influence of the imperial cult and the overall Romanization of this eastern city of Asia Minor played a larger and larger role in driving home the connection between Artemis, Androclos, the imperial cult, and civic identity for the

---

128. *IEph.* 4.1351. Cited by Horsley, "The Inscriptions of Ephesos," 108.
129. Wilson, *Biblical Turkey*, 214.
130. Murphy-O'Connor, *St. Paul's Ephesus*, 95; Stefan Feuser, "A Stroll along the Sea: The Processional Way in Ephesus and the Littoral," *Center for Hellenic Studies Research Bulletin* 3.1 (2014): 2.1–2.6, https://research-bulletin.chs.harvard.edu.

Ephesians.[131] Frequently along this route, in places where the original paving stones remain, you can find crosses and ICHTHUS Christograms.

The Harbor Way/Arcadian Street

Leading from the huge Ephesian theater in the west to the harbor in the east was an elaborate colonnaded street, often called Harbor Street, the Harbor Way, or Arcadian Street (sometimes the Arcadiane). At the western end of the street was the harbor, and at the eastern end of the street is still the intersection with Theater Street and then the theater. To the north of this street lay two extensive gymnasium areas with bathhouses— the Theater Gymnasium and the Harbor Gymnasium—and an exercise field referred to as the Xyster or the Halls of Verulanus. This street was an early feature of Ephesus that boasted colonnaded walkways and shops on both sides, as well as pagan god statues on pedestals lining the way. On this short stretch of paved road, from the Harbor Gymnasium entrance up to the intersection with Theater Street, there are ten regular ICHTHUS Christograms, three modified ICHTHUS Christograms (with loops across the arches), and one equilateral cross within a circle (see figs. 5-26 and 5-27). The ICHTHUS Christograms along Harbor Street are grouped into two clusters: one near the intersection with Theater Street and the Theater Gymnasium; the other near the entrance to the Harbor Gymnasium. This paved road was also the main entryway into the city from the harbor.

The name "Arcadian Street" comes from the Christian Byzantine

Fig. 5-26 Ephesus, Arcadian Street (Harbor Street): ICHTHUS Christogram (Theater in the Background)

Fig. 5-27 Ephesus, Arcadian Street (Harbor Street): ICHTHUS Christogram

---

131. Harrison, "An Epigraphic Portrait of Ephesus," 3–7, 12–17.

Emperor Arcadius (ruled 395–408). He rebuilt this street (perhaps in response to lingering effects of the severe earthquake in 359) and apparently raised it in elevation slightly. There is little doubt that he reused most of the original paving stones, but we have no way of knowing if his project placed them back in the same location (which is unlikely). Thus, the original location of the many paving stones along this road that contain ICHTHUS wheels cannot be determined. Those paving stones could have been anywhere along this street when the ICHTHUS symbol was etched into them. Likewise, we cannot be certain that the ICHTHUS Christograms were inscribed prior to Arcadius's renovations. This emperor erected statues on this street honoring the four apostles instead of pagan gods, underscoring the dramatic transformation that took place during the Christianization of Ephesus. Perhaps the Christograms were inscribed after the renovations as part of the dedication of the street. While we do not know for certain, it seems plausible for the Christograms to have been inscribed before the street renovations by Arcadius, perhaps in the mid-fourth century when the Christians were removing pagan idols and inscribing crosses and Christograms to drive away the demons.

The Olympieion and the Church of St. Mary

About halfway down Harbor Street (Arcadian Street) a path to the right cuts across what had been the Harbor Baths. Walking a few hundred yards along this path, you arrive at the northwest corner of the walled city, where the huge Temple of Hadrian Zeus Olympios (Olympieion) stood. This temple was constructed around 130 for the imperial cult of Emperor Hadrian. Apart from the gigantic Temple of Artemis, this Temple of Hadrian was, by far, the largest temple in Ephesus. The temple itself measured 280 feet (85 m) by 188 feet (57 m) and stood 82 feet (25 m) high—the roof supported by seventy-four huge columns. An impressive stoa, or colonnaded porch, surrounded the temple on all four sides, enclosing a courtyard. In front of the southern section of the stoa, a basilica (a large building with a vaulted ceiling) was constructed, functioning as the entrance to the temple complex. This basilica measured 858 feet (260 m) in length and ran east-west, paralleling Harbor Street. Some scholars maintain that in 211 this stoa-basilica structure was renovated and adopted as a separate imperial cult temple venerating Caracalla and Geta. Other scholars disagree, arguing that this structure served as the banking center for the Olympieion, while others argue that it was "the Court of the Muses," an educational/cultural center.[132]

We do not know whether the Christians in the mid-fourth century stormed into this gigantic Olympieion temple to remove, deface, and behead the idol statues and to carve crosses and ICHTHUS wheels, because in the late fourth century, the Christians completely leveled this temple, right down to its foun-

---

132. Miszczak, *The Secrets of Ephesus*, 88–90; Matthews, *Greco-Roman Cities*, 246–48; and Wilson, *Biblical Turkey*, 220–23.

dations. They also carried away and reused all of the blocks and columns (or destroyed them). Today, practically nothing remains of this huge ancient temple. A significant portion of the lengthy basilica on the southern side of the temple, however, which had served as the entrance, was renovated and converted into a church dedicated to Saint Mary. This church also underwent several renovations and modifications, including the conversion and separation of the eastern portion to serve as the bishop's residence and palace.

In 431, a stormy church council held in Ephesus was said to meet in the Church of St. Mary. More than 250 delegates attended. This third ecumenical council determined the special theological relationship between Mary and Jesus—that she was the *Theotokos*, the "bearer of God," a relationship embraced both in Eastern Orthodoxy and Roman Catholicism. In 449, another, smaller council was held at Ephesus, also in the Church of St. Mary.[133]

Archaeologists working at this site, however, have concluded that most of the significant renovations at the Church of St. Mary site, especially that which conclusively changed the Roman basilica into a Christian church, did not occur until the end of the fifth century—after both of these Ephesus church councils. The purpose of this renovation may have been to construct a church that was truly worthy of the Virgin Mary after discussing her importance. Other renovations occurred even later, in the sixth century.[134] Much of what you see at the Church of St. Mary on a visit today was not there at the time of the 431 council, even though the council records refer to meeting in a Church of St. Mary. The size of the council (250 delegates) implies a fairly spacious structure. The un-renovated, yet remaining, Roman basilica on the south side of the ruined Olympieion was still there at that time. Some propose that the council actually met in this facility and that the decision to convert this basilica into a church dedicated to St. Mary was made shortly thereafter.[135]

Discovered in the ruins of the Church of St. Mary and visible today when one visits the site are several stone wall panels that had been at floor level in the front central nave of the church, each connected on both ends to columns. This portion of the church renovation dates to the end of the fifth century. These wall panels are inscribed professionally and were part of the church symbolic architecture.[136] One panel contains a typical Christian cross, and

---

133. Wilson, *Biblical Turkey*, 221–22. For the letters and documents relating to the 431 council at Ephesus, see "Chapter 23—Cyril, Nestorius and the Council of Ephesus, 431," in *Creeds, Councils and Controversies: Documents Illustrating the History of the Church, AD 337–461*, ed. J. Stevenson, rev. ed. by W. H. C. Frend (Grand Rapids: Baker, 2012), 330–70.

134. Angelica Degasperi, *Die Marienkirche in Ephesos: Die Bauskulptur aus frühchristlicher und byzantinischer Zeit*, Ergänzungshefte zu den Jahresheften des Österreichischen Archäologischen Instituts in Wien 14 (Wien: Österreichischen Archäologischen Instituts, 2013), 21–23, 61.

135. Matthews, *Greco-Roman Cities*, 247.

136. Degasperi, *Die Marienkirche in Ephesos*, 21–23, 61. Degasperi, 21–23, notes that other, smaller, wall panels with different geometric designs were also discovered, but they were part of later renovations and not part of the central nave.

the other panel contains an ICHTHUS Christogram (see fig. 1-2). These two symbols were used in parallel as important Christian symbols located in an important and centrally visible part of the church.

The Temple of Artemis

By far the most famous pagan temple in Ephesus was the Temple of Artemis (Artemis is sometimes referred to with the Latin name Diana). This temple was located to the west and slightly north of the city, connected to the city's North Gate (near the stadium) by the Sacred Way. The earliest phase of the construction of this temple dates to the eighth century BC. The main expansion of the temple and the version of the temple that became so famous worldwide was built in the sixth century BC, probably during the reign of King Croesus of Lydia (ruled 585–546 BC). Built entirely of marble, the temple itself was 380 feet long (115 m) and 151 feet wide (46 m). It contained 127 marble columns, each about 63 feet (19 m) high. It was included in the list by Herodotus in the fifth century BC of the seven wonders of the ancient world, and it was the biggest building in Italy, Greece, or Asia at this time, earning fame throughout the Mediterranean world.[137] It was badly damaged by a fire in 356 BC on the same night that Alexander the Great was born. The legend developed, recorded by Plutarch, that Artemis was too occupied overseeing the successful birth of Alexander to defend her temple from the fire. Reconstruction of the damaged temple started in 323 BC, the year of Alexander's death, and stretched over a number of years.[138] It was probably this rendition of the temple, still quite spectacular, that stood as the pride of Ephesus when the apostle Paul and his colleagues arrived with the gospel of Christ to challenge its supremacy in the first century AD.

In AD 262 Ephesus was devastated by a severe earthquake. Six years later, invading Goths captured Ephesus and looted the temple. The extent of the damage is not known for certain, but one literary source mentions that the Goths set fire to the famous Temple of Diana (Artemis) at Ephesus.[139] This means that in the mid-fourth century, as Christians were removing, destroying, or defacing the pagan idols of Ephesus and cleansing the temples and other areas of the city from demons associated with the pagan gods, the status and standing of the Temple of Artemis is not known. Even if the temple was not completely restored, it was probably functioning, especially since it was so tightly connected to the annual festival celebration of the city. It most likely still contained an altar and idols, especially the central idol of Artemis. Yet recall that back in the center of the city near the Library of Celsus at the Triodos intersection once stood a statue of Artemis that had been removed by a Christian named Demeas, who added his own inscription to the base on which Artemis

---

137. For a discussion and references to this temple in ancient literature, see Murphy-O'Connor, *St. Paul's Ephesus*, 20–24.
138. Miszczak, *The Secrets of Ephesus*, 185–220.
139. Miszczak, *The Secrets of Ephesus*, 222.

had stood, indicating that this "demonic Artemis" had been driven away by God and the cross.[140] It is unlikely that such statues of Artemis stood at city intersections if the temple itself did not also hold a statue of Artemis. So, it is probable that as Christians like Demeas destroyed the pagan statues of Artemis in the center of the city, others would have destroyed the idols at the Temple of Artemis itself and probably also tried to cleanse this famous pagan sacred space of associated demons through the name of Jesus Christ and the cross. This likely included the etching of crosses and ICHTHUS Christograms on the stones of the temple (and perhaps painting crosses and Christian symbols as well), similar to what we see in the Temple of Apollo at nearby Didyma.

As discussed in more detail below, on one of the stone blocks used to construct the nearby Basilica of St. John is an ICHTHUS Christogram. Since much of this church was built using stone blocks from the abandoned Temple of Artemis, it is likely that this Christogram was chiseled into this stone while it served as part of the paving for the Temple of Artemis, and it could have been part of the Christian effort to cleanse the Artemis temple of its evil spirits.

The Basilica (Church) of St. John

Not far outside of Ephesus stands a small hill overlooking the site where the Temple of Artemis once stood. According to early church tradition, the apostle John was buried on this hill. Early in the fourth century, after Constantine legalized Christianity, a small, four-posted, domed wooden structure was built over his gravesite, perhaps funded by Constantine's mother Helena.[141] Later, during the reign of Theodosius II (ruled AD 408–450), the son of Arcadius (who rebuilt Arcadia Street in the center of Ephesus), a larger, more significant basilica was built over the site. This structure was later damaged by earthquakes. During the reign of Emperor Justinian (AD 527–565), a huge cross-shaped basilica was built to replace the earlier structure. This basilica had six domes, four of them covering the long portion of the cross shape and two of them covering the portions that formed the arms of the cross. Measuring 132 feet wide (40 m) and 430 feet long (130 m), in the sixth century the Basilica of St. John was one of the largest and most important churches outside of the capital, Constantinople.[142]

One of the economic problems facing Ephesus when the Temple of Artemis was closed was the loss of revenue that came in from all of the people who visited Ephesus during the annual festival of Artemis. Indeed, this problem was multiplied across the Greco-Roman world in cities that had huge annual festivals centering on one of their gods. One of the things that replaced these

---

140. *IEph* 4.1351. Cited by Horsley, "The Inscriptions of Ephesos," 108; Wilson, *Biblical Turkey*, 214.

141. Wilson, *Biblical Turkey*, 224.

142. Miszczak, *The Secrets of Ephesus*, 251–61; Joseph D. Alchermes, "Art and Architecture in the Age of Justinian," in Maas, *The Cambridge Companion to the Age of Justinian*, 357–60; Wilson, *Biblical Turkey*, 223–25; Matthews, *Greco-Roman Cities*, 252–53.

annual festivals during the early Christian era, at least in regard to bringing in revenue from visiting people, was Christian pilgrimage. After the legalization of Christianity by Constantine in 312, both he and his mother, Helena, provided a huge impetus to pilgrimages by identifying sites and erecting shrines at sites associated with the life of Jesus. Soon sites associated with the apostles and other holy saints also became popular pilgrimage destinations, and an entire network of hostels and monasteries sprang up to serve the needs of the pilgrims.[143] Pilgrimage visits to the Basilica of St. John in Ephesus (i.e., the grave of the apostle John) became popular as early as the mid-fourth century. This popularity as a pilgrimage site probably played a role in the two major expansions and renovations of this church.[144]

Archaeologists working at the Basilica of St. John have uncovered and reconstructed a significant and impressive portion of the walls and columns of the church, including the baptistry and the location of the tomb of St. John. While none of the six domed roofs remain, portions of the support walls, along with columns and entryways, do remain and have been restored. On a stone block located about fifteen feet above ground level in one of the massive wall supports for one of the domes is an ICHTHUS wheel, similar to those occurring on the stone pavement all across nearby Ephesus (see fig. 5-28). It is highly improbable that someone etched this Christogram fifteen feet high after the support wall was built. These walls were also probably covered with plaster and then painted, and neither the paint nor the plaster has survived the years of weathering. Yet it is important to note that most of the stone blocks used in the two major construction phases of the Basilica of St. John were secondary-use blocks. That is, most of the material used to construct this church came from the Temple of Artemis (and also, perhaps, from the stadium).[145] It is probable

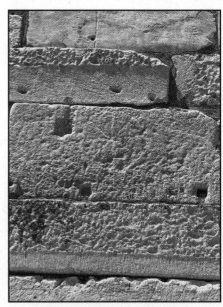

Fig. 5-28 Ephesus, Church of St. John, Exterior Vertical Wall: ICHTHUS Christogram

143. Georgia Frank, "Pilgrimage," in Harvey and Hunter, *The Oxford Handbook of Early Christian Studies*, 826–41.

144. Andreas Pülz, "Archaeological Evidence of Christian Pilgrimage in Ephesus," *Journal on Hellenistic and Roman Material Culture* 1 (2012): 225–60.

145. Wilson, *Biblical Turkey*, 223; Miszczak, *The Secrets of Ephesus*, 256; Fairchild, *Christian Origins in Ephesus*, 120.

Fig. 5-29 Ephesus, Church of St. John, Column Capital: Equilateral Cross

Fig. 5-30 Ephesus, Church of St. John, Column Capital: Iota-Chi Christogram

Fig. 5-31 Ephesus, Church of St. John, Column Capital: ICHTHUS Christogram

that this ICHTHUS Christogram was initially inscribed on this stone block while it was part of the Temple of Artemis (or the stadium). This would probably have occurred in the mid-fourth century as part of the Christianizing process occurring across the Roman Empire.

Several interesting features at the Basilica of St. John are relevant to our study. Dozens of stone capitals[146] were discovered in the excavations. Common decorative features on these capitals are variations of crosses placed inside of circles. There are three styles: 1) a common equilateral cross (see fig. 5-29); 2) a six-spoked wheel—that is, the Greek letters *iota* and *chi*, the first letters in Jesus Christ (*Iēsous Christos*) (see fig. 5-30); and 3) an eight-spoked wheel, the ICHTHUS Christogram (see fig. 5-31). This is another strong example of the eight-spoked ICHTHUS Christogram being used in parallel with other cross symbols in church architecture.

---

146. The square piece that goes on top of a column that transfers the load from the roof horizontal beams to the column.

Fig. 5-32 Ephesus, Church of St. John, Column Capital: Monogram of the Emperor Justinian

Fig. 5-33 Ephesus, Church of St. John, Column Capital: Monogram of the Empress Theodora

In addition, several of the capitals (a number of which have been restored) have the complicated monograms of Emperor Justinian (see fig. 5-32), who funded the construction, and his wife Theodora (see fig. 5-33), who was also perhaps active in funding the project. As noted in chapter 2, these monograms are evidence that the early Christians frequently used complex letter combinations and abbreviations.

On the exterior of the church there is a small pool basin, which probably served as a water source for those visiting the church, especially the many pilgrims. There are crosses professionally engraved on the stone wall panels that make up the sides of this basin (see fig. 5-34). These are similar to the crosses that were engraved on the stone slabs that stood at the front of the water pool in the renovated fountain from the Heroon of Androclos, once again providing an example of crosses being connected to water sources.

LABRAUNDA

The City of Labraunda

The ancient city of Labraunda was located along one of the major roads connecting the coast of the Aegean Sea with the inland areas of Anatolia—about 100 miles (160 km) southeast of Ephesus and about 50 miles (80 km) east of Didyma and the southwestern coast of Turkey. The site was dedicated to the Greek god Zeus as early as the sixth century BC. The name of the city is derived from the double-headed axe carried by Zeus called a *labrys*. Unlike

Fig. 5-34 Ephesus, Church of St. John:
Small Fountain with Crosses

most of the other cities we are discussing in this region of southwest Turkey, Labraunda was not a populous urban city but a religious center associated with the Temple of Zeus. For most of its history, its primary residents were priests and other workers from the temple. The population swelled considerably during the festivals associated with Zeus. Differing from the surrounding cities we have been discussing, where many of the existing buildings and facilities date from AD 100 to 600, most of the remaining archaeological structures that are visible today date to the fourth century BC. The few structures that were constructed during late antiquity (AD 200–600) include a bathhouse and two Christian churches. The churches date from 400 to 425.[147]

The Two Christian Churches

Although the presence of two churches at this site suggests a resident population of Christians either in Labraunda or in the surrounding cities,[148] Blid argues that these churches primarily served a pilgrimage clientele, much like the earlier Temple of Zeus had catered to temporary visitors who had come for the festivals.[149] Blid notes that in many of the residential cities, as the area was transformed from pagan control to Christian control, the Christians often built churches in the old pagan temples or converted the pagan temples (and other buildings like bathhouses) for Christian use. In Labraunda, however, the two new churches were located across the city from the pagan Temple of Zeus and along the well-traveled roadway. The two churches served to block off the old pagan temple from regular travelers, as well as providing service for these travelers. The east church had running water and was adjacent to a bathhouse.[150]

In the remains of the west church, archaeologists discovered a broken stone slab that had served as the chancel screen. Sometimes referred to as a *templon*, this stone made a low wall that divided the main sanctuary from the apse or front of the church. On this broken piece of the chancel screen, you can

147. Jesper Blid, "Sacred Movement to Labraunda: An Archaeological Perspective," *Journal on Hellenistic and Roman Material Culture* 1 (2012): 159–60, 171–73, 178–80. Blid suggests that there may have been three churches.
148. Matthews, *Greco-Roman Cities*, 347.
149. Blid, "Sacred Movement to Labraunda," 190–91.
150. Blid, "Sacred Movement to Labraunda," 164, 171–73, 180, 190–91.

see the top portion of a professionally inscribed ICHTHUS Christogram,[151] similar to the one discovered in the Church of St. Mary in nearby Ephesus, as well as the one in the church at Stobi (North Macedonia). A sketch of what the front of this church at Labraunda probably looked like is provided by Blid. It depicts the central altar flanked by low stone wall panels containing the ICHTHUS Christogram.[152] Here we see another example of the ICHTHUS wheel used in a very visible and highly important location of a church.

LAODICEA

The City of Laodicea

The city of Laodicea is located about ninety-six miles (155 km) inland (to the east) of Ephesus, near Aphrodisias, Hierapolis, and Colossae. It was built at an important intersection of two major trade routes—the road from Ephesus going east to the interior of Anatolia and the road from Sardis going south to the southern coast of Anatolia.

Unlike many of the ancient cities in western Anatolia, Laodicea was not founded by ancient Greek colonists. Alexander the Great died (323 BC) shortly after he conquered this area, and his general Seleucus became the ruler of Anatolia and Syria. Antiochus II Theos (286–246 BC), the grandson of Seleucus, founded Laodicea and named it after his wife Laodice. In 133 BC, it came under the rule of the Roman Empire. Located at an important trade intersection, the city flourished during the Roman era and became quite wealthy.[153]

The archaeological exploration, excavation, and discussion of many of the other cities that we cover in this book began more than one hundred years ago. The excavations of Laodicea, however, only began in earnest in 2003. The archaeologists excavating Laodicea have proceeded at a remarkable speed to uncover and restore this breathtaking site. Extensive excavations and restorations are ongoing, and important discoveries continue to be made nearly every year. This makes almost any discussion of Laodicea quickly out of date.

The spectacular ruins of Laodicea cover almost two square miles (five square km) and include the largest stadium in Anatolia, two theaters, four bathhouses, four agoras, five monumental public water fountains, a council meetinghouse, temples, at least twenty churches, an extensive fresh water supply and drainage system, walls, gates, paved streets, and residential areas.

Christianity probably was first proclaimed in Laodicea around AD 53, after Paul and his colleagues Priscilla and Aquila arrived in the area (Acts 18:18–19:10). During Paul's two-year stay at Ephesus, the gospel spread throughout

---

151. See the picture and suggested sketch of the original complete wall in Blid, "Sacred Movement to Labraunda," 181; and the discussion and pictures in Jesper Blid, *Felicium Temporum Reparatio: Labraunda in Late Antiquity (c. AD 300–600)* (Stockholm: Stockholm University, 2012), 114, 119, 135.
152. Blid, *Labraunda in Late Antiquity*, 119.
153. Matthews, *Greco-Roman Cities*, 160–61.

the province of Asia (Acts 19:10), which is likely when the church was planted in Laodicea (along with other cities in this area). Colossians—the letter written to the church in the nearby city of Colossae—credits Epaphras as playing a central role in planting the church in Laodicea at the same time as he was planting it in Colossae (Col. 1:7; 2:1; 4:12). At the end of Colossians, Paul greets the Laodicean Christians specifically. In particular, he mentions a woman named Nympha and the church that met in her house (Col. 4:15). By the early 60s, when Paul writes Colossians while a prisoner in Rome, not only is there a church in Laodicea, but there is a particular house church already known by the benefactor, Nympha, in whose house the church was meeting. Furthermore, not only does Paul tell the Colossians to share their letter from him with the Christians in Laodicea, he exhorts the Colossian Christians to read the letter he wrote to the church in Laodicea (Col. 4:16), a document that has not survived.

Laodicea is one of the seven churches in Asia Minor addressed in Revelation 2 to 3. The address to Laodicea (Rev. 3:14–22) implies that the church there was wealthy in human terms but lacking—described as "lukewarm" (Rev. 3:16)—in regard to the true spiritual life. It is to the Laodicean church that Jesus addresses his famous proposition, "Here I am! I stand at the door and knock. If anyone hears my voice and opens the door, I will come in and eat with that person, and they with me" (Rev. 3:20). The next verse employs the Greek word *nikaō* ("to be victorious, to overcome") twice, encouraging the Laodicean Christians that "to the one who is *victorious*, I will give the right to sit with me on my throne, just as I was *victorious* and sat down with my Father on his throne" (Rev. 3:21, emphasis added).

Nonetheless, the church at Laodicea developed into an influential church. As early as the 160s the bishop Sargaris of Laodicea was known to have been martyred. Likewise, a bishop of Laodicea named Theophilus was martyred during the Great Persecution along with many others. In fact, more than fifty Christian martyrs from Laodicea are known.[154]

In the year 2012, a fascinating funerary block from a tomb in the western necropolis (cemetery) was discovered. The inscription on the block (in Latin) identifies the deceased as Aurelius Marianianus, and his comrade, the one who built the tomb, as Aurelius Dinianus. Both were soldiers—horsemen in the Roman legion named *Legio VII Claudia*. Celal Şimşek and Alister Filippini argue that here is strong evidence that this legion was part of the army of Constantine and that elements of it were sent to Laodicea (then the capital of the province of Phrygia) in 324, after major battles at Byzantium and Chrysopolis. This means the death of this soldier and the creation of this funeral block can be dated between 324 and 350.[155]

---

154. Tabbernee, "Asia Minor and Cyprus," 287–88.
155. Celal Şimşek and Alister Filippini, "The Funerary Altar of the Christian Soldier Aurelius Marinianus (Early 4th Cent.) from Viminacium to Chrysopolis and Laodikeia," in *Laodikeia Çalişmalari 5:15. Yilinda Laodikeia (2003–2018)*, ed. Celal Şimşek (Istanbul: Ege Yayinlari, 2019), 187–204.

What is particularly relevant for our study is that this funerary block has an engraved picture of a Roman horseman and his horse. This soldier and his horse both have their feet on a snake (with a human head). The soldier has a halo (often called a nimbus) and is holding a flag that has an equilateral cross. The combination of these three signs provides strong evidence that this soldier was a Christian (or that at this time soldiers in Constantine's army depicted themselves with Christian symbology).[156] While this is only one example, it is evidence that in the early to mid-fourth century (AD

Fig. 5-35 Laodicea, Syria Street

325–350) there were Christian soldiers from Constantine's army stationed in Laodicea who identified with the Christian cross and who saw themselves as the defeaters of the forces of evil.

After the Great Persecution and throughout the fourth century, Laodicea functioned as an important episcopal see (seat of a bishop). Between 343 and 381, several important, but local, ecclesiastical councils were held there.[157]

As occurred in other cities in this region, Laodicea was struck with earthquakes. From 27 BC to AD 610, Laodicea experienced nine earthquakes that appear in literary or archaeological records. Three of these were particularly devastating, destroying much of the city. These three were in AD 60, 494, and 602 to 610. The final earthquake around 602 to 610 led to the complete relocation of the city and the abandonment of this particular site.[158]

Syria Street and the Fountain of Severus
The major street running east and west (designated in Roman urban planning as the Decumanus Maximus) was Syria Street (see fig. 5-35). On the eastern end of the street was the Syria Gate, and on the western end of the street was the Ephesus Gate. This paved street, lined with columns, shops, temples, fountains, and the central agora, is one of the best preserved (and restored) ancient Greco-Roman streets in all of the Roman East.

Along Syria Street, right in the center of the city, the Central Agora (the largest of Laodicea's agoras) lay adjacent to the street, to the south. Across

---

156. Şimşek and Filippini, "The Funerary Altar of the Christian Soldier," 190, 205–16.

157. Tabbernee, "Asia Minor and Cyprus," 287–88.

158. Celal Şimşek, *Church of Laodikeia: Christianity in the Lykos Valley* (Denizli, Turkey: Denizli Metropolitan Municipality, 2015), 9.

Fig. 5-36 Laodicea, Near the Fountain of Severus: Chi-Rho Christogram and Three Equilateral Crosses in Circles

Fig. 5-37 Laodicea, Near the Fountain of Severus: ICHTHUS Christogram

the street from the Central Agora was a public monumental fountain, usually referred to as the Fountain of Severus (emperor AD 193–211). Statues of Athena, Tyche, and other pagan gods stood in niches in the walls of the two-story structure overlooking the rectangular pool. Several of the decorative wall panels were covered with sculpted scenes of people and gods. Water flowed from the pool into three basins that provided water for the agora area. Near the fountain was a decorative monumental gateway.

In this area, on the north side of the street (across from the agora and next to the Fountain of Severus and the propylon), etched into the pavement of the street or on blocks adjacent to the street, are numerous Christian symbols: four circles with equilateral crosses inside, one regular cross with flared ends, one Chi-Rho Christogram inside of a circle (see fig. 5-36), and one eight-spoked ICHTHUS Christogram (see fig. 5-37). These are also three four-square boxes that, as suggested in chapter 2, are probably crosses or Christian symbols.[159]

Throughout the excavations of Laodicea, headless statues of pagan gods, famous people, and Roman emperors were discovered, and, alternately, several heads without bodies were discovered. A number of these are from this area, especially the Fountain of Severus. On the forehead of one of these heads, belonging to a goddess statue, a cross is inscribed. On another head,

159. See Testa, *Il Simbolismo Dei Giudeo-Cristiani*, 304–9.

the entire face has been removed, the surface flattened, and then a Tau-Rho Staurogram, along with the letters *alpha* and *omega*, has been inscribed on the stone surface, replacing the face. The head and part of the leg from a statue of the Emperor Augustus, worshiped as part of the imperial cult, was discovered in the public latrine on Stadium Street, a suggestive disposal area.[160] It is probable that the act of inscribing Christian symbols on the pavement could be associated with the removal and destruction (defacing/beheading) of the pagan idols that dominated the fountain and the street in this area.

While it is possible at some sites that broken pagan idol statues were damaged by earthquakes, the absence of their associated heads, along with the defacing and addition of Christian symbols etched on them, suggests otherwise. Obviously, an earthquake was not responsible for depositing the severed head of Augustus in the latrine across town.

Also discovered in this area is a stone column section on which is informally etched a Jewish menorah (seven-branched lampstand). Etched above the menorah and extending down into it (and thus defacing it slightly) is a Christian cross. This column was part of the lower colonnade of the two-story Fountain of Severus.[161] This short column section is now set up in the agora just across Syria Street.

The cross graffiti on this column certainly fits in with other Christian graffiti in this area. As noted above, there are at least seven other Christian symbols etched in the pavement as graffiti in this area (and columns with similar cross graffiti were discovered at nearby Aphrodisias). The puzzling issue relates to the presence of the Jewish menorah and the relationship between the menorah and the cross. Menorahs are not unknown in the graffiti of this era,[162] but the purpose and function of this one—on a column of the Fountain of Severus—is enigmatic.

The disparate—and often quite speculative—scholarly opinions about this column vary widely, and there is nothing close to a consensus.[163] Usually the discussion is focused on the sensitive topic of early Jewish-Christian relationships, and frequently, the important archaeological context slides to the background. Yet it is important to keep in mind that this column was part of the Fountain of Severus and was discovered at that location. There is no evidence that it was used in a synagogue or that this public fountain was ever used as

---

160. Celal Şimşek, "Laodikeia Yontuculuğu" [Eng. "Laodicea Sculpting"], in *Laodikeia (Laodicea ad Lycum). Laodikeia Çalişmalari 2*, ed. Celal Şimşek (Istanbul: Ege Yayinlari, 2013), 460–63 (see figs. 653, 654, 661 [Athena], 662 [Aphrodite], 669, and 670).

161. Celal Şimşek, "A Menorah with a Cross Carved on a Column of Nymphaeum A at Laodicea ad Lycum," *Journal of Roman Archaeology* 19 (2006): 343.

162. Fine cites examples of menorah graffiti at Aphrodisias, Sardis, Ephesus, and Hierapolis. Steven Fine, "The Menorah and the Cross: Historiographical Reflections on a Recent Discovery from Laodicea on the Lycus," in *New Perspectives on Jewish-Christian Relations*, ed. Elisheva Carleback and Jacob J. Schacter, Brill Reference Library of Judaism 33 (Leiden: Brill, 2012), 31–33.

163. See the discussion of the wide range of views by Fine, "The Menorah and the Cross," 31–50.

a Jewish building. That is, the presence of the menorah does not necessitate that this column was in a building used by Jews. In this same exact location, the pagan idols of this fountain were defaced and destroyed and dozens of Christian symbols were etched into the pavement. It is highly likely that this cross and probably both symbols (cross and menorah) were inscribed as part of the same phenomenon.

Yet puzzling questions remain. Was the Jewish menorah graffiti being used in a similar fashion as Christian symbols—to drive away demons or to protect areas from the demons associated with the pagan gods, especially at water fountains? Was the cross inscribed over the top of the menorah as a sign of Christian victory or triumph over the Jews[164] (puzzling in this location), or was it used in an apotropaic way as crosses were used in graffiti elsewhere?

The Fountain of Trajan

Going around the corner from the Central Agora and the Fountain of Severus and then continuing south on Stadium Street, you come to the newly discovered (2015) and reconstructed Fountain of Trajan (emperor AD 98–117). Inscriptions found at this fountain date the initial construction of the fountain and associated statues to 113 to 115. This complex included five fountains and a towering (over nine feet) statue of Trajan in the center.[165]

In the fourth century, the Christians took possession of this fountain complex and reconfigured it as a Christian fountain. They reused the statue of Trajan but renamed it Constantine, the emperor who ended the Great Persecution and gave his support to Christianity. They engraved Latin crosses on the stone panels of water basins and elsewhere in the fountain complex.[166] This is similar to the crosses added to the front panels of the water basin for the fountain associated with the Heroon of Androclos in Ephesus.

The Central Church of Laodicea

Twenty churches and chapels have been discovered and excavated at Laodicea.[167] One expansive church in particular, often called the Laodicean Church (or the Central Church), has been excavated and extensively restored and preserved. It is a complicated structure with several apses and naves, three water fountains with pools, numerous rooms, and a baptistry. Built in a central part of the city, it was located just to the east of one of the main temples dedicated to Apollo, Artemis, Aphrodite, and later to the Roman imperial cult. Archaeologists date this church to the early fourth century, shortly after Constantine issued the edict of

---

164. Fine suggests this as part of his tentative conclusion ("The Menorah and the Cross," 50).
165. Celal Şimşek, "Statue Group of Trajan with Cuirass (lorika-thoraks)," in Şimşek, *Laodikeia Çalışmaları 5*, 89–90.
166. Şimşek, "Statue Group of Trajan with Cuirass," 98–99.
167. Mark R. Fairchild, "Laodicea's 'Lukewarm' Legacy: Conflicts of Prosperity in an Ancient Christian City," *Biblical Archaeology Review* 43.2 (2017): 67.

Milan (AD 313), legalizing Christianity. This was probably the first officially sanctioned church built in Laodicea and one of the earliest—perhaps *the* earliest—churches built in Anatolia after the Great Persecution.[168] Şimşek argues that the Council of Laodicea (AD 363–364) would have met in this facility.[169]

As part of its water system, this church facility had two exterior fountains that provided water not only for parishioners entering and exiting the church but for people in the neighborhood. Both of these fountains have engraved crosses on the stone-walled water pools, a feature that occurs at the pools of water fountains in other locations (Ephesus, Sardis).

In the center of the church, in the naos[170] proper, right at the altar, another small fountain was located. This fountain was probably to supply holy water, especially for pilgrims. This water was provided for the pilgrims in small bottles, so that they could take this special water home. Indeed, a number of these bottles were uncovered in the excavations. A marble vessel was also discovered in the area of this fountain and probably served as part of the distribution system of this water. There is a dedicatory vow inscribed on the marble vessel, using the Greek word εὐχὴ (*euchē*, "vow, dedication, prayer"). Although some of the inscription is damaged, the readable part translates: "as a vow for himself and all of his family."[171] This dedicatory inscription is probably associated with the donor who funded this part of the water system and the altar. Note the similarity between this water fountain and dedicatory vow using εὐχὴ and the similar situation in the synagogue of Sardis (discussed below).

The Peristyle House Church

Very recently, near the reconstructed North Theater, a different type of church was discovered. A peristyle house (peristyle refers to a house with an open middle courtyard with columns around the perimeter) was discovered, dating to the first century AD. The lead archaeologist Celal Şimşek has determined that this house structure served as a home (and a shop for business) for the first few centuries but then was used as a house church in the early days of Christianity (while probably still functioning as a home and shop). This probably happened before Christians could legally build permanent churches. This would be before the time of Constantine, or shortly after he came to power, but before money could be raised or designated for the construction of an official church structure. It is also possible that, when the Central Laodicean Church was built in the early fourth century, this house became the residence of the newly empowered Christian bishop.[172]

---

168. Regarding the date of this church, see Şimşek, *Church of Laodikeia*, 59, 84–85. See also Fairchild, "Laodicea's 'Lukewarm' Legacy," 67.

169. Şimşek, *Church of Laodikeia*, 84.

170. In church architecture, the naos was the main sanctuary area or the central hall in front of the altar.

171. Şimşek, *Church of Laodikeia*, 37.

172. *Hürriyet Daily News*, "House with church unearthed in Laodicea" (October 27, 2020), https://www.hurriyetdailynews.com/house-with-Church-Unearthed-in-Laodicea-159481.

Fig. 5-38 Laodicea, Street Pavement in Front of the Peristyle House Church: ICHTHUS Christogram

Fig. 5-39 Laodicea, Entrance to the Peristyle House Church: The ICHTHUS Christogram Is on the Second Stone Block out from the Doorway

It will be interesting to see if the archaeologist Celal Şimşek can determine when exactly this home became a house church. Recall that in Colossians 4:15, Paul explicitly sends his greetings to a church in Laodicea associated with the house of a woman named Nympha. From the earliest days of Christianity, there were house churches in Laodicea. Now that archaeologists have identified one (and a large one), we will wait expectantly for them to try to date the time when this house became a house church (if possible).

There are two ICHTHUS Christograms integrated into this early house church. Right after you enter it, you encounter a floor paved with terra-cotta bricks that are laid in patterns and shapes. There are two panels with designs side by side. One panel contains a depiction that is clearly a fish. The adjacent panel contains an eight-spoked ICHTHUS Christogram. Because the brick paving is somewhat fragile, and due to the possibility of visitors and tourists damaging this part of the floor as they walk through the house church, this part of the floor is currently (June 2023) covered with a protective tarp and not visible to tourists. Although this floor panel has not been published yet, Cenk Eronat, a Turkish tour guide and vice president of TUTKU Educational Travel, graciously showed me a picture of this remarkable side-by-side fish and ICHTHUS Christogram. This church floor provides extraordinarily strong evidence of the association of the eight-spoked wheel with the fish symbol.

The other ICHTHUS Christogram is etched informally on the pavement of the road running alongside the front of this house church (Temple East Street), lined up to be precisely centered with the threshold for the doorway entering into the church (see figs. 5-38 and 5-39). The appearance of this

ICHTHUS wheel on the street directly in front of the doorway to the house church is significant and intriguing. It is unlikely that a church worship gathering of any size could have been kept completely secret, so it is doubtful that this was a secret church or that the eight-spoked wheel was a secret sign. The size and luxuriousness of the house implies that the owner was wealthy and, without doubt, influential. Perhaps those intent on oppressing Christians in the Great Persecution—city officials and pagan temple personnel— simply looked the other way. On the other hand, people of high standing also suffered during this time, so it is more likely that this house served as a Christian church before the Great Persecution of 303–313, and again after the persecution ended, but not during the middle of it.

At any rate, it is plausible that the ICHTHUS Christogram on the pavement in front of the house church served as an identification marker, noting the place where the Christians met while at the same time proclaiming the core truths held by those who met there (Jesus Christ God's Son Savior). While it seems unlikely that the purpose was to cleanse an unholy area or to drive demons away, this Christogram near the doorway could still be serving as a protective symbol, using the power of the name of Jesus Christ and the cross to protect those within from the many evil forces that still lurked throughout the streets of this pagan city filled with idols and pagan temples. Inside the church, the floor-paving pattern of the fish gives a clear explanation of the eight-spoked wheel: it is ICHTHUS, the Greek word for fish, and an acronym for Jesus Christ, God's Son, Savior.

PRIENE

The City of Priene
The city of Priene is close to the coast of western Anatolia, approximately thirty-three miles (fifty-four km) due south of Ephesus. Founded by Greek colonists in the twelfth century BC, the city was originally built on the banks of the Maeander River. By the fifth century BC, the river had eroded the edges of the city, and in the fourth century BC, the citizens of Priene moved the entire city from the location in the river valley where the city had been for seven hundred years up to a higher elevation. Here they completely rebuilt the city.[173]

Priene was brought into the Roman Empire in 133 BC. By that time it was a fairly wealthy city, but much smaller than Ephesus or Miletus, since it no longer had a harbor and port. With a population around 50,000 to 60,000, it still boasted significant architectural structures and facilities, including the Temple of Athena, multiple smaller temples, city walls and gates, an agora with administrative offices and meeting council chamber, two gymnasiums,

---

173. Matthews, *Greco-Roman Cities*, 264–66.

a theater, plush residences, and a significant water supply system with aqueducts, pipes, and fountains.[174]

Although Priene is not mentioned in the Bible, Christianity probably arrived in Priene around AD 54 to 55, during the two years that Paul was in nearby Ephesus. Acts 19:10 states that "all the Jews and Greeks who lived in the province of Asia heard the word of the Lord." A church of some size definitely developed there, for, starting in 431, bishops from Priene are mentioned in church council records under the overall authority of the bishop at Ephesus.[175]

The Temple of Athena

When the new, relocated city of Priene was planned, at the heart and center of the city's urban design was the Temple of Athena Polias. Like Athens, the goddess of the city of Priene was Athena. "Athena Polias" means "Athena, goddess of the city." Construction began on the temple in the fourth century BC. Alexander the Great (and his army) arrived in Priene in 334 BC, and Alexander offered to pay for the completion of the construction. In fact, he personally dedicated the temple to Athena. The ensuing chaos and unsettled situation in this region delayed the completion of the temple for almost two hundred years. The Romans arrived in 133 BC, and the temple was finally completed during the reign of Augustus (ruled 27 BC–AD 14), probably with his financial support. No doubt driven by financial and political practicality, the Temple of Athena was dedicated to the imperial cult, and the veneration of Caesar Augustus was added to the worship of Athena.[176]

Fig. 5-40 Priene, The Temple of Athena

Not quite on the same gigantic scale as the temples of Artemis at Ephesus or at Sardis, or of the Temple of Apollo at Didyma, this temple of Athena was, nonetheless, quite impressive (see fig. 5-40). The

---

174. Matthews, *Greco-Roman Cities*, 266–87; see also Frank Rumscheid, *Priene: A Guide to the "Pompeii of Asia Minor"* (Istanbul: Ege Yayinlari, 1998).

175. Rumscheid, *Priene*, 22.

176. Wolf Koenigs, *Der Athenatempel von Priene*, Archäologische Forschungen 33 (Wiesbaden: Reichert Verlag, 2015), 12–13. Koenigs notes, however, that while there is an inscription indicating the dedication to Augustus, there is no evidence that a statue of Augustus was added to the main sanctuary where the statue of Athena stood (13).

main temple area was enclosed with a high stone wall and surrounded by thirty-four columns nearly four feet in diameter and thirty-eight feet tall.[177] At the present time, five of these columns have been set back in place (although these reconstructed columns are about ten feet shorter than the originals),[178] and pieces of other columns lie on the ground in the nearby vicinity.

Approaching the temple from the front, going up the main steps and then turning to the right and walking around to the north side of the main sanctuary area, between the foundation blocks for the temple wall and the column bases, you will find two ICHTHUS Christograms: one at the western end of this paved area and one at the eastern end (see fig. 5-41). There are also two clear regular crosses and two (perhaps three) equilateral crosses inscribed inside circles. There is at least one square box with a cross inscribed within it (i.e., a four-square box), with a regular cross inscribed in the stone just

Fig. 5-41 Priene, The Temple of Athena: ICHTHUS Christogram

inches away.[179] Once again, we see Christian crosses and ICHTHUS Christograms inscribed together in the same stone pavement at a pagan temple.

This is additional evidence that these symbols were placed there by Christians, probably at some time after the Great Persecution ended and after Constantine came to power and gave imperial support to Christianity. It is possible that the Temple of Athena fell into disuse first due to economic and political pressure as Christians became more powerful in city and regional politics. Or at some point, perhaps the temple lost its ability to provide guards, and with Christian administrators now ruling the city along with zealous bishops growing in power, a group of Christians entered the temple with hammer and chisel and began etching crosses and the eight-

---

177. For a detailed architectural and archaeological description of the temple, including a detailed floorplan, see Koenigs, *Der Athenatempel von Priene*.

178. Koenigs, *Der Athenatempel von Priene*, 6.

179. On my visit to this site in June 2023, in addition to the graffiti inscriptions mentioned above, I found an inscribed bird, a rough drawing of a person, and a drawing of what looks like a tent with a circle above it. In several places there were undecipherable texts. In the appendix of Koenigs, *Der Athenatempel von Priene*, Beilage (Supplement) 2, there is a detailed floorplan of the temple with most of the graffiti shown. This drawing shows only one eight-spoked wheel, however, along with three C2 circles (with crosses inside), the bird, the tent with the circle above it, four four-square boxes, and three indistinguishable sketches—two of which are perhaps people. It does not show either of the crosses. See also Theodor Wiegand et al., *Priene: Ergebnisse der Ausgrabungen und Untersuchungen in den Jahren 1895–1898* (Berlin: Georg Reimer, 1904), 88.

spoked Christogram, thus proclaiming the identity and power of "Jesus Christ God's Son Savior."

Also discovered at Priene, near the Temple of Demeter, is a statue of a priestess named Nikeso who served in that temple. This statue apparently stood at the entrance to the temple. She is headless and has a cross inscribed on her back.[180] This type of cleansing or claiming victory in the nearby Temple of Demeter probably occurred at the same time or under the same circumstances as the etching of the ICHTHUS wheels and the crosses in the Athena temple.[181]

In the fifth century, when the Christians built their first substantial church structure in Priene along with the bishop's residence, they did not locate it in the Temple of Athena but near the theater and adjacent bathhouse. They did, however, take loads of stone blocks and columns from the temple precinct and reused them in the new church.[182] The remains of the church include several stone wall panels (or chancel screen panels) with crosses inside of circles.

SAGALASSOS

The City of Sagalassos

Sagalassos was an important, ancient city in the region of Pisidia in what is now southwest Turkey. It was located along the busy north-south Roman road called the Via Sebaste, the main roadway in Pisidia linking the port of Perga in Pamphylia with the city of Pisidian Antioch, north of Sagalassos. In Acts 13:13–14, when Paul and his companions sail from Paphos on Cyprus to Perga in Pamphylia and then go overland from Perga to Pisidian Antioch, they would probably have passed through Sagalassos, though it is not mentioned in Acts.

During the reign of Emperor Hadrian, Sagalassos was awarded the high status of being the temple warden for the imperial cult and was designated as the first city of Pisidia. Sagalassos remained the leading city of Pisidia up until Emperor Diocletian (AD 284–305) reorganized the province and designated nearby Pisidian Antioch as the capital.[183]

The archaeological site of Sagalassos is one of the best-preserved sites in Turkey, similar to Ephesus, Laodicea, and Aphrodisias. Structures on the site include a theater, a stadium, an Odeon (a small theater-like facility for meetings), several pagan temples, bathhouses, monumental public fountains,

180. Troels Myrup Kristensen, "Addenda to T. M. Kristensen, 'Miraculous Bodies,'" *Late Antique Archaeology* 15 (2021): 1–3.

181. Early archaeologists reported evidence that the wooden roof of the temple had been burned. They suggest that perhaps the Christians were responsible for the fire. Wiegand et al., *Priene*, 83.

182. Matthews, *Greco-Roman Cities*, 280–81; Rumscheid, *Priene*, 35.

183. M. Waelkens, P. Talloen, and I. Jacobs, "Sagalassos," in Finney, *The Eerdmans Encyclopedia of Early Christian Art and Archaeology*, 2:444–47; Peter Talloen, "The Rise of Christianity at Sagalassus," in *Early Christianity in Asia Minor and Cyprus: From the Margins to the Mainstream*, ed. Stephen Mitchell and Philipp Pilhofer, Ancient Judaism and Early Christianity 109 (Leiden: Brill, 2019), 164–66.

streets, mansions, government buildings, fortified walls and gates, two agoras, and eight churches.[184]

By the fourth century, Sagalassos was an important center of Christianity with influential bishops residing and ministering there. As in other cities across the Roman Empire in the fourth century and into the fifth century, after Constantine legalized Christianity and provided imperial support for churches and bishops, Sagalassos underwent a transition from a pagan-dominated city to a Christian-dominated city. All the pagan temples in the city were systematically closed and replaced by a growing number of churches. One of these churches was built in the middle of what had been a public government building.[185]

Beginning in the early stages of the Christianization of Sagalassos, a wide range of Christian graffiti incorporating a variety of symbols (equilateral crosses, Latin crosses, Chi-Rho Christograms, etc.) appears. Soon after, professionally inscribed crosses appear as part of officially sponsored Christian renovation and construction. For example, a number of stone blocks with professionally inscribed equilateral crosses (inside circles) were discovered at one of the public monumental fountains in the upper agora. In addition, Christian symbols such as crosses and fish appear on several oil lamps. Statues of pagan gods that had been destroyed, beheaded, or defaced were also discovered in the excavations.[186]

The Upper Agora (Market Area)

Along with a number of crosses—some in circles and some without circles—two eight-spoked ICHTHUS Christograms were discovered, both inscribed on the pavement of the upper agora.[187] The location near the public agora is similar to the location of wheel graffiti at Ephesus, Laodicea, and Philippi. In the lower agora at Sagalassos there is a large (about eighteen in.) inscribed circle with an equilateral cross in it.[188] As argued above, these simple equilateral crosses inscribed within circles are most likely Christian crosses. After the Great Persecution of the early 300s ended and the legalization of Christianity, Christians started Christianizing Sagalassos. As a critical part of this

---

184. Waelkens, Talloen, and Jacobs, "Sagalassos," 444–46; Talloen, "The Rise of Christianity at Sagalassus," 180–81.
185. Talloen, "The Rise of Christianity at Sagalassus," 164–65, 176–84.
186. Peter Talloen, "From Pagan to Christian: Religious Iconography in Material Culture from Sagalassos," *Late Antique Archaeology* 7.1 (2011): 584–86; Talloen, "The Rise of Christianity at Sagalassus," 176–84; Jacobs, "Cross Graffiti," 202–4.
187. Lavan, "The Agorai of Sagalassos," 333–43. On 334 n. 48, Lavan uses Bell and Roueché's classification for circle graffiti, identifying these two as C4 ("circle with eight spokes"). Lavan, 334–35, assumes these circles are game boards but does not provide any evidence other than citing Bell and Roueché. Interestingly, Lavan, 334–35, notes the presence of these circles right as he is discussing Christian graffiti. As noted throughout this book, the frequent use of the eight-spoked wheel alongside crosses, in churches, and with the acrostic ΙΧΘΥΣ argues strongly that this symbol is a Christogram and not a game board.
188. Lavan, "The Agorai of Sagalassos," 336.

transformation, they apparently used the ICHTHUS Christogram, along with the more traditional cross, as one of their powerful tools for cleansing, driving away the demons, and claiming victory over the pagan forces.

SAMOS

The Island/City of Samos

In Acts 20:15, as Paul and his companions were returning to Jerusalem after his third missionary journey (about AD 56), they were traveling by ship down the west coast of Asia, hopping from port to port. "The next day we set sail from there [Assis] and arrived off Chios. The day after that we crossed over to Samos, and on the following day arrived at Miletus." Although there is no literary evidence for Paul himself doing missionary activity on Samos (in Acts 20:15 he appears to leave the next day), there is a tradition on the island that Paul himself preached the gospel here and made Christian converts.[189] Keep in mind that Ephesus is quite close, and ship traffic back and forth from Samos to Ephesus was frequent and common. In Acts 19:10, Luke writes that Paul spent two years in Ephesus, "so that all the Jews and Greeks who lived in the province of Asia heard the word of the Lord." It is likely that during this time a church was planted at Samos.

Samos is one of a number of small islands that lie just off the coast of Turkey but that remain under the jurisdiction of Greece. In fact, Samos lies only about one mile off the Turkish coast, located about halfway between Ephesus and Miletus. Samos had a good harbor and was a busy port. Ships traveling up and down the coast of Asia frequently stopped there for the night (as Paul did).

Samos is the name of both the island and the city there. Settled by the ancient Greeks, by the sixth century BC the city of Samos, with its large fleet of ships, was a major naval power in the Aegean Sea and an important geopolitical power in the region. The city was sometimes referred to as Pythagoria, named after one of its famous citizens, Pythagoras. When the Romans gained control of this area, Samos was included in the administrative region of Asia.[190]

Although poorly preserved, Samos' archaeological remains include a stadium, a theater, an agora, a bathhouse, several pagan temples, city walls, and city gates. The most famous religious site associated with Samos is the Heraion, an extensive complex that was about four miles away, connected by the Sacred Road. There were numerous temples here, some of which date back as early as the eighth century BC. At the center of this complex, and by far the largest and most dominating structure, is the great Temple of Hera (the wife of Zeus). When originally built (around 570 BC), it was 300 feet (91 m) long and 150 feet (45 m) wide with 160 columns (eight rows of twenty each). A gigantic altar, approximately 110 feet (33 m) by 50 feet (15 m), stood in

---

189. Fant and Reddish, *Biblical Sites in Greece and Turkey*, 118.
190. Fant and Reddish, *Biblical Sites in Greece and Turkey*, 116–17.

front. The citizens of Samos, along with visitors and pilgrims, held an annual festival known as Heraia, celebrating the wedding of Hera to Zeus, which centered around a ceremonial procession from the city along the Sacred Road to the temple.[191]

The Churches on Samos

Across the Roman Empire, after Constantine achieved sole power as emperor and provided recognition, legality, and imperial support for Christianity, churches start to appear frequently in the archaeological record. This continues throughout the fourth to sixth centuries, with new churches and renovations being built on top of earlier structures. The remains of at least four churches have been identified on Samos in the main city area down by the port, one of which was dedicated to St. Paul. This church, dating to the sixth century, was built inside a complex that had earlier been a gymnasium, and a baptistry was built over the remains of a Roman bath.[192]

Up from the port, Christians built a church in the middle of the Heraion, which had been dominated by the Temple of Hera. In fact, most of the church occupied what had been the forecourt of the pagan temple. It was built between the main temple proper and the altar in front. Dating perhaps to the fifth century, this church was constructed almost entirely with reused finished stones (often referred to as *spolia*) from the temples and associated buildings of the Heraion, implying that these buildings and temples had either fallen into disuse and were sitting empty or were destroyed and dismantled by the Christians. Reused material in this church has been identified as coming from eight different surrounding structures. Furthermore, the church itself incorporated several adjacent buildings into its structure. It was also situated so that the Sacred Road from the lower city terminated right at the church.[193]

During the excavations of the church, large pieces and smaller fragments coming from seven professionally carved and finished stone wall panels were discovered. For five of these wall panels, enough material remains to be able to reconstruct the look of the panel. The standard pattern reflects an eight-spoked wheel in the center flanked by crosses. In two of the panels, the outer circle of the Christogram is a laurel wreath, and in three of them it looks like the plain rim of a wheel.[194]

These stone wall panels with the ICHTHUS Christogram discovered in this church are similar to the stone panels with the same Christogram discov-

191. Fant and Reddish, *Biblical Sites in Greece and Turkey*, 121–23.
192. Cornelius Steckner, "Samos," in Finney, *The Eerdmans Encyclopedia of Early Christian Art and Archaeology*, 2:453.
193. Stephan Westphalen, "Die frühchristliche Basilika im Heraion von Samos und ihre Ausstattung," Sonderdruck aus den Mitteilungen des Deutschen Archäologischen Instituts Athenische Abteilung, vol. 109 (Berlin: Gebr. Mann Verlag, 1994), 302–5.
194. Westphalen, "Die frühchristliche Basilika im Heraion," 320–22. For a drawing that reconstructs what these panels looked like, see 321. For pictures of some of the fragments, see tables 78–81.

ered at the Church of St. Mary in nearby Ephesus and in a church at Stobi across the Aegean Sea in Macedonia. While the panels here on Samos have the Christogram flanked by crosses on one panel, at Ephesus, there is a sole panel with the Christogram flanked by two panels that each have a cross. The design—and, no doubt, the significance—of these occurrences is similar. As was the case in Ephesus, and probably in Stobi, these wall panels are from the front area of the church, either part of the chancel screen that divided the congregation area (the naos) from the front altar area (the apse), enclosing the altar on three sides, or they were the panels on each interior side of the church walls at the beginning of the apse. Either way, it is clear that these panels and the symbols they depicted were being stressed and were placed in prominent areas of the church. The eight-spoked Christogram was being used in a similar, parallel context as was the cross, and sometimes it was even placed in the focal area flanked by crosses.

SARDIS

The City of Sardis

The city of Sardis was located to the northeast of Ephesus and about sixty miles (ninety-seven km) inland from the west coast of Turkey and the port city of Smyrna (modern Izmir). An ancient city whose origins go back as far as 1400 BC, Sardis was the capital of the Lydian Empire, famous for the gold of legendary King Croesus (560–546 BC). In 189 BC, it came under the control of the Attalid dynasty of the city of Pergamum, but in 133 BC, it was incorporated into the Roman Empire. A terrible earthquake devastated Sardis in AD 17, but a generous donation from the Roman emperor Tiberius assisted it in rebuilding. The region around Sardis was associated with the ancient Anatolian earth mother goddess Cybele, who had been transformed into the goddess Artemis by the Greeks, who had also settled in the area.[195]

Sardis was prosperous and growing throughout the second and into the third century AD. The famous gymnasium and bathhouse were built in several phases during the second century. The spectacular facade for the bathhouse, which has been reconstructed and is visible to visitors today, rises two stories high and is filled with niches that once held statues of pagan gods. By the beginning of the fourth century, the city of Sardis was prosperous, with a population as high as 60,000 to 100,000. Archaeological excavations have revealed the remains of a theater, a stadium, city walls and gates, a gymnasium and bathhouse, a public latrine, the huge Artemis temple, shops and residences, and a water supply/drainage system.[196]

---

195. Wilson, *Biblical Turkey*, 296–97.
196. George M. A. Hanfmann, Fikret K. Yegül, and John S. Crawford, "The Roman and Late Antique Period," in *Sardis: From Prehistoric to Roman Times: Results of the Archaeological Exploration of Sardis 1958–1975*, ed. George M. A. Hanfmann (Cambridge, MA: Harvard University Press, 1983), 140–46.

Christianity came to Sardis very early. Indeed, Sardis is one of the seven churches John addresses in Revelation 2–3, although he had mostly negative things to say about the church there. By the end of the first century, Sardis was already the seat of a bishop. In the mid-second century, it was the home of the prolific Christian writer and bishop Melito. Two martyrs, Therapon and Apollonius, are known from third-century literary sources. The bishop of Sardis attended the Council of Nicaea (AD 325), where he was ranked as the sixth highest in the orthodox hierarchy.[197]

The remains of four Christian churches have been discovered at Sardis. Based on the presence of datable coins, archaeologists have dated one of the churches (referred to as Church EA) as early as the mid-fourth century. One of the other churches, often referred to as Church M, is attached to the ruins of the Temple of Artemis and likewise dates quite early, either to the fourth or fifth century.[198]

Although George Hanfmann and Hans Buchwald argue that the de-paganization and the Christianization of Sardis went slowly and dragged on for several centuries,[199] the abandonment and destruction of her famous Temple of Artemis took place quickly. By the middle of the fourth century, it had been completely abandoned, and part of it was buried by the deposits left from the flooding of a nearby stream. In fact, the church that was built adjacent (and attached) to the temple lies on top of nearly three feet of sediment deposited by the stream (and left unremoved). While perhaps pockets of paganism survived for a while in Sardis, it is significant to note that the most public, most famous, and most central temple in the city was abandoned rather quickly (by around 350), similar to the fate of many other temples in the Roman Empire.

This archaeological evidence corroborates the account of Eunapius, a writer living in Sardis in the mid-fourth century. In his *Lives of the Philosophers and Sophists,* he recounts that in 375 an official came to Sardis to try to revive pagan worship but only found "traces" of pagan temples.[200]

There are three visible eight-spoked ICHTHUS Christograms inscribed as graffiti at Sardis, along with more than twenty-five crosses of various shapes and sizes. Some of these crosses are inside of circles, creating four-spoked wheels.

The Temple of Artemis

Sardis boasted a spectacular temple dedicated to the goddess Artemis. Built and expanded over the years 300 BC to AD 150, it was the fourth

197. Marcus L. Rautman, "Sardis," in Finney, *The Eerdmans Encyclopedia of Early Christian Art and Archaeology,* 2:474; Tabbernee, "Asia Minor and Cyprus," 283–84; George M. A. Hanfmann and Hans Buchwald, "Christianity: Churches and Cemeteries," in Hanfmann, *Sardis: From Prehistoric to Roman Times,* 191.
198. Clive Foss, *Byzantine and Turkish Sardis* (Cambridge: Harvard University Press, 1976), 48–49; Hans Buchwald, with Anne McClanan, *Churches EA and E at Sardis,* Archaeological Exploration of Sardis (Cambridge: Harvard University Press, 2015), xiii–xv.
199. Hanfmann and Buchwald, "Churches and Cemeteries," 191–96.
200. Hanfmann and Buchwald, "Churches and Cemeteries," 194.

Fig. 5-42 Sardis, The Temple of Artemis

largest Ionic temple in the Greco-Roman world. During the Roman era, around the year AD 150, Sardis was granted permission to have an imperial cult temple, as at Ephesus, and emperor worship was added to the Temple of Artemis. The temple was modified to have two sacred rooms (called *cella*) where the statues of the idol gods and deified emperors stood. In one room, Artemis (Greek goddess) and Faustina (Roman empress) were worshiped, and in the other room, Zeus (Greek god) and Antoninus Pius (Roman emperor) were worshiped.[201] These two sacred inner rooms were aligned in an east-west direction and were accessed by stairway entrances at either end (visitors today typically approach the temple at the west entrance). This temple boasted huge columns—sixty-four in the Roman era—and several of these are still standing today (see fig. 5-42).

During the fourth century, as Christianity ascended politically, the temple at Sardis was apparently abandoned and allowed to be flooded and inundated with silt. During this time, the ongoing preventative measures and maintenance to protect the Temple of Artemis from flooding was halted, as well as the cleanup activities after the flooding. Hanfmann and Buchwald suggest that the dismantling and removal of parts of this temple for reuse elsewhere may have begun as early as the reign of Constantine.[202]

The temple was probably not abandoned simply due to the unstoppable flooding and sediment deposits. Flooding from major rivers sometimes was unstoppable, but at Sardis the flooding came from a small stream, maybe as a result of heavy rain or flash flooding. With the level of resources available, the authorities in Sardis could have contained the flooding or even rerouted the stream. Likewise, the cleanup effort after a flood would be minimal—not at all on the same level of repair needed after a major earthquake. This indicates the temple was either first abandoned (as other temples were in the fourth century) and then experienced flooding and sedimentation that was not cleaned up, or its financial resources had dried up due to Christian ascendancy, and it was then unable to address the flooding and the sedimentation problem.

At the same time or shortly afterward, the Temple of Artemis was de-demonized by the inscribing of twenty-five crosses (as graffiti), most of which are on the vertical stone doorway jambs for the eastern entrance

---

201. Wilson, *Biblical Turkey*, 296–98; Matthews, *Greco-Roman Cities*, 125–28.
202. Hanfmann and Buchwald, "Churches and Cemeteries," 193.

into the eastern *cella* (see figs. 5-43 and 5-44). Several crosses are also inscribed on the floor paving in this area. In addition to the crosses, the two Greek words "light" (φῶς, *phōs*) and "life" (ζωή, *zōē*) are informally inscribed—no doubt references to Jesus Christ. Several graffiti inscriptions combining "light" and "life," along with crosses, occur at Aphrodisias too.[203]

There are two ICHTHUS Christograms in this temple inscribed informally as graffiti. One is at the western entryway, located in the southwest corner on the main floor stone paving right after you step up onto the floor level. The other ICHTHUS Christogram is located at the other end of the temple, near the collection of crosses. It is inscribed on the floor stone slab of the threshold for the eastern entrance—the entryway into the eastern sacred room—where the idol statues of the gods stood (see fig. 5-45).

Fig. 5-43 Sardis, The Temple of Artemis, Eastern Entrance Threshold: ICHTHUS Christogram

Connected to the temple, a small church was built but on the southeastern edge of the temple, not in the midst of it. Its small size suggests that it was probably a chapel for the nearby cemetery. It also could have served as part of the temple cleansing and reclaiming. Archaeologists date this church to the fourth or fifth centuries.[204]

It is difficult to determine when the crosses and ICHTHUS Christograms were inscribed. They would not necessarily need to be connected to the time of the church construction. It is clear that all across the empire, once the pagan temples lost their power to defend themselves, Christians quickly removed their idols and cleansed the temples of demons through the power of the cross and the name of Jesus Christ. They were also proclaiming victory over the pagan forces and over the forces that oppressed them during the Great Persecution. It is likely, therefore, that around 350 or perhaps earlier, the Christians of Sardis, probably led by their bishop, marched into this temple to cleanse it from demons. They destroyed the idols and carved

203. Rouché, *Aphrodisias in Late Antiquity*, 183, 188; Hanfmann and Buchwald, "Churches and Cemeteries," 193.
204. Foss, *Byzantine and Turkish Sardis*, 48–49; Hanfmann and Buchwald, "Churches and Cemeteries," 193–95.

crosses and eight-spoked wheels into the stone floors, thresholds, and doorways of the temple, where the demons were believed to congregate and exert their influence.

At about the same time, many of the limestone columns of the temple were dismantled and burned to make lime (which was mixed with volcanic ash to make pozzolana cement), further desecrating the pagan temple.[205]

The Synagogue

A strong Jewish presence in Sardis, dating centuries before the coming of Christianity, continued into the Christian era. The synagogue discovered, excavated, and restored at Sardis is the largest known synagogue in the Roman Empire.

The synagogue is located on the main street of the city, adjacent to the equally impressive gymnasium. In fact, the main exterior walls of the synagogue were originally part of the gymnasium, probably used as dressing rooms, similar to (and parallel with) those that can be seen directly across the exercise field of the gymnasium to the north. The synagogue comprised a colonnaded entrance court (the forecourt, including a fountain) and a long assembly hall. Overall, it is over 250 feet (76 m) long and 60 feet (18 m) wide.[206] This synagogue was constructed in four major renovation and expansion states, reaching its final form in the mid-fourth century (with perhaps a few minor repairs completed in the fifth century). The forecourt was one of the final features added to the synagogue during the mid- to late fourth century (AD 360–380), a date determined by the coins discovered in that area.[207]

This synagogue has more than eighty inscriptions. Most of them occur either as professionally installed floor mosaics or as professional inscriptions written on stone (usually marble plaques) mounted on the walls. Six fragments are in Hebrew; the rest are in Greek. Most of the inscriptions honor synagogue members who financed construction of the various aspects of the synagogue's interior: "the mosaics on the floor, the marbling of the walls, and a number of architectural and ritual furnishings."[208] There are also a few inscribed menorahs.[209]

Peculiarly, an ICHTHUS Christogram graffito appears in the forecourt to this synagogue (see figs. 5-46 and 5-47). This Christogram is inscribed on

---

205. Wilson, *Biblical Turkey*, 129–30; Hanfmann and Buchwald, "Churches and Cemeteries," 193.

206. Andrew R. Seager and A. Thomas Kraabel, "The Synagogue and the Jewish Community," in Hanfmann, *Sardis: From Prehistoric to Roman Times*, 168–70, and see figs. 248–280; Foss, *Byzantine and Turkish Sardis*, 29–30.

207. Seager and Kraabel, "The Synagogue," 172–73; L. Michael White, *The Social Origins of Christian Architecture*, vol. 2, *Texts and Monuments for the Christian Domus Ecclesiae in Its Environment*, Harvard Theological Studies 42 (Valley Forge, PA: Trinity Press International, 1997), 318–21.

208. John H. Kroll, "The Greek Inscriptions of the Sardis Synagogue," *HTR* 94.1 (2001): 5.

209. Seager and Kraabel, "The Synagogue," 171.

a marble slab in the center of the entrance, right in front of the fountain and in a prominent location. It is similar in size to the many other eight-spoked Christogram graffiti found across the Greco-Roman world. This one is different in that it has a Greek letter inscribed in each pie-shaped segment of the wheel. Although some of the letters are not completely clear (due to wear), they appear to read: ΕΥΧΗΜΑΠΑ (probably to be read as: Εὐχὴ ΜΑΠΑ; euchē ΜΑΡΑ).

Fig. 5-44 Sardis, Synagogue/Fountain Courtyard: ICHTHUS Christogram with Letters

Although there is no clearly marked place in the circle where one is to start, John Kroll has suggested a logical starting point and arrangement as shown above, based on the recognizable and common word Εὐχὴ (ΕΥΧΗ, euchē).[210] This Greek word can mean "prayer," but in inscriptions it often refers to a vow or the fulfillment of a vow. Frequently, it refers to an offering or donation that was given. In nearby Aphrodisias, there are a number of inscriptions using the word Εὐχὴ (ΕΥΧΗ) to express

Fig. 5-45 Sardis, Synagogue/Fountain Courtyard: ICHTHUS Christogram Is in the Foreground, in Front of the Fountain, Between the Columns

a prayer or a vow, often accompanied with a cross at the beginning and end of the inscription.[211] This word also appears in other inscriptions in the synagogue at Sardis.[212]

The second half of the text, ΜΑΠΑ (ΜΑΡΑ), could perhaps be a name ("vow of Mapa"?), although there is no evidence elsewhere that Mapa is a name. Also, the letter M is not clear; it could possibly be an N.[213] Keep in mind that names are frequently abbreviated in inscriptions, especially graffiti inscriptions. That would be particularly appropriate here, where there are

---

210. Kroll, "The Greek Inscriptions of the Sardis Synagogue," 47.
211. See the discussion of this word, which occurs frequently in the inscriptions and graffiti of Aphrodisias, in Roueché, *Aphrodisias in Late Antiquity*, 172–75.
212. Kroll, "The Greek Inscriptions of the Sardis Synagogue," 16–45.
213. Several of these letters have experienced continuing deterioration and are difficult to read now. The discussions on which letters appear are based on pictures from twenty years ago.

only four remaining spaces in the pie of the wheel. At nearby Aphrodisias, where the abundant informal inscriptions provide an extensive database for comparison, many names are abbreviated. Because they are abbreviations, the specific translations of these names are often a bit speculative, but it is more certain that they are indeed names. Aphrodisias includes many examples where M, MA, Π, and ΠA appear to be name abbreviations. For example, one inscription in the Odeon reads MAYKOM: "Markos, Aurelios, Kometic."[214] Another graffiti inscription at Aphrodisias includes three symbols arranged vertically. The first is a cross. The next symbol looks like a fish symbol stood on its head, but in reality, it is the abbreviation for the common dual-letter combination of Greek ου. The final symbol is a capital M, probably an abbreviation for a name. Reynolds, Rouché, and Bodard suggest that this combination might mean "place of M"[215] but, no doubt, with a Christian identification due to the cross. For an example of ΠA as an abbreviation, an inscription in the Temple-Church area of Aphrodisias contains an abbreviated list of several names, with ΠA (PA) perhaps abbreviating the name Palmas.[216]

Working with both Latin and Greek graffiti in Rome, Guarducci explicates the complicated cryptography often used in the tomb of St. Peter, again frequently in association with known Christian symbols such as the Chi-Rho Christogram or the Tau-Rho Staurogram. She notes that M or MA often abbreviates Maria (Mary), P (Π in Greek) often represents Peter, A often refers to Christ from the *alpha-omega* usage (even if the A stands alone), and N often refers to the Greek νικα (*nika*, "victory").[217] The word Εὐχὴ (*euchē*, "prayer, vow, dedication") used next to a name can also be the "prayer of someone" or the "prayer to someone," so the MAΠA (MAPA) abbreviation can be the one praying or making the vow, or the one to whom the prayer or vow is dedicated.

At Aphrodisias, abbreviations for Mary (M) and for Peter (Π) occur in Christian inscriptions often alongside crosses and sometimes as part of monograms, along with numerous appearances of N as part of or abbreviating νικα (*nika*).[218] Furthermore, sometimes the letters M, A, and P are used in significant settings in association with crosses but without any clear indication of what the letters abbreviate. For example, one inscription contains a cross with a letter next to the end of each of the cross's four arms. The letter M stands next to the horizontal arms, and next to the two vertical arms is the letter A. Rouché tentatively suggests that it means "[gift of?] Mamas," but

214. Reynolds, Rouché, and Bodard, eds., *Inscriptions of Aphrodisias* (2007), See https://insaph.kcl.ac.uk/insaph/iaph2007/inscriptions/index.html; Banes, "A Comparative Approach to Graffiti," 379.
215. *IAph2007* 4.14; Banes, "A Comparative Approach to Graffiti," 429.
216. *IAph2007* 1.33ii; Banes, "A Comparative Approach to Graffiti," 369.
217. Guarducci, *The Tomb of St. Peter*, 100–106.
218. Rouché, *Aphrodisias in Late Antiquity*, 172–90.

Guarducci's study of inscriptions in Rome might suggest to us Mary for M and *alpha* (i.e., the Lord Jesus Christ) for A.[219]

Of special interest is one of the inscriptions on a theater seat at Aphrodisias, for it contains both the terms EYXH ("vow, prayer") and NIKA ("victory, triumph"). On one part of the seat is inscribed EYXHCTEΦANA (Eὐχὴ Στεφανα; vow/prayer of Stephana) and on another part, inscribed at a 90-degree angle to this first text, reads NIKAHTYXHTWN (Νικα ἡ τύχη των; "Victory is the fortune of . . .").[220] Next to this inscription is an ICHTHUS Christogram, with a Chi-Rho added to it,[221] adding to the plausibility, at least, of the word NIKA being associated with an ICHTHUS wheel.

In conclusion, we see that suggested understandings of these four letters in the ICHTHUS Christogram in the Sardis synagogue are tentative at best. Not only is it unclear exactly which letters are shown, but even if the letters are identified, abbreviated strings of letters can be next to impossible to decipher.

Aphrodisias may provide us with another helpful parallel situation for comparison. The famous temple to Aphrodite was converted to a Christian church around the year 500. The temple underwent an extensive renovation as part of this conversion to a church. When completed, this church had a number of combinations of crosses and Christian monograms informally inscribed on the vertical stone doorway threshold blocks. Throughout the church, there are professionally and formally constructed inscriptions honoring the major donors of the renovation. There are also several informal graffiti etchings using the word Eὐχὴ (*euchē*; "vow, prayer, dedication") followed by a name (vow of so-and-so) and then often a description of the person (deacon, lector, lute player). This is then followed by a series of single-letter abbreviations, which scholars have been unable to translate with any certainty. These informal inscriptions often have a cross at the beginning and at the end. Roueché notes that these informal inscriptions likewise honor donors.[222] This arrangement also occurs in Aphrodisias at the southern end of the western portico of the agora, where informally inscribed graffiti-style texts are honoring the donations and funding of the building by a Christian man named Albinus.[223]

These two examples from Aphrodisias seem to match the situation in the synagogue in Sardis, which has a number of formally and professionally inscribed tributes to the major financial donors who paid for renovations and expansions, along with the one informal eight-spoked wheel with Eὐχὴ located in a prominent place at the entryway. Adding plausibility to this

219. Roueché, *Aphrodisias in Late Antiquity*, 162. On page 163, Roueché presents a similar cross inscription that has adjacent to its four arms the letters Π, A, K, and the fish-looking symbol that represents Greek ου.

220. *IAph2007* 8.57.2a and 8.57.2bii; Banes, "A Comparative Approach to Graffiti," 414.

221. *IAph2007* 10.32Y.ii; Banes, "A Comparative Approach to Graffiti," 391.

222. Roueché, *Aphrodisias in Late Antiquity*, 172–77.

223. Roueché, *Aphrodisias in Late Antiquity*, 125–36.

theory, Jacobs cites several instances in late antiquity where donors were cele-brated after the completion of the architecture they financed by the addition of informal graffiti inscriptions. It could be concluded that this eight-spoked wheel may also be connected to a donor.[224]

The prominent placement of this eight-spoked wheel in the synagogue of Sardis is also interesting. Kroll, perhaps comparing this inscription to the many professionally inscribed, monumental-type inscriptions found else-where in the Sardis synagogue, concludes with a curious statement: "This humble, isolated graffito is presumably little more than a record of its inscrib-er's piety, for it seems impossible that it could refer to any part of the Syna-gogue's construction or ornamentation."[225] Kroll's use of the terms "humble" and "isolated" is rather puzzling, for this inscription is the most prominently placed and most noticeable inscription in the entire synagogue. It is located right in the entryway at the center of the forecourt, directly in front of the fountain. If practicing Jews washed their hands in that fountain (which had running water),[226] they would have to step over this inscription every time they entered the synagogue. Kroll is correct that this inscription is different from others in the synagogue, for the others all appear to be connected to the construction and ornamentation of the synagogue. Yet he never attempts to answer why this inscription is placed in such a prominent location. Indeed, the examples from Aphrodisias cited above, along with the prominent loca-tion, are fairly strong evidence that this εὐχή (euchē) inscription in Sardis was most likely placed here in front of the fountain by a major financial donor.

The Sardis synagogue presents several puzzling anomalies—features that set it apart from most other known synagogues of late antiquity (AD 200–600). First is its size: it is by far the largest synagogue known from late antiquity. Another peculiarity is the synagogue's location—right next to the gymna-sium, adjacent to the expansive field where athletes trained and competed while naked. The location is rather shocking in light of Jewish sensitivities regarding naked men competing in public (although by the time this syna-gogue was constructed, athletic training in gymnasiums all across the eastern Roman Empire was on the decline or had ceased altogether).

Furthermore, at the front of the main hall of the synagogue is an unusual marble table. Seager and Kraabel note that this feature is unique in syna-gogues, as far as they know. It is not the Torah shrine, which was apparently located at the other end of the synagogue in a niche on the wall closest to Jerusalem—that is, the easternmost wall, as was tradition. Seager and Kraabel propose that this marble table was perhaps used as a lectern for readings.[227] Yet this table has odd ornamentations. Two Roman imperial eagles, standing

---

224. Jacobs, "Cross Graffiti," 178.
225. Kroll, "The Greek Inscriptions of the Sardis Synagogue," 5.
226. Seager and Kraabel, "The Synagogue," 169.
227. Seager and Kraabel, "The Synagogue," 169–70.

upright and clutching thunderbolts, are built into the supporting legs, prominently visible. Calling this a "lectern" perhaps plays down the inappropriateness of the Roman imperial eagles supporting the table upon which the Torah was placed for reading (keep in mind that worship of the Roman imperial cult had been added to the nearby Temple of Artemis).

Besides eagles, there are two pairs of marble lions guarding each side of the table—images that probably were originally associated with the goddess Cybele (popular throughout Asia Minor) and probably taken from the Temple of Cybele.[228] Seager and Kraabel summarize the uniqueness of this synagogue. "Taken as a whole," they write, "the building has no close parallels." It is much larger than any other known synagogue. It lacks benches along the walls of the assembly hall, and it apparently lacks a women's gallery, all features typically present in extant synagogues, although there is not complete uniformity in synagogue architectural structure.[229]

Another oddity of this synagogue is the paucity of Jewish names in the inscriptions, even though Greek names are not unexpected in diaspora synagogues. Among the eighty inscriptions found in the Sardis synagogue, thirty names are mentioned, but only two of them are Jewish names; the rest are Greek.[230]

The final, and perhaps the most interesting, anomaly is an inscription, often called "the Regina inscription." Written in all Greek capitals, it translates in part: "with my wife Regina and our children, in fulfillment of a vow, I gave out of the gifts of Almighty [παντοκράτορος; pantokratoros] God all the . . ." This was followed by a short list of the things they apparently paid for. Unfortunately, this part of the inscription is damaged or missing. The word "God" (θεοῦ, theou) is abbreviated as ΘΥ (ThU), with a line clearly drawn above this abbreviation. This is a nonambiguous example of nomina sacra (see fig. 5-48).[231]

As discussed in chapter 2, nomina sacra show up regularly in early Christian literature as well as in inscriptions, in which divine names (and other related terms) are abbrevi-

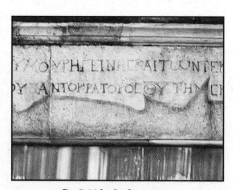

Fig. 5-46 Sardis, Synagogue: Inscription Using *Nomina Sacra*

228. Seager and Kraabel, "The Synagogue," 170.
229. Seager and Kraabel, "The Synagogue," 177.
230. Kroll, "The Greek Inscriptions of the Sardis Synagogue," 8.
231. James R. Edwards, "'A Nomen Sacrum' in the Sardis Synagogue," *JBL* 128.4 (2009): 814–15. For a picture of the inscription fragments placed together, see Seager and Kraabel, "The Synagogue," fig. 270. For a picture of the cast reproduction, see Edwards, 815.

ated (usually keeping the first and last letters) and then marked with an over-head line. *Nomina sacra* appear in church mosaics as well. Although recognizing that the driving force behind the origins of this Christian practice may be indebted to the way Jewish scribes handled the divine name, Hurtado concludes that "along with the codex, the *nomina sacra* should be counted among our earliest extant evidence of a visual and material 'culture' that can be identified as Christian."[232] That is, everywhere else—and there are so many examples—that this practice occurs, the *nomina sacra* is in a Christian context. Why, then, is this common Christian literary practice being used in a synagogue?

Equally unusual for a synagogue, and much more to be expected in a Christian context, is the use in this same inscription of the Greek word παντοκράτορος (*pantokratoros*, "Almighty, ruler over everything"). In the Septuagint (the Greek translation of the Old Testament), this word is used frequently to translate the Hebrew word *Saboath* ("Almighty"), so *pantokratoros* is certainly in the Jewish repertoire of Greek words to use for God. Yet none of the other Jewish inscriptions in the Sardis synagogue use the word *pantokratoros* for referencing God. Instead, ten times they use the term πρόνοια (*pronoia*; "Providence").[233]

On the other hand, this Greek word (the root is παντοκράτωρ, *pantokratōr*) plays a huge role in Christian literature and theology. It appears nine times in the book of Revelation (1:8; 4:8; 11:17; 15:3; 16:7, 14; 19:6, 15; and 21:22), referring to the Lord as *pantokratōr*. Wilhelm Michaelis writes that in Christian patristic literature, "it was used to express the universalist claim of Christianity."[234] Revelation 1:8 reads, "'I am the Alpha and the Omega,' says the Lord God, 'who is, and who was, and who is to come, the Almighty [παντοκράτωρ, *pantokratōr*].'" The *alpha* and *omega* became two of the most widely used and most recognizable Christian symbols in early Christianity. The term *pantokratōr* was closely associated with the *alpha* and *omega* symbolism, as well as with the claim of Christian victory and the universal rule of Christ. Indeed, the term *pantokratōr* appears frequently in Christian inscriptions.[235] Likewise, the opening line of the Nicene Creed (AD 325) reads, "I believe in God, the Father, Almighty [*pantokratōr*]." In the

---

232. Hurtado, *Earliest Christian Artifacts*, 120–21. Examples of *nomina sacra* are common in the early Christian papyri (e.g., P45, P46, P66, P75). See the pictorial evidence in Hurtado, *Earliest Christian Artifacts*, 233–38. Early inscriptional evidence for *nomina sacra*, perhaps the earliest (tentatively dated to the third century AD), is from a mosaic floor inscription discovered at Kefar 'Othnay near Megiddo in Israel. See Tepper and Di Segni, *A Christian Prayer Hall*, 34–41.

233. Edwards, "Nomen Sacrum," 816.

234. Wilhelm Michaelis, "παντοκράτωρ," *TDNT* 3:914–15.

235. Citing only those inscriptions that include the Greek term *pantokratōr* along with clear Christian identification (such as crosses or the name Jesus Christ) include *ICG* 278; *SEG* 30:1064; *SEG* 1:139; *IG* II 13517; *RIChrM* 15; *IG* X 289.80; *IG–XI* Bandy 106; *IG–XI* Bandy 98; *MAMA* I.170; *MAMA* III.577a; *IGLSyr* 5.2541 (this inscription has an *alpha* and *omega* following the word *pantokratōr*); *IGchrEg* 64; *IGchrEg* 634; Milne, *Cairo Mus.* 32,9273; *SB* 3:6186; *SEG* 24:1194; *Faras* IV 26,4; and *IG* XIV 187.

Orthodox Christian tradition, the name Christ *Pantokrator* continues to be a common and iconic reference to the Lord Jesus Christ.

In the case of the synagogue, the use of *pantokratōr* in an inscription that also uses the *nomina sacra* certainly suggests Christian involvement. If this inscription had been discovered anywhere except in a synagogue, it would have been identified as Christian without question.

What are the possible explanations? Were Regina and her husband Christian patrons of the synagogue? Or perhaps the mason who chiseled the inscription was a Christian, or at any rate familiar with the Christian practice of *nomina sacra* and the connotations of the word *pantokratōr*. Perhaps the division between Christians and Jews was not as clear-cut as sometimes assumed, especially in material culture. Or perhaps, as Edwards concludes, the most plausible interpretation is to see this particular inscription as evidence pointing to a Jewish origin for the *nomina sacra*.[236]

Yet everywhere else in the Greco-Roman world throughout the early Christian era *nomina sacra* usage is interpreted to be a sign of Christian provenance, just as the eight-spoked ICHTHUS Christogram was a symbol used by the Christians in much the same way as the cross was used. Taken by themselves, each of these could perhaps be dismissed as an anomaly; taken together, they support each other in their Christian identity.

A few other observations about Sardis are worthwhile to mention, although this data does not necessarily lead to any firm conclusions about why someone took a hammer and chisel and inscribed an eight-spoked wheel in the entryway of the synagogue. In the late second century, Melito, bishop of Sardis, writes *Peri Pascha*, one of the most explicit early Christian works judging Israel for executing Jesus Christ. A generation later, the Jews in Sardis build the largest, most expensive, and most visible synagogue known in the Greco-Roman world. Is there a connection between these two events? Some scholars have surmised that Melito's message must have come out of the social setting in Sardis (hostility between Christians and Jews, with the Christian perhaps being jealous of the high social and economic standing of the Jews in Sardis). Others, drawing from the scattered material evidence from the archaeology of the site, have argued against this thesis, stressing that the relationship between Jews and Christians in Sardis during the early church era was friendly and congenial.[237] Both points, however, are probably moot, for Melito's second-century *Peri*

---

236. Edwards, "Nomen Sacrum," 820. Yet note that Christian usage of *nomina sacra* is attested to earlier than this synagogue inscription.

237. See the discussions by A. Thomas Kraabel, "Impact of the Discovery of the Sardis Synagogue," in Hanfmann, *Sardis: From Prehistoric to Roman Times*, 178–90; Keir E. Hammer and Michele Murray, "Acquaintances, Supporters, and Competitors: Evidence of Inter-Connectedness and Rivalry among the Religious Groups in Sardis," in *Religious Rivalries and the Struggle in Sardis and Smyrna*, ed. Richard S. Ascough (Waterloo, ON: Wilfrid Laurier, 2005), 175–95.

Pascha has absolutely nothing to do with the social, religious, and economic situation of third-century Sardis.[238]

Yet it is interesting to note that the date for the forecourt entrance expansion, the installation of the fountain with running water, and the eight-spoked wheel came in the second half of the fourth century, after the Great Persecution had ended and Constantine had elevated the power and fortune of Christianity. The timing seems to at least suggest a Christian influence or reaction behind the eight-spoked wheel, which in so many other contexts is clearly used as a Christogram.

Complicating matters is an article written by Israeli archaeologist Jodi Magness in which she challenges the widely accepted fourth-century date for the construction and renovation of this area into a synagogue. The archaeologists who excavated and restored the synagogue found many coins dating to the fourth century under the floor paving and mosaics, driving them to conclude that the project occurred primarily in the fourth century. The cutoff date they give, based on these coins, is 380. Magness points out that they also found several coins dating after 380, a number of which date to the fifth and even sixth centuries. Interestingly, most of these were found in the forecourt, although a few were found in the main hall. Magness concludes that the Sardis synagogue, and the forecourt in particular, was constructed, renovated, or converted into a synagogue in the sixth century, challenging the earlier, widely held view.[239]

Did Christians take over the synagogue at some point? This is commonly rejected by those writing on Sardis and the synagogue (although they are probably unaware that the eight-spoked wheel is most likely a Christogram). Yet Hanfmann and Buchwald write, "More remarkable is the fact that the Synagogue was not transformed into a Christian Church."[240] In quite a few places throughout the empire, not only temples, but also synagogues were destroyed or replaced by churches, a phenomenon that became more prevalent in the sixth century.[241]

---

238. Lynn Cohick, "Melito of Sardis's *PERI PASCHA* and Its 'Israel,'" *HTR* 91.4 (1998): 351–72.

239. Jodi Magness, "The Date of the Sardis Synagogue in Light of the Numismatic Evidence," *American Journal of Archaeology* 109.3 (2005): 443–75.

240. Hanfmann and Buchwald, "Churches and Cemeteries," 194.

241. Fine cites a number of instances throughout the area where, in new church construction, the Christians reused *spolia* (finished stones from earlier structures) that came from Jewish facilities, most likely synagogues. See Steven Fine, "Synagogues as Foci of Multi-Religious and Ideological Confrontation? The Case of the Sardis Synagogue," in *Jerusalem and Other Holy Places as Foci of Multireligious and Ideological Confrontation*, Jewish and Christian Perspectives 37, ed. Pieter B. Hartog et al. (Leiden: Brill, 2020), 104–5. For a discussion on a specific case, see Estēe Dvorjetski, "The Synagogue-Church at Gerasa in Jordan: A Contribution to the Study of Ancient Synagogues," *Zeitschrift des Deutschen Palästina-Vereins* 121.2 (2005):158–59. Dvorjetski, 158–59, notes that synagogues were converted to churches at Stobi, Gerasa, and Apamea (based on archaeological evidence) and at Callinicum, Adessa in Asia Minor, Ravenna, and elsewhere in Italy, Mauritania, Spain, Gaul, and Syria (based on literary sources).

Hammer and Murray present another interesting and plausible scenario. They note that in 364 in the nearby city of Laodicea, a group of Anatolian bishops held a council and issued a number of canons. Several of these canons were directed at Christians who seemed to have embraced Jewish practices or who were participating with the Jews in worship activities. Hammer and Murray argue that these canons suggest that the intermixing of Christian and Jewish practice must have been a significant problem of the church in western Anatolia, since the bishops saw fit to address it specifically. They note that these regulations imply that Christians were not just embracing some Jewish practices but were worshiping with them.[242] This could explain the use of the *nomina sacra* in the Regina inscription from the Sardis synagogue, which dates to a similar time period.[243] These benefactors could be Christian patrons (and probably participants) worshiping in, or at least financially supporting, the synagogue. Yet this scenario doesn't quite answer the eight-spoked wheel usage. If that wheel stands for "Jesus Christ God's Son Savior," it is hard to imagine that the Jewish leadership in the synagogue would allow a Christian to inscribe that symbol right in the main entryway without a compelling reason.

Perhaps the most plausible explanation for the presence of an ICHTHUS wheel in the forecourt of the synagogue relates to the nature of the fountain and the status of the forecourt in relation to the rest of the synagogue that the presence of the fountain implies. Among the many inscriptions discovered in the city of Sardis, there is one that lists out the public fountains of the city, including the Fountain of the Synagogue. If this is a reference to the big basin in the forecourt of the synagogue—as seems likely—then that area (the forecourt) would most likely have been a public fountain and would have functioned as civic space. Technically, it would not have been viewed as part of the synagogue.[244]

The purpose of the fountain-list inscription in Sardis seems to be connected to the issue of authority given to the entities associated with each fountain to use the city water system, along with, in some cases, the actual specified quantity of water that could be used (the inscription has some damage, and some portions are not legible). This is not unusual, for typically the supply of water to a populous Roman-era city and the way it

---

242. Hammer and Murray, "Acquaintances, Supporters, and Competitors," 190–91. For example, Canon 29 reads, "Christians must not judaize by resting on the Sabbath, but must work on that day." Canon 38 reads, "It is not lawful to receive unleavened bread from the Jews, not to be partakers of their impiety." Translations from Philip Schaff and Henry Wace, eds., *Nicene and Post-Nicene Fathers*, vol. 14, *The Seven Ecumenical Councils* (New York: Charles Scribner's Sons, 1900; repr., Peabody, MA: Hendrickson, 2004), 148–51.

243. Based on the datable coins found throughout the synagogue excavations, Seager and Kraabel conclude, "The Synagogue in its final form thus seems to have taken shape beginning a decade or two before the middle of the fourth century, perhaps a bit earlier, (i.e., 320–340), with installation of the mosaics continuing a decade or more after mid-century" ("The Synagogue," 173).

244. Seager and Kraabel, "The Synagogue," 169. See the inscription and translation in W. H. Buckler and David M. Robinson, *Sardis: Publications of the American Society for the Excavation of Sardis; Greek and Latin Inscriptions*, vol. 7, part 1 (Leiden: Brill, 1932), 39.

was distributed was tightly controlled and regulated.[245] In nearby Laodicea, for example, the Fountain of Trajan contains an extensive inscription dealing with "Water Law." It "states the usage of water, its control, preservation, distribution, the officials in charge, and the fines for those causing damage, contamination and unfair distribution, as well as those not abiding by the rules."[246]

Unlike today, cities like ancient Sardis did not have water lines in every street to which any house or business could connect. This narrows down the possibilities for the fountain in question. Since 1) a public fountain was designated as the "Fountain of the Synagogue," 2) this fountain in the forecourt was connected into the city water system (and the city sewer system), and 3) this fountain was in a significant and strategic location, then almost certainly this fountain was a public fountain and not restricted to synagogue usage only.[247]

Expanding on this argument, note that the term used in the city inscription for this Fountain of the Synagogue (and the other fountains) is κρήνη (krēnē), the common term used for monumental public fountains during this era. Second, common to public fountains, this fountain was accessible to many people. This fountain and its associated courtyard (perhaps the term "forecourt" is misleading and the term "courtyard" should be used)[248] is along the main roadway of Sardis. Actually, it is at the *intersection* of two main streets—one along the south side of the synagogue, shops, and public latrine, and one along the east side of the synagogue and gymnasium. This courtyard with the fountain was accessible from both streets.

Supporting this is that the fountain courtyard had two entrances. Along with the main entrance to the courtyard from the east—the entrance that aligned straight with the entrance to the synagogue—there was another, smaller (yet still eight to ten feet wide) entrance from the south, allowing access from the main road. A secondary entrance from the south is another anomaly for synagogues.

Furthermore, all along the south side of the fountain courtyard and the synagogue, indeed even sharing the southern wall of the courtyard and

---

245. Buckler and Robinson, *Sardis*, 39. It is interesting to note that in the British Museum is a papyrus document (No. 1,177) dating to 113 that reflects an accounting by the water commissioners of the town of Arsinoë, an important city in Egypt. In this document the commissioners list out water distributions to different fountains and other locations, along with who paid for each allocation. One payment comes from "the officers of the synagogue of the Theban Jews." Another payment is for water at "the house of prayer." For the text of this papyrus document, see Naphtali Lewis and Meyer Reinhold, eds., *Roman Civilization: Selected Readings*, vol. 2, *The Empire*, 3rd ed. (New York: Columbia University Press, 1990), 243–44.

246. Şimşek, "Statue Group of Trajan," 89–90.

247. See the extensive study of public fountains in the Roman East (where Sardis is located) in Richard, *Monumental Fountains in the Roman East*.

248. That is, if this fountain is for public use, then this area around the fountain does not serve as the "forecourt" to the synagogue but just as a public courtyard.

synagogue, was a group of small shops and residences.[249] This fountain most likely served these shops and residences through the southern entrance. This fountain would have served the many travelers along these main two roads, along with the many participants in the synagogue (capacity for over a thousand people).[250]

This evidence strongly implies that this fountain and the courtyard were in public space and not just there for Jews to perform purification rituals before entering the synagogue. Note that the courtyard division and the addition of the fountain were part of the final stage in the development of the synagogue. A likely scenario for its installation could be that the Jewish community wanted clean running water at their beautiful, prominent synagogue, and the people living in that area and working in those shops also wanted a nearby, reliable clean water supply (an improvement over the roof and rainwater collection system they were using).[251] That kind of water was only available through the city-controlled supply. To get it, the synagogue (and the shop owners) had to place the fountain in a public area, probably along with paying for it. The location at the intersection of two main thoroughfares would have had its appeal to the city planners. Thus, a courtyard at the front of the synagogue was designated for this and renovated accordingly, with the addition of a barrier wall and a new entrance to the synagogue. The fountain was installed, and running water from the city system was connected. The runoff from this fountain went to an arched sewer that ran along the wall between and below the shops and the synagogue. This drain then turned north to cross under the synagogue and under the entire exercise field of the gymnasium. This theory means the so-called forecourt of the synagogue was really a courtyard containing the public Fountain of the Synagogue.

It is possible that the donor who paid for this fountain and the courtyard renovations may not have even been connected to the synagogue but rather a Christian who undertook this project as part of a vow. Since it was public space, if the donor was a Christian, then he or she may have been allowed to use a Christian symbol as part of their dedication. Inscriptions of dedica-

249. For a discussion of these shops and residences, see John Stevens Crawford, "The Byzantine Shops," in Hanfmann, *Sardis: From Prehistoric to Roman Times*, 161–67; and John Stevens Crawford, *The Byzantine Shops at Sardis*, Archaeological Exploration of Sardis 9 (Cambridge, MA: Harvard University Press, 1990). For pictures and layout of the entrance to the fountain courtyard coming from the shop area, see *The Byzantine Shops at Sardis*, fig. 4–5, pp. 559–560, and 576.
250. For a discussion of the terminology for public monumental fountains during the era and in this region, along with a discussion of the frequent location of public fountains near thoroughfares and public spaces like market areas and near clusters of shops, see Richard, *Monumental Fountains in the Roman East*, 1–2, 20–27, 189–214. Richard, 211–12, specifically addresses this cluster of shops at Sardis. For a discussion regarding the relationship between urban workshops and urban water supply systems of this era, see López, "Water Supply to Urban Workshops in Roman Times."
251. López, "Water Supply to Urban Workshops in Roman Times," underscores the important reliance of urban workshops on city public water systems, https://doi.org/10.1007/s12685-023-00323-4.

tion by private donors and benefactors were common for public monumental fountains during the time and in this region.[252]

It is also possible that this Christogram was not placed by the one who paid for the initial construction of the fountain but by the ones who were paying the ongoing fee for using the water when the inscription was made. Every year someone had to pay for the city water that was being used, and these benefactors would change over time.[253] There were a number of complicated legal water-rights issues involved with constructing and operating a public fountain that used city water. Often the users—not the city water commissioners—were responsible for paying to maintain the system.[254] This might explain the somewhat informal look of the inscription, which may have been placed by a fountain benefactor after the initial construction of the fountain. This benefactor could easily have been a Christian and agreed to this benefaction in relation to a vow taken.

Although it may seem strange (and anti-Semitic) to us today, another factor to consider is that many Christian leaders and writers of this era viewed Jewish synagogues as equally evil as the pagan temples and as places that needed cleansing and the driving away of demons.[255] This Christogram could be serving the purpose of cleansing the fountain area from the synagogue-associated demons.

Related to this, and noted throughout this study, is the observation that a variety of crosses, as well as ICHTHUS Christograms, appear in water-related facilities. One study noted that in twenty-one water storage facilities (reservoirs and cisterns) in Israel dating to late antiquity, thirty-five crosses had been inscribed or painted.[256] This study proposes several possible explanations for why crosses appear in association with water installations. Possibly it was to protect the facility (water systems were prone to break down, and the possibility of earthquakes was a reality throughout the region). Relatedly, perhaps the crosses were to drive away demons, often associated with water systems. Finally, perhaps the crosses were there to provide a certain purification function. These three reasons can be interrelated; they are not mutually exclusive.[257]

252. Richard, *Monumental Fountains in the Roman East*, 239–42.

253. As noted above, there is a papyrus from Egypt indicating that accounts were kept by a city's water commissioners, listing out water distributions to different fountains along with who paid for each allocation. Many of the payments were from individual benefactors. For the text of this papyrus document, see Lewis and Reinhold, *Roman Civilization*, 243–44.

254. For a good discussion on the complicated issue of water rights and water usage in the Roman Empire, especially in regard to time commitments from both the supplier and the user, see Cosima Möller, "Time as an Argument in Roman Water Law," *Water History* 15 (2023).

255. See, for example, the homilies entitled *Adversus Judaeos* (*Against the Jews*) by John Chrysostom (347–407), bishop of Antioch. For a discussion on John Chrysostom and his view of the synagogue as a place for demons, see Kalleres, *City of Demons*, 93–112.

256. Humphreys, "Crosses as Water Purification Devices," 229–46.

257. Humphreys, "Crosses as Water Purifications Devices," 229–46. See also Crow, "Monumental Aqueduct Bridge," 157–80.

Another water facility of interest is the Heroon of Androclos in Ephesus (a heroon was a monument honoring a hero). This heroon included a fountain with a large rectangular water basin from which people could draw water. At some point in early Christianity, the Christians replaced the front four stone panels of this water basin with panels that contained crosses, as at other fountains in Ephesus and Laodicea.[258] The fountain in Ephesus also has an ICHTHUS wheel etched on the street directly in front of and adjacent to the wall panels that have crosses. This is one of the few eight-spoked Christograms that, like the one in the synagogue at Sardis, has letters in it. There are two clear, legible letters in the eight-spoked wheel at the fountain in Ephesus: π (*pi*) and ε (*epsilon*). Although we do not know for certain what the letters represent, it is plausible that the ε (*epsilon*) represents εὐχὴ (*euchē*, "prayer, vow, dedication"), as in the eight-spoked wheel in the synagogue in Sardis, and the π (*pi*) represents the name of someone. At any rate, the similarities are significant: eight-spoked wheels etched into the stone pavement directly in front of a fountain, one with the word εὐχὴ (*euchē*) and one with the letter ε (*epsilon*) that could mean *euchē*.

Finally, in one of the shops of Sardis that shared a wall with the synagogue, a water basin was formed by reusing two large flat stones with inscriptions on them. The inscriptions were rubbed down slightly to make them less legible and to allow for a new inscription. Then two Latin crosses were inscribed on the stones. This cross-inscribed water basin is similar to those found at Ephesus and Laodicea that have crosses inscribed on the front stone wall panels. Crawford suggests that these crosses in the shop at Sardis identify it as Christian with Christian owners,[259] but there may be more to it than that. It is possible that the crosses carry some special connection to protecting or purifying the water in the basin.

In conclusion, although the exact meaning of the letters inscribed in the graffito remain uncertain, it seems highly likely that this eight-spoked wheel in this fountain courtyard next to the Sardis synagogue is an ICHTHUS Christogram, similar to the dozens of others we have examined in this study, including those inscribed in the nearby Temple of Artemis. The location of the fountain, the identification of a "Fountain of the Synagogue" connected to the city water supply, and the presence of an additional doorway all suggest that this area with the ICHTHUS Christogram was not viewed strictly as the forecourt but as a water distribution courtyard open to all in that community. In all likelihood, this Christogram was produced by a Christian benefactor to honor their Christian faith, proclaim the name of Jesus Christ, and to cleanse the fountain, synagogue, and street intersection of evil forces.

---

258. Miszczak, *The Secrets of Ephesus*, 143–44.
259. Crawford, *The Byzantine Shops of Sardis*, 18. See the picture in fig. 68.

CHAPTER 6

THE EIGHT-SPOKED ICHTHUS
CHRISTOGRAM IN THE BALKAN PENINSULA
(GREECE, MACEDONIA, AND PANNONIA)

INTRODUCTION

In Acts 16:6–10, God gave Paul a vision, calling him from Asia Minor into Macedonia. Paul and his colleagues quickly complied, and in Acts 16–18 they planted churches in Macedonia (Philippi, Thessalonica, Berea) and Greece (Corinth). Acts 18:11 records that Paul stayed in Corinth for a year and a half. No doubt during this time the gospel continued to spread throughout the region, including north up to Pannonia. In Romans 15:19b, Paul summarized his ministry at that time as follows: "So from Jerusalem all the way around to Illyricum, I have fully proclaimed the gospel of Christ." Illyricum was the name of the Roman province that included this area, north of Greece, up to and including Pannonia.

By the beginning of the fourth century, Christianity was firmly established throughout this region. Although almost no church structures remain from this early time (the Christians were still meeting in private houses), Christian symbols and epitaphs appear on funerary monuments produced throughout the third century, and there are literary records of bishops being appointed in cities throughout this region. Further indicating the presence of Christianity at the beginning of the fourth century, literary records indicate that many Christians in this region were martyred in the Great Persecution (AD 303–313).[1]

---

1.   Julia Valeva and Athanasios K. Vionis, "The Balkan Peninsula," in Tabbernee, *Early Christianity in Contexts*, 321–66.

The Christianization of this region in the fourth and early fifth centuries progressed similarly as in other areas. Pagan idols were removed, beheaded, or defaced. Pagan temples were closed or destroyed, their expensive columns and building blocks reused in other structures. Churches and other Christian buildings (bishop residences, hospitals, monasteries, etc.) were built all across the region, especially in the cities. The number of Christians in the region mushroomed, churches grew, and the number of appointed bishops expanded. Throughout this time, more and more secular rulers and administrators, as well as wealthy landowners and public benefactors, became Christians, adding impetus for the removal of the pagan statues and the cleansing of the pagan temples with Christian symbols.

DELPHI

The Sacred Complex at Delphi
Delphi was a small, ancient, and influential city located in the province of Achaia, the southern part of Greece. It was to the northwest and across the Gulf of Corinth from the nearby city of Corinth (capital of Achaia). It was primarily a sacred city, built up around its central feature and asset, the Temple of Apollo. This temple was the home of the most famous oracle in the ancient world, the so-called Pythia, a priestess who officiated at the temple and was believed to receive pronouncements and oracles from Apollo himself, using bubbling water from a spring in the temple's interior. With a history reaching back a millennium before the advent of Christianity, Delphi, the Temple of Apollo, and the Pythia oracle appear frequently in ancient Greek literature from the sixth century BC on. The ancient Greeks considered Delphi the "center of the world."[2] The Temple of Apollo and the Pythia oracle associated with it composed perhaps the most famous pagan sacred site in the Greco-Roman world as the Christian era dawned. It now draws more than two million visitors per year.

As the Romans conquered Greece and expanded their empire to the east, Delphi achieved somewhat of an independent status. Many of the Roman emperors either visited Delphi, consulted the Pythia oracle there, or honored the city with money and dedications. As imperial cult worship spread throughout the Roman Empire, statues of deified Roman emperors were added to the streets and temples of Delphi. The Pythian Games, perhaps the most famous temple-related festival in the early Roman Empire, were held every four years.[3] Although the Temple of Apollo and several other pagan temples dated back centuries before the Romans, much of the rest of the city

---

2. For a good discussion of the possible origins of Delphi, references to it in ancient Greek literature, and a history of the site and the oracle, see Michael Scott, *Delphi: A History of the Center of the Ancient World* (Princeton, NJ: Princeton University Press, 2014).
3. Scott, *Delphi: A History*, 200–239.

was built or seriously renovated during the first and second centuries, as was true of many cities in the Roman Empire. This included the addition of a theater, hippodrome, colonnaded streets, fountains, pools, an agora, and a gymnasium with bathhouses.

Delphi started into a period of slow decline as early as the third century, so the city entered the fourth century—that century when all across the Roman Empire pagan temples were challenged, closed, cleansed of demons, and abandoned or destroyed—already in a slightly weakened position. Yet Delphi and the Temple of Apollo retained their power and fame; the institution would not be taken down easily. In the fourth century, Delphi continued to erect statues in the agora honoring each ruling emperor of the Roman Empire as they came to throne, even though, after Constantine, most of these emperors were Christians and several issued edicts against paganism. No doubt the fourth century was tense in Delphi.

Writing in the early fourth century, Eusebius, a bishop and church historian for Constantine, noted that in his time only the oracles of Delphi, Claros, and Didyma (i.e., the three most famous) were still operating (*Preparation for the Gospel* 5.16). From this we know that the Pythian oracle at Delphi was still functioning in the early fourth century. In spite of the rising Christian hostility against the pagan temples, and even though the emperor was a strong supporter of Christianity, as late as 342 to 344 Delphi received an encouraging reply from the emperor Constantius II, the son of Constantine, that the Temple of Apollo and the oracle could continue.

After Constantius's death, however, Julian the Apostate became emperor. He championed pagan worship and wanted to minimize Christianity and return the Roman Empire to paganism. Accordingly, he was a strong supporter of Delphi and of the Pythia oracle at the Temple of Apollo. Julian sent one of his advisors and friends to Delphi to consult with the Pythian priestess about his imperial matters. Although there is some controversy about the response, many scholars take this to be the last oracle of the Pythia at the Temple of Apollo. The oracle stated: "Tell the king the fair wrought hall is fallen to the ground. No longer has Phoebus [a reference to Apollo] a hut, nor a prophetic laurel, nor a spring that speaks. The water of speech even is quenched." Julian only reigned a few short years (AD 361–363); he was killed in battle shortly after this oracle.[4] With him died any hope the pagan institutions had of being restored to power. This oracle was bleak, and there is no record of any further activity from the Pythia at Delphi after this. In fact,

---

4. Scott, *Delphi: A History*, 243. For a good discussion of the literary sources involved in retrieving this oracle and of the controversy surrounding whether this was an oracle from Delphi or from Daphne, see Timothy E. Gregory, "Julian and the Last Oracle at Delphi," *Greek, Roman and Byzantine Studies* 24.4 (1983): 355–66. Defending the Delphi location, Gregory, 366, notes that "Delphi was the pagan oracle *par excellence*" and was a "convenient symbol of opposition" to Christianity. In this final oracle, the Christians probably saw this "confession of its powerlessness" as "a significant victory for Christianity."

some surmise that this oracle itself is an indication that prophetic activity by the Pythia at Delphi had already ceased and that the Temple of Apollo was no longer functioning. Indeed, Gregory of Nazianzus, archbishop of Constantinople, proclaims not long after this: "No longer does the oak shine . . . nor does the Pythia provide information. Again Kastalia [the water source used by the Pythian priestess] has been silenced, and is silent, and the water is not prophetic but laughable" (*Oratio in laudem Basilii*, 5.25).[5]

In 365, just two years after Julian's death, a severe earthquake struck Greece, severely damaging Delphi and the Temple of Apollo. In the early 370s, the city of Delphi erected statues in the agora honoring the emperors Valentinian (ruled briefly in AD 364) and Valens (ruled AD 364–378), continuing their tradition of honoring the ruling emperors. The inscription on the bases of these statues thanked them for being benefactors. Perhaps the emperors had provided money to help the city recover from the earthquake, though it is unlikely that they repaired the Temple of Apollo. One significant and revealing change appears in these inscriptions. Earlier inscriptions honoring emperors and other benefactors in Delphi referred to the city with a technical term that meant "sacred place" (Gr. *hiera*), but these two inscriptions lack that reference, perhaps indicating that the temple was no longer functioning.[6]

In one of his poems (AD 405), Paulinus of Nola, a member of the Roman senatorial aristocracy who had converted to Christianity in 378, exults in the victory of Christianity over paganism throughout the Roman Empire. He writes, "Holiness has gained the ascendant in almost every nation. . . . All Rome is called by Christ's holy name. . . . Egypt will not stupidly worship cattle under the name of Apis . . . nor Greece superfluously consult any longer a Delphi now silent, but rather despise and grind underfoot her own Olympus as she mounts higher to Sion [Zion], where Christ sets high His soft yoke on a lofty summit of this kindly hill."[7]

It is not known exactly when Christianity arrived in Delphi, but Paul, along with Priscilla, Aquila, Silas, Timothy, and Apollos, ministered in Achaia from Corinth for several years in the mid-first century (Acts 18), spreading Christianity throughout the region. A church was definitely planted here, for at some point Delphi became the seat of a bishop.[8] French and Greek archaeologists have been working in Delphi for over one hundred years.[9] A local village had spread out over a portion of the ancient city, making archaeological remains for this time period sparse for some areas, but there is archaeo-

5.   Cited by Gregory, "Julian and the Last Oracle at Delphi," 360.
6.   Scott, *Delphi: A History*, 244.
7.   Paulinus of Nola, *Poems* xix, in P. G. Welsh, *The Poems of St. Paulinus of Nola* (New York: Newman, 1975); cited by Lewis and Reinhold, eds., *Roman Civilization: Selected Readings*, 617.
8.   Amandry, "Chronique delphique," 736.
9.   Scott, *Delphi: A History*, 269–85.

logical evidence that there were three churches built in Delphi during the late fifth to sixth centuries.[10]

The Temple of Apollo and the Altar of the Chians

Writers throughout the classical Greek and Roman eras extolled the grandeur and beauty of the Temple of Apollo at Delphi. The Pythia at Delphi and her oracles also are mentioned numerous times in Greco-Roman literature. Like the other great temples at Ephesus, Didyma, and Pirene, the exterior was comprised of gigantic columns—six across and fifteen deep, huge in both diameter and height. The temple was approximately 73 feet (22 m) wide and 192 feet (58 m) long. Today you can only catch a glimpse of what the ancient temple looked like. The basic floor foundations remain, and archaeologists have stacked some broken column pieces to semi-restore a handful of columns.

Of special interest to this study is the altar in front of the Temple of Apollo (see fig. 6-1). This huge altar, often referred to as the Altar of the Chians, measured approximately 28 feet (8.6 m) long by 16.8 feet (5.1 m) wide by 6 to 10 feet high (1.8–3.0 m). It was funded by the city of Chios, perhaps in the third century BC (although there is some disagreement about this date). Much of this altar has been reconstructed from the original stones discovered nearby, and it stands prominently in front of the Temple of Apollo. Yet what we

Fig. 6-1 Delphi, Temple of Apollo, Altar of the Chians in the Foreground

see reconstructed today is only the platform on which the actual altar stood. That is, missing from this reconstruction are the steps up to this platform (on which the priests stood) and the elaborate square altar structure (perhaps measuring about 4 by 4 by 3 ft. high) on which they sacrificed animals.[11] About one-third of the large, flat, dark gray marble stones that comprised the top level of the altar, on which the priests stood, were discovered and placed in the reconstruction. These

10. Vincent Déroche and Platon Pétridis, "Delphi," in Finney, *The Eerdmans Encyclopedia of Early Christian Art and Archaeology*, 1:409–10; Platon Pétridis and Kalliopi Dimou, "La redécouverte de Delphes protobyzantine," *PALLAS* 87 (2011): 267–81; and Vincent Déroche, "Delphes: la christianisation d'un sanctuaire paien," in *Actes du XIe congrès international d'archéologie chrétienne* (Rome: École Française de Rome, 1989), 2713–23.

11. See the drawing that proposes what the original platform, steps, and altar actually looked like in Didier Laroche, "L'autel d'Apollon à Delphes: éléments nouveaux," in *L'espace Sacrificiel dans les Civilisations Méditerranéennes de L'Antiquité*, ed. Roland Etienne and Marie-Thérèse Le Dinahet (Lyon: Université Lumière, 1991), 112 (plate XXIb).

six stones are in an L shape and are about 14 feet (4.2 m) long by 7.5 feet (2.2 m) wide.

Etched into the top of these altar platform paving stones are over one hundred crosses, three equilateral crosses inside of circles, and five eight-spoked ICHTHUS Christograms. Because of the dark stone and the weathering of time, the circles and crosses are just barely visible today, especially in pictures (see fig. 6-2), but Pierre Amandry, one of the major French archaeologists and scholars of Delphi, has provided a helpful drawing, showing all of these engraved crosses and Christograms.[12] Amandry notes that he found several other locations at Delphi where these "radiating" circles were engraved alongside crosses. He concludes that these are Christograms and not games ("*d'un chrisme, et non d'un jeu*").[13]

Fig. 6-2 Delphi, Temple of Apollo, Altar of the Chians: Numerous Crosses and ICHTHUS Christograms Are Inscribed All Across the Top Slabs of the Altar

Other scholars have also made note of these cross inscriptions on this altar. For example, Déroche and Pétridis write: "The Apollo temple . . . had been neutered, its resident daimones [demons] exorcised and driven out, and cruciform signs were marked on the altar of the temple."[14] In another article, Déroche writes that the altar of the Chians was covered with "cross graffiti." He notes that a block from the southwest corner of the temple also had this "same mark," without clarifying whether this mark was a cross, the ICHTHUS Christogram, or the four-spoked circle.[15]

The crosses on the altar vary in size from about two to eight inches (5.08 cm to 20.32 cm) high. The majority are equilateral crosses, most with flared ends on their arms. The ICHTHUS Christograms vary in size from about four to six inches (10.16 cm to 15.24 cm) in diameter. These wheels were apparently etched rather hurriedly. They are informal in the sense that a pre-drawn pattern or template was not used, but rather the circles and spokes were etched freehand. The implications are that this was done by people

12. Amandry, "Chronique delphique," 739–40.
13. Amandry, "Chronique delphique," 733, 740.
14. Déroche and Pétridis, "Delphi," 410.
15. Déroche, "Delphes," 2720.

untrained in stonework. That is, this is not the action of professionals hired to undertake this project over time but probably the action of a group of Christians, perhaps a congregation led by a zealous bishop, as appears in some of the literature discussed in chapter 4. With about two-thirds of the platform surface missing, one wonders if those stones also were covered with crosses and ICHTHUS Christograms.

In all likelihood, these crosses and ICHTHUS Christograms were etched on this famous pagan altar sometime after the mid-fourth century as Christians in Delphi (and throughout the Roman/Byzantine Empire) sought to cleanse and de-demonize this famous temple. Certainly the graffiti was completed before the end of the fourth century. Perhaps these Christians were also making a proclamation of victory as they etched more than one hundred crosses and five ICHTHUS wheels on the top of this altar platform. Déroche notes that the Christians destroyed the innermost sacred part of the Temple of Apollo and etched all of these crosses and Christograms on the altar, as well as on other parts of the temple, but they did not destroy the main part of the temple itself.[16]

Crosses appear on several other stone blocks that were discovered during excavations of Delphi, although their scattered locations make it difficult to determine which structures these blocks were part of when these crosses were added. Amandry presents pictures of some of these inscriptions, suggesting that these blocks with crosses came from either a fountain or a bathhouse.[17]

PANNONIA

The Region of Pannonia

Pannonia refers to a region in the Roman Empire that was located in the Balkans. For much of the Roman imperial period, this region was divided into two provinces—Pannonia Inferior and Pannonia Superior. In 296 to 297, however, it was slightly reconstituted and renamed as Pannonia Valeria (or sometimes, Pannonia Savia) in the north and Pannonia Secunda in the south. Pannonia Valeria included regions in modern Hungary and Croatia. Pannonia Secunda included areas in modern Serbia, Croatia, and Bosnia and Herzegovina. Pannonia controlled much of the overland east-west travel and commerce in the Roman Empire. In the second century, it experienced a surge in urban construction and growth, and a number of cities were given the status of Roman colonies. Influential elites in the region embraced Roman culture and practices and assisted in Roman governance.[18]

---

16. Déroche, "Delphes," 2720.
17. Amandry, "Chronique delphique," 733.
18. Craig H. Caldwell, "The Balkans," in *The Oxford Handbook of Late Antiquity*, ed. Scott Fitzgerald Johnson (Oxford: Oxford University Press, 2012), 95–96; Mirja Jarak, "The History of Early Christian Communities in Continental Croatia," in Demo, *Early Christianity in Continental Croatia*, n.p.

In the late third century, when the Roman Empire was split up into four regions (called the Tetrarchy), the city of Sirmium in Pannonia Secunda was designated as one of the four imperial capital cities with an imperial pala-tial residence. It became a populous, prosperous city. In addition, four of the Roman emperors who ruled in the third century were from Sirmium or the surrounding area.[19]

Christianity was well-established in Pannonia by the end of the third century. This is evidenced by the large number of Christian inscriptions discovered on grave markers and in tombs. At Sirmium, living in close prox-imity to an imperial residence produced a rather dangerous situation for the Christians during the Great Persecution. There are literary records and legends of several martyrs who were executed in Pannonia during this time. For example, in 304 a young bishop named Irenaeus (different from the more famous bishop and prolific writer Irenaeus of Lyon, France) refused to sacri-fice to the gods and consequently was beheaded—his body dumped into the nearby river. Church leaders from the nearby cities of Cibalae and Singidu-num also were said to have been martyred during this time.[20] Cibalae was in Pannonia Secunda. Here the famous Battle of Cibalae was fought in 316, a battle in which Constantine defeated his former ally, Licinius, and soon after-ward became sole emperor of the Roman Empire.[21]

As mentioned above, Christianity spread into Pannonia early, and during late antiquity, it was an important region of Christianity along the northern boundary of the empire. Bevelacqua references 140 Christian inscriptions, primarily from the early fourth to sixth centuries.[22] Throughout the fourth to sixth centuries, this region was frequently overrun by various groups (often Arian Christians) from the north (Goths, Huns, Ostrogoths). While Arianism was popular in Pannonia in the early fourth century, in the 380s Pannonia was brought back into Nicene orthodoxy, primarily through the work of Ambrosius, the bishop of Mediolanum (modern Milan), although throughout late antiquity Pannonia experienced continual theological controversies and disputes.[23]

Funerary Inscriptions

Many Christian inscriptions have been discovered in Pannonia. Almost all are written in Latin and date from the fourth to the sixth centuries. They are almost exclusively found in funerary contexts. There are more than twenty

19. Caldwell, "The Balkans," 96.
20. Caldwell, "The Balkans," 99. See also Hajnalka Tamas, *Hagiography, the Cult of Martyrs, and the Formation of Christian Identity in Late Antique Pannonia* (Cluj-Napoca, Romania: Cluj University Press, 2022).
21. Linski, "The Reign of Constantine," 59–74.
22. Bevelacqua, "Christian Epigraphy in Pannonia," 75–78.
23. Olivér Gábor, "Early Christian Buildings in the Northern Cemetery of Sopianae," *Studia Patristica* 73 (Leuven: Peeters, 2014), 45; Caldwell, "The Balkans," 99.

occurrences of some type of cross-related symbol—crosses, Tau-Rho Stauro-grams, Chi-Rho Christograms (sometimes with *alpha* and *omega* on either side), and Iota-Chi symbols.[24]

One of the grave markers from the city of Cibalae has an inscription iden-tifying a Christian couple (Venatorinus and Martoria).[25] Below the inscrip-tion is an eight-spoked wheel. The vertical line of the wheel (the *iota*) has a small loop at the top, making it into the letter *rho*, similar in form to a typical Chi-Rho symbol. But this circle also has a horizontal line through the middle (the horizontal line of the letter *theta*, Θ). It appears to be a combination of the eight-spoked ICHTHUS Christogram and the Chi-Rho Christogram.[26] As noted in chapter 2, the early Christians often combined different Christo-grams together in creative ways.[27]

PHILIPPI

The City of Philippi

The city of Philippi is located in the northern part of the modern coun-try of Greece. Although people had been living in the general vicinity for hundreds of years, Philippi itself was originally founded in 360 BC as a Greek colony named Krenides. In 356 BC, Philip II of Macedonia captured the city and renamed it Philippi. Although small in size, nearby gold and silver mines made Philippi prosperous. The Romans conquered the region in the second century BC and organized the area into a Roman province, likewise called Macedonia.

In 42 BC, an important and famous battle took place near Philippi. After the Roman Senators Brutus and Cassius murdered the emperor Julius Caesar (attempting to keep Rome as a republic ruled by the Senate), a civil war broke out. Just outside Philippi, the armies of Octavian (later known as Caesar Augustus) and Mark Antony defeated the armies of Brutus and Cassius, resulting in the death of both senators and signaling the end of the Roman Republic. A few years later, Octavian (Augustus) defeated his former ally, Mark Antony. This began the Roman imperial age, in which the Roman emperor had much more power than the Roman Senate.[28]

24. Bevelacqua, "Observations on Christian Epigraphy in Pannonia," 75–81. For pictures of these Christian symbols, see pp. 103–111.

25. Migotti notes that this epitaph is unusual in that it does not give this couples' age or the date of their death. He suggests they had been martyred and that the church later erected this inscribed monument in their honor. They could also have been killed during the intense strife between Arianism and Orthodox Niceanism. See Branka Migotti, "The Archaeological Material of the Early Christian Period in Continental Croatia," in Demo, *Early Christianity in Continental Croatia*, n.p.

26. This inscription is catalogued as ILJ 283. For a picture of it, see Bevelacqua, "Observations of Christian Epigraphy," fig. 19, p. 109. It is now located in the Vinkovci Municipal Museum in Croatia.

27. Kraus, "Christograms," 222–23.

28. Fant and Reddish, *Biblical Sites in Greece and Turkey*, 100–101.

Octavian designated Philippi as a Roman colony and a place for retired Roman soldiers to settle. Located along the major east-west Roman highway (the Via Egnatia) that connected Rome to the eastern regions of the Roman Empire, the city flourished, and during the second century AD, significant building projects were undertaken throughout the city, patterned on typical Roman urban models. Much of the archaeological remains at Philippi that can be seen today date from this period. There was a large rectangular forum (or agora), a sizable theater (expanded during the Roman era and modified to handle gladiator and wild animal fights), bathhouses, public latrines, pagan temples (including temples dedicated to the imperial cult), gates, and walls.[29] During this era both Latin and Greek were commonly spoken and also used for civic inscriptions.

During the first century, the two major cities of Macedonia were Philippi and Thessalonica. When Paul received a vision calling him to go to Macedonia (Acts 16:9), Paul and his coworkers soon arrived in Philippi and also visited Thessalonica. In Acts 16, a businesswoman named Lydia (along with her entire household) and a jailer (along with his entire household) embraced Christianity, and they probably formed the beginning of the new church in Philippi. Paul visited Philippi at least two more times (Acts 19:21–22; 20:1–6) and wrote one of his famous epistles to the church at Philippi.

During the second century, Philippi was visited by Ignatius, the well-known Christian writer and bishop of Antioch. Christians at Philippi also corresponded with the early church leader Polycarp, bishop in Smyrna (modern Izmir in Turkey) and direct disciple of John, requesting copies of the letters of Ignatius. Both Ignatius and Polycarp were martyred in the mid-second century. Polycarp addresses an epistle to the "church" at Philippi, indicating that there was a church congregation there, but it was apparently too small to warrant a bishop. Tertullian, another early church leader and writer who lived in North Africa, also mentions the church at Philippi. These very early Christian writers (Paul, Polycarp, and Tertullian) all say positive things about the church at Philippi. So while it may have remained small during the second century, it appears to have been faithful from the beginning and throughout the century.[30]

As in many Greco-Roman cities that contained early Christian communities, the climate of sporadic persecutions, climaxing in the empire-wide Great Persecution initiated by Diocletian in the early 300s, prohibited the Christians in Philippi during this period from building permanent church structures. Indeed, even when churches were built during this era, they were often confiscated for reuse or destroyed altogether within a few years, mean-

---

29.   Eduard Verhoef, *Philippi: How Christianity Began in Europe—The Epistle to the Philippians and the Excavations at Philippi* (London: Bloomsbury; T&T Clark, 2013), 57–63; Fant and Reddish, *Biblical Sites in Greece and Turkey*, 101, 104–10.

30.   Verhoef, *Philippi*, 53–56.

ing the little archaeological evidence of Christians in the third century is usually limited to funerary inscriptions.[31]

After Constantine gains sole rule of the Roman Empire in the early fourth century, however, churches start to show up in the archaeological record all across the Roman Empire. Church sanctuaries—both newly constructed and renovated from earlier temples and other buildings—continue to be built in significant numbers throughout the fourth to the sixth centuries. The situation for the Christians at Philippi reflects this pattern. The remains of four different church buildings, with indications of several phases of renovations, have been excavated at Philippi.[32]

The Churches at Philippi

The earliest church in Philippi dates to the mid-300s, perhaps as early as 320, and was dedicated to the apostle Paul. It is also referred to as Basilica B. Located on the south side of the forum, it was fairly small. This church was apparently destroyed in a fire at the end of the fourth century, and in 400, a much larger church was built on the same site. It is referred to as the Octagon Church due to its shape. This church incorporated several rooms from the adjacent bathhouse into the church and added a stone baptistry in the shape of a Maltese cross.[33] One of the stone wall panels (or perhaps the chancel screen) discovered in the excavations contains a wreathed Iota-Chi Christogram (a six-spoked wheel).

Another fourth-century church (Basilica C) was located outside of the city walls, past the Neapolis gate, in what is now the village of Krenides. Next to this church was a cemetery containing an abundance of Christian inscriptions. Interestingly, throughout the fourth century and into the fifth, the use of Latin seemed to die out and was replaced with Greek. Most of the Christian funerary inscriptions discovered are in Greek.[34]

The largest church in Philippi, referred to as Basilica A, was built by the end of the fifth century, just to the north of the Via Egnatia and the agora. This church was expansive—180 feet by 89 feet (55 m by 27 m)—and seated up to one thousand people.[35]

---

31. A large number of Christian funerary inscriptions, dating from the third century to the seventh century, were discovered at Philippi. In the database *Inscriptiones Christianae Graecae*, see numbers *ICG* 3243 to 4056.

32. For a good discussion of the early church at Philippi, see Julien M. Ogereau, "The Social Constituency and Membership of the First Christian Groups at Philippi: A Literary and Epigraphic Survey," in *The First Urban Churches 4: Roman Philippi*, Writings from the Greco-Roman World Supplement 13, ed. James R. Harrison and L. L. Wellborn (Atlanta: SBL Press, 2018), 79–122; and Verhoef, *Philippi*, 53–87.

33. Verhoef, *Philippi*, 71–74.

34. Verhoef, *Philippi*, 74–75.

35. Verhoef, *Philippi*, 78.

ICHTHUS Graffiti at Philippi

Three eight-spoked ICHTHUS Christograms have been identified in the archaeological remains of Philippi. Two of them follow the common pattern of being a plain inscribed circle, roughly eighteen to twenty inches in diameter (45.72 cm to 50.8 cm), with eight spokes.[36] Both of these are inscribed on the paving stones of the Via Egnatia. One is right next to the agora (see figs. 6-3 and 6-4), and the other is near the theater (see fig. 6-5).[37]

Fig. 6-3 Philippi, The Agora: With the Via Egnatia (highway) in the Foreground

The other ICHTHUS wheel is unique. It was discovered in the *macellum* (a covered market area often called the commercial agora), which lies on the south side of the forum between the forum and the church referred to as Basilica B. As the crow flies, it is more or less directly across the forum, due south from the ICHTHUS Christogram on the Via Egnatia. This ICHTHUS Christogram is about the same size as the other two Christograms, but this one has eight curved arcs drawn from point to point where the radial arms touch the circle perimeter, a variation of the eight-spoked ICHTHUS Christogram seen at Ephesus.[38] Similar to the ICHTHUS Christogram in the fountain court-yard next to the synagogue at

Fig. 6-4 Philippi, Paving of the Via Egnatia (highway): ICHTHUS Christogram

Sardis, this Christogram has letters inscribed in each pie-shaped segment.

---

36. This is the circle shape designated as C4 in Bell and Roueché, "Graeco-Roman Pavement Signs," 13.

37. Séve and Weber present a picture of a similar but somewhat peculiar circle in that it has nine spokes, along with five loop-type arches up against the perimeter of the circle in five of the pie-shaped spaces. See Michel Séve and Patrick Weber, *Guide du forum de Philippes*, Sites et Monuments 18 (Athens: École française d'Athènes, 2012), 75. This is the only example of a nine-spoked wheel that I am aware of. See also, Bell and Roueché, "Graeco-Roman Pavement Signs," 107–8; they list out twenty different circle-shaped graffiti inscriptions, none of which has nine spokes.

38. This is the circle shape designated as C6 in Bell and Roueché, "Graeco-Roman Pavement Signs," 13.

Fig. 6-5 Philippi, Near the Theater: ICHTHUS Christogram

But uniquely, this Christogram has two words (two sets of letters)— one set inscribed close to the outer perimeter of the circle (between the arc and the outer perimeter) and one set inscribed in each pie-shaped segment right next to the center (wheel-hub) of the circle. The outer word is IⲰANNOⲨ ('Ιωάννου, John). It is in a grammatical form that translates as "of John." Note that this word only has seven letters. Since there are eight pie-shaped spaces, the eighth spot is filled with a Latin-style cross. The inner word is MAΓ(space)POⲨ (μαγ[space]ρου), which is probably a slightly abbreviated form of μάγειροσ (*mageiros*), a Greek word that can be translated as "cook," "butcher," or "seller of meat." This word only has six letters. One of the eight spaces is left blank (where the letter ι would be expected), and in the other space there is a Latin-style cross. Today the letters are faint and difficult to read (foot traffic from the forum to Basilica B crosses the inscription), but the eight-spoked wheel remains recognizable.[39] For pictures of this Christogram, see the database *Inscriptiones Christianae Graecae*, ICG 3250. Also helpful is the drawing from 1946 that clearly shows the eight-spoked circle along with all of the letters and crosses.[40] Dating such inscriptions with precision is always difficult. The *Inscriptiones Christianae Graecae* database dates it 300 to 555. Peter Pilhofer likewise estimates fourth to fifth century.[41]

Working off of the poorly supported presupposition that all inscribed graffiti circles and rectangles are game boards, Ogereau assumes that this circle is a game board, and he even calls it a "hopscotch game." He assumes that the genitive Greek "of John" implies that the text means "hopscotch gameboard of John the butcher."[42] This interpretation is highly unlikely and has no evidence to support it. As presented throughout this book, there is strong evidence that the eight-spoked wheel is a Christogram for the acrostic

39. Peter Pilhofer, *Philippi*, vol. 2, *Katalog der Inschriften von Philippi*, WUNT 119 (Tübingen: Mohr Siebeck, 2000), 263–64.

40. Jacques Coupry, "Un joueur de marelle au marché de Philippes," *Bulletin de correspondance hellénique* 70 (1946): 104.

41. Pilhofer, *Philippi*, 263.

42. Ogereau, "The First Christian Groups at Philippi," 91. In Ogereau's defense, earlier scholarship had made the same assumption, and he is following their conclusions. For example, note the title of Coupry's article in 1946, "Un joueur de marelle au marché de Philippes" ("a hopscotch player in the market of Philippi"). Even more recently, Pilhofer, *Philippi*, 263, refers to this inscription as "Das Spiel des Metzgers Johannes" (the game of the butcher John).

IXΘΥC (ICHTHUS). The presence of two crosses inside this particular eight-spoked circle adds to the argument, indicating that this circle in particular was associated with Christianity.

The implied subject of the inscription "of John, the butcher" is not specified, and we cannot know for certain to whom or to what the reference is. As discussed in more detail in chapter 3, in her discussion of circle graffiti in Aphrodiasias, Roueché cautions against assuming that all graffiti shapes are game boards, noting that some of the graffiti are probably serving as place markers.[43] That is a possibility here, especially in the context of the market location. Perhaps John the butcher marked the place in the market where his stall would regularly be. As a Christian, he marked it with strong Christian symbols: the ICHTHUS Christogram (similar to the others in the city) inscribed with two additional crosses.

However, Pilhofer presents seven other inscriptions discovered in the *macellum*. None of them appear to be place markers for anyone's stall. Some of these inscriptions are in Latin, and some are in Greek. Some of them are dedications to one or more pagan gods, and some are dedications honoring people who have paid for something.[44] This means the genitive "of John, the butcher" could also be translated as "by John the butcher" in the sense of it being a dedication to Jesus Christ God's Son Savior "by John the butcher." In this sense, this inscription shares some similarities with the ICHTHUS Christogram in the fountain courtyard near the synagogue at Sardis (see chapter 5).

This Christogram in the market area of Philippi could perhaps be serving an apotropaic function as well.[45] Since several other inscriptions in this market area, which measures 174 feet by 27 feet (53 m by 8.2 m), were dedications to pagan gods (Apollo, Artemis), perhaps it was an area involved in pagan worship rites. The dedications to these gods themselves might have been viewed by the Christians as desecrating or contaminating the area, bringing along the demons associated with the pagan gods.

The actual word IXΘΥC also appears several times throughout the province of Macedonia. As noted in the next section, at the nearby city of Stobi, IXΘΥC appears as an acrostic in the mosaics of a church floor. In Thessalonica, IXΘΥC occurs in the epitaph on a Christian gravestone, dated between 200 and 400. The letters ΦZ occur right next to the IXΘΥC acrostic, probably abbreviations for φως (*phōs*, light) and ζωή (*zōē*, life).[46]

---

43. Roueché, "Game Boards at Aphrodisias," 100.
44. Pilhofer, *Philippi*, 262–71.
45. Orgereau, "The First Christian Groups at Philippi," 91, notes that at Philippi crosses were apparently used in an apotropaic manner on the acropolis, the city gates, and the altar of Isis.
46. *ICG* 3090. These two words (φως (light) and ζωή (life) appear together on a Christian epitaph in Philippi. See Pilhofer, *Philippi*, 328. Along with numerous crosses, these two words are also inscribed on the doorjamb side panels in the back of the Temple of Artemis in Sardis and likewise alongside crosses at Aphrodisias.

STOBI

The City of Stobi

The ancient city of Stobi is located about 160 miles northwest of Thessalonica, in what is now the country of North Macedonia. Located at an intersection of two major roads, it was part of the Macedonian Empire until the Romans conquered the area in 168 BC. In 69 BC, it received the status of *municipium*, which allowed the city to mint its own coins. This status also gave Roman citizenship to Stobi's inhabitants. When the area was later reorganized into a province called Macedonia Salutaris, Stobi was made the capital of the province. It was a prosperous, significant city until the late sixth century, when it was abandoned for unknown reasons and never rebuilt.[47]

As Christianity spread into the area, Stobi was already a thriving urban city with pagan temples, bathhouses, fountains, and a theater seating 7,600 people. Although we do not know how and when exactly the church was planted in Stobi, we can assume that Christianity spread to Stobi from the nearby churches at Thessalonica and Philippi. By the early fourth century, it was an important center of Christianity. There was a bishop from Stobi (Boudias) at the council of Nicaea in 325. Later in the century (AD 388) the emperor Theodosius I visited Stobi and resided there for a short while. Stobi was also represented by bishops at several later church councils (Chalcedon, 451; Constantinople, 553).[48]

The Episcopal Basilica

The earliest church discovered in Stobi, often called the Episcopal Basilica, dates to the first half of the fourth century and was probably constructed during the service of bishop Boudias. This church was adjacent to the theater. It was renovated later in the fourth century while Eustatios was bishop (he is mentioned in a floor mosaic inscription), probably just prior to the visit by Theodosius I in 388.[49] Reused as construction materials in the expansion phase of the church were stone seats from the nearby theater, indicating that at some time toward the end of the fourth century, the theater was abandoned. The stone seats from the theater were reused not only in the church renovation but in the construction of the new fortification wall on the eastern side of the city.[50]

---

47. Carolyn S. Snively, "Stobi," in Finney, *The Eerdmans Encyclopedia of Early Christian Art and Archaeology*, 2:546; James Wisemen and Djordje Mano-Zissi, "Stobi: A City of Ancient Macedonia," *Journal of Field Archaeology* 3.3 (1976): 269–70.

48. Elizabeta Dimitrova et al., *Early Christian Wall Paintings from the Episcopal Basilica in Stobi* (Gradsko: NI Stobi, 2012), 9; Snively, "Stobi," 546.

49. Dimitrova et al. proposes these dates, while recognizing that some scholars advocate for slightly later dates (*Episcopal Basilica in Stobi*, 11–14).

50. This information comes from the website maintained by the archaeological project currently working at Stobi—Archaeological Site Stobi: National Institution Stobi, Stobi.mk/Templates/Pages/Excavations.aspx?Page=160.

The Episcopal Basilica has a beautiful, complex mosaic floor comprising a wide variety of shapes and patterns. Directly in the center of the floor, in view right as one enters the church, are the letters IXΘYC followed by a cross.[51] This IXΘYC acrostic is similar to the one in the floor mosaics from the same era discovered in the Church of the Nativity in Bethlehem, as discussed in chapter 7.

Also discovered in the Episcopal Basilica was a stone wall panel that was part of the chancel screen at the front of the basilica. This panel contains an eight-spoked ICHTHUS Christogram professionally inscribed in the center of the panel with traditional crosses on both sides. Most scholars view this panel as part of the renovation that took place at the end of the fourth century (perhaps the early fifth century).[52]

During the fourth century, here in Stobi—a church center and seat of a prominent bishop—the ICHTHUS acrostic is used in the floor mosaics of a church and placed in a prominent location where all would see it as they entered the church, while the eight-spoked ICHTHUS Christogram (a visual representation of the ICHTHUS acrostic) was placed at the very front of the church as part of the chancel screen that divided the altar area in the nave from the seating area. The additions of regular crosses on each side of the eight-spoked wheel provide further evidence that this ICHTHUS Christogram was functioning in a similar fashion symbolically as the crosses.

Also discovered at Stobi were several other stone wall panels, which the archaeologists concluded were from a different part of the church. One of the designs on these panels is a six-spoked Iota-Chi Christogram inside a victory wreath.[53]

---

51. ICG 3311. See Ruth E. Kolarik, "Mosaics of the Early Church at Stobi," Dumbarton Oaks Papers 41 (1987): 296–99; and Dimitrova et al., Episcopal Basilica in Stobi, 11–12.

52. Dimitrova et al., Episcopal Basilica in Stobi, 14–18; Kolarik, "Mosaics of the Early Church at Stobi," 295–96.

53. Ernst Kitzinger, "A Survey of the Early Christian Town of Stobi," Dumbarton Oaks Papers 3 (1946): 90–92. See the picture of this stone panel in fig. 141.

CHAPTER 7

THE EIGHT-SPOKED ICHTHUS
CHRISTOGRAM IN ISRAEL/PALESTINE

INTRODUCTION

After the disastrous Jewish revolts against Rome in AD 66–70 and again in 132–136, Jerusalem and Judea were almost completely emptied of Jewish residents. The region of Judea was renamed and incorporated into Syria Palaestina. A sizable population of Jews still remained in Galilee, parts of Samaria, and across the Jordan in cities of the Decapolis like Pella. By and large, during the second to third centuries, most cities of this area and, to some extent, the countryside as well, became Greco-Roman in character, much like other cities in the Roman Empire. This was true even though the Christian population was growing and the Jewish population in some cities outside of Judea remained significant. Yet of the twenty-five cities in Syria Palaestina located west of the Jordan River, only Tiberias and Sepphoris had a Jewish majority. The cities of Scythopolis (Beth Shean), Caesarea, and perhaps Lydda had significant Jewish minority populations.[1] Pagan temples and associated pagan structures, such as monumental fountains and bathhouses, became prominent features in most cities but perhaps not to the extent that occurred in Asia Minor.[2]

Christianity continued to grow during the years 100–300, despite periodic persecution. By 300, there was a substantial Christian population in the

---

1. Günter Stemberger, *Jews and Christians in the Holy Land: Palestine in the Fourth Century*, trans. Ruth Tuschling (Edinburgh: T&T Clark, 2000), 18.
2. Stoehr lists forty-seven known and identifiable pagan temples in Palestine at this time. Gregory William Stoehr, "The End of Pagan Temples in Roman Palestine" (PhD diss., University of Maryland, 2018), 196, 202, 209.

185

area, and Eusebius notes that quite a few of the martyrs who died in the Great Persecution of 303 to 313 were in the cities of Caesarea Maritima or Gaza. Eusebius also mentions a number of other cities in Syria Palaestina whose Christians experienced martyrdom at this time—Ashcalon, Scythopolis (Beth Shean), and Iamnia.[3] In fact, in his study of the Great Persecution, Shin states that there were ninety-two martyrs executed in this region.[4] This evidence suggests a strong Christian population, yet still probably in the minority.

Further testifying to the presence of Christians even prior to the Great Persecution is the presence of Christian graffiti scrawled on the walls of the house church at Capernaum, known as the Church of St. Peter (believed to be the site of St. Peter's house). While some of this graffiti dates to the fourth to fifth centuries, the earliest graffiti dates to the early third century. This suggests that there were already some Christian pilgrims coming to Capernaum to see the house of St. Peter as early as the third century.[5]

After Constantine came to power in the early fourth century, significant changes took place. He personally ordered the destruction of several pagan temples in Jerusalem. In conjunction with his mother Helena's pilgrimage to Syria Palaestina (still the name of the province at that time), Constantine immediately ordered the construction of several impressive churches in Jerusalem along with one in Bethlehem. Soon the region was flooded with pilgrims from across the empire, and Christian building activity increased dramatically. From 350 to 400, churches were constructed throughout the province. The construction of monasteries, convents, hostels, and more churches continued over the next two hundred years. Through conversions, immigration, and pilgrimages, the Christian population in Syria Palaestina grew dramatically throughout the latter two-thirds of the fourth century,[6] and by the year 400, Christians composed the majority of the population.[7]

In 361, however, Julian the Apostate became emperor and tried to take the Roman Empire back to Hellenistic (Greek) paganism, and he declared that a temple for the Jews should be rebuilt on the Temple Mount in Jerusalem. We do not know for certain whether construction had started or not, but in 363, a terrible earthquake damaged this region. Julian died the next month in a battle with the Sasanians (Persians). Christian writers interpreted both the earthquake and Julian's death as God's response to Julian's attempt

---

3. Joseph Patrich, "The Early Christianization of the Holy Land: The Archaeological Evidence," in Olof Brandt and Gabriele Castiglia, *Constantino E I Constantinidi: L'Innovazione Constantiniana, Le Sue Radici E I Suoi Sviluppi*, Studi Di Antichità Cristiana 66 (Rome: Pontificio Istituto di Archeologia Cristiana, 2016), 266.
4. Shin, *The Great Persecution*, 169–80.
5. Patrich, "The Early Christianization of the Holy Land," 270.
6. Stemberger, *Jews and Christians in the Holy Land*, 20–21, 48–85.
7. Yoram Tsafrir, "The Fate of the Pagan Cult Places," in Hayim Lapin, *Religious and Ethnic Communities in Later Roman Palestine* (Bethesda: University of Maryland Press, 1998), 198. For bib., see pp. 197–218.

to revive paganism, as well as his plans to rebuild the Jewish temple.[8] Many of the remaining pagan temples throughout the region were damaged by this earthquake, never to be rebuilt.[9]

Around the year 400, the province of Syria Palaestina was split into two regions: Palaestina Prima, with its capital at Caesarea Maritima (whose power was to be challenged by the growing influence of Jerusalem), and Palaestina Secunda, with its capital at Scythopolis (Beth Shean). Other important cities in the province of Palaestina Secunda were Sepphoris and Hippos.

There are many eight-spoked ICHTHUS Christograms in this region, both as informally inscribed graffiti and in formal floor mosaics. The acrostic letters ΙΧΘΥϹ (ICHTHUS) appear twice in floor mosaics. Jerusalem has three ICHTHUS Christograms. Bethlehem has an ICHTHUS acrostic, as does the convent at Beth-Hashitta. Sepphoris and Scythopolis contain eight-spoked wheels prominently displayed in mosaics in public areas, while Hippos contains an eight-spoked wheel on the floor mosaics of the central church there. The convent at Beth-Hashitta also has an ICHTHUS Christogram in the floor mosaics. Finally, there is a peculiar, somewhat enigmatic geometric figure, much like the eight-spoked ICHTHUS Christogram, in the floor mosaics of a synagogue at Magdala.

BETH-HASHITTA

Not far from Scythopolis (Beth Shean), just to the northwest, is the kibbutz of Beth-Hashitta. Near the kibbutz, archaeologists discovered and excavated a small two-room chapel (or cloister), dating to the 400s, that apparently was associated with a Christian convent. Perhaps the most fascinating feature of this discovery is the floor mosaics. The mosaics of one room contain an equilateral cross (with slightly flared ends) within a circle, centered in the room. Just below this cross and circle and to the lower right is an eight-spoked wheel.[10]

Adjacent and to the right is the second room. The floor of this room contains a mosaic grid of seventy squares (ten squares by seven squares). Each square contains a design. These may simply be random, geometric designs, but that is unlikely. The peculiar look of these designs, when compared to the cryptic-like symbols used within early Christianity discussed in chapter 2 (also similar to those in the Baths of Neptune at Ostia, as discussed in chapter 8) suggest that these are cryptic Christian symbols, a view embraced

---

8. Stemberger, *Jews and Christians in the Holy Land*, 201–16.

9. Kenneth W. Russell, "The Earthquake of May 19, A.D. 363," *Bulletin of the American Schools of Oriental Research* 238 (1980): 47–64; Walter D. Ward, "The 363 Earthquake and the End of Public Paganism in the Southern Transjordan," *Journal of Late Antiquity* 9.1 (2016): 132–70.

10. See drawings depicting this eight-spoked wheel in Y. Aharoni, "Excavations at Beth-Hashitta," *Bulletin of the Israel Exploration Society* 18 (1954): 210; and Brandenburg, "Christussymbole," 124.

by a number of scholars who have studied the strange mosaics.[11] Several squares simply have an X in them, probably the Greek letter *chi*, reflecting either a cross or the first letter of *Christos* (Christ). One square contains a six-spoked wheel, probably an Iota-Chi Christogram (i.e., an abbreviation for Jesus Christ). Israeli archaeologist Aharoni, along with several other scholars, suggests that some of the squares have designs that are letters and word abbreviations reflecting common Christian word inscriptions (*kurios*, "Lord"; *boētheō*, "help"). Although the letters are not completely clear, these scholars suggest that one of the squares appears to contain the Greek letters IXΘΥC.[12]

Thus, in the first room of this fifth-century Christian chapel, there is a large cross and a small eight-spoked wheel, and in the other room, along with dozens of cryptic Christian symbols and abbreviations, there is a square with the acrostic IXΘΥC. It is highly likely, therefore, that the eight-spoked wheel in the first room, right alongside the cross, is the eight-spoked ICHTHUS Christogram. The IXΘΥC acrostic in the next room certainly strengthens this identification.

BETHLEHEM

In 300, at the beginning of the fourth century, Bethlehem was a small village, located a few miles south of, and in the territory of, Aelia Capitolina (the new Roman name for Jerusalem; see the discussion below). Since Emperor Hadrian had killed or expelled all Jews from Jerusalem and the surrounding area of Judea after the Bar Kokhba revolt in 135 to 136, the village of Bethlehem was probably devoid of Jewish residents. Under the influence of the new Roman colony at Aelia Capitolina, the village of Bethlehem became a primarily pagan village. In 395, Jerome writes that prior to the time of Constantine, a sacred grove of trees and a worship center venerating the Greco-Roman god Adonis had been on the holy site, desecrating that holy location of the Lord's birth in Bethlehem.

In 325 to 326, Empress Helena, the mother of Constantine, took a pilgrimage to the Holy Land to locate sites and relics from the time of Jesus. Consulting with local Christians, Helena located the sites of Jesus's birth (in Bethlehem) and death and burial (in Jerusalem). Constantine quickly ordered that churches be constructed on each site. As noted above, Helena's pilgrimage was not in isolation. First hundreds and then thousands of Christian pilgrims flocked to the land of Jesus.

One of the early Christian pilgrims (known as the Pilgrim of Bordeaux, France) notes in his written account of his travels (dated AD 333) that

---

11.   Aharoni, "Beth-Hashitta," 209–15; Brandenburg, "Christussymbole," 123–25. In the epigraphical corpora database, see *SEG* 20 (1964): 460.

12.   Aharoni, "Beth-Hashitta," 213–15; Brandenburg, "Christussymbole," 123–24; Testa, *Il Simbolismo Dei Giudeo-Cristiani*, 85–90. Aharoni, 213, Brandenburg, 124, and Testa, 85, all present drawings of the mosaics.

Constantine had built a basilica on the site of Jesus's birth at Bethlehem. This puts a significant structure there already by 333; the Church of the Nativity was officially dedicated in 339.[13]

Soon monasteries and hostels were built to aid in providing services for the huge crowds of pilgrims. In 384, Jerome arrived, to be joined two years later by his benefactor, a wealthy Roman woman named Paula, along with her daughter. Paula funded a convent for women (which she directed) and a monastery for men, where Jerome resided, and together they built Bethlehem into an important monastic center. Here in this monastery next to the Church of the Nativity, Jerome produced the famous and influential Latin Vulgate translation of Scripture.[14]

In the early sixth century, Emperor Justinian renovated and expanded the Church of the Nativity. Unlike the Church of the Holy Sepulcher in nearby Jerusalem, which was damaged and extensively modified several times throughout history, the Church of the Nativity has remained largely intact with only minor renovations taking place in the twelfth and seventeenth centuries.[15]

In the apse of the Church of the Nativity, in the front of the church that lies over the cave below where it was believed that Jesus was born, a portion of the original floor mosaics from the Constantinian church (AD 326–339) has survived. This is not to be confused with the recent mosaic renovations on the walls carried out in the Church of the Nativity, which restored mosaics from the twelfth century (and also contain a beautiful eight-spoked Christogram). The old floor mosaics in the apse, dated to the early fourth century, contain the word IXΘΥC. There is no doubt that this is the IXΘΥC acrostic standing for "Jesus Christ God's Son Savior."[16] Not only was this IXΘΥC acrostic placed on the floor of the apse—that is, at the focal point of the basilica—but it was over the center of the earlier pagan shrine, which, according to Jerome, had been located over the cave where Jesus had been born. This IXΘΥC acrostic, proclaiming the name of Jesus and the cross, was placed into these mosaics only a few years after that very site had been a functioning pagan worship center. Not only did that acrostic make a clear christological proclamation about Jesus Christ, but it probably served to cleanse and sanctify the pagan site, driving away any remaining demons.

---

13. Murphy-O'Connor, *The Holy Land*, 231–32; R. W. Hamilton, *The Church of the Nativity Bethlehem* (Jerusalem: Department of Antiquities, 1947), 11–12.

14. Murphy-O'Connor, *The Holy Land*, 232–33.

15. Jodi Magness, *The Archaeology of the Holy Land: From the Destruction of Solomon's Temple to the Muslim Conquest* (Cambridge: Cambridge University Press, 2012), 335–36.

16. Andrew M. Madden, *Corpus of Byzantine Church Mosaic Pavements from Israel and the Palestinian Territories*, Colloquia Antiqua 13 (Leuven: Peeters, 2014), 37–38; Brandenburg, "Christussymbole," 97–98; and Franz Joseph Dölger, "Die IXΘΥC-Formel in dem neuentdeckten Fußboden-Mosaik der Konstantinischen Basilika von Bethlehem," *Antike und Christentum: kultur und religionsgeschichtliche Studien* 5 (1936): 81–86. Dölger, 85, dates this mosaic to 330. Likewise dating this mosaic to the fourth century is Hamilton, *The Church of the Nativity Bethlehem*, 93.

HIPPOS

The City of Hippos

The remains of the ancient city of Hippos are located on the hilltop of Sussita Mountain on the eastern shore of the Sea of Galilee near Kibbutz Ein Gev. Although evidence of an earlier settlement has been discovered, the city itself developed primarily during the Hellenistic period (323–63 BC). During the Roman imperial period (63 BC–AD 324) Hippos flourished, particularly during the first, second, and most of the third centuries. It was included as one of the cities of the Decapolis.[17] During the fourth century, as elsewhere in the Roman/Byzantine Empire, Christianity became more dominant in the city, and Hippos was designated as an episcopal see (home to the regional bishop). Some brief archaeological exploration and excavation at Hippos was done in the 1950s, and the project has recently been renewed. These excavations have revealed that at least five churches, and perhaps as many as seven, were built during the fourth to sixth centuries in Hippos.

The Southwest Church at Hippos

One of the most recent churches to be discovered and excavated is located in the southwest portion of the city. It has variously been referred to as "the Burnt Church" (due to evidence that the roof had burned), the "Martyrion of Theodoros" (due to an inscription on the floor indicating this function), or "the Southwest Church," in accordance with how the other churches were named. Excavations began in 2007, and progress picked up in 2022 and 2023, especially in regard to uncovering and cleaning the mosaic floors of the church and adjoining rooms.[18] Based on the dedicatory inscriptions in the mosaics (along with coins discovered), the construction of this church is dated to the mid-sixth century. The extensive floor mosaics showcase many designs and patterns, but located centrally in the entryway (i.e., the narthex of the church) is an eight-spoked ICHTHUS Christogram.[19] Among the other designs in the mosaics are birds (including peacocks), date palms, crosses, and at least three fish.[20]

JERUSALEM

The City of Jerusalem (Aelia Capitolina)

Jerusalem was destroyed by the Romans in AD 70, and the complete dismantling of major buildings and fortifications continued over the next several

---

17. Michael Eisenberg, *A Visitor's Guide to Ancient Hippos: Above the Sea of Galilee* (Israel: Millennium Ayalon, 2021), 8–9.

18. Gregor Staab, "Hippos: was Mosaik-inschriften Verraten; Auf den Spuren einer christlichen Gemeinde," *Welt und Umwelt der Bibel* 2 (2023): 62–65.

19. The ICHTHUS Christogram can be seen in the bottom left corner of the aerial picture of the church shown in Staab, "Hippos: was Mosaik-inschriften Verrate," 62.

20. Staab, "Hippos: was Mosaik-inschriften Verrate," 64; Eisenberg, *Hippos*, 54–55.

years. This included not only the Jewish temple but the Antonia Fortress, most of the walls and gates, and practically all monumental buildings, palaces, and residences. Most of the city's population who did not flee earlier were either killed or enslaved. Afterward, just to be certain that the Romans maintained firm control, they stationed an entire legion (the Tenth Legion) in Jerusalem. This huge military unit settled into the southwest area of the city (mostly in what is now the Armenian Quarter), and Jerusalem became primarily a military outpost with supporting services. Later on, the barracks and activities of the Tenth Legion spread eastward into what is now the Jewish Quarter (near the Temple Mount).[21] Very little rebuilding took place over the next sixty years outside of what was needed to support the Tenth Legion.

Emperor Hadrian came to power in 117 and ruled until 138. He spent much of his rule traveling across the empire, battling Rome's enemies but also fortifying the empire. He sponsored and initiated a great deal of building projects. Monumental buildings (like triple arches) were often built specifically in honor of his visits. In 129–130, Hadrian arrived in the eastern part of his empire (now composed of Syria, Lebanon, Jordan, Israel, the Palestinian Territories, and the Gaza Strip). In Jerash (modern-day Jordan), one of the substantial Greco-Roman cities of the Decapolis, a huge monumental triple arch was built in his honor. This structure, with one large central arch and two small flanking arches, is still standing and in very good condition.

Jerusalem, however, remained mostly in ruins. Hadrian decided to rebuild the city but to reconstruct it in a more traditional Greco-Roman pagan style—a Roman colony, devoid of any Jewish association whatsoever. He renamed it Aelia Capitolina. The term "Aelia" came from Hadrian's family name, and the term "Capitolina" came from the Temple of Jupiter Capitolinus in the Forum in Rome. Although the exact sequence of events is uncertain, as are the exact cause and effect, this announcement led to another serious Jewish revolt against Rome, the Bar Kokhba revolt (AD 132–136).[22] It took Hadrian and several Roman legions four to five years to defeat the Jews, and casualties, especially for the Jews, were catastrophic. Other serious consequences ensued—Jews were prohibited from living in Jerusalem at all, and Judea itself was emptied of practically all of its Jewish population. Hadrian changed the name of the province from Judea to Syria Palaestina and began rebuilding the city of Aelia Capitolina—now a Roman colony to be settled primarily with retired soldiers.[23] No doubt there were a significant number of

21. On the camp of the Tenth Legion, see the discussion in Shlomit Weksler-Bdolah, *Aelia Capitolina: Jerusalem in the Roman Period in Light of Archaeological Research*, Mnemosyne Supplements: History and Archaeology of Classical Antiquity 432 (Leiden: Brill, 2020), 19–50.
22. Weksler-Bdolah, *Aelia Capitolina*, 51–60.
23. Magness, *The Archaeology of the Holy Land*, 257–60; Robert Schick, "Aelia Capitolina," in *The Oxford Encyclopedia of the Bible and Archaeology*, ed. Daniel M. Master, 2 vols. (Oxford: Oxford University Press, 2013), 1:1–2.

non-Jewish people, including Christians, who moved here for jobs and business connections over the following years.[24]

Although the ancient sources are not consistent and modern scholars disagree, Hadrian probably built a temple of Jupiter on the Jewish Temple Mount (which was at the time unoccupied—the Jewish temple had been completely destroyed in AD 70). He also built a temple to Aphrodite (Latin/Venus) on top of the site that Christians believed to have been the tomb of Christ.[25] At least when Helena, the mother of Constantine, came to Jerusalem in 326, the local Christians there pointed her to this temple as the location of the empty tomb of Jesus. Perhaps Hadrian built the Temple of Aphrodite in that location specifically to destroy the Christians' sacred site. This is the conclusion of Eusebius, a contemporary with Helena and Constantine, who lived in nearby Caesarea and wrote in the early fourth century (*Life of Constantine* 3.26). This is also the conclusion of Jerome (who lived in nearby Bethlehem) who, writing around 395 about the statue of Venus (Aphrodite), states, "The original persecutors, indeed, supposed that by polluting our holy places they would deprive us of our faith in the passion and in the resurrection" (*Epistle* 58.3). Many other pagan temples and shrines were built too. A temple of Asclepius (god of healing and medicine) was built at the site of the pool of Bethesda, and there is evidence in Jerusalem of a cult site that worshiped Mithras, a cult especially popular among Roman soldiers.[26]

The Christian church at Jerusalem starts in the early chapters of the book of Acts. The church continues to expand through the early church era, although it appears to be primarily Jewish-Christian in composition in the latter part of the first century. James, the brother of Christ, is considered the first bishop. He was martyred in 62. When the Jews rebelled against Rome in 66, the church in Jerusalem dispersed, and most of the Jewish Christians fled. Many of them settled in the area around Pella, one of the cities of the Decapolis across the Jordan River (in modern Jordan). This group continued to call themselves the "church of Jerusalem," even in exile, and they continued to appoint bishops. After the Bar Kokhba revolt, however, as Gentile Christians began to move into Jerusalem in significant numbers, a Gentile bishop was appointed, and all of the bishops after 135 were Gentiles.[27] While not nearly as large as the church at Caesarea Maritima (the nearby provincial capital), there was, nonetheless, a bishop and a small growing church in Jerusalem throughout the second and third centuries.

---

24. Magness, *The Archaeology of the Holy Land*, 257–60, 271.
25. Schick, "Aelia Capitolina," 5; Magness, *The Archaeology of the Holy Land*, 272; Hershel Shanks, *Jerusalem: An Archaeological Biography* (New York: Random House, 1995), 202–3.
26. Magness, *The Archaeology of the Holy Land*, 277–79; Weksler-Bdolah, *Aelia Capitolina*, 126.
27. F. F. Bruce, "The Church of Jerusalem," *Christian Brethren Research Fellowship Journal* 4 (1964): 5–14. Eusebius refers to the bishops prior to 135 (the coming of Hadrian and the revolt) as "bishops of the circumcision" and "of Hebrew descent" (*Ecclesiastical History* 5.2–5).

Around 300, Emperor Diocletian transferred the Tenth Legion south to Aqaba and replaced them in Aelia Capitolina (Jerusalem) with a much smaller garrison. This would have had a drastic impact on the population of Jerusalem and the many businesses and activities that had been dedicated to serving the Tenth Legion. The population in Jerusalem at this time probably decreased significantly. During the Great Persecution, there is documentation of several Christian leaders being tortured and killed in nearby Caesarea and in Gaza, both of which had sizable Christian populations. No doubt, times were equally difficult for Christians in Jerusalem.

Evidence for Christians living in Jerusalem in the first half of the fourth century comes from the recent excavations in the Givati Parking Lot, an area just south of the Old City walls, not far from the Dung Gate. In these excavations, a mansion dating to the Roman era was discovered. The house suffered serious damage in the earthquake of 363 and was never rebuilt. Apparently, during the earthquake the plaster on the walls fell off in massive pieces, which were then buried in the debris and preserved. Twenty-three of these plaster pieces have informal, graffiti-style inscriptions written on them. Several are clearly Christian in character, containing the word *kyrios* ("Lord"), the Chi-Rho Christogram, palm branches, and crosses.[28]

In 313, Constantine legalized Christianity, and in 324, he became the sole ruler of the Roman Empire, moving his capital from Rome to Byzantium and renaming it Constantinople. In the years that followed, things changed quickly and dramatically in Jerusalem. As noted above, Constantine's mother, Empress Helena (now a fervent Christian), arrived in Jerusalem in 326, looking for relics and sites related to Jesus. The Christians there told her that the Temple of Aphrodite (constructed by Hadrian) lay over the tomb of Jesus, and according to legend, she found the true, original cross at that location. Constantine, no doubt in consultation with his mother, decided immediately to raze the pagan temple to the ground and to build an expansive, impressive Christian church on that site. Eusebius informs us that Constantine was so concerned about the demonic defilement of the site that not only were all of the stones removed and disposed "as far away as possible" but even the soil ("polluted by the foul impurities of demon worship") was to be excavated to a "considerable depth" and transported far away (*Life of Constantine*, 3.27). Constantine sent letters both to the current bishop of Jerusalem and to the governor over the province stressing the importance of this church. Construction began before the end of the year, and the Church of the Holy Sepulcher (called the Church of the *Anastasis* [Greek: "resurrection"] at the time) was built. It was dedicated in 335.

---

28. Lena Naama Sharabi, Yana Tchekhanovets, and Doron Ben Ami, "Early Christian Graffiti from Fourth Century Jerusalem," in *Holy Land, Archaeology on Either Side: Archaeological Essays in Honor of Eugenio Alliata, ofm*, ed. A. Coniglio and A. Ricco, Collectio Maior 57 (Milan: Edizioni Terra Santa, 2020), 295–302.

Through the centuries, this church was rebuilt, remodeled, renovated, and expanded many times, resulting in the complicated, rambling, subdivided church that is there today. Constantine also built a church on the Mount of Olives (the Eleona Church) and a church at Bethlehem (Church of the Nativity), as discussed above.[29]

Backed by the imperial family and other wealthy benefactors, Jerusalem quickly transformed from a Roman pagan city primarily inhabited by a Roman legion and retired legionnaires into an important, influential, and thriving Christian city. It became a primary destination for Christian pilgrims, who came by the thousands from all over the Roman Empire. There is Christian graffiti left by pilgrims dated as early as 330. The famous Bordeaux Pilgrim, who traveled from Bordeaux, France, to Jerusalem in 333 to 334, documented his pilgrimage in a literary account that has been preserved. Over the next three hundred years numerous churches, monasteries, convents, hostels, and residences were built, and the population grew significantly. The Temple Mount, however, was left vacant.

The power of the bishop in Jerusalem grew as well over these years, and during the reign of Justinian (AD 527–565), Jerusalem was designated as one of the five patriarchates (region-ruling churches with a region-ruling ecclesiastical leader), along with Rome, Constantinople, Alexandria, and Antioch.

The Sasanid Persians captured Jerusalem in 614 and destroyed many of the churches there. The Byzantine emperor recaptured Jerusalem in 629, but Muslim Arabs soon overran the entire area, capturing Jerusalem in 638. Jerusalem was ruled by Muslims for the next 1,300 years, with a brief 100-year interruption by the Crusaders (who left their mark archaeologically). In 1516, the Ottoman Turks captured Jerusalem, ruling over this region until World War I. It was the Ottoman ruler Suleiman the Magnificent who rebuilt the complete perimeter of Old City walls and gates that you can see today.[30]

Understandably, then, the archaeology of Jerusalem is extraordinarily complicated. First of all, the city is very old, and it has been completely destroyed and rebuilt a number of times. Stones cut and placed during the huge building program during the reign of Herod the Great (37–4 BC), for example, were relocated and reused several times in numerous locations over the next 1,500 years. Other reuse examples abound. A stone pedestal with a dedicatory Latin inscription that likely held a statue of the Roman Emperor Hadrian (ruled AD 117–138) was probably inscribed and set up around 135. That same pedestal can now be seen and still read (upside down) as part of the southern wall of the Temple Mount, just above the southern

---

29. Magness, *The Archaeology of the Holy Land*, 323–24; Gregory T. Armstrong, "Jerusalem," in Finney, *The Eerdmans Encyclopedia of Early Christian Art and Archaeology*, 1:728–29; Johnson, "Architecture of Empire," 293–94.
30. Shanks, *Jerusalem*, 233–43.

steps in a portion of the wall that was rebuilt by the Muslim Umayyads around 660–750.[31]

The other complicating factor is that the Old City part of Jerusalem is currently occupied, filled with houses, streets, stores, churches, mosques, schools, and offices. Often areas that archaeologists would love to excavate are inaccessible. In addition, most of the current street level in modern Old City Jerusalem is about ten feet above the street level during the era in which we are interested (AD 100–600).

The Eight-Spoked ICHTHUS Christogram—The Ecce Homo Station and Damascus Gate Triple-Arches and Paved Plazas

Perhaps the most famous eight-spoked wheel graffito is the one in Jerusalem, located underneath the Ecce Homo station of the Via Dolorosa in the Convent of the Sisters of Zion. It is etched into a large paving flagstone, alongside two small, square grids (probably game boards) and what might be the Greek letter B (*beta*) (see fig.7-1). For years, this stone paving area (varying from eight to thirteen feet below the current ground level) was claimed to be the

"place known as the Stone Pavement [Λιθόστρωτον; *lithostrōton*]" (John 19:13), supposedly where Pilate said, "Here is the man!" (John 19:5), or in the Latin Vulgate: *Ecce homo*— the name of the station. People thought that this stone pavement with the eight-spoked wheel and the square grid game boards etched on it was the exact place where the Roman soldiers gambled for Jesus's robe and that they used these very game boards for that gambling event. For support, this speculative claim added that the Greek letter B (*beta*) stood for *basileus*, the Greek word for "king," and that the game was "the king's game."

Over the past forty years, however, archaeologists have come to the conclusion that this particular area was part of the construction activities surrounding the visit of Hadrian and his rebuilding of

Fig. 7-1 Jerusalem, Convent of the Sisters of Zion: ICHTHUS Christogram (Plexiglas Protective Cover Makes It Difficult to Distinguish All of the Spokes of the Wheel)

---

31. Hershel Shanks, *Jerusalem's Temple Mount: From Solomon to the Golden Dome* (New York: Continuum, 2007), 48–51.

Jerusalem into Aelia Capitolina in the years that followed the end of the Bar Kokhba revolt (i.e., after 135)—more than one hundred years after the death of Christ. So, obviously, it cannot be the spot where the Roman soldiers gambled for Jesus's robe. Furthermore, at present there is no literary or archaeological evidence that I am aware of that there even was such a "king's game" in the ancient world. Finally, it is not at all certain that the symbol etched into the paving is the Greek letter *beta*; it may be part of a box. Even if it is the letter *beta*, there is no inscriptional evidence that B by itself would be an abbreviation of *basileus* ("king"). During the Roman era, when *basileus* was abbreviated in inscriptions, it normally appeared as ΒΑΣ or ΒΑC.[32] On the other hand, as discussed above, the early Christians often used the Greek word βοηθέω (*boētheō*, "help") in both graffiti and in inscriptions, and they frequently abbreviated this word with the single capital letter B, especially when it appears next to some kind of symbol, like a cross or an anchor.[33]

In his discussion of the symbols on these paving stones in the Convent of the Sisters of Zion, Michael Sebbane dates the inscriptions vaguely as between the first half of the second century up to the seventh century. He also notes that the "game boards" were not all inscribed at the same time. He surmises that the eight-spoked wheel, which he views as a game board, was inscribed first.[34]

Based on a few remaining structures, limited excavations, and the famous Madaba mosaic map of Jerusalem (in a church in Jordan, dating to 600), archaeologists have been able to determine the central street layout constructed in the time of Hadrian (early second century). These streets and other identifiable landmarks remained in the same locations down into the seventh century, and the Madaba mosaic map lines up remarkably well with the archaeological data. Even though the current street level in Old Jerusalem is approximately eight to thirteen feet higher in elevation, several current streets are still aligned along similar routes. This means we can determine fairly accurately many of the central streets and monuments that Hadrian built—facilities that would have still been in place as the tumultuous fourth century began.[35]

On the north side of the Old City of Jerusalem, where the famous Damascus Gate currently stands, Hadrian built an impressive triple-arched monu-

32.   McLean, *An Introduction to Greek Epigraphy*, 52.

33.   See the examples cited and presented in drawing form in Testa, *Il Simbolismo Dei Giudeo-Cristiani*, 396–400. One particularly interesting and relevant door lintel inscription that Testa cites has the word ΙΧΘΥC, followed by a Tau-Rho Staurogram, followed by the abbreviated words "hear" and "Lord," followed by the letter B, which in this case abbreviates the word for "help" (*boētheō*) (399).

34.   Michael Sebbane, "Board Games from the Eastern Cardo," in *Jerusalem: Western Wall Plaza Excavations*, vol. 1, *The Roman and Byzantine Remains: Architecture and Stratigraphy*, IAA Reports 63, ed. Shlomit Weksler-Bdolah and Alexander Onn (Jerusalem: Israel Antiquities Authority, 2019), 153–54.

35.   Magness, *Archaeology of the Holy Land*, 271–76. See the map of Aelia Capitolina at this time on p. 272. See another similar map in Armstrong, "Jerusalem," 728.

Fig. 7-2 Jerash, Triple-Arched Monumental Gate Honoring Emperor Hadrian

Fig. 7-3 Jerusalem, Damascus Gate: One of the Small Side Openings Remaining from the Original Triple-Arched Gate Can Be Seen in the Lower Left

ment. It is not certain whether this (and other similar monuments he built in Jerusalem) were built by others to honor him or built by him as monuments of his triumph over the Jews in the Bar Kokhba revolt. As noted above, there is one of these triple-arched (one large central arch and two smaller side arches) monuments from the time of Hadrian still standing in good condition not too far away in Jerash (now in modern Jordan) (see fig. 7-2).[36] In Jerusalem, the current Damascus Gate is built on top of the Hadrian-era triple-arch monument, with current ground level about ten feet above the old ground level. The high, middle arch of the original monument has been replaced with the actual entryway part of the Damascus Gate. Yet one of the smaller side arches still remains and can be seen today, about ten feet down on the east side of the Damascus Gate (see fig. 7-3).[37]

Just inside this triple-arched monument (it was only attached to rebuilt walls as a gate much later), Hadrian built an expansive oval-shaped paved stone plaza with a towering column in the center. There was probably a statue of Hadrian (or one of the later Roman emperors) on the top of that column.[38]

From this monument and plaza on the north side of the new city Aelia Capitolina, Hadrian built two primary north-south paved colonnaded streets (called "cardos"). One ran due south (the so-called West Cardo). The street on top of this route now is Suq Khan Ez-Zeit. The entrance to the Temple of Aphrodite (now replaced by the Church of the Holy Sepulcher) faced this

---

36. Weksler-Bdolah, *Aelia Capitolina*, 60–63.
37. Magness, *Archaeology of the Holy Land*, 273–76.
38. Weksler-Bdolah, *Aelia Capitolina*, 65–66.

street, built on the west side of the street. After continuing south, this West Cardo terminated, making a T at an intersection with an east-west street (major east-west streets in Roman cities were called "decumanus") that ran from Wilson's Arch at the Temple Mount westward to what is now the Jaffa Gate in the west. Later, during the Byzantine era and after the departure of the Tenth Legion, this ancient West Cardo was continued south from the termination at the intersection into what is now the western edge of the Jewish Quarter. A portion of the street in this area has been excavated and partially restored (simply referred to as "the Cardo") and is a popular tourist site.[39]

The other north-south cardo built by Hadrian (called the East Cardo) angled slightly from the plaza and the triple-arched monument at the Damascus Gate to the southeast, in the direction of the Temple Mount. The current street, lying approximately eight to thirteen feet above the ancient one, is called HaGai or El-Wad. During various excavations in this area (for sewer lines, etc.), remains of the ancient street have been discovered in twenty different locations.[40] After a short distance southeast, this street formed an intersection with an east-west street (the North Decumanus) that ran on the north side of the abandoned Temple Mount, from an eastern gate (now the Lion's Gate) through the ruins of the Antonia Fortress, along the route that is now the Via Dolorosa. A short distance after the intersection with this North Decumanus, the East Cardo turns slightly to the right and goes straight south, paralleling the Temple Mount and terminating just south of it.

On the North Decumanus, which now lies underneath the Via Dolorosa to the north of the Temple Mount, Hadrian built another triple-arch monument. The top part of the high central arch can still be seen today above the street. Popularly it is called the Ecce Homo arch. Anyone who has walked this part of the Via Dolorosa has passed underneath the central section of this arch (see fig. 7-4). It is difficult at first to recognize it as a monumental triple arch because stores and residences have been built into it and around it and the current ground level is several

Fig. 7-4 Jerusalem, Via Dolarosa, Ecce Homo Arch

39. Magness, *Archaeology of the Holy Land*, 273–76; Weksler-Bdolah, *Aelia Capitolina*, 67–71.
40. Weksler-Bdolah, *Aelia Capitolina*, 68–69, 76–88.

feet above the original street. One of the smaller side arches can still be seen inside the Convent of the Sisters of Zion, down below current street level.[41]

Just to the east (toward the east gate—now the Lion's Gate) of this triple-arch monument, Hadrian built a broad square paved area, most likely as a forum. Temples, such as the nearby Temple of Asclepius, probably bordered this paved forum area. Sections of this area can be seen today below ground level in the Convent of the Sisters of Zion and in the Chapel of the Condemnation in the Franciscan Monastery of the Flagellation. Portions of this area were built above an earlier water pool (the Struthion Pool) using arches, some of which can still be seen today.[42]

We can conclude with some confidence that, in the mid-second century and into the early fourth century, there was a triple-arch monument and paved plaza area at the location where the Damascus Gate now stands and another triple-arch monument with a paved forum area where the Ecce Homo arch can be seen on the Via Dolorosa.

There is a clear eight-spoked ICHTHUS wheel etched into the stone paving of this forum near the Ecce Homo arch (the famous one in the Convent of the Sisters of Zion). Michael Sebbane, an Israeli archaeologist and museum curator for the Israeli Antiquities Authority, actually documents three eight-spoked wheels on the Hadrianic-era paving stones associated with these two monumental triple arches in the northern part of Aelia Capitolina (Old City Jerusalem): one in the Convent of the Sisters of Zion (as noted above); one in the nearby Chapel of the Condemnation; and one in the oval plaza associated with the triple-arch monument at the Damascus Gate location.[43]

While there can be no certainty about how these eight-spoked wheel graffiti came to be etched onto these paving stones, as we have argued throughout this book, the events taking place in the early fourth century provide a plausible context for their appearance. Note that these two triple-arch monuments contained niches that held pagan idols. The monuments also served as the most visible and prominent entrances to the city. As we have seen in other cities from this era, it is likely that following the Great Persecution, after Constantine declares Christianity legal and then actually throws his imperial support in their favor, Christians in Jerusalem (as in Ephesus, Laodicea, and other cities throughout the empire) sought to cleanse and Christianize their city, perhaps with some feelings of retribution and victory as well. The Christians in Jerusalem were probably emboldened by Constantine's decree that the Temple of Aphrodite be completely destroyed and removed. They probably first destroyed the many idols in the city, beheading and defacing pagan idol statues as well as (and especially) imperial cult statues. At the

41. Weksler-Bdolah, *Aelia Capitolina*, 100–106.

42. Murphy-O'Connor, *The Holy Land*, 35–36; Magness, *Archaeology of the Holy Land*, 276–79; Weksler-Bdolah, *Aelia Capitolina*, 100–106.

43. Sebbane, "Board Games from the Eastern Cardo," 162.

same time, they sought to drive out the demons associated with pagan gods at entrances, intersections, and water facilities, using the name of Jesus and the sign of the cross. The three ICHTHUS Christograms near the two triple-arched monuments were probably etched at this time as well. The appearance of the ICHTHUS acrostic in the floor mosaics of the Church of the Nativity in Bethlehem, as discussed above, attests to the fact that ICHTHUS was a widely known acrostic and symbol of Jesus Christ at this time in this particular area.

Due to the complications listed above, we have limited archaeological records in Jerusalem from this time (AD 100–600). The entire Temple of Aphrodite, as well as any of the pagan shrines or temples that were built elsewhere in the city, were destroyed and removed by Constantine from 325 to 335. In the limited remains of the triple-arch monuments and the stone paving plaza associated with them, it is remarkable that there are three eight-spoked ICHTHUS Christograms. Undoubtedly, based on this limited evidence, there must have been many more of these Christograms inscribed throughout the city, even if the actual numbers of Christians in the city at this time may have been small.

MAGDALA (TARICHEAE)

The Village/City of Magdala (Taricheae)

The archaeological site popularly referred to as Magdala lies on the northwestern shore of the Sea of Galilee at the base of Mount Arbel just to the north of Tiberias. It is often identified as the home village of Mary Magdalene, a place that was almost certainly visited by Jesus.

As the ongoing archaeological excavations at this site continue to uncover a larger and larger urban center, questions have come up about whether this is indeed the *village* of Magdala and whether this site is really connected to Mary Magdalene.[44] Some scholars have argued that this urban center being excavated is not the village of Magdala but rather the city of Taricheae, a significantly sized fortified city mentioned several times by Josephus.[45] Some of the archaeologists currently working the site argue to keep both identifications—that in Aramaic the site was known as Magdala, in Hebrew it was Migdal, and in Greek it was known as Taricheae, the city to which Josephus refers.[46] This is also the view of Richard Bauckham and all of the contributors to the book *Magdala of Galilee*; Bauckham claims it is the "scholarly consensus."[47]

---

44. Joan E. Taylor, "Missing Magdala and the Name of Mary 'Magdalene,'" *PEQ* 146.3 (2014): 205–23; Elizabeth Schrader and Joan E. Taylor, "The Meaning of 'Magdalene': A Review of Literary Evidence," *JBL* 140.4 (2021): 751–73.

45. Joan E. Taylor, "Magdala's Mistaken Identity," *BAR* 48.3 (2022): 55–58.

46. Marcela Zapata-Meza, Andrea Garza, Diaz Barriga, and Rosaura Sanz-Rincón, "The Magdala Archaeological Project (2010–2012): A Preliminary Report of the Excavations at Migdal," *'Atiqot* 90 (2018): 83–125.

47. Richard Bauckham, "Magdala as We Now Know It," in *Magdala of Galilee: A Jewish City in the Hellenistic and Roman Period*, ed. Richard Bauckham (Waco, TX: Baylor University Press, 2018), 7.

Magdala/Taricheae was established around 200 BC during the Hasmonean period. From the beginning, it was associated with the fishing industry. The meaning of the Greek name of the city, Taricheae, is related to the processing of fish. In the mid-first century BC, to gain firm control of this region and especially the roads passing through Magdala/Taricheae, the Romans established an army camp here. Throughout the first century BC and into the first century AD, Magdala/Taricheae flourished and grew. It was a Jewish stronghold during the first Jewish revolt (AD 66–70) and was captured by the Romans in 67. The city, however, did not participate in the Bar Kokhba revolt in 132 to 136 and continued to function in the second century.

Like many of the cities in this region, Magdala/Taricheae was seriously damaged by the earthquake of 363, and the archaeological evidence suggests a certain amount of depopulation then. However, as the Christianization of the region continued throughout the fourth and into the fifth century, Magdala/Taricheae recovered and grew. The city was said to be the birthplace of Mary Magdalene, and it became a popular pilgrimage site. Catering to the pilgrims no doubt added to its growth. Indeed, a sizable Christian monastery from this era was discovered in the excavations of the city.[48]

The Synagogue

In 2009, the excavation team working in Magdala/Taricheae uncovered what they have identified as a synagogue. This identification was based on the shape of the building, a block of stone in the center of the main room with a menorah etched on it (probably the base for a wooden stand to hold the Torah while it was being read or studied), and two nearby *mikva'ot* (Jewish ritual baths, below ground level, with descending steps). They dated this synagogue to the Second Temple period, making this one of the earliest synagogues discovered to date and bringing a certain amount of fame to the site. In fact, they suggest that this synagogue went out of use by the latter half of the first century AD, probably during the Jewish revolt against Rome in 66–70.[49]

The central room in this synagogue has a mosaic floor. In addition to a swastika meander–type perimeter edging, there is one circular-shaped symbol, placed prominently at the center of the pattern in one of the most visible and central locations in the entire synagogue. This circle appears to have eight spokes, although two of the spokes are thinner than the others, and there are four triangles with an arc on one edge (similar to pizza slices) in four of the eight spaces formed by the spokes (see fig. 7-5). In discussing this mosaic, Mordechai Aviam makes the following, somewhat misleading statement: "The mosaic floor of the eastern side contains the decoration of a colored rosette [i.e., the eight-spoked wheel] and swastika meanders, a design similar to that of other mosaic floors of first century CE palaces and private

48. Bauckham, "Magdala as We Now Know It," in Bauckham, *Magdala of Galilee*, 21.
49. Mordechai Aviam, "The Synagogue," in Bauckham, *Magdala of Galilee*, 127–33.

houses. A mosaic with an identical design and size was uncovered by Virgilio Corbo in the southern area of Magdala in what we now know to be a room in the baths."[50]

After tracking down Aviam's sources and the pictures they show, it is clear that Aviam's statement, "a design similar to that of other mosaic floors of first century CE palaces and private houses," refers *only* to the swastika meanders and *not* to the "colored rosette" (the eight-spoked wheel). That is, the perimeter edging ("swastika meanders") is a recognizable feature of mosaics from this time period and in this region. Yet, while the perimeter edging design in the mosaics can be found in other places, I have been unable to locate any kind of eight-spoked wheel among all of

Fig. 7-5 Magdala (Taricheae), Synagogue Floor Mosaics

the first–second-century floor mosaics that I have viewed in Israel to date.[51] Furthermore, while rosettes are fairly common decorative features in buildings and in funerary inscriptions, these rosettes are quite different than the eight-spoked wheel in the mosaics at Magdala; they lack the dark lines that look like wheel spokes. Six-segmented rosettes, for example, are inscribed into the "synagogue stone" (also called the Magdala Stone) likewise discovered in this synagogue, but these differ significantly from the eight-spoked wheel in the mosaics of the main room of the synagogue.[52]

The Magdala archaeology project director notes that another, similar circular mosaic was discovered in the *mikva'ot* (Jewish ritual baths) area at Magdala. Calling them both rosettes, she presents an extensive comparison of the two, noting that while similar, there are some clear differences. Nonetheless, she states that they are both the same geometric shape, just different

50. Aviam, "The Synagogue," 130.

51. Besides the numerous sites that I have visited (Sepphoris, Scythopolis, etc.), there is no evidence of an eight-spoked wheel in any of the mosaics found in the following: Ernst Kitzinger, *Israeli Mosaics of the Byzantine Period* (New York: UNESCO, 1965); Zvi Gal, *The Splendor of Mosaics in Israel's National Parks* (Industrial Park, Israel: Rahash, 2012); and Michal Dayagi-Mendels and Silvia Rozenberg, eds., *Chronicles of the Land: Archaeology in the Israel Museum, Jerusalem*, 2nd edition (Jerusalem: The Israel Museum, 2011). Zodiac circles are quite common but not anything resembling an eight-spoked wheel.

52. Mordechai Aviam and Richard Bauckham, "The Synagogue Stone," in Bauckham, *Magdala of Galilee*, 136–38.

in quality. She concludes that, overall, "The rosette was a frequent motif in Jewish art during the early Roman period, and it is strictly decorative, devoid of ancient symbolism, but inherited by oriental designs."[53] Yet when she presents the rosettes side by side,[54] one can see clearly that the pattern from the *mikva'ot* is a traditional rosette and lacks the dark radial arms that the eight-spoked figure in the synagogue contains. Furthermore, while traditional rosettes may be "strictly decorative," it seems premature to conclude that this rather unique eight-spoked wheel shape in a prominent, central, and most visible location is "strictly decorative" and "devoid" of "ancient symbolism."

For now, this eight-spoked circle mosaic in the synagogue at Magdala remains an enigma, and to date I haven't found any satisfactory, or even plausible, published explanation for it. The discovery of this synagogue is fairly recent, and books such as Bauckham's *Magdala of Galilee* are based on preliminary reports. Often in archaeology, in the years that follow, the initial conclusions of the original archaeologists are challenged and refined. Here at Magdala/Taricheae, even the identification of the city has been challenged. Furthermore, in December 2021, the Israel Antiquities Authority announced that another, second synagogue was discovered at Magdala.

At the time of this writing, a final, comprehensive archaeological report on the first synagogue (with the eight-spoked wheel) has not been published, meaning many of the conclusions that have been drawn by scholars are tentative.[55] The initial dating of the synagogue was based on coins that were discovered in the excavation (minted in Tiberias, dated 42–43). Yet keep in mind that coins can only establish a firm limit for the earliest date of the constructed area. The area certainly underwent some dramatic transitions, and at the present time most of the archaeologists associated with the site believe that the synagogue was abandoned or destroyed in the mid-first century (perhaps in 67 during the Jewish revolt).[56] That creates a very narrow window for when the eight-spoked wheel was placed in the mosaics of this synagogue. Or was this design added later? If it is a Jewish design, what does it mean? Is it mere decoration? Why was it placed in such a prominent, visible area?

SCYTHOPOLIS (BETH SHEAN)

The City of Scythopolis
In the Old Testament, this site was known as the city of Beth Shean. It was one of the oldest continuously occupied cities in the ancient Near East. The

---

53. Rosaura Sanz-Rincón, "An Early Roman Mosaic Floor in the Jewish Village of Magdala, Galilee," *European Journal of Science and Theology* 16.3 (2020): 129–38.
54. Sanz-Rincón, "An Early Roman Mosaic Floor," 136 (fig. 8).
55. Aviam, "The Synagogue," 128, reminds his readers of this back in 2018.
56. Aviam, "The Synagogue," 133.

stratified remains of this ancient city now form the huge tel, a mountain shaped by successive layers of destroyed and rebuilt cities. The tel looms over the newer Greco-Roman city that lies at its base. After the Assyrians destroyed the city in 732 BC, the upper part of the city, which was elevated on top of the tel, was abandoned and unoccupied until the Hellenistic period (following the conquest of the area by Alexander the Great in 332 BC).[57]

Beth Shean was strategically located at one of the most important north-south and east-west highway intersections in the region. During the third century BC it became an administrative center and military stronghold. It was renamed Scythopolis, and sometimes it was referred to as Nysa-Scythopolis. The term "Nysa" was related to the pagan god Dionysius, the god of this city. It was inhabited primarily by a Greek-speaking, non-Jewish population, and the city took on a Hellenistic character. It was included as one of the cities of the Decapolis, a loose confederation of ten Hellenistic cities in this region on both sides of the Jordan River.[58]

The Romans conquered the area in 64 to 63 BC, and Scythopolis, the most populous city of the Decapolis at that time, became an important part of the Roman Empire. At this time in history (the so-called Pax Romana), the security of cities within the Roman Empire against outside attack was provided by the legions of Rome, meaning the elevation and walls of cities became less important security features. For the city of Scythopolis, this is evidenced by its move down off the elevated heights and to the area at the foot of the ancient tel. As the city became more and more Roman in character, this move was essential, for Roman cities needed water for pools, monumental fountains, and bathhouses. It was nearly impossible to bring that much water to the top of the ancient tel, and so the city continued to move down to lower-lying areas, where plentiful water could be delivered.

Following the visit of the emperor Hadrian (AD 129–132) and the Roman victory over the Jewish Bar Kokhba revolt (AD 132–136), Scythopolis entered a period characterized by rapid expansion and the continuous construction of new, monumental structures. This continued into the third century. By the end of the third century, Scythopolis had numerous paved, colonnaded streets; two theaters (the huge southern theater seating up to ten thousand people); a hippodrome; an Odeon (small amphitheater for governmental meetings); two bathhouses; a plethora of temples, including some associated with the imperial cult; several monumental fountains; an expansive agora with a multitude of shops; a basilica (for administrative and judicial operations); two bridges over the nearby streams; an extensive aqueduct system; five monumental freestanding gates; and plenty of residences. As in typical

---

57. Nava Panitz-Cohen, "Beth-Shean, Bronze and Iron Age," in Master, *The Oxford Encyclopedia of the Bible and Archaeology*, 1:118.

58. Gabriel Mazor, "Beth-Shean, Roman and Byzantine Period," in Master, *The Oxford Encyclopedia of the Bible and Archaeology*, 1:119–20.

Greco-Roman cities at this time, the gates, temples, fountains, streets, and monuments contained statues of Greco-Roman gods.[59]

When the Great Persecution started in 303, there was apparently a strong Christian church there. Eusebius recounts the martyrdom in 303 of Procopius, a leader of the church in Scythopolis, who held the office of "reader, translator, and exorcist" (a term that perhaps underscores the serious concern over demons that the early church had). Eusebius also mentions the martyrdom of a woman from Scythopolis named Manathas.[60] After Constantine came to power, Christianity expanded rapidly throughout the region, and as in other cities, the Christianization of Scythopolis continued over the next two hundred years.

Soon there were powerful, influential, and often highly controversial bishops presiding over the church at Scythopolis. In the early years of the fourth century, for example, soon after Constantine came to power and called the famous Council of Nicaea (AD 325), the bishop of Scythopolis was Patrophilus, a friend and outspoken supporter of Arius, whose teachings were rejected as heresy at the council. He even gave refuge to Arius after he was exiled by the Council of Nicaea.[61] This particular region—both Palaestina Secunda (Galilee, etc.) and Palaestina Prima (Jerusalem, Judea, etc.)—was a hotbed of theological controversy during the christological battles running throughout the fourth and fifth centuries, not only those addressed at the Council of Nicaea but also those addressed at the Council of Chalcedon (AD 451). The theological beliefs and sympathies of both bishops and provincial governors became critical aspects of appointment and tenure, as well as within church council and imperial court conspiracy and intrigue; tensions were almost always high. All of this took place while the Christians were trying to convert all the non-Christians in the area and to change the nature of the cities from pagan to Christian.

In 363, in the middle of the fourth-century Christianization process, the city of Scythopolis was hit by a devastating earthquake. Those temples that had not been destroyed by the Christians or abandoned for economic reasons were seriously damaged and not repaired. By the early fifth century, all the temples in Scythopolis had been abandoned or completely removed.[62] A number of defaced or headless pagan god statues from this time were discovered in the excavations, implying that here, as elsewhere, the Christians destroyed the

---

59. Mazor, "Beth-Shean, Roman and Byzantine Period," 120–26.
60. Eusebius, *The Martyrs of Palestine* 1.1–2; 9.6–8. See the discussion in Yoram Tsafrir and Gideon Foerster, "Urbanism at Scythopolis-Bet Shean in the Fourth to Seventh Centuries," *Dumbarton Oaks Papers* 51 (1997): 107.
61. Katharina Heyden, "Beth Shean/Scythopolis in Late Antiquity: Cult and Culture, Continuity and Change," in *One God—One Cult—One Nation: Archaeological and Biblical Perspectives*, BZAW 405, ed. Reinhard Kratz and Hermann Spieckermann (2010): 308–9; Tsafrir and Foerster, "Urbanism at Scythopolis-Bet Shean," 108.
62. Mazor, "Beth-Shean, Roman and Byzantine Period," 126.

pagan gods of the city (or at least most of them).[63] Furthermore, new Christian churches were built on top of, or in close proximity to, the earlier pagan temples. This typically involved reusing many of the stone blocks and columns from the destroyed temples.[64] As in other cities across the Roman Empire, the Christianization process spread beyond temple cleansing and conversion to the removal of public idols and the attempt to cleanse all of the areas of the city that had been affected by paganism and its associated demons.

Over the next two hundred years, Scythopolis continued to grow. It was an important ecclesiastic, economic, and administrative center. Not only churches but several monasteries were built, along with new and renovated monumental structures. The city probably reached its population and building-activity peak during the reigns of the Byzantine emperors Anastasius (AD 491–518) and Justinian I (AD 518–527).

A bubonic plague devastated the population in 541 to 542. In 614, the Sasanid Persians conquered the region and captured Scythopolis, followed by the Muslim Arabs in 635 to 636, who moved the provincial capital to Tiberias. Scythopolis was damaged by another earthquake in 660 and then almost totally destroyed by an even more severe earthquake in 749, after which the city was abandoned.[65]

The Western Bathhouse

As the fourth century began, bathhouses were a regular and important facility in cities across the Roman Empire. The fate of these bathhouses during the Christianization process of the fourth and early fifth centuries varied from city to city. In general, Christians discouraged the bathhouses, especially some of the immoral activities associated with them, but no monolithic view was taken toward them. In some areas, after certain modifications, the public bathhouses continued to operate with popularity throughout this time period.[66]

While the bathhouses, like other structures associated with idols, were assumed to be the abode of demons, this could be corrected and the facility cleansed. Consistently, the Christians removed and destroyed the idol statues of the bathhouses and removed or painted over the offensive and often immoral wall paintings. Crosses, along with other Christian symbols and inscriptions, were often etched into the doorjambs and walls of the bathhouses, cleansing the facility and driving out the demons, in similar fashion to the pagan temples.

There is considerable evidence from sites throughout the Roman/Byzantine Empire that, in the fourth to sixth centuries, Christians began using the

---

63. Mazor, "Beth-Shean, Roman and Byzantine Period," 126. For pictures of several of these defaced or beheaded statues, see Tsafrir and Foerster, "Urbanism at Scythopolis-Bet Shean," figs. 37–38.

64. Chambers, "The Origin and Expansion of the Decapolis Churches," 233.

65. Heyden, "Beth Shean/Scythopolis in Late Antiquity," 328–29.

66. Yegül, Bathing in the Roman World, 201–2.

public bathhouses (a standard central and prestigious facility in every city of any size) for purposes other than public bathing. "Baptistries often replaced bathing installations. . . . The educational spaces of the Greek gymnasium were also often adapted to Christian pedagogical purposes. . . . In the 5th and 6th c. Christians also inserted their administrative institutions into the architecture of bath-gymnasium complexes."[67]

While in some cities the bathing function of the bathhouse was replaced with administrative or pedagogical activities, in other cities mixed bathing and immoral activities were banned but the basic bathing and social interaction function of the bathhouse was retained. Sometimes the church itself took over the operation of the bathhouse. In cities like Scythopolis, which experienced a huge influx of pilgrims and other visitors, the bathhouses were apparently kept operational and were even expanded during the late fourth and fifth centuries to accommodate the new crowds.[68]

Many bathhouses had associated gymnasium facilities where athletes practiced and trained, often naked. In general, however, gymnasiums were already in decline by the beginning of the fourth century, due to the trend in the Roman era to replace the Greek-era athletic competitions with chariot races and gladiatorial contests. During the Christianization process in the fourth century, most of the few remaining operating gymnasiums were closed.[69]

This transition or rededication and reuse of the bathhouses is strongly suggested by the multiple Christian inscriptions (often with crosses) that appear in bathhouses throughout the Roman/Byzantine world. An example of this can be seen at the Hadrianic Baths at Leptis Magna in North Africa. In this bathhouse is an inscription containing a Latin cross, a branch, and a name.[70] As discussed in chapter 5, at Aphrodisias, multiple Christian inscriptions can be found in both the Theater Baths and the Hadrianic Baths.[71] One of these inscriptions contains a cross with the Greek word τουτο ("this") written above and νικα ("is victorious, triumphant") written under its arms (i.e., "the cross is victorious").[72] Both bathhouses at Aphrodisias apparently underwent some type of Christian transformation, or at least were modified with

---

67. Cornelius Steckner, "Bath: Christian Reuse of," in Finney, *The Eerdmans Encyclopedia of Early Christian Art and Archaeology*, 1:177. Note also that Severus, the influential Patriarch of Antioch in the early sixth century, who had started out his adult service to God as a monk, rejected the use of the luxurious bathhouse that came with his official residence and ordered that it be torn down. *Anonymous Life of Severos (Attributed to John of Beth Aphtonia)* trans. Sebastian Brock and Brian Fitzgerald in *Two Early Lives of Severos, Patriarch of Antioch* by Sebastian Brock (Liverpool: Liverpool University Press, 2013), 58. See also Iain R. Torrance, *Christology after Chalcedon: Serverus of Antioch and Sergius the Monophysite* (Eugene, OR: Wipf & Stock, 1998), 5.

68. Yegül, *Bathing in the Roman World*, 201–4; Tsasfrir and Foerster, "Urbanism at Scythopolis-Bet Shean," 131.

69. Yegül, *Bathing in the Roman World*, 206.

70. Inscriptions of Roman Tripolitania database, no. 832, https://inslib.kcl.ac.uk/irt2009/.

71. Roueché, *Aphrodisias in Late Antiquity*, 187–88, 233–34.

72. Roueché, *Aphrodisias in Late Antiquity*, 188.

Christian influence. Several scholars have suggested that the conversion of bathhouses to some type of Christian use is suggested by cross patterns in the mosaics of the bathhouses both at Sardis and Aizanoi,[73] as well as other Christian symbols in the mosaics of the baths of Neptune at Ostia.[74]

In Scythopolis, just west of the main north-south Palladius Street and to the northwest of the theater, is a well-preserved bathhouse (the Western Bathhouse). Archaeologists at Scythopolis in 1994 dated its construction to the late fourth century,[75] but as of 2013, they have modified the date to be somewhat ambiguous, stating that it was "built in the Roman period according to the spacious pattern of imperial bathhouses and enlarged in the Byzantine period."[76]

Fig. 7-6 Scythopolis (Beth Shean), Western Bathhouse: Niche with Cross and Alpha-Omega

One of the small rooms connected directly to the bathhouse on the northwest side contains a curved-roof niche with a small pool. There is a large, red, Latin-style cross painted on the plastered wall below the curved roof and above the pool (see fig. 7-6). This cross has slightly flared ends and the letters *alpha* and *omega* appear to be suspended from its cross (although portions of the two letters are missing). Branches and leaves are depicted next to this cross. This pool may have served as a "bathing basin,"[77] or it may have served more generally as an exterior fountain pool. Some suggest that this may have been converted by the Christians to be used as a baptistry or perhaps a martyrium,[78] but this is unlikely.

73. For this suggestion regarding the bathhouse/gymnasium complex at Sardis, see Buchwald, *Churches EA and E at Sardis*, 43. For similar views of the bathhouse conversion at Aizanoi (located in Phrygia, northeast of Sardis), see Rudolf Naumann, "Aizanoi: Bericht über die Ausgrabungen und Untersuchungen 1983 und 1984," *Archäologischer Anzeiger* (1987): 303–40, cited by Buchwald, *Churches EA and E at Sardis*, 43.
74. Longenecker, *The Cross before Constantine*, 76–81.
75. G. Mazor and R. Bar-Nathan, "Scythopolis—Capital of Palaestina Secunda," *Qadmoniot* 107–8 (1994): 124. For bib. see 117–37.
76. Mazor, "Beth-Shean, Roman and Byzantine Period," 125.
77. Mazor and Bar-Nathan, "Scythopolis—Capital of Palaestina Secunda," 126.
78. Miriam Feinberg Vamosh, *Beit She'an: Capital of the Decapolis*, Israel Nature and National Parks Protection Authority (Tel Aviv: ERETZ Ha-Tzvi, 1996), 23.

Often these curved-roof niches in Greco-Roman cities held small pagan statues, and this may have been the case here. The pool below the niche seems to be an exterior pool or fountain, perhaps providing water for activities and use outside of the bathhouse. Pagan statues were frequently placed at pools and fountains, so perhaps after removing the pagan idol in the niche, the Christians cleansed the area of the idol's demonic influence with a painted cross.

This is one of the few places where the original plaster and paint from an ancient wall remains, allowing us to see what was painted by the early Christians and not just what was etched in stone or laid in mosaics. There is a similar red cross painted in a niche at a public monumental fountain (the Antonine Nymphaeum) at Sagalassos in Anatolia, and another one painted on a wall frieze in between pagan gods in the theater of Perge on the southern coast of Asia Minor. The fact that, of the few plastered walls that are preserved, several of them bear painted crosses suggests that there probably were quite a number of crosses painted throughout the pagan cities as the Christians sought to Christianize them.[79] Yet whichever of these purposes this cross in the Western Bathhouse served, the painted cross clearly indicates a Christian function for that room or an attempt to cleanse and Christianize the room.

Later, in 538, Flavius Theodorus, the governor of Palaestina Secunda, rebuilt and expanded the Western Bathhouse.[80] This included a colonnaded basilica-shaped structure that extended across its southern edge. While some earlier scholars referred to this as a *palaestra*, an exercise area and part of a gymnasium, many scholars today identify it as a basilica.[81] This is due to the shape of the structure—a long narrow hall and a semi-circular apse at the front (usually on the west end)—and to the fact that few *palaestra* were functioning anymore at this time.

This basilica, probably serving an administrative function, contained "living rooms" on its western side and an open-air colonnaded stoa along the eastern side. The floor of the long hall was paved with mosaics, and while part of the floor has been damaged, many of the mosaics remain. In addition to several inscriptions about the assistance the provincial governors had provided (like Flavius Theodorus), the mosaic floor contains multiple eight-spoked wheels. These wheels are generally located next to the inscriptions or along the eastern edge of the stoa—in prominent view as you step into the basilica from the open-air side (see fig. 7-7). These wheels are nearly identical to the eight-spoked ICHTHUS Christogram in the mosaics of the Southwest Church at Hippos (as discussed above), another one of the cities

79. Jacobs, "Cross Graffiti," 179.
80. Vamosh, *Beit She'an*, 23; Heyden, "Beth Shean/Scythopolis in Late Antiquity," 319.
81. Heyden, "Beth Shean/Scythopolis in Late Antiquity," 319; Tsafrir and Foerster, "Urbanism at Scythopolis-Bet Shean," 131; Gabriel Mazor, "The City's [Scythopolis] Appearance at the Beginning of the 6th Century," Israel Antiquities Authority, www.antiquities.org.il/Article_eng.aspx?sec_id=17&sub_subj_id=326&id=651.

of the Decapolis, located just on the other side of the Sea of Galilee and built at about the same time. It is highly probable that the many eight-spoked wheels in this basilica are also ICHTHUS Christograms.

By the end of the fourth century, Scythopolis had become a highly Christianized city. As noted above, in the beginning it was known as a center for Arianism. During the fifth and sixth centuries, especially after the Council of Chalcedon (451), this influential city became embroiled in the widespread theological and political battle over the nature of Christ. In 452 to 453, during a visit to Jerusalem, Severianus, bishop of Scythopolis, was assassinated for defending Chalcedonian Christology.[82] At the time of the construction of the Western Bathhouse basilica

Fig. 7-7 Scythopolis (Beth Shean), Western Bathhouse Basilica Mosaics: ICHTHUS Christogram

with the eight-spoked wheel pattern in the mosaics (AD 538), the bishop of Scythopolis was a pro-Chalcedon priest called John of Scythopolis.[83] Although the provincial governor Flavius Theodorus paid for the expansion, the bishop may have had some input on the theological symbols used. While we cannot conclude with any degree of certainty, it is at least possible that the eight-spoked wheel placed repeatedly on the floor of the basilica of the Western Bathhouse near the Christian niche with a cross reflected a theological statement supporting Chalcedonian orthodoxy.

Related to this is the observation that at Sepphoris (discussed in the next section), Flavius Theodorus is mentioned in an inscription along with the bishop of Sepphoris (Marcellinus). They apparently worked together to repair a church (Greek: *basilica*), showing that the provincial governor and local bishop collaborated to build or repair a Christian structure.[84]

On the other hand, as we have argued in this work, throughout early Christianity the eight-spoked ICHTHUS Christogram carried similar meanings and nuances as the traditional cross did. One of the symbolic statements

82. Heyden, "Beth Shean/Scythopolis in Late Antiquity," 308–10, 315.
83. Paul Rorem and John C. Lamoreaux, "John of Scythopolis on Apollinarian Christology and the Pseudo-Areopagite's True Identity," *Church History* 62.4 (1993): 469–82.
84. James F. Strange, Thomas R. W. Longstaff, and Dennis E. Groh, *Excavations at Sepphoris*, vol. 1, University of South Florida Probes in the Citadel and Villa (Leiden: Brill, 2006), 28.

frequently associated both with the cross and the ICHTHUS Christogram was that of "victory" (Greek, νίκη)—victory over the pagan world, including the demons and gods associated with it; over the hostile Roman emperors and their persecutions; and in the case of the bathhouses, perhaps victory over the immorality of the pagan Greco-Roman world that was symbolized in each city by their bathhouses. The ICHTHUS wheel was used to drive out demons and to keep them away. Yet these purposes (proclamation of victory and cleansing from demons) fit better in the fourth century during Phase I of the Christianization process than they do in the sixth century (as the mosaics here) during Phase III.

SEPPHORIS

The City of Sepphoris
Located in Galilee, Sepphoris was already an important fortified city when Herod the Great (37–4 BC) conquered the area. His son, Herod Antipas, inherited Galilee from his father, designated Sepphoris as his capital, and began a serious reconstruction of the city. Nazareth, a small village at this time, was not far away, and it is likely that Joseph, the father figure of Jesus, worked at Sepphoris as part of this huge construction project. As Jesus grew old enough to help, it is probable that he joined his father in trekking to Sepphoris every day to work on Herod Antipas's new capital city.[85]

During the Jewish revolt of AD 66 to 70 and the Bar Kokhba revolt of 132 to 137, the city of Sepphoris sided with the Romans. Indeed, during the reign of Hadrian (AD 117–139) the city changed its name to Diocaesarea ("Caesar is divine"), apparently in honor of Hadrian. It is probably at this time that a pagan temple was built in the center of the city, most likely dedicated to Zeus.[86] The city, however, managed to sustain a majority Jewish population, and Jewish writers continued to call the city by its Hebrew name, Tzipori or Zippori ("bird"). While maintaining peace with Rome throughout the third century, Sepphoris also became a center of Jewish academic study and the home of several rabbinic scholars. While there was a significant Gentile (pagan) population in the city, the Jews appeared to remain in the majority. There is little evidence of Christianity in the city until after Constantine (early fourth century).[87]

The city was built on the side of a hill. Although most of the population was Jewish, in regard to architecture and urban planning, most aspects of the city

---

85. Murphy-O'Connor, *The Holy Land*, 467–68.
86. Carol Meyers and Eric M. Meyers, "Sepphoris," in Master, *The Oxford Encyclopedia of the Bible and Archaeology*, 2:343.
87. Zeev Weiss, "Sepphoris," in Finney, *The Eerdmans Encyclopedia of Early Christian Art and Archaeology*, 2:492–94, and "Sepphoris," *Oxford Classical Dictionary*, doi.org/10.1093/acrefore/9780199381135.013.8039; Patrich, "The Early Christianization of the Holy Land," 267.

looked like other Greco-Roman cities. The lower part of the city was laid out in typical Roman fashion, with a central north-south street (the Cardo Maximus) intersecting the major east-west street (the Decumanus Maximus). Near this intersection was the forum, a pagan temple, two bathhouses, and several residences. Also nearby, built into the side of the hill, was a theater, and on top of the hill was a lavish residence with floor mosaics depicting typical scenes from Greco-Roman mythology, such as Hercules and Dionysius in a drinking contest. Indeed, beautiful floor mosaics were found in several buildings at Sepphoris.

One major difference between Sepphoris and other Greco-Roman cities is that only two fragments of pagan idols have been discovered in the extensive archaeological excavations. There is a literary reference by a rabbi to an idol in the bathhouse, but no idols or statue fragments have been discovered there. This strongly implies that the use of statuary, both of idols and honored individuals, was less prevalent in Sepphoris than in other cities, no doubt due to the strong Jewish influence. Another difference is that, as far as archaeologists can tell, there was only one pagan temple, although it was located at the heart of the city.[88] No doubt that temple contained at least one idol, but during the Christian era the temple itself was totally removed and replaced with a church, and no trace of the temple's original central idol has been discovered.

After Constantine came to power in the early fourth century, things started to change all across this region, and the Christian population and influence started to grow. In Sepphoris, due perhaps to the majority Jewish population, the big changes apparently were delayed until the fifth and sixth centuries—later than in most of the other cities we have studied. Sepphoris was severely damaged by the earthquake of 363 but was able to rebuild. Perhaps some of the fifth-century construction mentioned below was part of the reconstruction.

In the fifth century, many changes took place in the main forum area (lower area) of the city. The main north-south street (the Cardo Maximus) was rebuilt and improved, especially by adding a colonnaded, mosaic-paved sidewalk and storefront area (stoa) along the street (see fig. 7-8). The central pagan temple in the forum area—probably lying in ruins since the earthquake of 363—was completely destroyed and removed, and a church was built on top of it. Other churches were built as well. The Jewish presence also continued, and a new synagogue was built.

Fig. 7-8 Sepphoris, Cardo Maximus: Sidewalk with Mosaics to the Right of the Columns

88.   Zeev Weiss, "Greco-Roman Influences on the Art and Architecture of the Jewish City in Roman Palestine," in Lapin, *Religious and Ethnic Communities in Later Roman Palestine*, 244–46.

The Cardo Maximus

The rebuilt Cardo Maximus had a wide sidewalk and storefront area (stoa) that was colonnaded, covered, and paved with mosaics. Near the intersection with the Decumanus Maximus (this is the street that visitors walk on as they enter the site today), in the mosaics of the stoa is a dedicatory inscription circumscribed with a large circle. The inscription reads: "Under our most saintly father Eutropius the Bishop, the whole work of the mosaic [pavement] was done."[89] Architecturally and stratigraphically, the street renovation is related to the construction of the two new churches, one of which was just to the west of the inscription and one of which was to the east (built on top of the pagan temple).[90]

Many Christian bishops from 300 to 600 are named in the accounts of church historians and the records of the church councils. Bishop Marcellinus of Diocaesarea (Sepphoris), for example, is recorded as attending the synod of Jerusalem in 518. A dedicatory inscription mentioning Marcellinus was also discovered on a limestone block in Sepphoris, further verifying his tenure as bishop. This inscription, probably dating from 517 to 518, attributes the renovation and repair of a church to Marcellinus.[91] In all probability this is one of the two churches that was originally built by Eutropius.

Bishop Eutropius, however, is not mentioned anywhere else other than in these mosaic inscriptions near the central intersection of Sepphoris. Since Eutropius probably built the two nearby churches, and Marcellinus is said to have repaired one of these churches in 517 to 518 (while Flavius Theodorus was governor and perhaps with his help), the implication is that Eutropius built the churches and rebuilt the street (with its mosaics) prior to that time. Therefore, most scholars tend to estimate Eutropius's tenure as bishop to the late fifth to early sixth centuries.[92]

The mosaic pavement in the stoa area that parallels the Cardo Maximus is decorated with squares placed at forty-five-degree diagonals with the street. Each square has a design in the center composed of nine diamonds placed in a three-by-three square. Disrupting this pattern are the circle-circumscribed inscriptions regarding Bishop Eutropius, along with one eight-spoked ICHTHUS Christogram, likewise placed in a prominent location near the main intersection (see fig. 7-9). The inscription of Bishop Eutropius and the ICHTHUS Christogram certainly seem to be connected.

89. Translation from Murphy-O'Connor, *The Holy Land*, 473. Weiss, in "Sepphoris," *Oxford Classical Dictionary*, notes that there are actually three different "medallion" type inscriptions referring to Eutropius.

90. Weiss, "Sepphoris," in Finney, *The Eerdmans Encyclopedia of Early Christian Art and Archaeology*, 2:494.

91. M. Avi-Yohan, "A Sixth-Century Inscription from Sepphoris," *Israel Exploration Journal* 11.4 (1961): 184–87.

92. Meyers and Meyers, "Sepphoris," 2:343.

The construction of the two churches and the inscription crediting the street improvements to Bishop Eutropius paired with this ICHTHUS Christogram are the earliest archaeological and architectural evidence for strong Christian influence in Sepphoris. Within the historical context that we know, we can suggest a plausible scenario as to how these events came about.

As noted above, when Constantine came to power, things began to change immediately in many cities of Syria Palaestina. By 335, the pagan temple of Aphrodite in Jerusalem had been completely destroyed, and the new Church of the Holy Sepulcher had been completed. As the fourth century progressed, more and more bishops were appointed. Churches, monasteries, and hostels

Fig. 7-9 Sepphoris, Cardo Maximus Sidewalk Mosaics: ICHTHUS Christogram

were built. Thousands of Gentile Christian pilgrims flocked to the Holy Land, and many of these Christians moved there to stay.

Sepphoris, on the other hand, probably because of its dominant Jewish population, was not part of this fourth-century Christianizing frenzy. Perhaps it was last on the list of priority cities to receive a bishop and to undergo the Christianization process. Since no other bishops are mentioned anywhere, it is plausible, at least, to assume that Eutropius was the first appointed bishop, perhaps as early as 450 to 475. Arriving in Sepphoris (Diocaesarea), he found a city with a strong Jewish population, a smaller pagan population, and an even smaller Christian population. As he set to work, the extent of his power and his relationship to the power structures already in the city were probably tentative at best and constantly evolving. Fortunately, he was wealthy enough to play the role of civic benefactor and pay for the reconstruction of the most central and visible street in the city. His dedication inscription was therefore placed prominently.

The Temple of Zeus, located near Bishop Eutropius's inscription and reconstructed street, was completely destroyed at about this time. Perhaps it had suffered damage from the earthquake in 363 and had been abandoned then. At any rate, Eutropius completely razed the temple, as Constantine did to the Temple of Aphrodite in Jerusalem. This action implies an attempt to cleanse or sanctify the area desecrated by the temple activities and the associated demonic influences. In addition, although the Christians and Jews in Sepphoris were apparently able to live together amicably, the rhetoric of Christian bishops and influential writers at this time was still quite harsh against Judaism and often depicted Jews as being connected to demons in much the same way as the pagans were. When Eutropius moved into this city dominated both by Jews and pagan Gentiles, with a temple of Zeus still standing prominently in the center of town (a rarity at this late date [450–475] in the empire), it is plausible that as he replaced the pagan temple with a sacred church, he also placed an ICHTHUS Christogram in front of the temple area and near the (probably demon-haunted) intersection of the city. The ICHTHUS Christogram combined a cross-like symbology and the name of Jesus, which was used elsewhere to drive away demons at street intersections and at pagan temples, as well as made a proclamation that there was now a strong Christian presence in this formerly pagan and Jewish city.

CHAPTER 8

THE EIGHT-SPOKED ICHTHUS CHRISTOGRAM IN ITALY

INTRODUCTION

No one knows exactly how the Christian church was planted in Italy, but a plausible explanation is that Jews from Italy (especially Rome) were converted to Christianity at Pentecost (Acts 2:1–41) and carried the gospel with them back to Italy. The book of Acts implies that the Jewish Christians Aquila and Priscilla, early church leaders and church planters, were living in Rome in 49 when the emperor Claudius evicted the Jews from Rome. This forced Aquila and Priscilla to move to Corinth, where Paul met them around 51 to 52 and built a close working relationship with them. By the time Paul wrote Romans (around 56–57) there was a substantial church in Rome, probably meeting in house churches across the city (Rom. 16:3–5). In Acts 28:13–16, as Luke recounts Paul's arrival (under guard) in Italy, he mentions Christians both from the seaport Puteoli and from Rome who welcomed Paul. In the year 66, there were enough visible and known Christians in Rome that Nero could blame them for the great fire (Tacitus, *Annals* 15.44).[1]

By the end of the first century, there was a strong church in Rome led by an active bishop, Clement I (bishop AD 88–99), who was martyred by Trajan.[2] Afterward, both literary accounts and funerary inscriptional evidence from the many Christian catacombs indicate that the church in Rome continued to grow, especially in the third century. Being the bishop

---

1. Benko, *Pagan Rome and the Early Christians*, 14–18.
2. L. L. Welborn, "Early Christianity at Rome as Reflected in the So-Called First Epistle of Clement," in Harrison and Wellborn, *The First Urban Churches 6: Rome and Ostia*, 137–99.

of Rome—in the capital of the Roman Empire and the largest city in the world at that time—carried considerable prestige and power, but it was also hazardous. We noted in chapter 4 that prior to the Great Persecution there were smaller persecutions of shorter duration. While the severity of these persecutions varied across the empire, they tended to be severe in the capital city of Rome. Of the thirty-plus bishops of Rome who held office prior to the end of the Great Persecution (AD 67–313), almost all were killed in one of the persecutions.[3]

When Constantine was first rising to power, he captured the city of Rome. Showing his favor to the Christians, Constantine bequeathed the royal palace in Rome, called the Lateran Palace (actually owned by his wife Fausta), to the bishop of Rome. For centuries afterward this remained the primary residence of the bishop of Rome (the pope). This underscored the prestige of the bishop of Rome, even early in the reign of Constantine. Slightly later in the fourth century (AD 381), Emperor Theodosius I convened a church council at Constantinople, where it was recognized that the bishop at Constantinople was second in honor, behind the bishop of Rome.[4] Although the authority of the bishop of Constantinople in the east was often challenged by the bishop of Alexandria (in Egypt), the basic division between the bishop of Rome in the west and the bishop of Constantinople in the east that developed in the late fourth century foreshadowed the upcoming division of the church into a Roman (Catholic) church and an eastern (Orthodox) church.

Yet the bishop of Rome was not the only influential bishop in Italy. Bishop Ambrose in Milan (a powerful city in northern Italy), who served as bishop from 374 to 397, was extraordinarily articulate and influential, as noted in the discussion below regarding Ambrose's efforts to have the altar and the idol of the goddess Victoria removed from the Senate building in Rome.

Geopolitically during this period, the Roman Empire lost control of much of what is now Western Europe. Indeed, Rome itself was captured and sacked five times in the fifth and sixth centuries by the so-called barbarians. Note that most of these groups (Visigoths, Ostrogoths, Vandals, etc.) were Arian Christians, following a stream of Christianity that had been ruled to be heretical by the church councils of Nicaea (AD 325) and Chalcedon (AD 451).[5] Nonetheless, these invasions were often quite destructive and, no doubt, set back the timeline for the construction of new churches.

---

3. Hastings, "150–550," 31–34; Matilda Webb, *The Churches and Catacombs of Early Christian Rome* (Eastbourne, UK: Sussex Academic, 2010), 291–92.
4. Hastings, "150–550," 36–39.
5. Michael Maas, "Roman Questions, Byzantine Answers: Contours of the Age of Justinian," in Maas, *The Cambridge Companion to the Age of Justinian*, 10–11.

OSTIA

The City of Ostia

Ostia, along with the city of Puteoli farther to the south (now modern Puzzuoli), served as the major port city for Rome. Located only about twenty miles (thirty km) from Rome, Ostia was the closest port and was integrally connected to the economic, political, and religious life of Rome. A wide range of pagan gods were venerated at Ostia, and the city also contained "crossroad shrines" where spirits and demons (Latin: *lares*) were placated and worshiped.[6]

Due to the silting up of the river channel, problems with flooding, and various economic factors, Ostia declined from the fifth century to the ninth century, when it was practically abandoned. Unlike Puteoli and many other ancient cities, these same problems prohibited the continued habitation and the construction of a modern city over the ancient city, which left much of ancient Ostia preserved. The archaeological site of Ostia Antica is expansive, and there are hundreds of ancient shops and houses still standing. The city had a big theater, several temples and fountains, and a number of bathhouses. At one point in the Roman imperial era, it became the coastal location in which many wealthy Roman families built lavish secondary homes. While many houses and shops remain, along with bathhouses and floor mosaics, very few large, monumental structures like temples and fountains can be seen. As the city declined, and as the temples fell out of use, the beautiful marble columns, wall paneling, and floor paving were used in construction elsewhere.

Christianity probably spread to Ostia at the same time as it was being established in nearby Rome. Based on evidence from funerary monuments and tombs, along with graffiti, inscriptions, and other literary records (especially the recording of martyrdoms), it is clear that Christianity was firmly planted there by the mid-third century.[7] As noted in chapter 2, for example, the baths of Neptune at Ostia, dating from the third or perhaps early fourth century, contain several Christian symbols in the floor mosaics, including a rather clever and cryptic monogram-type symbol representing the name of Jesus.[8]

As at many sites, there is evidence of the Christianization and de-paganization process in Ostia, most of which occurred in the fourth century. For example, near the lavish House of Diana is a small plaza with one of the crossroad shrines—a small building with a water basin and a cylindrical marble altar in

6.   James R. Harrison, "Ostia, Harbor Port of Rome: An Epigraphic and Archaeological Portrait," in Harrison and Welborn, *The First Urban Churches 6: Rome and Ostia*, 113–17.

7.   For discussions on early Christianity in Ostia, see Harrison, "Ostia, Harbor Port of Rome," 67–136; Maria Floriani Squarciapino, "Considerazioni su Ostia Cristiana," *Studi Romani* 27.1 (1979): 15–24; and Raisa Calza, "Le Sculture e la Probabile Zona Cristiana di Ostia e di Porto," *RendPontAc* 37 (1964–65): 155–257.

8.   Longenecker, *The Cross before Constantine*, 76–81; Squarciapino, "Considerazioni su Ostia Cristiana," 22.

front.[9] The top part of this altar has been smashed, and several of the pagan images on the lower part of the altar have been defaced, likely by the Christians in the fourth century.[10] Many of the statues that were discovered at Ostia were headless, and their heads have not been discovered (perhaps they were totally smashed). Several of these statues are on display at Ostia today (see fig. 8-1). One particular statue was beheaded and then buried upside down.[11]

Fig. 8-1 Ostia: Headless Statue

In the latter part of the fourth century or early fifth century, a small church was built over the bath of Mithras. There is a Tau-Rho Staurogram within a wreathed circle with an *alpha* and *omega* under the arms of the Tau, etched on one of the columns from this bathhouse that had been converted to a church.[12]

As part of the Christianization process in the fourth century and into the fifth, several churches were built, along with a monument venerating Christian martyrs who had died in Ostia. Also, a professionally and formally inscribed Chi-Rho Christogram was discovered on the tall ornamental door lintel that stretches across two columns of a lavish house (see fig. 8-2). This

Fig. 8-2 Ostia, Christian Basilica: Artist's Reproduction of Door Lintel and Chi-Rho Christogram

building is often called the Christian Basilica because of the Chi-Rho Christogram. Perhaps it was a house church or was converted into a church. The

9. On crossroad shrines at Ostia, often referred to in Latin as *compita*, see Jan Theo Bakker, *Living and Working with the Gods: Studies of Evidence for Private Religion and Its Material Environment in Ostia (AD 100–500)*, Dutch Monograph on Ancient History and Archaeology 12 (Amsterdam: Gieben, 1994), 118–33; 195–204.

10. Harrison, "Ostia, Harbor Port of Rome," 116. For online pictures, see Jan Theo Bakker, "Regio 1—Piazza dei Lari (Square of the Lares)," https://www.ostia-antica.org/regio1/forum/lari.htm.

11. Squarciapino, "Considerazioni su Ostia Cristiana," 21.

12. Squarciapino, "Considerazioni su Ostia Cristiana," 21; Calza, "Le Sculture e la Probabile Zona Cristiana," 239.

city was also well-known as being the place where St. Monica, the mother of Augustine, died and was first buried.[13]

The Christian Graffiti

Much of the graffiti in Ostia has been photographed, digitized, and indexed by Eric Taylor in the Ostia Graffiti Project, and I will use his numbering system to refer to specific graffiti.[14] While some of the graffiti is crude with sexual connotations (this was a busy seaport) and some of it is undecipherable, there is a significant amount of graffiti that is Christian in nature, probably etched in the fourth century as the Christians tried to Christianize the city and drive out and keep out the demons associated with pagan worship.

For example, in the Forum Bathhouse there is a Chi-Rho Christogram. On the steps of the nearby Capitolium, the largest temple in Ostia, there is a simple, regular cross, as well as an equilateral cross inside of a circle (a four-spoked circle). There is also a cross inside of a square (a four-square box; see chapter 2). Elsewhere on site there are other equilateral crosses within circles.[15] Furthermore, there is an entire row of crosses etched into the stone at the nymphaeum (monumental fountain).[16]

Among these Christian symbols at Ostia are two, or perhaps three, eight-spoked ICHTHUS Christograms. The clearest one is on the pavement of the Schola del Traiano.[17] This building was probably one of the guild meeting houses, perhaps for ship builders. It would have contained pagan statues and been the site of guild banquets, which often involved sacrifices and pledges of fidelity to the gods. Another eight-spoked wheel is in the Casa delle Volte Dipinte (House of the Painted Vaults), which was perhaps a hotel. This wheel actually has sixteen radial lines, but it is fairly clear that two lines are used to define each spoke, forming an eight-spoked wheel.[18] The third eight-spoked wheel is faint but still legible. It is located in the Santuario della Bona Dea, a temple dedicated to a goddess of agriculture and health.[19]

The graffiti at Ostia is similar to that of Ephesus and Aphrodisias, but less plentiful. Examples indicate that the ΙΧΘΥC (ICHTHUS) acrostic and associated eight-spoked wheel were well-known in nearby Rome. The cultural, religious, and political setting in Ostia would be similar to that in Rome. Thus, there is strong evidence that these three eight-spoked wheels in Ostia reflected the ICHTHUS acrostic and proclaimed "Jesus Christ God's Son Savior," driving out the demons by the name of Jesus and the sign of the

---

13. Calza, "Le Sculture e la Probabile Zona Cristiana," 164.
14. "The Graffiti per Building," Ostia Graffiti, www.ostia-antica.org/graffiti/graffiti-list.htm.
15. From Eric Taylor's numbering system, these are: G0001, G0002, G0003, G0010 (img.9410), G0064, G0072, G0229, and G0342.
16. G0341.
17. G0396.
18. G0165, G0166.
19. G0347.

cross and proclaiming victory over the pagan system that had been behind the Great Persecution. The inscribing of this ICHTHUS Christogram graffiti, along with the other Christian inscriptions, as well as the destruction and defacing of pagan idols, probably occurred in the mid- to late fourth century.

RAVENNA

The City of Ravenna

After the death of Emperor Theodosius I in 395, administration of the Roman Empire was split again into two (east and west, with capital cities at Constantinople and Rome), with his two sons ruling over the two halves. Honorius, the emperor in the west, moved the capital of the western Roman Empire to Milan. Then in 402, after Milan was in danger of being captured by the invading Visigoths, Honorius moved the capital to Ravenna, a northern provincial capital on the east coast of Italy on the Adriatic Sea—more defensible than Rome or Milan.[20]

For the next few decades, the western half of the Roman Empire was ruled from Ravenna by emperors who were either inept or underage. When they were declared to be emperor, for example, Honorius was age ten and Valentinian III was age six. For much of the mid-fifth century, however, the Empress Galla Placidia, followed by Neon, the bishop of Ravenna, managed affairs well, and under their direction, the city of Ravenna flourished. A number of impressive churches and other buildings were constructed during this time.[21]

In 490, an invading migration of Ostrogoth troops and dependents, along with a Visigoth contingent, arrived in northern Italy and laid siege to Ravenna. Their leader, King Theodoric the Great, probably had conspiratorial approval for this invasion from Emperor Zeno, the ruler of the Eastern Roman Empire (with its capital at Constantinople). After a three-year siege, Ravenna fell, and the Arian Ostrogoth, King Theodoric, became the ruler over most of Italy along with several provinces to the north. Rather than destroy, loot, and return home, Theodoric was determined to settle down and rule as the Roman emperor in northern Italy along with his 80,000-plus countrymen.[22] His empire included Italy, Sicily, much of North Africa, and much of what is now Central Europe (the Balkans, Hungary, etc.). He continued to support the construction of new churches and other buildings.

In 533, Justinian, the emperor now ruling in the east from Constantinople, sent an army and navy to the west to regain control of Italy and the western part of the empire. Under his capable general Belisarius, Justinian's forces recaptured North Africa and Sicily and then moved into Italy from the

---

20. See the discussion by Judith Herrin, *Ravenna: Capital of Empire, Crucible of Europe* (Princeton, NJ: Princeton University Press, 2020), 9–13.
21. Herrin, *Ravenna*, 46–68. For a more negative critique of Galla Placidia's abilities and rule, see Malafarina, ed., *The Basilica of San Vitale*, 95–96.
22. Herrin, *Ravenna*, 90–98.

south. In 536, they captured Rome, and in 540, with reinforcements from Constantinople, they entered Ravenna and reestablished their rule over Italy. Ravenna would remain the administrative government capital for Italy for the next two hundred years,[23] even though Rome would continue to be the home of the powerful bishop of Rome.

The Churches of Ravenna

During these tumultuous times (AD 450–550), a number of beautiful churches were built in Ravenna. Three of the most spectacular of these structures contain early Christian symbols relevant to our study. These include: the Mausoleum of Galla Placidia, the Basilica of Sant'Apollinare in Classe, and the Basilica of San Vitale. Similar to other churches constructed in this era, these churches are rather plain when viewed from the outside but filled with impressive colorful wall and ceiling mosaics on the inside.

Mausoleum of Galla Placidia (Chapel Dedicated to St. Lawrence)

Although popularly known as the Mausoleum of Galla Placidia, that title is probably a misnomer, for it is unlikely that Galla Placidia was ever interred in this room. This was a cross-shaped chapel, constructed by the Empress Galla Placidia between the years 425 and 450. Originally, it was part of a larger church called the Basilica of the Holy Cross, which was later destroyed, leaving only this smaller attached chapel. Galla Placidia dedicated this small chapel to St. Lawrence, a famous and popular martyr who had been executed in Rome back in 258.[24]

Fig. 8-3 Ravenna, Mausoleum of Galla Placidia: Chi-Rho Christogram with Alpha-Omega, Inside Victory Wreath

The interior walls and domed ceiling of this chapel are covered with beautiful, colorful mosaics, filled with biblical depictions and Christian symbols. There are several standard crosses along with a Chi-Rho Christogram with the letters *alpha* and *omega*, within a victory wreath (see fig. 8-3). The central dome has a cross at the center and is covered with stars along with symbols for the four evangelists.

---

23. Herrin, *Ravenna*, 151–59.
24. Herrin, *Ravenna*, 46–47, figs. 6–8.

The side domes are dominated by two elaborate circle patterns. Embedded in the center of one of these patterns is a cross shape, and in the center of the other is an eight-spoked wheel. There are several floral patterns in this mosaic, and it could be possible that the eight-spoked wheel is only an eight-petaled flower. Yet since this eight-division circle is in parallel with the cross embedded circle, the floral explanation is less likely and interpreting this symbol as an eight-spoked Christogram seems more plausible, yet still uncertain (see fig. 8–4).

Basilica of Sant'Apollinare at Classe

Right on the coast, just a few miles from Ravenna, was the city of Classe. This city served as the port for Ravenna, both for commercial shipping and as the home station for military fleets. The name Classe comes from the Latin word *classis*, which means "fleet."

After Justinian recaptured Ravenna (and Classe) in 540, a wealthy Greek citizen named Julianus, probably a banker, financed two of the most spectacular and beautiful churches in the area—the Basilica of Sant'Apollinare at Classe and the Basilica of San Vitale in Ravenna. These two churches are only about three miles apart.

Completed in 549, the Basilica of Sant'Apollinare is dedicated to Saint Apollinaris, traditionally viewed as the first bishop of Ravenna and Classe. Some traditions place him as early as the first century, claiming he was a disciple and bishop-appointee of Peter. At some point in the early Christian era he was martyred, and throughout the following centuries Christians continued to venerate him.

Fig. 8-4 Ravenna, Mausoleum of Galla Placidia: Ceiling Mosaics

The Basilica of Sant'Apollinare has a beautiful nave (main congregation area) lined with twenty-four solid marble columns. In the apse, high on the wall where often the resurrected Christ is portrayed (as at the Basilica of San Vitale), the mosaics have a tall, gem-studded Latin cross inside of a circular victory wreath. The background area between the cross and the circle is filled with stars against a blue background. At the center intersection of the arms of the cross is the face of Jesus Christ. Written below the cross in Latin is

Fig. 8-5 Ravenna, Basilica of Sant' Apollinare Mosaics: Latin Cross with IXΘYC (ICHTHUS) Written Above

the phrase *Salus Mundi* ("Salvation of the World"). Written above the cross in Greek is the word IXΘYC (see fig. 8-5).[25]

This fascinating use of the Greek word IXΘYC in Latin-speaking Italy underscores how widely known the acrostic was. Coupled with the other occurrences of IXΘYC in Italy, it provides additional evidence that Christians used this acrostic frequently, both in the eastern part of the empire and in Italy. Its use in the parallel context of "Salvation of the World" emphasizes the connection with "Jesus Christ God's Son *Savior*." Note also the close connection between the word IXΘYC and the cross.

The Basilica of San Vitale

Just a few miles away, in Ravenna, is the beautiful Basilica of San Vitale. This magnificent church, built at about the same time as the Hagia Sophia in Constantinople, was named after St. Vitalis of Milan, who was martyred in Ravenna in the early days of the church (either first or second century). Venerated widely across Italy, he was also the patron saint of Ravenna.

Construction on this church started back in 527, led by Bishop Ecclesio, while King Theodoric and the Ostrogoths controlled Ravenna. From the beginning of construction, the main nave was laid out in an octagonal shape. Construction continued throughout the term of the next bishop, Victor (AD 537–544), and through the transition in leadership after Justinian's army drove out the Ostrogoths. With imperial support from Justinian and serious financing from the benefactor Julianus, Bishop Maximian completed and dedicated the church in 547. While the overall octagonal shape of the church was set in the early days of construction, the spectacular wall and ceiling mosaics come from the Maximian and Justinian era, and both of them (along with Empress Theodora) are depicted on the wall mosaics.[26]

There are dozens of crosses and variations of cross patterns in the mosaics and on the columns throughout the church along with several Chi-Rho Christograms. In addition, the complex monogram of Emperor Justinian is inscribed on the capitals above the eight main columns. There are several

25. Kessler, "Bright Gardens of Paradise," 128–29; Gianfranco Bustacchini, *Ravenna: Mosaics, Monuments and Environment*, rev. ed., ed. Franco Gàbici (Ravenna: Salbaroli, 2022), 140–41.

26. Malafarina, ed., *The Basilica of San Vitale*, 7–9; Irina Andreescu-Treadgold and Warren Treadgold, "Procopius and the Imperial Panels of S. Vitale," *The Art Bulletin* 79.4 (1997): 708; Herron, *Ravenna*, 160–66; Bustacchini, *Ravenna*, 26–27.

sarcophagi in the outer hallway of the church bearing crosses and Chi-Rho Christograms.

At the front of the church, connected to the octagonal-shaped nave, is a circular-shaped apse with a short, wide hallway (sometimes called the *presbytery*) connecting the apse to the large, central octagonal room. This apse is the focal point of the room, both architecturally and theologically. As one approaches the apse through the short hallway, on the right is a scene depicting Abel

Fig. 8-6 Ravenna, Basilica of San Vitale: Winged Angels Holding a Cross Inside of a Victory Wreath

and Melchizedek with Moses and Isaiah just above on either side. Above this scene are two angels with wings (similar in appearance to earlier depictions of the goddess Victoria) holding a victory wreath between them. Inside the victory wreath is a Latin cross, and hanging from each arm of the cross is the letter ω (*omega*), from the *alpha* and *omega* reference to Christ in Revelation 1:8, 21:6, and 22:13.

On the left side of the hallway, the mosaics are parallel but with different biblical characters. There is a mosaic depicting scenes from the life of Abraham with Jeremiah and Moses just above to the left and right. The angels above this panel are identical to those on the right side (see fig. 8-6).

With these two scenes on the right and left, at the front is the climactic scene of the church. The exalted, victorious Jesus Christ sits on a globe with a cross-shaped halo behind his head. In his left hand, he holds a scroll sealed with seven seals, and in his right hand, he holds a crown, which he is handing to the martyr Vitalis. Directly above Jesus Christ is a victory wreath containing the Iota-Chi Christogram. Directly above this, and directly above the exalted Jesus Christ, are two winged angels, similar to those in the hallway. These angels are holding a circle, but inside of this circle is not the Latin cross with the letter *omega*, but an eight-spoked wheel with the letter *alpha* in the center (see fig. 8-7).[27]

Once again, we see the ICHTHUS Christogram used in specific parallel with regular crosses inside victory wreaths and in parallel with the encircled Iota-Chi Christogram. Here in the Basilica of San Vitale—as in other churches like the Church of St. Mary in Ephesus—the ICHTHUS wheel is placed in the central location of all of the cross symbols.[28] It is clearly not simply a geometric pattern, but a symbol worthy of its climactic location. The ICHTHUS acrostic, proclaiming "Jesus Christ God's Son Savior," is certainly a declaration worthy of this placement.

27. Malafarina, *The Basilica of San Vitale*, 28–92; Bustacchini, *Ravenna*, 30–59.
28. Malafarina, *The Basilica of San Vitale*, 79, calls it a "Christological monogram."

Fig. 8-7 Ravenna, Basilica of San Vitale: The Exalted Christ, with an Iota-Chi Christogram Above, and Winged Angels Overhead, Holding an ICHTHUS Christogram

Other interesting and relevant features in the Basilica of San Vitale are the floor mosaics in the octagonal nave. The overhead dome is supported by eight columns. The floor mosaics incorporate variations of the octagonal shape as the unifying theme along with variations of circles divided into eighths. The entirety of the floor is an octagon with eight radial spokes, resembling an eight-spoked wheel. In three of the pie-shaped panels on the floor are three variations of a circle with eight radial arms, looking exactly like an eight-spoked wheel. This is the main seating area of the church, and currently there are usually chairs on top of these floor mosaics, but Malafarina provides a good picture, capturing all of the floor mosaics in this room while the chairs are absent.[29]

The Ravenna Churches and Anti-Arian Theology?

One of Emperor Justinian's goals in recapturing Italy and driving out the heretical Arian-believing Ostrogoths was to unite the Roman Empire around the orthodox theology that was spelled out at the Council of Chalcedon. Some scholars argue that the symbols used in the Basilica of San Vitale and in the Basilica of Sant'Apollinare at Classe were not random but were used intentionally to convey orthodox theology.[30] Due to the specific context, especially here at Ravenna where the Arians had just been driven out, these scholars maintain that the scenes and symbology in these new churches advocated Chalcedonian orthodoxy but were also specifically anti-Arian.[31] Reiner Sörries states that the ΙΧΘΥϹ acrostic in particular,

---

29. Malafarina, *The Basilica of San Vitale*, 46–47.
30. Bente Kiilerich, "The State of Early Christian Iconography in the Twenty-First Century," *Studies in Iconography* 36 (2015): 121–26; Anne Karahan, "Byzantine Visual Culture: Conditions of 'Right' Belief and Some Platonic Outlooks," *Numen* 63.2–3 (2016): 217–20.
31. Reiner Sörries, *Die Bilder der Orthodoxen im Kampf gegen den Arianismus: Eine Apologie der orthodoxen Christologie und Trinitätslehre gegenüber der arianischen Häresie, dargestellt an den ravennatischen Mosaiken und Bildern des 6. Jahrhunderts*, Europäische Hochschulschriften Series 23, vol. 186 (Frankfurt and Bern: Peter Lang, 1983), 125–58, 203–220; Deborah Mauskopf Deliyannis, "The Mosaics of Ravenna," in Jensen and Ellison, *The Routledge Handbook of Early Christian Art*, 358–60.

with the meaning of "Jesus Christ God's Son Savior," purposely countered Arian theology.[32]

ROME

By the end of the first century BC, Rome (founded in the eighth century BC) was the most populous and most powerful city in the world, ruling over an empire that not only dominated the entire Mediterranean world but stretched from Britain in the west to the border with Persia in the east. At the beginning of the fourth century, the landscape of Rome was dominated by pagan temples—both those dedicated to the traditional gods and those dedicated to deified personalities of the Roman imperial cult. Three hundred years earlier, Augustus (ruled 19 BC–AD 14) claimed to have restored eighty-two temples in Rome.[33] When Constantine came to power, he ended the Great Persecution and provided imperial support for Christianity. Constantine's successors, ruling from Constantinople, made Christianity the official religion of the empire, banning pagan worship. All across the empire, a Christianization process began as Christianity spread, often led by zealous bishops. Part of this process was the cleansing and removal of pagan temples, pagan idols, and all pagan influence from the cities and the countryside, replacing them with churches.

The speed and depth of the Christianization process varied across the empire, based on variables such as the competence, power, and zeal of the local bishops as well as the political and economic power of those who opposed the process. In Rome, the process began rather quickly in some aspects, but powerful opposition meant the transition in Rome dragged out a little longer than in other cities.

On his way to consolidating power and becoming the sole emperor of the Roman Empire, one of Constantine's most critical victories was the defeat of a rival emperor, Maxentius, right outside of Rome in the famous Milvian Bridge Battle in 312. After this battle, Constantine then entered Rome triumphantly. Yet Constantine did not want to be viewed as a conqueror but rather as a liberator—the true emperor of the Roman Empire who overthrew the usurper, Maxentius. Constantine wanted the support of the Roman Senate and other powerful people in Rome, and so he styled himself as a typical Roman emperor, placing his name on buildings and inscriptions and installing statues of himself in the city, especially in the Forum. The name of the defeated Maxentius, on the other hand, was erased in inscriptions all across Rome.

Yet Constantine's newfound Christian faith, or at least his strong sympathies toward Christianity, definitely made him different from the earlier

---

32. Sörries, *Die Bilder der Orthodoxen*, 219–20. Sörries, however, only discusses the IXΘΥC occurrence above the cross at Sant'Apollinare and does not make the connection between IXΘΥC and the eight-spoked wheel at San Vitale.
33. David Watkin, *The Roman Forum* (Cambridge, MA: Harvard University Press, 2009), 13.

emperors. Convinced that Christ had given him this crucial recent victory at the nearby Milvian Bridge, Constantine almost immediately sponsored the construction of a church, San Giovanni in Laterano, just to the southwest of the Forum. Despite legalizing and even supporting Christianity, he did not ban pagan worship. Therefore, Constantine did not build this first new church on top of a destroyed pagan temple (as he did slightly later in Jerusalem) but rather on top of the barracks that had housed Maxentius's imperial guard. This church became operational quite quickly, as Pope Sylvester (AD 314–335) used it as his primary cathedral.[34] Constantine also quickly built several smaller, shrine-like basilicas over the burial places of famous deceased saints, like St. Peter and San Sebastiano.[35] Yet, by and large, Constantine left the pagan temples and the statues of pagan gods in Rome alone.

There were powerful, wealthy people in Rome, many of them senators or from senatorial families, who opposed the closing of temples and the removal of idols and other statues. Some of them perhaps clung to pagan beliefs, but others saw the pagan gods and their trappings as a critical part of Roman heritage and identity. The literary and archaeological evidence indicates that the battle in Rome over closing down the pagan temples and removing all pagan idols, as well as other honorarium statues, dragged out well into the early fifth century, even as spectacular new churches were being built across Rome.

A well-documented example of how this struggle played out in Rome can be seen in the battle over the altar and statue of Victoria, located in the Senate building (known as Curia Julia, sometimes just called the Curia). Started by Julius Caesar, Augustus completed this building in 29 BC and installed the famous statue of Victoria (winged, barefooted, standing on a globe, and holding a victory wreath in her right hand) along with an altar in front of her. Although the power of the Senate was diminished in the years after Augustus, it remained important and influential. Upon entering the Curia to hold sessions, the members would first offer libations on the altar of Victoria and swear allegiance to the emperor. Victoria was the symbol of the empire, and especially the Senate's connection to the empire, so these rituals were both religious and political.[36] During the fourth century, as the Christianization process took place, this statue and altar became an issue, especially as more and more senators became Christians and as Christian bishops in Italy grew in power.

In the early years of the fourth century, Constantine, needing strong Senate backing in Rome, ignored the issue. His son, Emperor Constantius II (ruled AD 337–361), however, ordered the altar's removal, but he did not mention the idol. Twice during the years after Constantius II the altar was restored, only to be removed again. During the reign of Valentinus II (ruled

---

34. Webb, *Churches and Catacombs*, 40–44.
35. Webb, *Churches and Catacombs*, xvi–xvii.
36. Pohlsander, "Victory: The Story of a Statue," 590–93; Gregor Kalas, *The Restoration of the Roman Forum in Late Antiquity: Transforming Public Space* (Austin: University of Texas Press, 2015), 143–53.

AD 375–392), a heated argument broke out, in which opposing individuals in Italy presented their cases to him as he resided in Constantinople. Ambrose, the bishop of Milan, sent letters repeatedly, seeking authority to have the idol removed. These letters were rebutted and further arguments submitted by Quintus Aurelius Symmachus, the urban prefect of Rome, who argued that the statue of Victoria could be retained without any religious connotations; he argued the statue was a critical part of Rome's history and identity and provided current protection against another barbarian invasion. Also tied to this debate between Ambrose and Symmachus was the issue of imperial approval of continuing financial support (through estates and taxes, etc.) of the pagan temples and their personnel. Eventually Bishop Ambrose won both arguments. The statue was removed and financial support for temples was completely withdrawn.[37]

At other times and in other areas of Rome, Christian actions were more decisive. Both the Christian scholar Jerome, writing around 405 to 420, and the Roman Christian poet Prudentius, writing slightly earlier, recount that the prefect of Rome, a man named Gracchus, had become a Christian and then destroyed a shrine of Mithras in Rome (Jerome, *Epistles* 107.2; Prudentius, *Contra Symmachum* 1.561–65). This would have occurred around 376.[38] Some have suggested that Gracchus probably destroyed other gods in Rome as well.[39] It should also be noted that, while Rome had a long history of crowd action, as the fourth century progressed this "crowd" became decisively Christian, and its leaders were local bishops.[40]

During the latter half of the fourth century and into the early fifth, the Christianization process in Rome created quite a bit of tension and disagreement, but the process nonetheless moved forward steadily. While some pagan temples continued to function for a while, many others, along with their idols, were destroyed by the end of the fourth century. In addition, expansive, beautiful churches were built. There were at least seven identifiable large churches (or basilicas) built in Rome during the fourth century, with four more that were probably begun in the fourth but completed in the fifth century. Another five churches that we know of were built in the fifth century. Most of these churches, while originally built in the fourth or fifth centuries, have been modified and renovated several times over the centuries,[41] and much of what you can see today dates to a later time.

---

37. Kalas, *The Restoration of the Roman Forum*, 150–53.
38. T. D. Barnes and R. W. Westall, "The Conversion of the Roman Aristocracy in Prudentius' 'Contra Symmachum,'" *Phoenix* 45.1 (1991): 55.
39. Caroline Michel D'Annoville, "Rome and Imagery in Late Antiquity: Perception and Use of Statues," in *Pagans and Christians in Late Antique Rome*, ed. Michele Salzman, Marianne Sághy, and Rita Lizzi Testa (Cambridge: Cambridge University Press, 2016), 348.
40. Daniëlle Slootjes, "Crowd Behavior in Late Antique Rome," in Salzman, Sághy, and Testa, *Pagans and Christians in Late Antique Rome*, 178–94.
41. Webb, *Churches and Catacombs*, 6–213.

Note that some of the early Christian structures, especially in the Roman Forum, were removed or destroyed during the excavations and renovations carried out in 1928 to 1936 during the reign of Mussolini, who styled himself as another great Roman emperor and conqueror. He was interested only in the structures from the imperial Roman era (50 BC–AD 300), and he often ordered that later structures from the Christian era be cleared away to uncover buildings from the imperial era. Furthermore, Mussolini built a highway (the current multi-lane Via dei Fori Imperiali—the street that most tourists cross to get to the Forum) right through the Forum, destroying more than 428,000 square feet (40,000 sq. m) of some of the most historical remains of ancient early Christian and medieval Rome.[42] This is important to keep in mind during our study of the ICHTHUS Christogram. Several pre-Mussolini studies and observations note the presence of multiple eight-spoked wheels with a wide range of variation in the Roman Forum (they usually assume that these circles are game boards).[43] However, with the destruction of many of the structures by Mussolini, along with the continuing deterioration of the stone surfaces due to time and exposure, added to the problem that significant portions of the Forum are not accessible to the public, I was only able to locate and verify a handful of eight-spoked ICHTHUS Christograms in my 2023 visit. Nonetheless, these ICHTHUS Christograms are significant.

The Roman Forum

As in most other sizable cities across the Roman Empire, at the center of Roman political, religious, and economic life was the Forum (and remember that these three things—politics, religion, and economics—were tightly integrated and inseparable). Typical of forums throughout the empire, only on a larger scale, the Roman Forum included market areas (agoras); administrative buildings (for Senate meetings and legal hearings); several monumental arches; hundreds of statues honoring emperors, generals, and gods; special processional streets; and temples containing the idols of pagan gods (see fig. 8-8). Although the Roman emperors from Augustus to Constantine were continuously adding new buildings (and renovating or updating old ones) into the already crowded area, at the time when the Great Persecution ended and Christianity started to rise in political and civic power, major buildings in the Roman Forum included: the Basilica Julia for legal

Fig. 8-8 Rome, The Roman Forum

---

42. Watkin, *The Roman Forum*, 205–9.
43. Edward Falkener, *Games Ancient and Oriental and How to Play Them* (London: Longmans, Green and Co., 1892), 364–66; and Thédenat, *Le Forum Romain*, 216–24.

hearings and administrative activities; the Curia, where the Roman Senate met, although the Senate had been forced to be subordinate to the emperor since Julius Caesar and Augustus; the Rostrum, a raised platform eighty feet (24 m) long with columns and statues, for giving speeches and decrees; two monumental triple arches; and eight temples. There was also the Via Sacra ("sacred street") used for victory and religious processions.

After Constantine came to power, he added another monumental arch. A recently completed basilica, ironically originally dedicated to Maxentius, whom Constantine had just defeated, was rededicated to Constantine by the Roman Senate. A colossal statue of Constantine was placed in this basilica.[44]

Other impressive structures stood nearby, such as the Colosseum, the Circus Maximus, and the stadium, which entertained the Romans with chariot races, gladiatorial fights, and venationes (men against wild animals). On the adjacent Palatine and Capitoline Hills were lavish imperial palaces, fountains, and more temples.

As noted above, while the Christianization process (and the closing and cleansing of the pagan temples) in Rome, especially the central Roman Forum, perhaps took longer than elsewhere, the evidence is widespread that this process took place. Today, the Forum and the nearby museums are filled with headless statues of gods, goddesses, and people (see fig. 8-9). In some cases, heads have been discovered without bodies, and frequently their noses are missing, apparently having been knocked off with the blow of a hammer. This is true not only for freestanding statues but for the reliefs of gods and individuals engraved into monuments, like the famous Arch of Titus at the main entrance to the Forum today. This is typical of what we have noted all across the rest of the Roman Empire. Most of this beheading and defacing took place during the fourth century as the Christians came into power and sought to de-paganize and cleanse their cities from demonic influences as well as to proclaim victory over the pagan/imperial system that had killed so many of them during the Great Persecution.

As in other parts of the Roman Empire, inscribing ICHTHUS

Fig. 8-9 Rome, The Roman Forum: Headless Statue

---

44. Kalas, *The Restoration of the Roman Forum*, 68–70.

Fig. 8-10 Rome, The Roman Forum, Near the Forum of Nerva: ICHTHUS Christogram in Circle Form (left) and in Square Form (right)

Christogram graffiti was probably part of this process and even may have used the same hammers that defaced the pagan statues. There are a number of ICHTHUS wheels etched into the flat paving stones of the Forum and the surrounding vicinity. For example, although the large paving flagstone is broken, there appears to be an ICHTHUS Christogram in the main court-yard and entryway to the Temple of Mars Ultor in the Forum of Augus-tus (across the street—Via dei Fori Imperiali—from what is identified as the main Roman Forum Archaeo-logical Park today).

Crossing back over the street to the Forum, there is a clear eight-spoked Christogram on the stone pavement of the Forum of Nerva (a Roman emperor who ruled briefly at the end of the first century AD), near where a statue of Minerva had stood. Interestingly, adjacent to this eight-spoked wheel is a rectangular box also with eight spokes (see fig. 8-10). As we noted in chapter 2, many Greek (and Latin) letters in inscriptions had several vari-ant forms. One variant form of the letter Θ (*theta*) was a square (rectangular) form.[45] It is possible, even probable, that this rectangle with eight spokes is likewise the IXΘΥC Christogram, only using the square form of Θ (*theta*) as well as the square form of C (lunate form of *sigma*), instead of the rounded forms.

Fig. 8-11 Rome, The Roman Forum, The Arch of Severus

Another ICHTHUS wheel is in the Arch of Septimius Severus (a Roman emperor who ruled AD 193–211). This was a traditional triple-arch monument, a freestand-ing monumental gate, built by Severus in 203 to commemorate his victory over the Parthians (see fig. 8-11). The ICHTHUS Christogram is etched into the paving stones right in the center of the westernmost archway (see fig. 8-12). There are reports of other

---

45.   McLean, *An Introduction to Greek Epigraphy*, 41.

circles, both in this westernmost archway and in the easternmost archway, but I have been unable to verify these.[46]

The church historian Eusebius describes Severus as one who persecuted the churches and who martyred a number of church leaders (*Ecclesiastical History* 6.1). Even in the mid-fourth century, Christians would have had a negative attitude toward this monument honoring Severus. Furthermore, the Via Sacra (the special processional road) passed through the Arch of Septimius Severus on the north side of the Forum. The Arch of Septimius Severus, therefore, functioned not only as a monument to one of the emperors perceived to be one of the great persecutors of the church, but it functioned as a formal entryway into the Forum. Right beyond the arch is a

Fig. 8-12 Rome, The Roman Forum, The Arch of Severus: ICHTHUS Christogram (obscured slightly by accumulation of dirt and pavement cracks)

street intersection. The eight-spoked wheel is located exactly in the center of the western archway. As noted earlier, especially in the discussion of cities in Asia Minor (Ephesus, Aphrodisias), there was a common belief that demons inhabited entrances and intersections. As in Asia Minor, Christians in Rome believed that demons could be driven away and kept away through the name of Jesus and the sign of the cross, both of which are reflected in the ICHTHUS Christogram.

Apparently, there are a significant number of eight-spoked wheels (with several variations) in the Basilica Julia, an impressive building in the center of the Roman Forum used primarily for courts, hearings, and other administrative activities. In Thédenat's 1904 publication *Le Forum Romain*, he locates more than one hundred "game boards" on a map of the Basilica Julia, without differentiating between eight-spoked circle shapes and a wide variety of rectangular shapes as well as various configurations of cup-sized holes.[47] Writing in 1909, Hülsen states that most of the diagrams in the Basilica Julia are circles

---

46. Thédenat, *Le Forum Romain*, 235, lumping all circular shapes and rectangular shapes together as "game boards" notes that there are several in the Arch of Septimius Severus. Citing Thédenat, and likewise not distinguishing between circles and rectangles, Trifilò states that there are six board games in the western arch and one in the eastern arch. Trifilò, "Movement, Gaming, and the Use of Space in the Forum," 317.

47. Thédenat, *Le Forum Romain*, 217.

(and he presents an eight-spoked wheel, a variation type with an additional small half circle at each radial-arm intersection).[48] More recently, Trifilò has reproduced Thédenat's map and conducted a survey of the "game boards" in the Forum, although, to my knowledge, only a brief, preliminary report has ever been published. In that report, Trifilò claims to have located seventy-seven game boards, mostly in the Basilica Julia.[49]

According to these writers, most of the graffiti inscriptions are on the higher, main level of the Basilica Julia—inaccessible to the public today—so it is difficult to verify which actual shapes are there. Trifilò, however, does present a picture of one—an eight-spoked wheel with additional curved "flares" at the end of each spoke, a variation that occurs elsewhere.[50] On the other hand, the map presented by Thédenat and Trifilò that identifies the location of these "game boards" depicts thirteen on the steps of the Basilica Julia, and these steps are accessible and can be viewed. On my visit in 2023, I examined these steps quite carefully and did not see anything that I would classify clearly as a game board, and certainly there were no eight-spoked wheels. On one step there is a plain circle with some letters inside of it, but it is hard to imagine that this plain circle is a game board. Likewise, there is a small collection of fifteen to twenty small, cup-sized holes on one step, but they don't appear to be in any order or alignment (unlike some of the "hole" games in Asia Minor).[51] Other than these two, I was unable to find any graffiti of any shape on the steps of the Basilica Julia.

Nonetheless, there is at least some evidence from writers like Thédenat, Hülsen, and Trifilò that there are several eight-spoked wheels, including several variations, on the main floor of the Basilica Julia. The reason these eight-spoked wheel Christograms were inscribed on this floor probably relates to the situation found there in the early to mid-fourth century. The basilica was built in the first century BC and named in honor of Julius Caesar. In AD 284, there was a devasting fire that seriously damaged the building and destroyed its roof. The structure was rebuilt primarily by Diocletian and secondarily by Maximian—two of the principal architects of the Great

---

48. Christian Hülsen, *The Roman Forum: Its History and Its Monuments*, 2nd ed., trans. Jesse Benedict Carter (New York: G. E. Stechert & Co., 1909), 63–64. Hülsen also notes that the other style of diagram is rectangular, often with letters or symbols, usually in groups of six. This is similar to the rectangular games boards that appear in Asia Minor as well. See the discussion in chapter 3.

49. Trifilò, "Movement, Gaming, and the Use of Space in the Forum," 315–16; Trifilò, "The Forum Romanum Games Project: Preliminary Project Report" (University of Kent, 2012).

50. Trifilò, "The Forum Romanum Games Project," fig. 3. In the circle-graffiti typology developed by Bell and Roueché, "Graeco-Roman Pavement Signs and Game Boards," they label this style of eight-spoked wheel as CC.9.

51. Citing Trifilò ("Movement, Gaming, and the Use of Space in the Forum," 312–31) and Thédenat (*Le Forum Romain*, 216–21), Kalas, *The Restoration of the Roman Forum*, 111, states that there were lots of game boards in the Basilica Julia, but the only two pictures he provides are of the simple circle and the collection of holes noted above.

Persecution. As part of the renovation of the basilica, a row of statues was added across the front; no doubt Diocletian was well represented in this row.

Christians in Rome suffered tremendously during the Great Persecution. Based on literary records, Shin lists seventy Christian martyrs—men and women—executed in Rome during this time.[52] These are just the ones we know about in written records; the number of Christian martyrs in Rome must have been much higher in total. It is possible, even probable, that many of the trials that led to these executions took place in the Basilica Julia. At some point from the mid-fourth century to the mid-fifth century, Christians probably went through the Forum destroying pagan statues and attempting to cleanse the area of demons, as they did elsewhere throughout the empire. At this time, the ICHTHUS Christogram was probably inscribed on the pavement of the Arch of Septimius Severus, in the Forum of Nerva, and the Basilica Julia. No doubt there were other locations where this wheel was also inscribed.

The Villa of the Quintili

The famous ancient road known as the Via Appia was the primary road going south from Rome. In late antiquity, Rome was encircled with a city wall known as the Aurelian Wall, much of which remains today. From the gate exiting these walls, the Via Appia has stadia ("mile") markers along the way. Starting as early as the third century, Christians established extensive burial areas, especially underground catacombs, along the first three miles of the Via Appia. In the fourth and fifth centuries, memorial structures were built above ground as well. In these extensive underground catacombs, thousands and thousands of Christians were buried in the third to seventh centuries.[53] As discussed in chapter 2, one of the most famous of these tombs, dating to the late second to early third century, has the Greek word ΙΧΘΥϹ inscribed on the wall (*ICVR* 12899). Although the large catacombs are located within the first three miles, as the fourth century progressed into the fifth century, other Christian tombs and cemetery areas spread south along the Via Appia beyond the third mile.

Just a few miles beyond the Basilica of San Sebastiano, about five miles (eight km) south of the Aurelian Walls of Rome, was one of the most lavish and extensive residences in all of Rome. Originally built by two wealthy brothers from the Quintilius family in the mid-second century, this residence was known as the Villa of the Quintili. This facility was so nice that in AD 183 the Roman Emperor Commodus had the brothers executed so that he could confiscate the villa and reside there himself. The property stayed in the hands of the imperial family throughout the second and third centuries, retaining the name Villa of the Quintili.[54]

52. Shin, *The Great Persecution*, 149–50, 232–38.
53. Spera, "The Christianization of Space along the Via Appia," 23–43.
54. Paris, *Via Appia: The Villa of the Quintili*, 9–23.

Fig. 8-13 Rome, Villa of the Quintili: Necklace with Chi-Rho Christogram and Alpha-Omega

It is not known who owned or resided in this villa in the fourth century, but apparently it was a wealthy Christian family. As mentioned in chapter 2, during the excavations of this site, a piece of intact wall plaster was discovered in one of the residence areas. Inside a title box (called *tabula ansata*) is the Greek word IXΘΥC, and right above this title box is an eight-spoked wheel. The upper portion of the wheel is missing, but enough of the wheel remains to clearly establish that it is an eight-spoked wheel (see fig. 2–11). This is a fascinating and significant find, clearly associating the word IXΘΥC with the eight-spoked wheel and establishing that the eight-spoked wheel is indeed a Christogram standing for the acrostic IXΘΥC. There is little information available about the room and the context in which this piece of alabaster was found, but several scholars and archaeologists who have worked on this site propose a fourth-century date.[55] This piece of alabaster with the word IXΘΥC and the eight-spoked wheel are on display in the small museum at the Villa of the Quintili just south of Rome. Also on display in this small museum is a gold pendant necklace with a Chi-Rho (along with *alpha* and *omega*) Christogram, held by a gold chain (see fig. 8-14). Dated to the fourth century, this pendant necklace was found in one of the graves discovered on the villa property.

---

55. Spera, "The Christianization of Space Along the Via Appia," 107. The Epigraphic Database Bari (EDB633) dates this inscription from 300 to 399.

CHAPTER 9

SUMMARY AND CONCLUSIONS

EARLY CHRISTIAN SYMBOLS AND THE EIGHT-SPOKED ICHTHUS CHRISTOGRAM

This truth is perhaps obvious, but it bears repeating: from the very beginning of Christianity, at the center of the faith and practice of the church was the life, teaching, death, resurrection, ascension, return, and victorious rule of Jesus Christ, the Son of God, and the Savior of all who believe in him. The early Christian church, born into a culture that was already commonly using word abbreviations and clever, sometimes cryptic, letter combinations, developed a wide range of symbols, abbreviations, and sometimes cryptic letter combinations to represent and express critical aspects of their faith, especially regarding their Lord Jesus Christ.

The most common symbol, of course, was the cross, but throughout the earliest Christian era and into late antiquity, there was no standardized form of the cross but multiple variations—Latin crosses, equilateral crosses, crosses with flared ends, crosses inside circles, T-shaped crosses, and so forth. Perhaps not as commonly used as the cross, but nonetheless appearing frequently, were letter abbreviations for Jesus Christ—the Chi-Rho Christogram, the Iota-Chi Christogram, and the Iota-Eta Christogram. Closely related was the Tau-Rho Staurogram, abbreviating by letter and symbol the words relating to the cross and the crucifixion of Christ. Added into this mix and used especially alongside crosses, the Chi-Rho Christogram, and the Tau-Rho Staurogram, were the letters *alpha* and *omega*, connecting to the "beginning and end" identification of Christ in the book of Revelation. Also appearing frequently, especially in early biblical and other Christian manuscripts, were *nomina sacra* abbreviations, used to represent a wide range of divine related terms.

239

Many of these symbols, especially the equilateral cross, the Chi-Rho Christogram, and the Iota-Chi Christogram, often appear with a circle around them. With the equilateral cross this creates a four-spoked wheel, and with the Iota-Chi Christogram this creates a six-spoked wheel. Sometimes the outer circle in these symbols represents a victory wreath, associating Christ and his cross with his victory not only over death but over the evil powers of the pagan-temple and Roman-emperor-driven hostile Greco-Roman world.

Throughout the era from 200 to 600, these early Christian symbols were used in abundance across the Roman Empire: in Christian literature, including on book covers; in graffiti inscriptions on buildings, streets, theater seats, and especially temples; in church floor and wall mosaics; in funerary contexts (headstones, sarcophagi, catacomb walls, etc.); in personal jewelry, like rings and pendants; on lamps; on amulets; on door frames of houses; in church structural architecture, including capitals and stone wall panels, especially chancel screens; on aqueduct bridges; on public fountain pool walls; and on city walls and gates.

Very little Christian architecture remains from the years 100 to 300—that is, prior to Constantine and the legalization of Christianity. Christian symbols from that era are generally limited to literature, personal items (jewelry, etc.), and funerary contexts. After Constantine came to power in the early fourth century, however, and increasing throughout the rest of the fourth century, Christianity became more and more public, and Christian symbols and abbreviations appeared more and more frequently in churches and on other public structures.

The image of a fish was also used as an early Christian symbol, but even more popular than the depiction of a fish was the use of the Greek word for fish (ΙΧΘΥC; ICHTHUS), especially as an acrostic representing the first letters of the phrase "Jesus Christ God's Son Savior." This word was used symbolically in funerary contexts as early as the year 200. By the fourth century, the acrostic connection of ΙΧΘΥC to "Jesus Christ God's Son Savior" was popular and widely recognized by Christians. It was used frequently in a wide range of applications—in personal jewelry, on church floor mosaics, on funerary headstones, and in Christian literature. The appearance of the ΙΧΘΥC acrostic in the Sibylline Oracles was quoted by Christian writers as a prophetic proof for the coming of Jesus Christ.

Another Christian symbol that occurs frequently in the remains of ancient Greco-Roman cities, alongside the Christian crosses and other Christian symbols, is the eight-spoked wheel. As informal graffiti, this eight-spoked wheel appears frequently in pagan temples (on floors, at entrances and doorways, on altars) and streets in front of where idols once stood in cities across the Roman Empire. Incorporated formally as part of church architecture, the eight-spoked wheel appears in mosaics (floors, walls, and ceilings), as part of column capitals, and on stone wall panels, especially chancel screens. Added professionally and formally to public facilities, the eight-spoked wheel appears in sidewalk mosaics, bathhouse renovation mosaics, stone panels for water fountain pools, and on aqueduct bridges. Often the eight-spoked wheel is used in parallel with crosses, and sometimes it is given the prominent location in the center with crosses located on the side. Clearly, the eight-spoked wheel was a sacred Christian symbol, similar to the cross or the Chi-Rho Christogram.

It is almost certain that the eight-spoked wheel is a monogram type of letter combination that visually stands for the IXΘΥC acrostic, rendering "Jesus Christ God's Son Savior," and it should therefore be categorized as a Christogram. The arguments leading to this conclusion are many.

First of all, the IXΘΥC acrostic was well-known and popular among Christians. The connection would have been made by most Christians easily.

Second, the early Christians frequently used abbreviations and visual letter combinations to represent aspects of Jesus Christ and his name. So using the eight-spoked wheel as a composite for the letters in the word IXΘΥC is entirely plausible; it is similar to the way Christians were using other word combinations and symbols.

Third, the eight-spoked wheel was used frequently and widely as a highly regarded sacred Christian symbol, often in parallel to the cross. Based on the meanings of most other popular Christian symbols used by the early church, it is almost certain that this symbol was connected in some way to Jesus Christ and most likely to the name of Jesus Christ. The IXΘΥC identification fits this criterion and gives the symbol a significance and a meaning that is appropriate for the high level of sacredness in the contexts in which the eight-spoked wheel is often used within the church (e.g., at the focal points with the cross on either side; in parallel with the equilateral cross and the Iota-Chi Christogram, etc.).

Fourth, and perhaps most conclusive, is the piece of wall plaster from the Villa of the Quintili near Rome with the word IXΘΥC written in large letters within a title box right below an eight-spoked wheel. The most logical explanation for this is that the eight-spoked wheel is a composite of the letters in the word IXΘΥC.

Fifth, on the floor of the house church in Laodicea there is an eight-spoked wheel in the pattern of the brick flooring. Next to the panel with the eight-spoked wheel is a design of a fish. Being in a Greek-speaking area, it is likely that the connection between these two side-by-side designs is that the eight-spoked wheel is a composite letter combination of the acrostic IXΘΥC, the Greek word for fish. It is difficult to come up with a better, more plausible explanation for the side-by-side placement of these two designs.

Therefore, there is widespread, conclusive evidence that the eight-spoked wheel symbol was a Christogram, formed by combining the letters from the Greek word for fish (IXΘΥC), which was, in turn, an acrostic taken from the first letters of the divine name, "Jesus Christ God's Son Savior."

THE ICHTHUS CHRISTOGRAM AND THE
CHRISTIANIZATION OF THE PAGAN CITIES

Yet after identifying the eight-spoked wheel in graffiti and in church architecture as being a Christogram representing ΙΧΘΥϹ (ICHTHUS), important questions arise: Why was it used? When was it used? To answer this, we explored the historical, cultural, religious, and sociological background of late antiquity and then placed the many appearances of the ICHTHUS Christogram into this background setting, seeking the most plausible context that would best explain the phenomenon of the ICHTHUS Christogram as well as the other Christian symbols that we have encountered as informal graffiti.

All of the available evidence points to a setting in the tumultuous fourth century. At the beginning of the fourth century, the cities of the Roman Empire were dominated—visually, economically, and politically—by pagan temples. By the end of the fourth century, a drastic change had occurred. Practically all of the pagan temples were closed, having been either abandoned or destroyed. The vast majority of pagan idol statues, once plentiful, had been destroyed or defaced. Churches were being built all across the cities, sometimes on the very site where the ancient temple once stood, a process that accelerated even more into the fifth century. Practically every city of any size had a Christian bishop, often zealous in spreading Christianity and putting an end to paganism.

At the beginning of the fourth century, the emperor Diocletian and his co-rulers instituted the Great Persecution (AD 303–313), an attempt to remove Christianity from public life. As Constantine rose to power, he first ended the Great Persecution and legalized Christianity (AD 313), and then, as sole ruler of the Roman Empire (AD 326), he provided considerable imperial support for the Christian church. Throughout the rest of the fourth century and into the fifth century, his successors (with the exception of Julian the Apostate) used their imperial power to support and expand the Christian church and to end pagan worship.

Although the timing varied with city and region, depending on the various power dynamics, at some point during the fourth century the temples in each city could no longer stay open or defend themselves. Motivated by zeal to spread the Christian faith, proclaim victory over the evil forces that brought about the painful Great Persecution, and the desire to cleanse the temple and the rest of the city from evil demonic forces, Christians, often led by their bishops, marched into pagan temples to destroy and cleanse the temple. As part of this, Christians beheaded and defaced thousands of pagan statues across the empire. The Christians believed that the evil demonic forces associated with the pagan gods could be driven away and kept away by the power of the cross and the name of Jesus Christ. It was at this time, as the Christians were beheading idols and striving to cleanse the temples, that they most likely etched the ICHTHUS wheel graffiti on temple floors, altars, and entryways. As the Christians sought to cleanse the rest of the city, they removed, destroyed, or defaced the pagan idols that stood in public areas. This is also the likely context for the informal inscribing of the ICHTHUS Christogram on stone pavement in the streets at intersections and in front of monumental fountains—areas that had been associated with the realm of pagan gods and demons.

THE ICHTHUS CHRISTOGRAM IN EARLY CHURCH AND PUBLIC CHRISTIAN ARCHITECTURE

The eight-spoked ICHTHUS Christogram was also used in churches and in public architecture. These Christograms were not produced informally and quickly, as graffiti, but rather were made by skilled craftsmen following well-thought-out plans. Once again, our study of the historical, cultural, religious, and sociological background of this era is helpful in determining the significance and meanings that were conveyed by this symbol in these contexts.

After Constantine came to power, legalized Christianity, and even provided imperial support for the Christians, construction of new Christian churches began all across the empire. This started immediately in some areas (Rome, AD 314–315; Bethlehem, 325–330; Jerusalem, 335), where direct imperial funding and authority was provided. In other areas it took more time. The number of new churches being constructed continually increased throughout the fourth century and into the fifth century. As Christian bishops became more powerful in civic affairs, and as city and provincial governors along with the other financial benefactors of the city, transitioned from being pagan to being Christian, the rest of the city took on more of a Christian look with Christian symbols being used in public areas as well as in funerary contexts.

These symbols all pointed, first of all, to Jesus Christ, the center of the Christian faith. They served, in one sense, as symbols of identity. These symbols claimed these early Christians' cities for Christ.

No doubt these symbols also expressed connotations of victory; the word NIKA ("victory") continued to be popularly used in inscriptions throughout the fourth, fifth, and sixth centuries. Although the early, initial need of the fourth century to cleanse the temples and cities of demons had diminished, the belief in evil demons and their influence did not just disappear. This explains the appearance of the ICHTHUS wheel on sidewalks, on aqueduct bridges, and at church entrances; it probably continued to carry some apotropaic (power over the demons) connotations, even as its major meaning may have shifted somewhat.

There are a number of other possibilities of nuanced meaning expressed in the public display of the ICHTHUS Christogram. Furthermore, these possibilities are not necessarily mutually exclusive of each other. One strong possibility is that the ICHTHUS Christogram, with its rich christological affirmation of "Jesus Christ God's Son Savior," was used to make a more definite theological statement about orthodox Christology than could be made by the display of a simple cross. Recall that throughout the fourth through the sixth centuries, the church was constantly embroiled in serious theological conflict, much of it regarding Christology. Indeed, during this time, several of the major splits of Christianity started to appear, resulting in the Western Church, the Eastern Church, and the Monophysite (non-Chalcedonian) Church (in Egypt and Ethiopia).

The use of the ICHTHUS Christogram at San Vitale in Ravenna, for example, as well as the use of the Greek word ΙΧΘΥΣ above the jeweled cross at Sant'Apollinare at Classe, were probably being used to teach and proclaim orthodox Chalcedonian Christology in opposition to the Arianism of the previous rulers. It is therefore plausible that other usages of the ΙΧΘΥΣ acrostic, both in written form and in symbolic form (as found in the eight-spoked wheel), are theological statements countering not only Arianism but christological challenges to Nicene and Chalcedonian orthodoxy from other groups as well.

Another proposed connotation of the literary ΙΧΘΥΣ acrostic and the symbolic eight-spoked Christogram, although quite unlikely, is that it is connected to the Eucharist. There are some early Christian writings and funerary drawings (in the catacombs) that seem to associate "fish" with the eucharistic meal.[56] The shape of the eight-spoked ICHTHUS Christogram could resemble a loaf of bread sliced into eight pieces. The evidence—or plausibility—for this proposal, however, is weak.

As with the cross and other Christian symbols, there are perhaps basic pedagogical as well as apologetic connotations and usages associated with the ICHTHUS Christogram. Recall from chapter 2, for example, that Eusebius, Maximus of Turin, and Augustine all cited the ΙΧΘΥΣ acrostic in the Sibylline Oracles as an apologetic argument attempting to demonstrate that early prophecy prior to Christ predicted his coming. It seems plausible that the eight-spoked wheel may have been used in the same fashion, recalling the same argument. In an era where illiteracy or semi-literacy was still quite high, having a symbol that could be used to explain the basics of the faith would have been helpful. Related to this is Hurtado's observation regarding the function of the *nomina sacra* in early Christianity. He notes that this symbol was not just a scribal feature, but a "visual phenomenon." That is, semi-literate and even illiterate people could be shown the *nomina sacra*, identifiable by the line overhead, and be able to grasp with awe and respect that this symbol was the name of God (or Jesus Christ).[57] The ICHTHUS Christogram could have been used similarly while also allowing the teacher to go further and use the circle to explain the basics of Christology.

---

56. See the discussion in Jensen, "Fish Symbol," 280–87, who rejects the Eucharist connotation of the ICHTHUS acrostic.

57. Hurtado, *The Earliest Christian Artifacts*, 132–33.

As the fourth century progressed into the fifth and sixth centuries and the removal of the pagan idols became a past action, it is likely that the still visible eight-spoked ICHTHUS Christograms that had been etched on the streets and other pavement took on a new function. Keep in mind that throughout the fourth, fifth, and sixth centuries the number of Christians in the empire was rapidly growing. There was a constant push from many Christian leaders and laypeople to convert the unbelievers to Christ. Although we are speculating somewhat, it seems likely that Christians would have taken advantage of these ICHTHUS wheels (as well as the other Christian symbols) inscribed in public places across their cities and used them for pedagogical or evangelistic purposes. As one exited from the Lower Commercial Agora in Ephesus onto Harbor Street with a non-Christian acquaintance, for example, it would be evangelistically opportunistic to stop at one of the many ICHTHUS Christograms on that area of pavement and ask one's acquaintance if he or she knew what that symbol meant. This would certainly open the door for explaining who Jesus Christ is. Or as Christian parents came across these symbols on the streets with their children, stopping to explain what they meant would provide a meaningful pedagogical opportunity.

FINAL WORDS

The eight-spoked ICHTHUS Christogram (along with the other early Christian symbols), whether etched informally in the stone as graffiti or professionally inscribed into church architecture, is a testimony to the incredible spread of Christianity all across the Roman Empire (and beyond) in the fourth and fifth centuries. Wherever we Christians today live in the world, the events in the Roman Empire during the fourth century are part of our spiritual heritage. These Christograms were produced by real people who lived through real, complicated times. With the deaths of relatives and friends in the Great Persecution still fresh on their minds, Christians went into pagan temples—powerful and hostile institutions—to drive out the evil demonic forces behind the persecution and to proclaim victory through the name of Jesus Christ, God's Son, the Savior. Some of them took a hammer and chisel—perhaps they shared it and passed it around—and etched eight-spoked wheels in the entryway of the temple, proclaiming the name and power of Jesus Christ, the Son of God, the Savior. Fellow Christians inscribed crosses and other Christian symbols into the stone pavement, even as others knocked off the heads of existing idol statues and then toppled these statues to the ground. The pagan temples had come to an end. The world had changed—one of the more drastic and enduring changes in all of world history.

BIBLIOGRAPHY

Aharoni, Y. "Excavations at Beth-Hashitta." *Bulletin of the Israel Exploration Society* 18 (1954): 209–15.

Akşit, İlhan. *The History and Architecture of the Hagia Sophia*. Istanbul: Akşit Kültür Turizm Sanat Ajans Ltd. Şti., 2019.

Alchermes, Joseph D. "Art and Architecture in the Age of Justinian." Pages 343–75 in *The Cambridge Companion to the Age of Justinian*. Edited by Michael Maas. Cambridge: Cambridge University Press, 2005.

Amandry, Pierre. "Chronique delphique." *Bulletin de correspondance hellénique* 105.2 (1981): 673–769.

Andreescu-Treadgold, Irina, and Warren Treadgold. "Procopius and the Imperial Panels of S. Vitale." *The Art Bulletin* 79.4 (1997): 708–23.

Anonymous Life of Severos (Attributed to John of Beth Aphtonia). Translated by Sebastian Brock and Brian Fitzgerald. In *Two Early Lives of Severos, Patriarch of Antioch*. Liverpool: Liverpool University Press, 2013.

Armstrong, Gregory T. "Jerusalem." Pages 728-29 in vol. 1 of *The Eerdmans Encyclopedia of Early Christian Art and Archaeology*. Edited by Paul Corby Finney. Grand Rapids: Eerdmans, 2017.

Arnold, Clinton E. *Ephesians: Power and Magic: The Concept of Power in Ephesians in Light of Its Historical Setting*. SNTSMS 63. Cambridge: Cambridge University Press, 1989.

Ascough, Richard S., ed. *Religious Rivalries and the Struggle in Sardis and Smyrna*. Waterloo, Ontario: Wilfrid Laurier, 2005.

Aviam, Mordechai. "The Synagogue." Pages 127–33 in *Magdala of Galilee: A Jewish City in the Hellenistic and Roman Period*. Edited by Richard Bauckham. Waco, TX: Baylor University Press, 2018.

Aviam, Mordechai, and Richard Bauckham. "The Synagogue Stone." Pages 136–59 in *Magdala of Galilee: A Jewish City in the Hellenistic and Roman Period*. Edited by Richard Bauckham. Waco, TX: Baylor University Press, 2018.

Avi-Yohan, M. "A Sixth-Century Inscription from Sepphoris." *Israel Exploration Journal* 11.4 (1961): 184–87.

Bagnall, R. S., K. Broderson, C. B. Champion, and S. Huebner, eds. *The Encyclopedia of Ancient History*. London: Blackwell, 2013.

Bagnall, Roger S., Roberta Casagrande-Kim, Akin Ersoy, Cumhur Tanriver, and Burak Yolaçan. *Graffiti from the Basilica in the Agora of Smyrna*. New York: Institute for the Study of the Ancient World and New York University Press, 2016.

Bakker, Jan Theo. *Living and Working with the Gods: Studies of Evidence for Private Religion and Its Material Environment in Ostia (AD 100–500)*. Dutch Monograph on Ancient History and Archaeology 12. Amsterdam: Gieben, 1994.

Banes, Rachael Helen. "Scratch That: A Comparative Approach to Graffiti in the Late Antique Eastern Mediterranean c. 300–700 CE." PhD diss., University of Birmingham, 2022.

Barnes, T. D., and R. W. Westall. "The Conversion of the Roman Aristocracy in Prudentius' 'Contra Symmachum.'" *Phoenix* 45.1 (1991): 50–61.

Bauckham, Richard, ed. *Magdala of Galilee: A Jewish City in the Hellenistic and Roman Period*. Waco, TX: Baylor University Press, 2018.

———. "Magdala as We Now Know It." Pages 1–67 in *Magdala of Galilee: A Jewish City in the Hellenistic and Roman Period*. Edited by Richard Bauckham. Waco, TX: Baylor University Press, 2018.

Bauernfeind, O. "νικάω." *TDNT* 4:942.

Bayliss, Richard. *Provincial Cilicia and the Archaeology of Temple Conversion*. BAR International Series 1281. Oxford: BAR Publishing, 2016.

Beatrice, Pier Franco. "Monophysite Christology in an Oracle of Apollo." *International Journal of the Classical Tradition* 4.1 (1997): 3–22.

Behling, Claudia-Maria. "Der sog. Rundmühle auf der Spur—Zug um Zug zur Neudeutung römischer Radmuster." Pages 63–70 in *Akten des 14. Österreichischen Archäologentages am Institut für Archäologie der Universität Graz*. Edited by Elisabeth Trinkl. Wien: Phoibos, 2014.

Bell, R. C. "Notes on Pavement Games of Greece and Rome." Pages 98–99 in *Ancient Board Games in Perspective: Papers from the 1990 British Museum Colloquium, with Additional Contributions*. Edited by I. L. Finkel. London: The British Museum Press, 2007.

Bell, R. C., and C. M. Roueché. "Graeco-Roman Pavement Signs and Game Boards: A British Museum Working Typology." Pages 106–9 in *Ancient Board Games in Perspective: Papers from the 1990 British Museum Colloquium, with Additional Contributions*. Edited by I. L. Finkel. London: The British Museum, 2007.

Benko, Stephen. *Pagan Rome and the Early Christians*. Bloomington: Indiana University Press, 1986.

Bevelacqua, Gaetano S. "Observations on Christian Epigraphy in Pannonia." Pages 75–111 in *Studia Patristica* 73. Edited by A. Brent and M. Vinzent. Leuven: Peeters, 2014.

Birk, Stine, and Birte Poulsen, eds. *Patrons and Viewers in Late Antiquity*. Aarhus, Denmark: Aarhus University Press, 2012.

Blid, Jesper. *Felicium Temporum Reparatio: Labraunda in Late Antiquity (c. AD 300–600)*. Stockholm: Stockholm University, 2012.

_____. "Sacred Movement to Labraunda: An Archaeological Perspective." *Journal on Hellenistic and Roman Material Culture* 1 (2012): 159–80.

Blümlein, Carl. *Bilder aus dem römisch-germanischen Kulturleben*. München and Berlin: R. Oldenbourg, 1918.

Bolle, Katharina, Carlos Machado, and Christian Witschel, eds. *The Epigraphic Cultures of Late Antiquity*. Stuttgart: Franz Steiner Verlag, 2017.

Brandenburg, Hugo. "Christussymbole in frühchristlichen Bodenmosaiken." *Römische Quartalschrift für christliche Altertumskunde und Kirchengeschichte* 64 (1969): 74–138.

Brandt, Olof, and Gabriele Castiglia, ed. *Constantino E I Constantinidi: L'Innovazione Constantiniana, Le Sue Radici E I Suoi Sviluppi*. Studi Di Antichità Cristiana 66. Rome: Pontificio Istituto di Archeologia Cristiana, 2016.

Brent, Allen. *The Imperial Cult and the Development of Church Order: Concepts and Images of Authority in Paganism and Early Christianity before the Age of Cyprian*. Supplements to Vigiliae Christianae: Texts and Studies of Early Christian Life and Language XLV. Leiden: Brill, 1999.

Breytenback, Cilliers, Martin Goodman, Christoph Markschies, and Stephen Mitchell, eds. *Early Christianity in Asia Minor and Cyprus: From the Margins to the Mainstream*. Ancient Judaism and Early Christianity 109. Leiden: Brill, 2019.

Brown, Amelia R. "Crosses, Noses, Walls, and Wells: Christianity and the Fate of Sculpture in Late Antique Corinth." Pages 150–176 in *The Afterlife of Greek and Roman Sculpture: Late Antique Responses and Practices*. Edited by Troels Myrup Kristensen and Lea Stirling. Ann Arbor: University of Michigan Press, 2016.

Bruce, F. F. "The Church of Jerusalem." *Christian Brethren Research Fellowship Journal* 4 (1964): 5–14.

Buchwald, Hans, with Anne McClanan. *Churches EA and E at Sardis*. Archaeological Exploration of Sardis. Cambridge, MA: Harvard University Press, 2015.

Buckler, W. H., and David M. Robinson. *Sardis: Publications of the American Society for the Excavation of Sardis; Greek and Latin Inscriptions*, vol. 7, part 1. Leiden: Brill, 1932.

Bull, Christian H., Liv Ingeborg Lied, and John D. Turner, eds. *Mystery and Secrecy in the Nag Hammadi Collection and Other Ancient Literature: Ideas and Practices: Studies for Einar Thomassen at Sixty*. Leiden: Brill, 2012.

Bustacchini, Gianfranco. *Ravenna: Mosaics, Monuments and Environment.* Rev. ed. edited by Franco Gàbici. Ravenna: Salbaroli Publishers, 2022.

Caldwell, Craig H. "The Balkans." Pages 92–113 in *The Oxford Handbook of Late Antiquity.* Edited by Scott Fitzgerald Johnson. Oxford: Oxford University Press, 2012.

Calza, Raisa. "Le Sculture e la Probabile Zona Cristiana di Ostia e di Porto." *RendPontAc* 37 (1964–65): 155–257.

Cameron, Alan. *Circus Factions: Blues and Greens at Rome and Byzantium.* Oxford: Clarendon Press, 1976.

Carleback, Elisheva, and Jacob J. Schacter, eds. *New Perspectives on Jewish-Christian Relations*, Brill Reference Library of Judaism 33. Leiden: Brill, 2012.

Chambers, Adam C. "Re-Centering the Temple: The Origin and Expansion of the Decapolis Churches, 4th to 7th c. CE." PhD diss., Miami University, 2009.

Clark, John R. *Looking at Laughter: Humor, Power, and Transgression in Roman Visual Culture, 100 BC–AD 250.* Berkeley: University of California Press, 2007.

Cohick, Lynn. "Melito of Sardis's *PERI PASCHA* and Its 'Israel.'" *HTR* 91.4 (1998): 351–72.

Cole, Susan Guettel. "Greco-Roman Temples." *ABD* 6:380–82.

Collins, John J. "Sibylline Oracles." *ABD* 6:2–6.

Coniglio, A., and A. Ricco, eds. *Holy Land. Archaeology on Either Side: Archaeological Essays in Honor of Eugenio Alliata, ofm.* Collectio Maior 57. Milan: Edizioni Terra Santa, 2020.

Corcoran, Simon. "Before Constantine." Pages 35–58 in *The Cambridge Companion to the Age of Constantine.* Rev. ed. Edited by Noel Lenski. Cambridge: Cambridge University Press, 2012.

Coupry, Jacques. "Un joueur de marelle au marché de Philippes." *Bulletin de correspondance hellénique* 70 (1946): 102–5.

Crawford, John Stevens. "The Byzantine Shops." Pages 161–67 in *Sardis: From Prehistoric to Roman Times: Results of the Archaeological Exploration of Sardis 1958–1975.* Edited by George M. A. Hanfmann. Cambridge, MA: Harvard University Press, 1983.

———. *The Byzantine Shops of Sardis.* Archaeological Exploration of Sardis 9. Cambridge, MA: Harvard University Press, 1990.

Croke, Brian. "Justinian's Constantinople." Pages 60–86 in *The Cambridge Companion to the Age of Justinian.* Edited by Michael Maas. Cambridge: Cambridge University Press, 2005.

Crow, James. "Blessing or Security? Understanding the Christian Symbols of a Monumental Aqueduct Bridge in the Hinterland of Late Antique Constantinople." Pages 147–74 in *Graphic Signs of Identity, Faith, and Power in Late Antiquity and the Early Middle Ages.* Edited by Ildar Garipzanov, Caroline Goodson, and Henry Maguire. Turnhout: Brepols, 2017.

_____. "The Christian Symbols and Iconography of the Aqueducts of Thrace." Pages 157–80 in *The Water Supply of Byzantine Constantinople*. Edited by James Crow, Jonathan Bardill, and Richard Bayliss. Journal of Roman Studies Monograph 11. London: The Society for the Promotion of Roman Studies, 2008.

Crow, James, Jonathan Bardill, and Richard Bayliss. *The Water Supply of Byzantine Constantinople*. Journal of Roman Studies Monograph 11. London: The Society for the Promotion of Roman Studies, 2008.

Ćurčić, Slobodan. "Design and Structural Innovation in Byzantine Architecture Before Hagia Sophia." Pages 16–38 in *Hagia Sophia from the Age of Justinian to the Present*. Edited by Robert Mark and Ahmet Ş. Çakmak. Cambridge: Cambridge University Press, 1992.

D'Annoville, Caroline Michel. "Rome and Imagery in Late Antiquity: Perception and Use of Statues." Pages 343–57 in *Pagans and Christians in Late Antique Rome*. Edited by Michele Salzman, Marianne Sághy, and Rita Lizzi Testa. Cambridge: Cambridge University Press, 2016.

Dayagi-Mendels, Michal, and Silvia Rozenberg, eds. *Chronicles of the Land: Archaeology in the Israel Museum, Jerusalem*. 2nd ed. Jerusalem: The Israel Museum, 2011.

Degasperi, Angelica. *Die Mariekirche in Ephesos: Die Bauskulptur aus frühchristlicher und byzantinischer Zeit*. Ergänzungshefte zu den Jahresheften des Österreichischen Archäologischen Instituts in Wien 14. Wien: Österreichischen Archäologischen Instituts, 2013.

Deliyannis, Deborah Mauskopf. "The Mosaics of Ravenna." Pages 347–63 in *The Routledge Handbook of Early Christian Art*. Edited by Robin M. Jensen and Mark D. Ellison. New York: Routledge, 2018.

Demo, Zeljko, ed. *From the Invincible Sun to the Sun of Justice: Early Christianity in Continental Croatia*. The Archaeological Museum in Zagreb, 1994. Exhibition Catalogue.

Déroche, Vincent. "Delphes: la christianisation d'un sanctuaire paien." Pages 2713–23 in *Actes du Xie congrès international d'archéologie chrétienne*. Rome: École Française de Rome, 1989.

Déroche, Vincent, and Platon Pétridis. "Delphi." Pages 409–10 in vol. 1 of *The Eerdmans Encyclopedia of Early Christian Art and Archaeology*. Edited by Paul Corby Finney. Grand Rapids: Eerdmans, 2017.

Digeser, Elizabeth Depalma. "An Oracle of Apollo at Daphne and the Great Persecution." *Classical Philology* 99.1 (2004): 57–77.

_____. *A Threat to Public Piety: Christians, Platonists, and the Great Persecution*. Ithaca, NY: Cornell University Press, 2012.

Dimitrova, Elizabeta, Silvana Blaževska, and Miško Tutkovski. *Early Christian Wall Paintings from the Episcopal Basilica in Stobi*. Gradsko: NI Stobi, 2012.

Dölger, Franz Joseph. "Die ΙΧΘΥC-Formel in dem neuentdeckten Fußboden-Mosaik der Konstantinischen Basilika von Bethlehem." *Antike und Christentum: kultur und religionsgeschichtliche Studien* 5 (1936): 81–86.

———. ΙΧΘΥC. 2nd ed. 5 vols. Münster: Aschendorf, 1928–1943.

Drake, H. A. "The Impact of Constantine on Christianity." Pages 111–36 in *The Cambridge Companion to the Age of Constantine*. Edited by Noel Lenski. Cambridge: Cambridge University Press, 2012.

Dresken-Weiland, Jutta. "Response to Peter Lampe's *Paul to Valentinus: Christians at Rome in the First Two Centuries:* The Archaeology of *Die stadtrömischen Christen* in 2016." Pages 451–71 in *The First Urban Churches 6: Rome and Ostia*. Edited by James R. Harrison and L. L. Welborn. Writings from the Greco-Roman World Supplement Series 18. Atlanta: SBL Press, 2021.

Dvorjetski, Estēe. "The Synagogue-Church at Gerasa in Jordan: A Contribution to the Study of Ancient Synagogues." *Zeitschrift des Deutshcen Palästina-Vereins* 121.2 (2005):140–67.

Edwards, James R. "'A Nomen Sacrum' in the Sardis Synagogue." *JBL* 128.4 (2009): 813–21.

Eisenberg, Michael. *A Visitor's Guide to Ancient Hippos: Above the Sea of Galilee*. Israel: Millennium Ayalon, 2021.

Ellison, Mark D. "'Secular' Portraits, Identity, and the Christianization of the Roman Household." Pages 326–46 in *The Routledge Handbook of Early Christian Art*. Edited by Robin M. Jensen and Mark D. Ellison. New York: Routledge, 2018.

Elm, Eva, and Nicole Hartmann, eds. *Demons in Late Antiquity*. Transformationen der Antike 54. Berlin: de Gruyter, 2019.

Elm, Eva. "Introduction." Pages 1–14 in *Demons in Late Antiquity*. Edited by Eva Elm and Nicole Hartmann. Transformationen der Antike 54. Berlin: de Gruyter, 2019.

Engermann, Josepf. "Fisch, Fischer, Fischfang." Pages 959–1094 in *Reallexikon für Antike und Christentum: Sachworterbuch zur Auseinandersetzung des Christentums mit der antiken Welt*. Edited by Theodor Klauser, Ernst Dassman, and Georg Schöllgen. Stuttgart: Anton Hiersemann, 1969.

Erdemgil, Selahattin. *Ephesus Museum*. Istanbul, Turkey: Do-Gü, n.d.

Fairchild, Mark. R. *Christian Origins in Ephesus and Asia Minor*. 2nd ed. Peabody, MA: Hendrickson, 2017.

———. "Laodicea's 'Lukewarm' Legacy: Conflicts of Prosperity in an Ancient Christian City." *Biblical Archaeology Review* 43.2 (2017): 30–39, 67–69.

Falkener, Edward. *Games Ancient and Oriental and How to Play Them*. London: Longmans, Green and Co., 1892.

Fant, Clyde E., and Mitchell G. Reddish. *A Guide to Biblical Sites in Greece and Turkey*. Oxford: Oxford University Press, 2003.

Felle, Antonio E., and Bryan Ward-Perkins, eds. *Cultic Graffiti in the Late Antique Mediterranean and Beyond*. Turnhout: Brepols, 2021.

Felle, Antonio E. "Late Antique Christian Graffiti: The Case of Rome (Third to Fifth Centuries CE)." Pages 57–76 in *Cultic Graffiti in the Late Antique Mediterranean and Beyond*. Edited by Antonio E. Felle and Bryan Ward-Perkins. Turnhout: Brepols, 2021.

Ferguson, Everett. "Aberkios." Pages 2–3 in vol. 1 of *The Eerdmans Encyclopedia of Early Christian Art and Archaeology*. Edited by Paul Corby Finney. Grand Rapids: Eerdmans, 2017.

———. *Backgrounds of Early Christianity*. 3rd ed. Grand Rapids: Eerdmans, 2003.

———. *Church History*. Vol. 1 of *From Christ to Pre-Reformation*. Grand Rapids: Zondervan, 2005.

Feuser, Stefan. "A Stroll along the Sea: The Processional Way in Ephesus and the Littoral." *Center for Hellenic Studies Research Bulletin* 3.1 (2014): 2.1–2.6. http://nrs.harvard.edu/urn-3:hlnc.essay:FeuserS.A_Stroll_along_the_Sea.

Fine, Stephen. "The Menorah and the Cross: Historiographical Reflections on a Recent Discovery from Laodicea on the Lycus." Pages 31–50 in *New Perspectives on Jewish-Christian Relations*. Edited by Elisheva Carleback and Jacob J. Schacter, Brill Reference Library of Judaism 33. Leiden: Brill, 2012.

———. "Synagogues as Foci of Multi-Religious and Ideological Confrontation? The Case of the Sardis Synagogue." Pages 97–108 in *Jerusalem and Other Holy Places as Foci of Multireligious and Ideological Confrontation*. Edited by Pieter B. Hartog. Jewish and Christian Perspectives 37. Leiden: Brill, 2020.

Finkel, I. L., ed. *Ancient Board Games in Perspective: Papers from the 1990 British Museum Colloquium, with Additional Contributions*. London: The British Museum Press, 2007.

Finney, Paul Corby, ed. *The Eerdmans Encyclopedia of Early Christian Art and Archaeology*. Grand Rapids: Eerdmans, 2017.

Fitzgerald, G. M. *A Sixth Century Monastery at Beth-Shan (Scythopolis)*. Philadelphia: University of Pennsylvania Press, 1939.

Foerster, Werner. "σωτήρ." *TDNT* 7:1010–12.

Fontenrose, Joseph. *Didyma: Apollo's Oracle, Cult, and Companions*. Berkeley: University of California Press, 1988.

Foss, Clive. *Byzantine and Turkish Sardis*. Cambridge, MA: Harvard University Press, 1976.

———. *Ephesus after Antiquity: A Late Antique, Byzantine and Turkish City*. Cambridge: Cambridge University Press, 1979.

Frank, Georgia. "Pilgrimage." Pages 826–41 in *The Oxford Handbook of Early Christian Studies*. Edited by Susan Ashbrook Harvey and David G. Hunter. Oxford: Oxford University Press, 2008.

Friesen, Stephen J. *Twice Neokoros: Ephesus, Asia and the Cult of the Flavian Imperial Family*. Religions in the Graeco-Roman World 116. Leiden: Brill, 1993.

Gábor, Olivér. "Early Christian Buildings in the Northern Cemetery of Sopi-anae." *Studia Patristica* 73 (2014): 39–58.

Gal, Zvi. *The Splendor of Mosaics in Israel's National Parks.* Industrial Park, Israel: Rahash Press, 2012.

Garipzanov, Ildar, Caroline Goodson, and Henry Maguire, eds. *Graphic Signs of Identity, Faith, and Power in Late Antiquity and the Early Middle Ages.* Turnhout: Brepols, 2017.

Garipzanov, Ildar. "Monograms, Early Christians, and Late Antique Culture." Pages 109–30 in *Graphic Signs of Identity, Faith, and Power in Late Antiquity and the Early Middle Ages.* Edited by Ildar Garipzanov, Caroline Goodson, and Henry Maguire. Turnhout: Brepols, 2017.

_____. *Graphic Signs of Authority in Late Antiquity and the Early Middle Ages, 300–900.* Oxford: Oxford University Press, 2018.

Glahn, Sandra L. *Nobody's Mother: Artemis of the Ephesians in Antiquity and the New Testament.* Downers Grove, IL: IVP Academic, 2023.

Goodchild, Richard George. *Kyrene und Apollinia.* Zurich: Raggi, 1971.

Gregory, Timothy E. "Julian and the Last Oracle at Delphi." *Greek, Roman and Byzantine Studies* 24.4 (1983): 355–66.

Grig, Lucy. *Making Martyrs in Late Antiquity.* London: Duckworth, 2004.

Grundmann, Walter. "στέφανος." *TDNT* 7:615–36.

Guarducci, Margherita. *Epigrafia Greco IV: Epigraphi Sacre Pagane E Chris-tiane.* Rome: Instituto Poligrafico Dello Stato, 1978.

_____. *The Tomb of St. Peter: The New Discoveries in the Sacred Grottoes of the Vatican.* Translated by Joseph McLellan. New York: Hawthorn Books, 1960.

Gurtner, Daniel M. *Introducing the Pseudepigrapha of Second Temple Judaism.* Grand Rapids: Baker Academic, 2020.

Habas, Lehi. "Mosaic Floors of the Church at Ḥorbat Ḥadat, Israel." *Journal of Mosaic Research* 15 (2022): 167–84.

Hahn, Johannes. "The Conversion of the Cult Statues." Pages 333–65 in *From Temple to Church: Destruction and Renewal of Local Cultic Topography in Late Antiquity.* Edited by Johannes Hahn, Stephen Emmel, and Ulrich Gotter. Leiden: Brill, 2008.

_____. "Die Zerstörung der Kulte von Philae: Geschichte und Legende am Ersten Nilkatarakt." Pages 203–42 in *From Temple to Church: Destruc-tion and Renewal of Local Cultic Topography in Late Antiquity.* Edited by Johannes Hahn, Stephen Emmel, and Ulrich Gotter. Leiden: Brill, 2008.

Hahn, Johannes, Stephen Emmel, and Ulrich Gotter, eds. *From Temple to Church: Destruction and Renewal of Local Cultic Topography in Late Antiquity.* Leiden: Brill, 2008.

Hamilton, R. W. *The Church of the Nativity Bethlehem.* Jerusalem: Depart-ment of Antiquities, 1947.

Hammer, Keir E., and Michele Murray. "Acquaintances, Supporters, and Competitors: Evidence of Inter-Connectedness and Rivalry among the

Religious Groups in Sardis." Pages 175–95 in *Religious Rivalries and the Struggle in Sardis and Smyrna*. Edited by Richard S. Ascough. Waterloo, Ontario: Wilfrid Laurier, 2005.

Hanfmann, George M. A., ed. *Sardis: From Prehistoric to Roman Times: Results of the Archaeological Exploration of Sardis 1958–1975*. Cambridge, MA: Harvard University Press, 1983.

Hanfmann, George M. A., and Hans Buckwald. "Christianity: Churches and Cemeteries." Pages 191–210 in *Sardis: From Prehistoric to Roman Times: Results of the Archaeological Exploration of Sardis 1958–1975*. Edited by George M. A. Hanfmann. Cambridge, MA: Harvard University Press, 1983.

Hanfmann, George M. A., Fikret K. Yegül, and John S. Crawford. "The Roman and Late Antique Period." Pages 139–67 in *Sardis: From Prehistoric to Roman Times: Results of the Archaeological Exploration of Sardis 1958–1975*. Edited by George M. A. Hanfmann. Cambridge, MA: Harvard University Press, 1983.

Harley-McGowan, Felicity. "Picturing the Passion." Pages 290–307 in *The Routledge Handbook of Early Christian Art*. Edited by Robin M. Jensen and Mark D. Ellison. New York: Routledge, 2018.

Harrison, James R., and L. L. Welborn, eds. *The First Urban Churches 3: Ephesus*. Writings from the Greco-Roman World Supplement Series 9. Atlanta: SBL Press, 2018.

———. *The First Urban Churches 4: Roman Philippi*. Writings from the Greco-Roman World Supplement 13. Atlanta: SBL Press, 2018.

———. *The First Urban Churches 6: Rome and Ostia*. Writings From the Greco-Roman World Supplement Series 18. Atlanta: SBL Press, 2021.

Harrison, James R. "An Epigraphic Portrait of Ephesus and Its Villages." Pages 1–68 in *The First Urban Churches 3: Ephesus*. Edited by James R. Harrison and L. L. Welborn. Writings from the Greco-Roman World Supplement Series 9. Atlanta: SBL Press, 2018.

———. "Ostia, Harbor Port of Rome: An Epigraphic and Archaeological Portrait." Pages 67–136 in *The First Urban Churches 6: Rome and Ostia*. Edited by James R. Harrison and L. L. Welborn. Writings From the Greco-Roman World Supplement Series 18. Atlanta: SBL Press, 2021.

Hartog, Pieter B., ed. *Jerusalem and Other Holy Places as Foci of Multireligious and Ideological Confrontation*. Jewish and Christian Perspectives 37. Leiden: Brill, 2020.

Harvey, Susan Ashbrook, and David G. Hunter, eds. *The Oxford Handbook of Early Christian Studies*. Oxford: Oxford University Press, 2008.

Hastings, Adrian, ed. *A History of World Christianity*. Grand Rapids: Eerdmans, 1999.

Hastings, Adrian. "150–550." Pages 31–34 in *A History of World Christianity*. Edited by Adrian Hastings. Grand Rapids: Eerdmans, 1999.

Heimann, Florian Ulrich Maximilian and Ulrich Schädler. "The Loop within Circular Three Men's Morris." *Board Games Studies Journal* 8 (2014): 51–53.

Herrin, Judith. *Ravenna: Capital of Empire, Crucible of Europe.* Princeton, NJ: Princeton University Press, 2020.

Herring, Amanda. "Hekate of Lagina: A Goddess Performing Her Civic Duty." *Anatolian Studies* 72 (2022): 141–65.

Heyden, Katharina. "Beth Shean/Scythopolis in Late Antiquity: Cult and Culture, Continuity and Change." Pages 301–37 in *One God—One Cult—One Nation: Archaeological and Biblical Perspectives.* Edited by Reinhard Kratz and Hermann Spieckermann. BZAW 405. Berlin: de Gruyter, 2010.

Horsley, G. H. H. "The Inscriptions of Ephesos and the New Testament." *Novum Testamentum* 34.2 (1992): 105–68.

Hubbard, Moyer V. *Christianity in the Greco-Roman World.* Grand Rapids: Baker, 2010.

Hülsen, Christian. *The Roman Forum: Its History and Its Monuments.* 2nd ed. Translated by Jesse Benedict Carter. New York: G. E. Stechert & Co., 1909.

Humphreys, Stephen. "Crosses as Water Purification Devices in Byzantine Palestine." Pages 229–46 in *Trends and Turning Points: Constructing the Late Antique and Byzantine World.* Edited by Matthew Kinloch and Alex MacFarlane. The Medieval Mediterranean: Peoples, Economies and Cultures, 400–1500 117. Leiden: Brill, 2019.

Hürriyet Daily News. "House with Church Unearthed in Laodicea." October 27, 2020. https://www.hurriyetdailynews.com/house-with-church-unearthed-in-laodicea-159481.

Hurtado, Larry W. *The Earliest Christian Artifacts: Manuscripts and Christian Origins.* Grand Rapids: Eerdmans, 2006.

_____. "Earliest Christian Graphic Symbols: Examples and References from the Second/Third Centuries." Pages 25–44 in *Graphic Signs of Identity, Faith, and Power in Late Antiquity and the Early Middle Ages.* Edited by Ildar Garipzanov, Caroline Goodson, and Henry Maguire. Turnhout: Brepols, 2017.

Jacobs, Ine. "The Creation of the Late Antique City: Constantinople and Asia Minor During the Theodosian Renaissance." *Byzantion* 82 (2012): 113–64.

_____. "Cross Graffiti as Physical Means to Christianize the Classical City: An Exploration of Their Function, Meaning, Typographical, and Socio-Historical Contexts." Pages 175–21 in *Graphic Signs of Identity, Faith, and Power in Late Antiquity and the Early Middle Ages.* Edited by Ildar Garipzanov, Caroline Goodson, and Henry Maguire. Turnhout: Brepols, 2017.

Jarak, Mirja. "The History of Early Christian Communities in Continental Croatia." In *From the Invincible Sun to the Sun of Justice: Early Christianity in Continental Croatia.* Edited by Zeljko Demo. Zagreb: The Archaeological Museum in Zagreb, 1994. Exhibition Catalogue.

Jensen, Robin M. "Fish Symbol." Pages 275–80 in *From Celsus to the Catacombs: Visual, Liturgical, and Non-Christian Reception of Jesus in the Second and Third Centuries CE.* Edited by Chris Keith. Vol. 3 of *The Reception of Jesus in the First Three Centuries.* Edited by Chris Keith, Helen K. Bond, Christine Jacobi, and Jens Schröter. London: T&T Clark, 2020.

Jensen, Robin M., and Mark D. Ellison. *The Routledge Handbook of Early Christian Art.* London: Routledge, 2018.

Jensen, Robin M., Peter Lampe, William Tabbernee, and D. H. Williams. "Italy and Environs." Pages 379–432 in *Early Christianity in Contexts: An Exploration across Cultures and Continents.* Edited by William Tabbernee. Grand Rapids: Baker, 2014.

Johnson, Mark J. "Architecture of Empire." Pages 278–97 in *The Cambridge Companion to the Age of Constantine.* Rev ed. Edited by Noel Lenski. Cambridge: Cambridge University Press, 2012.

Johnson, Scott Fitzgerald, ed. *The Oxford Handbook of Late Antiquity.* Oxford: Oxford University Press, 2012.

Johnston, Sarah Iles. "Crossroads." *Zeitschrift für Papyrologie und Epigraphik* 88 (1991): 217–24.

Jones, Tamara. "Seating and Spectacle in the Graeco-Roman World." PhD diss., McMaster University, 1988.

Kalas, Gregor. *The Restoration of the Roman Forum in Late Antiquity: Transforming Public Space.* Austin: University of Texas Press, 2015.

Kalleres, Dayna S. *City of Demons: Violence, Ritual, and Christian Power in Late Antiquity.* Oakland: University of California Press, 2015.

Karahan, Anne. "Byzantine Visual Culture: Conditions of 'Right' Belief and Some Platonic Outlooks." *Numen* 63.2–3 (2016): 217–20.

Kearsley, R. A. "The Epitaph of Aberkios: The Earliest Christian Inscription?" Pages 177–81 in *New Documents Illustrating Early Christianity.* Edited by S. R. Llewlyn and R. A. Kearsley. Marrickville, NSW, Australia: Macquarie University, 1992.

Keener, Craig S. *Acts: An Exegetical Commentary, 15:1–23:35.* Grand Rapids: Baker, 2014.

Keith, Chris, ed. *From Celsus to the Catacombs: Visual, Liturgical, and Non-Christian Reception of Jesus in the Second and Third Centuries CE.* Vol. 3 of *The Reception of Jesus in the First Three Centuries.* Edited by Chris Keith, Helen K. Bond, Christine Jacobi, and Jens Schöter. London: T&T Clark, 2020.

Kessler, Herbert L. "Bright Gardens of Paradise." Pages 111–40 in *Picturing the Bible: The Earliest Christian Art.* Edited by Jeffrey Spier. New Haven, CT: Yale University Press, 2007.

————. "The Word Made Flesh in Early Decorated Bibles." Pages 141–68 in *Picturing the Bible: The Earliest Christian Art.* Edited by Jeffrey Spier. New Haven, CT: Yale University Press, 2007.

Kiilerich, Bente. "The State of Early Christian Iconography in the Twenty-First Century." *Studies in Iconography* 36 (2015): 121–26.

Kinloch, Matthew, and Alex MacFarlane, eds. *Trends and Turning Points: Constructing the Late Antique and Byzantine World.* The Medieval Mediterranean: Peoples, Economies and Cultures, 400–1500. Vol. 117. Leiden: Brill, 2019.

Kinross, Lord (John Patrick Balfour). *Hagia Sophia.* New York: Newsweek, 1972.

Kirbihler, François. "Ruler Cults and Imperial Cults at Ephesos: First Century BCE to Third Century CE." Pages 195–210 in *Religion in Ephesos Reconsidered: Archaeology of Spaces, Structures, and Objects.* Edited by Daniel Schowalter, Sabine Ladstätter, Stephen Friesen, and Christian Thomas. NovTSup 177. Leiden: Brill, 2020.

Kitzinger, Ernst. *Israeli Mosaics of the Byzantine Period.* New York: UNESCO, 1965.

———. "A Survey of the Early Christian Town of Stobi." *Dumbarton Oaks Papers* 3 (1946): 81–162.

Klauser, Theodor, Ernst Dassman, and Georg Schöllgen, eds. *Reallexikon für Antike und Christentum: Sachworterbuch zur Auseinandersetzung des Christentums mit der antiken Welt.* Stuttgart: Anton Hiersemann, 1969.

Klein, Nancy L. "How Buildings Were Constructed." Pages 105–18 in *A Companion Guide to Greek Architecture.* Edited by Margaret M. Miles. West Sussex, UK: Wiley and Sons, 2016.

Koch, Guntram. "Constantinople." Pages 358–63 in *The Eerdmans Encyclopedia of Early Christian Art and Archaeology.* Edited by Paul Corby Finney. Vol. 1. Grand Rapids: Eerdmans, 2017.

———. "Early Christian Sarcophagi Outside of Rome." Pages 56–72 in *The Routledge Handbook of Early Christian Art.* Edited by Robin M. Jensen and Mark D. Ellison. London: Routledge, 2018.

Koenigs, Wolf. *Der Athenatempel von Priene.* Archäologische Forschungen 33. Wiesbaden: Reichert Verlag, 2015.

Koester, Craig. "'The Savior of the World' (John 4:42)." *JBL* 109 (1990): 665–80.

Kolarik, Ruth E. "Mosaics of the Early Church at Stobi." *Dumbarton Oaks Papers* 41 (1987): 296–99.

Koloski-Ostrow, Ann Olga. *The Archaeology of Sanitation in Roman Italy: Toilets, Sewers, and Water Systems.* Chapel Hill: University of North Carolina Press, 2015.

Kontokosta, Anne Hrychuk. "Gladiatorial Reliefs and Elite Funerary Monuments at Aphrodisias." Pages 190–229 in *Aphrodisias Papers 4: New Research on the City and its Monuments.* Edited by C. Ratté and R. R. R. Smith. Journal of Roman Archaeology Supplement Series 70. Portsmouth, RI: Journal of Roman Archaeology, 2008.

Kraabel, A. Thomas. "Impact of the Discovery of the Sardis Synagogue." Pages 178–90 in *Sardis: From Prehistoric to Roman Times: Results of the*

Archaeological Exploration of Sardis 1958–1975. Edited by George M. A. Hanfmann. Cambridge, MA: Harvard University Press, 1983.

Kratz, Reinhard, and Hermann Spieckermann, eds. *One God—One Cult—One Nation: Archaeological and Biblical Perspectives.* BZAW 405. Berlin: de Gruyter, 2010.

Kraus, Thomas J. "Christianized Texts." Pages 387–400 in *From Thomas to Tertullian: Christian Literary Receptions of Jesus in the Second and Third Centuries CE.* Edited by Jens Schröter and Christine Jacobi. Vol. 2 of *The Reception of Jesus in the First Three Centuries.* Edited by Chris Keith, Helen K. Bond, Christine Jacobi, and Jens Schöter. London: T&T Clark, 2020.

———. "Christograms." Pages 221–34 in *From Celsus to the Catacombs: Visual, Liturgical, and Non-Christian Reception of Jesus in the Second and Third Centuries CE.* Edited by Chris Keith. Vol. 3 of *The Reception of Jesus in the First Three Centuries.* Edited by Chris Keith, Helen K. Bond, Christine Jacobi, and Jens Schöter. London: T&T Clark, 2020.

Kristensen, Troels Myrup, and Lea Stirling, eds. *The Afterlife of Greek and Roman Sculpture: Late Antique Responses and Practices.* Ann Arbor: University of Michigan Press, 2016.

Kristensen, Troels Myrup. "Addenda to T. M. Kristensen, 'Miraculous Bodies.' " *Late Antique Archaeology* 15 (2021): 1–3.

———. "Miraculous Bodies: Christian Viewers and the Transformation of 'Pagan' Sculpture in Late Antiquity." Pages 31–66 in *Patrons and Viewers in Late Antiquity.* Edited by Stine Birk and Birte Poulsen. Aarhus, Denmark: Aarhus University Press, 2012.

Kroll, John H. "The Greek Inscriptions of the Sardis Synagogue." *HTR* 94.1 (2001): 5–55.

Ladstätter, Sabine. "The So-Called Imperial Cult Temple for Domitian in Ephesos." Pages 11–40 in *Religion in Ephesos Reconsidered: Archaeology of Spaces, Structures, and Objects.* Edited by Daniel Schowalter, Sabine Ladstätter, Stephen Friesen, and Christian Thomas. NovTSup 177. Leiden: Brill, 2020.

Lanciani, Rodolfo. "Gambling and Cheating in Ancient Rome." *The North American Review* 155.428 (1892): 97–105.

Lapin, Hayim, ed. *Religious and Ethnic Communities in Later Roman Palestine.* Bethesda: University of Maryland Press, 1998.

Laroche, Didier. "L'autel d'Apollon à Delphes: éléments nouveaux." Pages 103–7 and plates XVII–XXII in *L'espace Sacrificiel dans les Civilisations Méditerranéennes de L'Antiquité.* Edited by Roland Etienne and Marie-Thérèse Le Dinahet. Lyon: Université Lumière, 1991.

Laurence, Ray, and David J. Newsome, eds. *Rome, Ostia, Pompeii: Movement and Space.* Oxford: Oxford University Press, 2011.

Lavan, Luke. *Field Methods and Post-Excavation Techniques in Late Antique Archaeology.* Leiden: Brill, 2013.

_____. "The Agorai of Sagalassos in Late Antiquity: An Interpretive Study." Pages 289–353 in *Field Methods and Post-Excavation Techniques in Late Antique Archaeology*. Edited by Luke Lavan and Michael Mulryan. Leiden: Brill, 2013.

_____. "The End of the Temples: Towards a New Narrative." Pages xv–lxv in *The Archaeology of Late Antique "Paganism."* edited by Luke Lavan and Michael Mulryan. Late Antique Archaeology 7. Leiden: Brill, 2011.

Lavan, Luke, and Michael Mulryan, eds. *The Archaeology of Late Antique "Paganism."* Late Antique Archaeology 7. Leiden: Brill, 2011.

Lee, A. D. "The Empire at War." Pages 113–33 in *The Cambridge Companion to the Age of Justinian*. Edited by Michael Maas. Cambridge: Cambridge University Press, 2005.

Lewis, Naphtali, and Meyer Reinhold, eds. *The Empire*. 3rd ed. Vol. 2 of *Roman Civilization: Selected Readings*. New York: Columbia University Press, 1990.

Lenski, Noel, ed. *The Cambridge Companion to the Age of Constantine*. Rev. ed. Cambridge: Cambridge University Press, 2012.

Lenski, Noel. "The Reign of Constantine." Pages 59–90 in *The Cambridge Companion to the Age of Constantine*. Edited by Noel Lenski. Rev. ed. Cambridge: Cambridge University Press, 2012.

Llewlyn, S. R., and R. A. Kearsley, eds. *New Documents Illustrating Early Christianity*. Marrickville, NSW, Australia: Macquarie University, 1992.

Long, Fredrick. "Ἐκκλησία in Ephesians as Godlike in the Heavens, in Temple, in γάμος, and in Armor: Ideology and Iconography in Ephesus and Its Environs." Pages 193–234 in *The First Urban Churches 3: Ephesus*. Edited by James R. Harrison and L. L. Welborn. Writings from the Greco-Roman World Supplement Series 9. Atlanta: SBL Press, 2018.

Longenecker, Bruce W. *The Cross Before Constantine: The Early Life of a Christian Symbol*. Minneapolis: Fortress, 2015.

_____. *The Crosses of Pompeii: Jesus-Devotion in a Vesuvian Town*. Minneapolis: Fortress, 2016.

Longenecker, Bruce W., and Chris Keith. "Cross Symbol." Pages 235–49 in *From Celsus to the Catacombs: Visual, Liturgical, and Non-Christian Reception of Jesus in the Second and Third Centuries CE*. Edited by Chris Keith. Vol. 3 of *The Reception of Jesus in the First Three Centuries*. Edited by Chris Keith, Helen K. Bond, Christine Jacobi, and Jens Schöter. London: T&T Clark, 2020.

López, Elena H. Sánchez. "Water and Production: Reflections on the Water Supply to Urban Workshops in Roman Times." *Water History* 15 (2023): n.p. https://doi.org/10.1007/s12685-023-00323-4.

Maas, Michael, ed. *The Cambridge Companion to the Age of Justinian*. Cambridge: Cambridge University Press, 2005.

Maas, Michael. "Roman Questions, Byzantine Answers: Contours of the Age of Justinian." Pages 3–27 in *The Cambridge Companion to the Age of Justinian*. Edited by Michael Maas. Cambridge: Cambridge University Press, 2005.

Madden, Andrew M. *Corpus of Byzantine Church Mosaic Pavements from Israel and the Palestinian Territories*. Colloquia Antiqua 13. Leuven: Peeters, 2014.

Maffia, Glenn. *Faint Whispers from the Oracle: Archaeological Environment Surrounding the Temple of Apollo at Didyma*. Knurów, Poland: Aslan, 2019.

Magness, Jodi. *The Archaeology of the Holy Land: From the Destruction of Solomon's Temple to the Muslim Conquest*. Cambridge: Cambridge University Press, 2012.

_____. "The Date of the Sardis Synagogue in Light of the Numismatic Evidence." *American Journal of Archaeology* 109.3 (2005): 443–75.

Maguire, Henry, ed. *Rhetoric, Nature and Magic in Byzantine Art*. Brookfield, VT: Ashgate, 1998.

Maguire, Henry. "Magic and Geometry in Early Christian Floor Mosaics and Textiles." Pages 265–88 in *Rhetoric, Nature and Magic in Byzantine Art*. Edited by Henry Maguire. Brookfield, VT: Ashgate, 1998.

Malafarina, Gianfranco, ed. *The Basilica of San Vitale and the Mausoleum of Galla Placidia in Ravenna*. 2nd ed. Modena: Franco Cosimo Panini, 2017.

Mark, Robert, and Ahmet Ş. Çakmak, eds. *Hagia Sophia from the Age of Justinian to the Present*. Cambridge: Cambridge University Press, 1992.

Mark the Deacon. *The Life of Porphyry, Bishop of Gaza*. Translated by G. F. Hill. Oxford: Oxford University Press, 1913.

Master, Daniel M., ed. *The Oxford Encyclopedia of the Bible and Archaeology*. 3 vols. Oxford: Oxford University Press, 2013.

Matthews, Henry. *Greco-Roman Cities of Aegean Turkey: History, Archaeology, Architecture*. Istanbul: Ege Yayinlari, 2014.

Mazor, Gabriel. "Beth-Shean, Roman and Byzantine Period." Pages 118–29 in vol. 1 of *The Oxford Encyclopedia of the Bible and Archaeology*. Edited by Daniel M. Master. 3 vols. Oxford: Oxford University Press, 2013.

_____. "The City's Appearance at the Beginning of the 6th Century." Israel Antiquities Authority. www.antiquities.org.il/Article_eng.aspx?sec_id=17&sub_subj_id=326&id=651.

Mazor, Gabriel and R. Bar-Nathan, "Scythopolis—Capital of Palaestina Secunda." *Qadmoniot* 107–8 (1994): 117–37.

McDavid, Allyson. "Renovation of the Hadrianic Baths in Late Antiquity." Pages 207–24 in *Aphrodisias Papers 5: Excavations and Research at Aphrodisias, 2006–2012*. Edited by R. R. R. Smith, J. Lenaghan, A. Sokolicek, and K. Welch. Journal of Roman Archaeology Supplement Series 103. Portsmouth, RI: Journal of Roman Archaeology, 2016.

McLean, B. H. *An Introduction to Greek Epigraphy of the Hellenistic and Roman Periods from Alexander the Great down to the Reign of Constantine (323 B.C.–A.D. 337)*. Ann Arbor: The University of Michigan Press, 2002.

Meijer, Fik. *The Gladiators: History's Most Deadly Sport*. New York: St. Martin's Press, 2003.

Meyers, Carol, and Eric M. Meyers, "Sepphoris." Pages 336–48 in vol. 2 of *The Oxford Encyclopedia of the Bible and Archaeology*. Edited by Daniel M. Master. 3 vols. Oxford: Oxford University Press, 2013.

Michaelis, Wilhelm. "παντοκράτωρ." *TDNT* 3:914–15.

Migotti, Branka. "The Archaeological Material of the Early Christian Period in Continental Croatia." Pages 1–27 in *From the Invincible Sun to the Sun of Justice: Early Christianity in Continental Croatia*. Edited by Zeljko Demo. Zagreb: The Archaeological Museum in Zagreb, 1994.

Miles, Margaret M., ed. *A Companion Guide to Greek Architecture*. West Sussex, UK: Wiley and Sons, 2016.

Miszczak, Izabela. *The Secrets of Ephesus*. Tan Travel Guide. Fairfield, CT: Aslan, 2020.

Mitchell, Stephen. "The Christian Epigraphy of Asia Minor in Late Antiquity." Pages 271–86 in *The Epigraphic Cultures of Late Antiquity*. Edited by Katharina Bolle, Carlos Machado, and Christian Witschel. Stuttgart: Franz Steiner Verlag, 2017.

Mitchell, Stephen, and Philipp Pilhofer, eds. *Early Christianity in Asia Minor and Cyprus: From the Margins to the Mainstream*. Ancient Judaism and Early Christianity 109. Leiden: Brill, 2019.

Möller, Cosima. "Time as an Argument in Roman Water Law." *Water History* 15 (2023): n.p. https://doi.org/10.1007/s12685-023-00325-2.

Morey, C. R. "The Origin of the Fish-Symbol: The Inscriptions of Abercius and Pectorius." *Princeton Theological Review* (1910): 282–89.

Murphy-O'Connor, Jerome. *The Holy Land: An Oxford Archaeological Guide*. 5th ed. Oxford: Oxford University Press, 2008.

———. *St. Paul's Ephesus: Texts and Archaeology*. Collegeville, MN: Liturgical Press, 2008.

Murray, H. J. R. *A History of Board-Games Other Than Chess*. Oxford: Clarendon Press, 1952.

Muss, Ulrike. *Die Archäologie der ephesischen Artemis: Gestalt und Ritual eines Heiligtums*. Vienna: Phoibos Verlag, 2008.

Naumann, Rudolf. "Aizanoi: Bericht über die Ausgrabunden und Untersuchungen 1983 und 1984." *Archäologischer Anzeiger* (1987): 303–40.

Nunn, Henry Preston Vaughan. *Christian Inscriptions*. New York: Macmillan, 1920.

Ogereau, Julien M. "The Social Constituency and Membership of the First Christian Groups at Philippi: A Literary and Epigraphic Survey." Pages 79–122 in *The First Urban Churches 4: Roman Philippi*. Edited by James R. Harrison and L. L. Welborn. Writings from the Greco-Roman World Supplement 13. Atlanta: SBL Press, 2018.

Otto, Walter. "Augustus Soter." *Hermes* 45.3 (1910): 448–60.

Paap, Anton Herman Reinier Everhard. *Nomina Sacra in the Greek Papyri of the First Five Centuries AD: The Sources and Some Deductions*. Leiden: Brill, 1959.

Panitz-Cohen, Nava. "Beth-Shean, Bronze and Iron Age." Pages 110–18 in *The Oxford Encyclopedia of the Bible and Archaeology*. Edited by Daniel M. Master. Oxford: Oxford University Press, 2013.

Paris, Rita, ed. *Via Appia: The Villa of the Quintili*. Milan: Electa, 2000.

Parlett, David. *Parlett's History of Board Games*. Updated edition of *The Oxford History of Board Games*. Brattleboro, VT: Echo, 2018.

Patrich, Joseph. "The Early Christianization of the Holy Land: The Archaeological Evidence." Pages 265–93 in *Constantino E I Constantinidi: L'Innovazione Constantiniana, Le Sue Radici E I Suoi Sviluppi*. Edited by Olof Brandt and Gabriele Castiglia. Studi Di Antichità Cristiana 66. Rome: Pontificio Istituto di Archeologia Cristiana, 2016.

Payton, James R., Jr. *The Victory of the Cross: Salvation in Eastern Orthodoxy*. Downers Grove, IL: IVP, 2019.

Penner, Ken, and Michael S. Heiser. "Old Testament Greek Pseudepigrapha with Morphology." Bellingham, WA: Lexham Press, 2008.

Pétridis, Platon, and Kalliopi Dimou. "La redécouverte de Delphes protobyzantine." *PALLAS* 87 (2011): 267–81.

Pilhofer, Peter. *Philippi*. Vol. 2 of *Katalog der Inschriften von Philippi*. WUNT 119. Tübingen: Mohr Siebeck, 2000.

Pohlsander, H. A. "Victory: The Story of a Statue." *Historia: Zeitschrift für Alte Geschichte* 18.5 (1969): 588–97.

Prentice, William Kelly. *Greek and Latin Inscriptions*. The Publications of the American Archaeological Expedition to Syria in 1899–1900. Part 3. New York: Century Co., 1908.

———. "Magical Formulae on Lintels of the Christian Period in Syria." *American Journal of Archaeology* 10.2 (1906): 138–48.

Price, S. R. F. *Rituals and Power: The Roman Imperial Cult in Asia Minor*. Cambridge: Cambridge University Press, 1984.

Pülz, Andreas. "Archaeological Evidence of Christian Pilgrimage in Ephesus." *Journal on Hellenistic and Roman Material Culture* 1 (2012): 225–60.

———. "Selected Evidence of Christian Residents in Late Antique Ephesos." Pages 73–89 in *Religion in Ephesos Reconsidered: Archaeology of Spaces, Structures, and Objects*. Edited by Daniel Schowalter, Sabine Ladstätter, Stephen Friesen, and Christian Thomas. NovTSup 177. Leiden: Brill, 2020.

———. "Von der Göttin zur Gottesmutter? Artemis and Maria." Pages 67–75 in *Die Archäologie der ephesischen Artemis: Gestalt und Ritual eines Heiligtums*. Edited by Ulrike Muss. Vienna: Phoibos Verlag, 2008.

Purcell, Nicholas. "Literate Games: Roman Urban Society and the Game of Alea." *Past and Present* 147 (1995): 3–37.

Rasimus, Tuomas. "Revisiting the *ICHTHYS*: A Suggestion Concerning the Origins of Christological Fish Symbolism." Pages 337–44 in *Mystery and Secrecy in the Nag Hammadi Collection and Other Ancient Literature: Ideas and Practices: Studies for Einar Thomassen at Sixty*. Edited by Christian H. Bull, Liv Ingeborg Lied, and John D. Turner. Leiden: Brill, 2012.

Ratté, C., and R. R. R. Smith, eds. *Aphrodisias Papers 4: New Research on the City and its Monuments*. Journal of Roman Archaeology Supplement Series 70. Portsmouth, RI: Journal of Roman Archaeology, 2008.

Rautman, Marcus L. "Sardis." Pages 474–75 in vol. 2 of *The Eerdmans Encyclopedia of Early Christian Art and Archaeology*. Edited by Paul Corby Finney. Grand Rapids: Eerdmans, 2017.

Reynolds, Joyce. "The Christian Inscriptions of Cyrenaica." *The Journal of Theological Studies* 11.2 (1960): 284–94.

Reynolds, Joyce, Charlotte Roueché, and Gabriel Bodard. *Inscriptions of Aphrodisias* (2007).

Richard, Julian. *Water for the City, Fountains from the People: Monumental Fountains in the Roman East*. Studies in Eastern Mediterranean Archaeology 9. Turnhout: Brepols, 2012.

Rieche, Anita. "Board Games and Their Symbols from Roman Times to Early Christianity." Pages 87–88 in *Ancient Board Games in Perspective*. Edited by I. L. Finkel. London: British Museum Press, 2007.

Rorem, Paul, and John C. Lamoreaux. "John of Scythopolis on Apollinarian Christology and the Pseudo-Areopagite's True Identity." *Church History* 62.4 (1993): 469–82.

Roth, Dieter T. "Staurogram." Pages 349–58 in *From Celsus to the Catacombs: Visual, Liturgical, and Non-Christian Reception of Jesus in the Second and Third Centuries CE*. Edited by Chris Keith. Vol. 3 of *The Reception of Jesus in the First Three Centuries*. Edited by Chris Keith, Helen K. Bond, Christine Jacobi, and Jens Schöter. London: T&T Clark, 2020.

Roueché, Charlotte. *Aphrodisias in Late Antiquity*. Journal of Roman Studies Monographs 5. London: The Society for the Promotion of Roman Studies, 1989.

_____. "Late Roman and Byzantine Game Boards at Aphrodisias." Pages 100–105 in *Ancient Board Games in Perspective: Papers from the 1990 British Museum Colloquium, with Additional Contributions*. Edited by I. L. Finkel. London: The British Museum, 2007.

Rumscheid, Frank. *Priene: A Guide to the "Pompeii of Asia Minor."* Istanbul: Ege Yayinlari, 1998.

Russell, Kenneth W. "The Earthquake of May 19, A.D. 363." *Bulletin of the American Schools of Oriental Research* 238 (1980): 47–64.

Salzman, Michele, Marianne Sághy, and Rita Lizzi Testa, eds. *Pagans and Christians in Late Antique Rome*. Cambridge: Cambridge University Press, 2016.

Sanz-Rincón, Rosaura. "An Early Roman Mosaic Floor in the Jewish Village of Magdala, Galilee." *European Journal of Science and Theology* 16.3 (2020): 129–38.

Saradi, Helen. "The Christianization of Pagan Temples in the Greek Hagiographical Texts." Pages 113–34 in *From Temple to Church: Destruction and Renewal of Local Cultic Topography in Late Antiquity.* Edited by Johannes Hahn, Stephen Emmel, and Ulrich Gotter. Leiden: Brill, 2008.

Schädler, Ulrich. "Games, Greek and Roman." Pages 2841–44 in *The Encyclopedia of Ancient History.* Edited by R. S. Bagnall, K. Broderson, C. B. Champion, and S. Huebner. London: Blackwell, 2013.

———. "Scripta, Alea, Tabula: New Evidence for the Roman History of 'Backgammon.'" Pages 73–98 in *New Approaches to Board Games Research: Asian Origins and Future Perspective.* Working Papers Series 3. Leiden: International Institute for Asian Studies, 1995.

Schäferdiek, Knut. "The Acts of John." Pages 152–212 in *New Testament Apocrypha.* Edited by Wilhelm Schneemelcher. Vol. 2. Louisville: Westminster John Knox, 1992.

Schaff, Philip, and Henry Wace, eds. *The Seven Ecumenical Councils.* Vol. 14 of *Nicene and Post-Nicene Fathers.* Peabody, MA: Hendrickson, 2004.

Schick, Robert. "Aelia Capitolina." Pages 1–8 in *The Oxford Encyclopedia of the Bible and Archaeology.* Edited by Daniel M. Master. Vol. 1. Oxford: Oxford University Press, 2013.

Schneemelcher, Wilhelm, ed. *New Testament Apocrypha.* 2 vols. Louisville: Westminster John Knox, 1992.

Schowalter, Daniel, Sabine Ladstätter, Stephen Friesen, and Christian Thomas, eds. *Religion in Ephesos Reconsidered: Archaeology of Spaces, Structures, and Objects.* NovTSup 177. Leiden: Brill, 2020.

Schrader, Elizabeth, and Joan E. Taylor. "The Meaning of 'Magdalene': A Review of Literary Evidence." *JBL* 140.4 (2021): 751–73.

Schröter, Jens, and Christine Jacobi, eds. *From Thomas to Tertullian: Christian Literary Receptions of Jesus in the Second and Third Centuries CE.* Vol. 2 of *The Reception of Jesus in the First Three Centuries.* Edited by Chris Keith, Helen K. Bond, Christine Jacobi, and Jens Schöter. London: T&T Clark, 2020.

Scott, Michael. *Delphi: A History of the Center of the Ancient World.* Princeton, NJ: Princeton University Press, 2014.

Seager, Andrew R., and A. Thomas Kraabel. "The Synagogue and the Jewish Community." Pages 168–90 and figs. 248–80 in *Sardis: From Prehistoric to Roman Times: Results of the Archaeological Exploration of Sardis 1958–1975.* Cambridge: Harvard University Press, 1983.

Sebbane, Michael. "Board Games from the Eastern Cardo." Pages 147–64 in *Jerusalem: Western Wall Plaza Excavations.* Vol. 1 of *The Roman and Byzantine Remains: Architecture and Stratigraphy.* Edited by Shlomit

Weksler-Bdolah and Alexander Onn. IAA Reports. No. 63. Jerusalem: Israel Antiquities Authority, 2019.

Seval, Mehlika. *Step by Step Ephesus*. Istanbul: Minyatür, 1988.

Séve, Michel, and Patrick Weber. *Guide du forum de Philippes*. Sites et Monuments 18. Athens: École française d'Athènes, 2012.

Shanks, Hershel. *Jerusalem: An Archaeological Biography*. New York: Random House, 1995.

_____. *Jerusalem's Temple Mount: From Solomon to the Golden Dome*. New York: Continuum, 2007.

Sharabi, Lena Naama, Yana Tchekhanovets, and Doron Ben Ami. "Early Christian Graffiti from Fourth Century Jerusalem." Pages 295–302 in *Holy Land. Archaeology on Either Side: Archaeological Essays in Honor of Eugenio Alliata, OFM*. Edited by A. Coniglio and A. Ricco. Collectio Maior 57. Milan: Edizioni Terra Santa, 2020.

Sheridan, James J. "The Altar of Victory: Paganism's Last Battle." *L'Antiquité Classique* 35 (1966): 186–206.

Shin, Min Seok. *The Great Persecution: A Historical Re-Examination*. Studia Antiqua Australiensia 8. Turnhout: Brepols, 2018.

Şimşek, Celal, ed. *Laodikeia (Laodicea ad Lycum). Laodikeia Çalişmalari 2*. Istanbul: Ege Yayinlari, 2013.

_____. *Laodikeia Çalişmalari 5:15. Yilinda Laodikeia (2003–2018)*. Istanbul: Ege Yayinlari, 2019.

Şimşek, Celal. *Church of Laodikeia: Christianity in the Lykos Valley*. Denizli, Turkey: Denizli Metropolitan Municipality, 2015.

_____. "Laodikeia Yontuculuğu" [Eng. "Laodicea Sculpting"]. Pages 456–66 in *Laodikeia (Laodicea ad Lycum). Laodikeia Çalişmalari 2*. Edited by Celal Şimşek. Istanbul: Ege Yayinlari, 2013.

_____. "A Menorah with a Cross Carved on a Column of Nymphaeum A at Laodicea ad Lycum." *Journal of Roman Archaeology* 19 (2006): 343–46.

_____. "Statue Group of Trajan with Cuirass (lorika-thoraks)." Pages 89–141 in *Laodikeia Çalişmalari 5:15. Yilinda Laodikeia (2003–2018)*. Edited by Celal Şimşek. Istanbul: Ege Yayinlari, 2019.

Şimşek, Celal, and Alister Filippini. "The Funerary Altar of the Christian Soldier Arelius Marinianus (Early 4th Cent. AD). From Viminacium to Chrysopolis and Laodikeia." Pages 187–204 in *Laodikeia Çalişmalari 5:15. Yilinda Laodikeia (2003–2018)*. Edited by Celal Şimşek. Istanbul: Ege Yayinlari, 2019.

Sitz, Anna M. "Hiding in Plain Sight: Epigraphic Reuse in the Temple-Church at Aphrodisias." *Journal of Late Antiquity* 12.1 (2019): 136–68.

_____. "Inscribing Caria: The Perseverance of Epigraphic Traditions in Late Antiquity." Pages 202–25 in *Early Christianity in Asia Minor and Cyprus: From the Margins to the Mainstream*. Edited by Cilliers Breytenback, Martin Goodman, Christoph Markschies, and Stephen Mitchell. Ancient Judaism and Early Christianity 109. Leiden: Brill, 2019.

Slootjes, Daniëlle. "Crowd Behavior in Late Antique Rome." Pages 178–94 in *Pagans and Christians in Late Antique Rome*. Edited by Michele Salzman, Marianne Sághy, and Rita Lizzi Testa. Cambridge: Cambridge University Press, 2016.

Smith, R. R. R., J. Lenaghan, A. Sokolicek, and K. Welch, eds. *Aphrodisias Papers 5: Excavations and Research at Aphrodisias, 2006–2012*. Journal of Roman Archaeology Supplement Series 103. Portsmouth, RI: Journal of Roman Archaeology, 2016.

Snively, Carolyn S. "Stobi." Pages 545–48 in *The Eerdmans Encyclopedia of Early Christian Art and Archaeology*. Edited by Paul Corby Finney. Vol. 2. Grand Rapids: Eerdmans, 2017.

Snyder, Graydon F. *Ante Pacem: Archaeological Evidence of Church Life before Constantine*. Macon, GA: Mercer University Press, 2003.

Sokolicek, Alexander. "The Magnesian Gate of Ephesos." Pages 108–22 in *Religion in Ephesos Reconsidered: Archaeology of Spaces, Structures, and Objects*. Edited by Daniel Schowalter, Sabine Ladstätter, Stephen Friesen, and Christian Thomas. NovTSup 177. Leiden: Brill, 2020.

Sörries, Reiner. *Die Bilder der Orthodoxen im Kampf gegen den Arianismus: Eine Apologie der orthodoxen Christologie und Trinitätslehre gegenüber der arianischen Häresie, dargestellt an den ravennatischen Mosaiken und Bildern des 6. Jahrhunderts*. Europäische Hochschulschriften Series 23. Vol. 186. Frankfurt: Peter Lang, 1983.

Spagnolo, A., and C. H. Turner. "Maximus of Turin: Against the Pagans/ Contra Paganos." *The Journal of Theological Studies* 17.7 (1916): 321–37.

Spera, Lucrezia. "The Christianization of Space along the Via Appia: Changing Landscape in the Suburbs of Rome." *AJA* 107.1 (2003): 23–43.

Spier, Jeffery. "The Earliest Christian Art: From Personal Salvation to Imperial Power." Pages 1–24 in *Picturing the Bible: The Earliest Christian Art*. Edited by Jeffrey Spier. New Haven, CT: Yale University Press, 2007.

_____, ed. *Picturing the Bible: The Earliest Christian Art*. New Haven, CT: Yale University Press, 2007.

Squarciapino, Maria Floriani. "Considerazioni su Ostia Cristiana." *Studi Romani* 27.1 (1979): 15–24.

Squire, Michael, and Christopher Whitton. "*Machina Sacra*: Optatian and the Lettered Art of the Christogram." Pages 45–108 in *Graphic Signs of Identity, Faith, and Power in Late Antiquity and the Early Middle Ages*. Edited by Ilday Garipzanov, Caroline Goodson, and Henry Maguire. Turnhout: Brepols, 2017.

Staab, Gregor. "Hippos: was Mosaik-inschriften Verraten; Auf den Spuren einer christlichen Gemeinde," *Welt und Umwelt der Bibel* 2 (2023): 62–65.

Stamper, John W. "Urban Sanctuaries: The Early Republic to Augustus." Pages 207–27 in *A Companion to Roman Architecture*. Edited by Roger B. Ulrich and Caroline K. Quenemoen. West Sussex, UK: Wiley and Sons, 2014.

Steckner, Cornelius. "Bath: Christian Reuse of." Pages 177–78 in *The Eerdmans Encyclopedia of Early Christian Art and Archaeology*. Edited by Paul Corby Finney. Vol. 1. Grand Rapids: Eerdmans, 2017.

———. "Samos." Page 453 in vol. 2 of *The Eerdmans Encyclopedia of Early Christian Art and Archaeology*. Edited by Paul Corby Finney. Grand Rapids: Eerdmans, 2017.

Stemberger, Günter. *Jews and Christians in the Holy Land: Palestine in the Fourth Century*. Translated by Ruth Tuschling. Edinburgh, T&T Clark, 2000.

Stevenson, J., ed. *Creeds, Councils and Controversies: Documents Illustrating the History of the Church, AD 337–461*. Rev. Edited by W. H. C. Frend. Grand Rapids: Baker, 2012.

Stinson, P. T. "New Incised Architectural Drawings from the Basilica." Pages 225–42 in *Aphrodisias Papers 5: Excavations and Research at Aphrodisias, 2006–2012*. Edited by R. R. R. Smith, J. Lenaghan, A. Sokolicek, and K. Welch. Journal of Roman Archaeology Supplement Series 103. Portsmouth, RI: Journal of Roman Archaeology, 2016.

Stoehr, Gregory William. "The End of Pagan Temple in Roman Palestine." PhD diss. University of Maryland, 2018.

Storch, R. H. "The Trophy and the Cross: Pagan and Christian Symbolism in the Fourth and Fifth Centuries." *Byzantion* 40.1 (1970): 105–18.

Strange, James F., Thomas R. W. Longstaff, and Dennis E. Groh. *Excavations at Sepphoris*. Vol. 1. University of South Florida Probes in the Citadel and Villa. Leiden: Brill, 2006.

Tabbernee, William. "Asia Minor and Cyprus." Pages 261–319 in *Early Christianity in Contexts: An Exploration across Cultures and Continents*. Edited by William Tabbernee. Grand Rapids: Baker, 2014.

———, ed. *Early Christianity in Contexts: An Exploration across Cultures and Continents*. Grand Rapids: Baker, 2014.

———. "Epigraphy." Pages 120–39 in *The Oxford Handbook of Early Christian Studies*. Edited by Susan Ashbrook Harvey and David G. Hunter. Oxford: Oxford University Press, 2008.

———. "Epigraphy: Clandestine and Crypto-Christian." Pages 476–81 in *The Eerdmans Encyclopedia of Early Christian Art and Archaeology*. Edited by Paul Corby Finney. Vol. 1. Grand Rapids: Eerdmans, 2017.

Talloen, Peter. "From Pagan to Christian: Religious Iconography in Material Culture from Sagalassos." *Late Antique Archaeology* 7.1 (2011): 573–607.

———. "The Rise of Christianity at Sagalassus." Pages 164–201 in *Early Christianity in Asia Minor and Cyprus: From the Margins to the Mainstream*. Edited by Stephen Mitchell and Philipp Pilhofer. Ancient Judaism and Early Christianity 109. Leiden: Brill, 2019.

———. "Rolling the Dice: Public Game Boards from Sagalassos." *Journal on Hellenistic and Roman Material Culture* 7.1–2 (2018): 97–132.

Talloen, Peter, and Lies Vercauteren. "The Fate of Temples in Late Antique Anatolia." Pages 347–58 in *The Archaeology of Late Antique "Paganism."* Edited by Luke Lavan and Michael Mulryan. Late Antique Archaeology 7. Leiden: Brill, 2011.

Tamas, Hajnalka. *Hagiography, the Cult of Martyrs, and the Formation of Christian Identity in Late Antique Pannonia.* Cluj-Napoca, Romania: Cluj University Press, 2022.

Taylor, Joan E. "Magdala's Mistaken Identity." *BAR* 48.3 (2022): 55–58.

——. "Missing Magdala and the Name of Mary 'Magdalene.'" *PEQ* 146.3 (2014): 205–23.

Tepper, Yotam, Leah Di Segni, and Guy Stiebel. *A Christian Prayer Hall of the Third Century CE at Kefar 'Othnay (Legio): Excavations at the Megiddo Prison 2005.* Jerusalem: Israel Antiquities Authority, 2006.

Testa, Emmanuele. *Il Simbolismo Dei Giudeo-Cristiani.* Publicazioni Dello Studium Franciscanum 14. Gerusalemme: Tipografia Dei PP. Francescani, 1962.

Teteriatnikov, Natalia B. *Justinianic Mosaics of Hagia Sophia and Their Aftermath.* Dumbarton Oaks Studies XLVII. Washington, DC: Dumbarton Oaks Research Library, 2017.

Thédenat, Henry. *Le Forum Romain et les Forums Impériaux.* Paris: Librairie Hachette, 1904.

Torrance, Iain R. *Christology after Chalcedon: Serverus of Antioch and Sergius the Monophysite.* Eugene, OR: Wipf & Stock, 1998.

Treu, Ursula. "Christian Sibyllines." Pages 652–85 in vol. 2 of *New Testament Apocrypha.* Edited by Wilhelm Schneemelcher. Rev. ed. 2 vols Louisville: Westminster John Knox, 1992.

Trifilò, Francesco. "The Forum Romanum Games Project: Preliminary Project Report." Kent: University of Kent, 2012.

——. "Movement, Gaming, and the Use of Space in the Forum." Pages 312–31 in *Rome, Ostia, Pompeii: Movement and Space.* Edited by Ray Laurence and David J. Newsome. Oxford: Oxford University Press, 2011.

Trinkl, Elisabeth, ed. *Akten des 14. Österreichischen Archäologentages am Institut für Archäologie der Universität Graz.* Wien: Phoibos70, 2014.

Trombley, Frank R. *Hellenic Religion and Christianization c. 370–529.* Vol. 1. 2nd ed. Religions in the Graeco-Roman World 115. Leiden: Brill, 1995.

Tsafrir, Yoram. "The Fate of the Pagan Cult Places." Pages 197–218 in *Religious and Ethnic Communities in Later Roman Palestine.* Edited by Hayim Lapin. Bethesda: University of Maryland Press, 1998.

Tsafrir, Yoram, and Gideon Foerster. "Urbanism at Scythopolis-Bet Shean in the Fourth to Seventh Centuries." *Dumbarton Oaks Papers* 51 (1997): 85–146.

Ulrich, Roger B., and Caroline K. Quenemoen, eds. *A Companion to Roman Architecture.* West Sussex, UK: Wiley and Sons, 2014.

Vakaloudi, Anastasia D. "ΔΕΙΣΙΔΑΙΜΟΝΙΑ and the Role of the Apotropaic Magic Amulets in the Early Byzantine Empire." *Byzantion* 70.1 (2000): 182–210.

Valevca, Julia, and Athanasios K. Vionis. "The Balkan Peninsula." Pages 321–66 in *Early Christianity in Contexts: An Exploration across Cultures and Continents*. Edited by William Tabbernee. Grand Rapids: Baker, 2014.

Vamosh, Miriam Feinberg. *Beit She'an: Capital of the Decapolis*. Israel Nature and National Parks Protection Authority. Tel Aviv: ERETZ Ha-Tzvi, 1996.

van der Linde, Dies. "Artemis Ephesia, the Emperor and the City: Impact of the Imperial Cult and the Civic Identity of Roman Ephesos." *Ancient Society* 46 (2016): 165–201.

van Opstall, Emilie M., ed. *Sacred Thresholds: The Door to the Sanctuary in Late Antiquity*. Religions in the Graeco-Roman World 185. Leiden: Brill, 2018.

Verhoef, Eduard. *Philippi: How Christianity Began in Europe—The Epistle to the Philippians and the Excavations at Philippi*. London: Bloomsbury; T&T Clark, 2013.

Waelkens, M., Peter Talloen, and Ine Jacobs. "Sagalassos." Pages 444–47 in vol. 2 of *The Eerdmans Encyclopedia of Early Christian Art and Archaeology*. Edited by Paul Corby Finney. Grand Rapids: Eerdmans, 2017.

Walter, Christopher. "IC XC NI KA: The Apotropaic Function of the Victorious Cross." *Revue des études byzantines* 55 (1997): 193–220.

Ward, Walter D. "The 363 Earthquake and the End of Public Paganism in the Southern Transjordan." *Journal of Late Antiquity* 9.1 (2016): 132–70.

Watkin, David. *The Roman Forum*. Cambridge, MA: Harvard University Press, 2009.

Webb, Matilda. *The Churches and Catacombs of Early Christian Rome*. Eastbourne, UK: Sussex Academic, 2010.

Wehrhahn-Stauch, Liselotte. "Christliche Fischsymbol von den Anfänger bis zum hohen Mittelalter." *Zeitschrift für Kunstgeschichte* 35 (1972): 54–68.

Weiss, Zeev. "Greco-Roman Influences on the Art and Architecture of the Jewish City in Roman Palestine." Pages 219–48 in *Religious and Ethnic Communities in Later Roman Palestine*. Edited by Hayim Lapin. Bethesda: University of Maryland, 1998.

_____. "Sepphoris." Pages 492–94 in vol. 2 of *The Eerdmans Encyclopedia of Early Christian Art and Archaeology*. Edited by Paul Corby Finney. Grand Rapids: Eerdmans, 2017.

_____. "Sepphoris." *Oxford Classical Dictionary*. doi.org/10.1093/acrefore/9780199381135.013.8039.

Weksler-Bdolah, Shlomit, and Alexander Onn, eds. *Jerusalem: Western Wall Plaza Excavations*. Vol. 1 of *The Roman and Byzantine Remains: Architecture and Stratigraphy*. IAA Reports. No. 63. Jerusalem: Israel Antiquities Authority, 2019.

Weksler-Bdolah, Shlomit. *Aelia Capitolina: Jerusalem in the Roman Period in Light of Archaeological Research*. Mnemosyne Supplements: History and Archaeology of Classical Antiquity 432. Leiden: Brill, 2020.

Welborn, L. L. "Early Christianity at Rome as Reflected in the So-Called First Epistle of Clement." Pages 137–99 in *The First Urban Churches 6: Rome and Ostia*. Edited by James R. Harrison and L. L. Welborn. Writings from the Greco-Roman World Supplement Series 18. Atlanta: SBL Press, 2021.

Welch, Katherine. "The Stadium at Aphrodisias." *American Journal of Archaeology* 102.3 (1998): 547–69.

Welsh, P. G. *The Poems of St. Paulinus of Nola*. New York: Newman, 1975.

Westphalen, Stephen. "Die Frühchristliche Basilika im Heraion von Samos und ihre Ausstattung." Sonderdruck aus den Mitteilungen des Deutschen Archäologischen Instituts Athenische Abteilung. 109. Berlin: Gebr. Mann Verlag, 1994.

White, L. Michael. *The Social Origins of Christian Architecture*. Vol. 2 of *Texts and Monuments for the Christian Domus Ecclesiae in its Environment*. Harvard Theological Studies 42. Valley Forge, PA: Trinity International, 1997.

Wicker, James R. "Pre-Constantinian *Nomina Sacra* in a Mosaic and Church Graffiti." *SWJT* 52.1 (2009): 52–72.

Wiedemann, Thomas. *Emperors and Gladiators*. New York: Routledge, 1992.

Wiegand, Theodor, and Hans Schrader. *Priene: Ergebnisse der Ausgrabungen und Untersuchungen in den Jahren 1895–1898*. Berlin: Georg Reimer, 1904.

Williamson, Christian G. "Filters of Light: Greek Temple Doors as Portals of Epiphany." Pages 309–40 in *Sacred Thresholds: The Door to the Sanctuary in Late Antiquity*. Edited by Emilie M. van Opstall. Leiden: Brill, 2018.

Wilson, Andrew. "Water, Nymphs, and a Palm Grove: Monumental Water Display at Aphrodisias." Pages 101–35 in *Aphrodisias Papers 5: Excavations and Research at Aphrodisias, 2006–2012*. Edited by R. R. R. Smith, J. Lenaghan, A. Sokolicek, and K. Welch. Journal of Roman Archaeology Supplement Series 103. Portsmouth, RI: Journal of Roman Archaeology, 2016.

————. "Water, Power, and Culture in the Roman and Byzantine Worlds: An Introduction." *Water History* 4 (2012): 1–9.

Wilson, Andrew, Ben Russell, and Andrew Ward. "Excavations in an Urban Park ('South Agora'), 2012." Pages 77–90 in *Aphrodisias Papers 5: Excavations and Research at Aphrodisia, 2006–2012*. Edited by R. R. R. Smith, J. Lenaghan, A. Sokolicek, and K. Welch. Journal of Roman Archaeology Supplement Series 103. Portsmouth, RI: Journal of Roman Archaeology, 2016.

Wilson, Mark. *Biblical Turkey: A Guide to the Jewish and Christian Sites of Asia Minor*. Istanbul: Ege Yayinlari, 2010.

_____. *The Victor Sayings in the Book of Revelation*. Eugene, OR: Wipf & Stock, 2007.

_____. *Victory through the Lamb: A Guide to Revelation in Plain Language*. Bellingham, WA: Lexham Press, 2019.

Wisemen, James, and Djordje Mano-Zissi. "Stobi: A City of Ancient Macedonia." *Journal of Field Archaeology* 3.3 (1976): 269–302.

Yamauchi, Edwin M. *Africa and the Bible*. Grand Rapids: Baker, 2004.

Yegül, Fikret. *Bathing in the Roman World*. Cambridge: Cambridge University Press, 2010.

Zapata-Meza, Marcela, Andrea Garza, Diaz Barriga, and Rosaura Sanz-Rincón. "The Magdala Archaeological Project (2010–2012): A Preliminary Report of the Excavations at Migdal." *'Atiqot* 90 (2018): 83–125.